C0-CCX-177

A Collector's Identification
And Value Guide
To

ANTIQUES

By
LAR HOTHEM

ISBN 0-89689-011-2

BOOKS AMERICANA

A Collectors Identification
And Value Guide To

ANTIQUES

ACKNOWLEDGEMENTS

The writer gratefully acknowledges the help of numerous persons in assembling this Priceguide to Antiques and Collectibles. Please see the book *Directory* for the complete addresses of all individuals and businesses who and which have contributed in some way to this book.

Tom King and Tom Porter, of GARTH'S AUCTIONS, Inc. (Delaware, Ohio) gave kind permission to use relevant selections from recent catalogs. These (see below) were of diverse and quality items from major collections and antiques accumulations. Their assistance to writers like myself no doubt adds to the high esteem in which they, and their auction house, are already held.

I am indebted to GARTH'S AUCTIONS for listings including—but not limited to—the following categories: Quilts, Historical Blue Staffordshire, Floor coverings, Artist's Originals, Weathervanes, Pewter, Lamps, Lighting devices, Silver, Furniture, Glass, Tole, Fraktur, Photographic, Iron (Cast & Wrought), Paperweights, Primitives, Mirrors, Clocks, Decoys & Shorebirds, Boxes, Baskets, Firearms, Chests, Samplers, Pottery, and more.

Also, to MORTON'S AUCTION EXCHANGE, Inc. (643 Magazine Street, New Orleans, Louisiana 70190) for catalogs that were most helpful in determining some of the major collecting fields of today.

William P. Weschler, of ADAM A. WESCHLER & SON, Inc., of Washington, D.C., gave gracious permission in several directions. These are book listings of highest-grade antiques (both domestic and foreign) including Asian and European art objects.

I am indebted to ADAM A. WESCHLER & SON for listings including—but not limited to—the following categories: Carved ivory, Chinese, Antiquities, Artist's originals, Tiffany, Lamps, Art Deco & Nouveau, Snuff containers, Silver, Oriental jades, Furniture, Glass, Japanese, Bronze Figures & Sculptures, Glass (Crystal & Other), Musical instruments, Netsuke, Clocks, Eastern & Oriental rugs, Boehm porcelain, Audubon prints, American sporting prints, and more.

ADAM A. WESCHLER & SON further permitted the use of a number of photographs illustrating some of the finest old and artistic creations available. This firm has been in the nation's capital since 1890. My special thanks to Mr. Weschler.

Further regarding photographs, my appreciation to two people and institutions for publication permissions: To Chris Brewer, Museum Aid, KERN COUNTY MUSEUM (California); and, Mary R. Maynard, Public Affairs Office, MYSTIC SEAPORT, Inc. (Connecticut).

Dealers who specialize in mail-order sales contributed greatly to this book, and they are hereby both acknowledged and thanked. Following is a chronological listing; during basic research, this is the order in which their information was received and selections assembled for book use.

Thanks to: Conway Barker, Osna and Jim Fenner, Maurice Nasser, Sallie and Bob Connelly, Richard Merlis, Barbara and Ron Hoyt, Peggy and Stan Hecker, Palmer V. Welch, John Sadler, Bea and James Stevenson, Clara Jean and Stan Davis, Charles DeLuca, Barbara and John Rudisill, Keith Schneider, Larry Eisenstein, Carol Secrist, Corinne and Sheldon Tucker, Linda Roberts, Walter Marchant, Jr., Aileen Wissner, Hugh W. Parker, F. W. Watson, Nancy and Al Schlegel, Dagmar and Spencer House, Dee and Ron Milam, E. London, Jack Cory, Linda and George LaBarre, and Bonnie Tekstra.

Intimate thanks also to private collectors who allowed photographs of top items in their collections. These appear both in the color section and in the black and white pictures associated with individual collecting areas.

In a more general way, I would like to thank John Mebane (now Editor Emeritus of *The Antiques Journal*) for being a good writing friend over the years. Also thanks to Dan Alexander, President of BOOKS AMERICANA, Inc., for fine attention to detail, inspired publishing decisions, and for making all the esoteric arrangements that have meant books that make marks.

Thanks also to my father, Luther C. Hothem of Wooster, Ohio, for helping instill an early and abiding interest in things antique and of listing worth.

In a very special way, thanks to my wife, Sue McClurg Hothem. She aided greatly in assembling listings, headings, and in compiling and making coherent some obscure information. She aided in contacts for photographs and in putting categories together. All this, understand, while teaching full-time and taking additional education courses.

If the writer has failed to acknowledge anyone who contributed in any way to this book, information or photographs, the error is mine, and will be corrected in subsequent editions.

INTRODUCTION

In doing this Priceguide the writer has attempted a slightly different route than some of the other books on related items of collector interest. While many different fields are covered in these pages (Some lightly, some in-depth), it was felt that an important contribution might be made in another way. And that is, whenever possible, the higher-valued objects are given the most description.

The book includes collecting areas that almost always appear (Shaker), some that may (Fireplace) and others that are rarely acknowledged (Soda fountain). New categories were developed to include objects that did not fit conveniently into standard groupings, such as Farm.

Whenever available an important measurement dimension is given, sometimes height, width and depth, as size is an important value determinate.

Please note that this is a *Guide* to Antiques and Collectibles and that the values listed, while accurate, do not constitute the final worth. Values in this book should be treated as a factual but general source of information.

Prices will vary somewhat depending on the geographic region. Many values in the book are Midwestern, and perhaps represent a sort of balance between East and West Coast values. These also vary according to item condition, and major flaws are listed whenever possible.

The designations preceding each dollar-figure in the book are of the below four types. A brief explanation follows.

A) **Auction.** These are the top-bid, realized prices from recent auctions.

C) **Collector.** A few listings came from people who have kept up with market conditions for their collecting area(s).

D) **Dealer.** These represent antiques listings from top dealers.

S) **Shows.** A few listings are from regional antiques exhibitions and sales.

The writer suggests two steps toward accumulating a good collection. One is purchasing from reliable dealers and auctions, for their very business depends on quality pieces at reasonable prices.

The other is learning as much as possible—via personal interchanges, books and magazines—about the items in areas of collecting interest. This makes collecting, either for enjoyment or investment, that much more satisfying.

Lar Hothem

ADVERTISING—*Calendars*

1889 pharmacy, child with wings, "Tuscarora Adv. Co.". **D-20.00**

1901 "Mrs. Dinsmore's Balsam", mother and child. **D-40.00**

1904 diecut cardboard, girl, sheaf of wheat, and dog. **D-40.00**

Perpetual desk calendar, advertising on brass plate. **D-5.00**

Studebaker **button.**

C/8-12

Old Conemaugh Whiskey. **Calendar. 1898.**

C/25

ADVERTISING—*Clocks*

Budweiser, shaped like pocket watch, lights, 14 in. diameter. **D-50.00**

Belfast Sparkling Water, electric, chrome 14 in. diameter. **D-125.00**

Canada Dry Sport Cola, needs starter for light, 13 x 18 inches. **D-25.00**

Cat's Paw, electric, cat picture, glass cracked. **D-45.00**

Calvert, owl picture, "Cool Heads Choose Calvert". **D-65.00**

Dr. Pepper, diamond-shaped, electric. **D-50.00**

Duquesne Pilsner, electric, officer holding beer, 12 in. diameter. **D-35.00**

Gem Safety Razor, eight-day windup, tin with wood grain finish, missing key, 13 x 30 inches. **D-650.00**

Hires Root Beer, electric, 14 in. diameter. **D-50.00**

Lux Animated Alarm Clock, spinning wheel, operating condition.   **D-55.00**

Pepsi Cola, wrought iron, electric, ca. 1950's, 18 in. diameter.   **D-35.00**

7-Up, electric, wrought iron.   **D-35.00**

7-Up, electric, wood frame 14 in. square.   **D-55.00**

Smith & Sons Jewelers, 13 in. diameter.   **D-35.00**

ADVERTISING—*Signs*

Anheuser Busch, light-up, man and woman, 18 x 24 inches.   **D-25.00**

A-1 Beer, framed cardboard, cowboys in saloon, 24 x 36 inches.   **D-150.00**

Budweiser, wall lamp, excellent condition.   **D-25.00**

Bevo, tin, (beverage), slight edge rust, 5 x 10 inches.   **D-75.00**

Burgermeister Burgie, bathing beauty, light-up, 12 x 16 inches.   **D-20.00**

Busch Bavarian Beer, light-up, hanging lamp.   **D-45.00**

Bartel's Brewing, tin, hops Trademark, 1920's, 18 in. diameter.   **D-50.00**

Burkhardt Beer, cardboard, 1930's 20 x 27 inches.   **D-35.00**

Beech-Nut Gum, cardboard, couple smoking, 10 x 20 inches.   **D-12.00**

Cunard Line, tin, rope design frame, 27 x 38 inches; Lusitania.   **D-575.00**

Cook's Beer, tin, lady with broad-brim hat, 22 x 28 inches.   **D-225.00**

Carling's Red Cap Ale, wood and metal, 9 x 11 inches.   **D-15.00**

Coor's Beer, light-up, lake in mountain scene, 18 x 24 inches.   **D-25.00**

Champale, light-up back bar sign; bottle and glass blink.   **D-40.00**

Camel Cigarettes, cardboard, pretty blonde, 11 x 20 inches.   **D-12.00**

Duffy's Malt Whiskey, tin, picture of chemist, 16 x 20 inches.   **D-225.00**

Dr. Pepper, porcelain, 10 x 27 inches.   **D-100.00**

Dr. Miles Nervine, cardboard under glass, 14 x 26 inches.   **D-175.00**

Dr. Meyer's Foot Soap, cardboard, hands and soap bars, 7 x 10 inches.   **D-5.00**

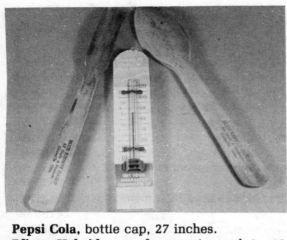

Advertising.
Fork and spoon, "Blue Ribbon Diary".
Both: C/7-10
Thermometer, working condition, "Standard Oil".
C/12-15
Lar Hothem photo

Pepsi Cola, bottle cap, 27 inches.	**D-25.00**
Pfister Hybrids, ear of corn, mirrored, 2 x 10 inches.	**D-35.00**
Salem Cigarettes, plastic, triangular.	**D-15.00**
Squirt, Squirt kit and embossed bottle, 4 x 14 inches.	**D-20.00**
Winston Cigarettes, raised pack, blue background.	**D-25.00**

ADVERTISING—*Trade Cards*

Dr. Thomas Electric Oil, "Cures Everything; Earache in 2 minutes".	**D-3.00**
E. O. Murphy/Harness Maker, "Concord, N. H.".	**D-2.00**
Judson's Mountain Herb Pill, children avoiding pain arrows.	**D-3.50**
Mrs. Pott's Cold-Handled Sad Iron, by Portland, Maine, firm.	**D-3.00**
Rose Quesnel Smoking Tobacco, mfg. by Rock City Tobacco Co., Ltd.	**D-2.50**
Shaker Family Pills/Cure Sick Headache, little girl with product.	**D-15.00**
Shaker Extract of Roots/Cures Dyspepsia, 3¼ x 5 inches.	**D-15.00**
Thomas Motor Bicycle, E. R. Thomas Motor Co., Buffalo, N.Y.	**D-10.00**
Turkish Trophies Cigarettes, rare jigsaw advertising puzzle.	**D-12.50**
Virginia Exposition tradecard, Walter A. Wood Farm Machinery.	**D-6.00**
Victorian tradecard scrapbook, embossed leather cover. Fifty pages with about 300 cards, all good, excellent condition.	**D-85.00**

Schusters Root Beer. **Tray.** 1920.
C/25

Dixie Beer. **Tray.** C/15

ADVERTISING—*Tip Trays [See also* **Bar Items***]*

Ballentine & Sons Brew., "50th Anniversary/Newark, 1915".	**D-45.00**
Bricker's Bread, Mr. Bricker's face in center, 4 in. diameter.	**D-30.00**
Clysmic Table Water, oval, nude lady on horse, burn marks.	**D-12.00**
Cottoline, Negro woman and child in cotton field, 4 in. diameter.	**D-40.00**
Dowagiac Grain Drills, grain on wood background.	**D-20.00**
Dubbleware, race horses around rim, lettering.	**D-25.00**
Fairy Soap, little girl sitting on bar of soap.	**D-35.00**
Globe Wernicke Bookcases, man and woman putting books into bookcase.	**D-25.00**
Tivoli Brewing Co., Detroit, "Altes Lager Bier".	**D-75.00**
Indianapolis Brew., Gold Medal Beer bottle, pre-Prohibition.	**D-50.00**
Liberty Beer, American Brewery, Rochester, pre-Prohibition.	**D-55.00**
Moxie, blonde holding glass, 5 in. diameter, some flakes.	**D-50.00**
Marilyn Monroe, nude picture, 5 in. diameter.	**D-20.00**
New England Furniture & Carpet Co., Priscilla Alden picture.	**D-40.00**
Oertel Brew. Cream Beer, lady with dove, "Purity".	**D-75.00**
Old Schenley, rectangular, 1940's, mint.	**D-10.00**

4

President Suspenders, picture of lady, 4 in. diameter.   **D-35.00**

Pratt's Cafe, stag picture, 4 in. diameter.   **D-30.00**

Presidential Insurance, oval, blue rim, 2 x 3 inches.   **D-10.00**

Ruppert's Beer, Hans Flato cartoon #1, people out on town.   **D-50.00**

Ruppert's Beer, Han Flato cartoon #3, arriving home.   **D-40.00**

S & H Green Stamps, picture of lady, 1917, 4 in. diameter.   **D-40.00**

Sears, Roebuck & Co., oval, picture of factory.   **D-35.00**

Simon Pure Beer, winged hops picture, red and white, 3 in. diameter.   **D-20.00**

Tally Ho Beer, (New York), stagecoach picture, 1930's.   **D-40.00**

White Rock Table Water, picture of Psyche, rectangular.   **D-45.00**

Welsbach Lighting, mother reading/child/lights, 4 in. diameter.   **D-40.00**

Welsbach Mantles, eagle on shield/lamps around rim.   **D-35.00**

ADVERTISING—*Trays [See also* **Bar Items***]*

Bissantz Ice Cream, oval, pretty girl, ca. 1900.   **D-75.00**

Beck's Brew., lettering, Buffalo, 13 in. diameter.   **D-15.00**

Baker's Chocolates, oval, products pictured.   **D-35.00**

Bardek Liquers, men drinking in tavern, ca. 1900, 12 in. diameter.   **D-35.00**

Eastside Beer, Los Angeles, pre-Prohibition.   **D-45.00**

Gentleman Brew., hand with glass of beer, 13 in. diameter.   **D-75.00**

Kreuger Beer, picture of Kreuger Bellboy, 1940's.   **D-20.00**

Miller High Life, girl on moon, 1940's, 13 in. diameter.   **D-45.00**

Narragansett Brew., 1940's, 12 in. diameter.   **D-20.00**

Neuweiler's Brew., man carrying tankard, 13 in. diameter.   **D-45.00**

Old Scenter Rye, hunting dogs in field, dated 1910.   **D-100.00**

Old Topper, man wearing top hat, 12 in. diameter.   **D-20.00**

Phoenix Brew., large, oval, phoenix bird on flames, pre-Prohibition, fine condition.   **D-275.00**

Piel's Beer, Bert and Harry Piel, dated 1957.   **D-15.00**

Pepsi Cola, Coney Island beach scene, 12 in. diameter.   **D-10.00**

Ruthstaller Brew., oval, brewery picture, pre-Prohibition.   **D-300.00**

Schaefer Brew., lettering, 1950's, excellent.   **D-7.00**

Sunshine Beer, "Wholesome As Sunshine", 1930's.   **D-50.00**

Tam O'Shanter, Amer. Brew. Rochester, 1933.   **D-35.00**

Valley Forge Beer, Washington's Headquarters, 1940's.   **D-30.00**

Yuengling's Beer, bottle and glass shown, 13 in. diameter.   **D-25.00**

ADVERTISING COLLECTIBLES—*General*

Cigar box label. "Radio Queen".
C/3

Old Abe Cigars. **Wooden box.** Rare.

Container, tin, advertising, 4 x 5 x 6 inches.

C/15-22.50

Photo courtesy Judy Morehead, Creative Photography, Lancaster, Ohio.

6

Dutch Masters Cigars, tin, oval, rusted, 9 x 11 inches.   **D-5.00**

Eastside Beer, framed paper under glass, 26 x 38½ inches.   **D-150.00**

Falstaff lamp, restored, tin, concave, 24 in. diameter.   **D-110.00**

Grape Ola, tin, basket of grapes, 15 x 20 inches.   **D-25.00**

Granger Tobacco, cardboard, WW-II soldier, 12 x 12 inches.   **D-12.00**

Harvester Cigars, tin, oval, 7 x 13 inches.   **D-15.00**

Howel's Root Beer, tin, bottle-shaped, 9 x 29 inches.   **D-35.00**

Illinois Watches, tin, "Always On Time", ca. 1910, 12 x 18 inches.   **D-325.00**

Kodak Film Sold Here, on chain, lights, 14 in. square.   **D-40.00**

Kellogg's Breakfast Cereals, lot of four different posters.   **D-15.00**

LaBatte's Beer, (Canada), light-up back bar sign.   **D-35.00**

Loose Wiles Chocolates, tin, die-cut of lady graduate and chocolates, 25 x 36 inches.   **D-700.00**

Mayo's Plug Tobacco, canvas, rooster, 24 x 40 inches.   **D-75.00**

Minard's Linemint, cardboard, two-fold store window sign.   **D-20.00**

Model Tobacco, tin, picture of man, 4 x 12 inches.   **D-25.00**

Old Jed Clayton Whiskey, paper framed under glass, 20 x 30 inches.   **D-375.00**

Old Milwaukee Beer, plastic, repairs; 15 x 22 inches.   **D-15.00**

Olympia Beer, light-up, mug bubbles, plastic, 14 x 20 inches.   **D-35.00**

Omar Cigarettes, tin, package, "20 for 15ᶜ", 8 x 14 inches.   **D-40.00**

Pabst Brewing Co., tin, hands holding bottle over brewery, "A Perfect Product From A Great Plant", 36 x 48 inches.   **D-600.00**

Pabst Blue Ribbon blackboard, 1950's, 17 x 26 inches.   **D-15.00**

Palace Livery Barn, cardboard, horse collar and lady, 12 x 18 inches.   **D-35.00**

Pickwick Ale, cardboard, stagecoach and tavern, 16 x 22 inches.   **D-20.00**

Piedmont Cigarettes, porcelain, two-sided, 13 in. square.   **D-60.00**

P. O. C. Pilsner Brewing, celluloid, 1930's, 9 in. diameter.   D-25.00

Raleigh Cigarettes, framed cardboard, dressed-up couple, 13 x 19 inches.   D-15.00

Reisch's Weiner Style Bottle Beer, tin, 6 x 13 inches.   D-15.00

Remington Arms, paper under glass, game chart, 21 x 29 inches.   D-65.00

Rheingold Beer, cardboard of Miss Rheingold, 14 x 18 inches.   D-10.00

Round Oak Stoves, cardboard, Indian head, 8 in. diameter.   D-10.00

Ruppert's Brewery, map of New York City and area, 22 x 30 inches.   D-75.00

Schenley Pure Rye, tin in wood frame, gentleman offering lady a drink; ca. 1900, 19 x 23 inches.   D-450.00

Schlitz Beer, metal, bracketed sign, 1940's.   D-80.00

Schlitz Malt Liquer light-up sign with bull.   D-35.00

Smith Piano & Organ Co., paper under glass, 23 x 31 inches.   D-275.00

South Bend Watches, tin, 1920's, 10 x 30 inches.   D-60.00

Target Tobacco, cloth, dated 1931, 30 x 56 inches.   D-45.00

Uncle John's Syrup, paper, U.J. and oxen, 11 x 21 inches.   D-10.00

Union Workman Tobacco, tin, 1950's, 17 x 23 inches.   D-25.00

Velvet Tobacco, tin, framed, ca. 1910, 23 x 31 inches.   D-350.00

Watch Repairing, framed paper under glass, 3½ x 12 inches.   D-10.00

Woo Chee Chong Import Co., paper hanger, 21 x 31 inches.   D-30.00

WW-II Poster, by Fisher Bodies, "Keep America Free Series".   D-15.00

Y-B Cigars, cardboard, giant cigar, 20 x 30 inches.   D-20.00

Yosemite Lager, stained and leaded glass window; one of seven made by San Francisco firm in 1970, 25 x 36 inches.   D-600.00

ADVERTISING—*Thermometers*

Camel Cigarettes, raised pack, fine condition.   D-25.00

Chesterfield Cigarettes, raised pack, some paint drops.   D-25.00

Hires, bottle-shaped, 27 in. high.   D-40.00

Bank, tin, in form of Red Circle coffee container. **S-7.00**

Booklet, childrens', by Chase & Sanborn Coffee and Tea Importers. **D-6.00**

Booklet, childrens', "Clark's O.N.T. Rhymes For All Times". **D-7.50**

Bottle, "Burnett's Standard Jamaica Ginger—75% alcohol". **D-8.50**

Bottle, full label, "Wintergreen/Shaker Village, N.H.". **D-45.00**

Bottle, paper label, "Shaker Witch Hazel"; ca. 1860. **D-55.00**

Bottle-opener, "Del Monte Hotel, Rock Island, Quebec". **D-1.50**

Box, "Clicquot Club Pale Dry Ginger Ale", 10½ in. deep. **D-7.50**

Box, "Corbett's Shaker Medicated Losenge", cardboard, ca. 1880. **D-20.00**

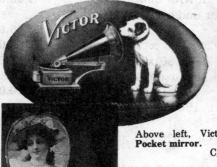

Above left, **Victor, Pocket mirror.** C/65

Bakery box, with additional label inside lid in pristine condition. Slight damage to lid corner, right; 10 x 14 x 22¾ inches. Private collection. C/35-55

Advertising paper. "Hood's Sarsaparilla Calendar", "Sweet Sixteen", dated 1894. C/25-35

Bottom, "Clark's O.N.T. Spool Cotton", Statue of Liberty front, one of two in series. C/15-25

Broadside, P. T. Barnum circus, ca. 1880; 31¼ in. high. **D-50.00**

Brochure on stiff cardboard, "Shaker Medicinal Spring Water". **D-49.50**

Button hook, "Walkover Shoes". **D-1.00**

Cake turner, "S & H Green Stamps...Discount", ca. 1910. **D-6.50**

Calendar, sketch of Boston Harbor, month of January, 1919. **D-4.00**

Chocolate box, tin, "Artstyle", 5 in. high. **S-7.50**

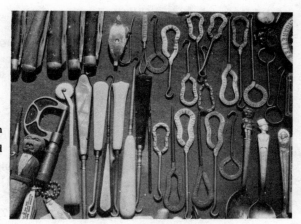

Cookbook, "The Dinner Calendar", Fannie M. Farmer, 1915. .... D-4.00

Cookbook, Dr. Sloan's Handy Hints (Mfgr. horse cure-alls), 1901. .... D-4.00

Cookbook, "Hood's Sasparilla", High Street, ca. 1880. .... D-6.00

Cookbook, by Golden Rule Food Products, 118 pages, 1916. .... D-3.50

Cook booklet, "Dwight's Cow Brand", Dwight's Soda, 1895. .... D-2.50

Cook booklet, "Occident Flour Tested Recipes", ca. 1940. .... D-1.50

Cookie and pastry tool, advertises Maine real estate firm, 1921. .... D-10.00

Cream pitcher, "Post Cereals Measured Creamer", child-size. D-10.00

Donut cutter, "Cottonlene For All Frying and Shortening". D-8.50

Envelopes, pair; advertising two different cigar brands. D-16.00

Fan, "Bissels 'Cyco' Ballbearing Carpet Sweeper", scenic. D-10.00

Fan, "Wheeler & Wilson Sewing Machines", shows Singer machine. D-4.00

Frying pan, give-away, "Grand Union Tea Co.", 9 in. diameter. D-24.50

Knife sharpener, "Bull Moose 5ᶜ Cigar/Skowhega, ME". D-20.00

Match safe, Garfield Memorial. D-20.00

Match safe, chrome, "Gillette".   D-10.00
Match safe, "Knapsack Matches/Licensed".   D-8.00
Match safe, "Niagara Falls", two different views.   D-25.00
Match safe, "Sharples Cream Separator Works".   D-35.00
Measure, tin, "Miss Princine Baking Power", minor
rust.   D-10.00
Medallion, brass, "International Harvester Co.",
half-dollar size.   D-6.50
Mirror, pocket; "Diamond Saw Stamping Works",
two in. diameter.   D-12.50
Mirror, advertising; "Duffy's Pure Malt Whiskey".   S-20.00
Paperweight mirror, "Aetna" Insurance, 3½ in.
diameter.   D-12.50
Mixing bowl, "Diamond Crystal Shaker Salt", 7¾ in.
diameter.   D-12.50
Nut set, "Mr. Peanut", one bowl, three servers.   D-10.00
Pen, oversized, wood; "Stylografic", 20 in. long.   A-22.50
Penknife, three-bladed, "Sunshine Biscuits", yellow
handle.   D-6.00

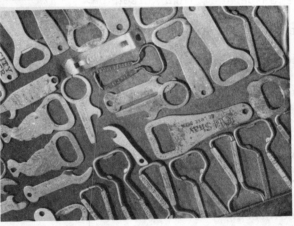

Advertising.
Bottle-opener collection.
C/Unlisted
Lar Hothem photo

Pocket box, "Gold Tip Peppermint Gum", cigarette
form.   D-5.50
Pin tray, "The Prudential Ships The Strength of
Gibralter".   D-12.50
Potholder, for "Glenwood Ranges" and
"Heaters...Hot Iron Holder".   D-3.00
Pottery mug, Orphan Annie, by "Ovaltine"; 4 in.
high.   S-16.00
Rag doll, Aunt Jemima", holding plate of hotcakes.   D-45.00
Rag doll, "Jack Frost", 18 in. high.   S-24.00

Rag doll, "Kellogg's Papa Bear", 13 in. high.   D-39.00
Rag doll, "Mr. Peanut", by Planter Peanuts, 20 in. high.   D-22.50
Rag doll, "Snow King Baking Powder", 12 in. high.   S-18.00
Sample miniature tin, "Condo Silver Polish", lithotin.   D-1.00
Sewing tape, "Boot 'n' Shoe Workers Union", ca. 1900.   D-18.50
Shoe brush, "Bill Nye 5ᶜ Cigar", hardwood, 2½ x 8½ inches.   D-22.50
Shoe horn, "Kennedy's—The Live Store".   D-1.50
Sign, "A.T. Cross Stylografic", 17 in. long, round.   S-45.00
Sign, "Drink Granite Rock Beverages", 9 x 19½ inches.   D-16.50
Sign, "Enjoy Kist Beverages/Take Home a Carton", 18 in. wide.   D-35.00
Sign, "Home Life Insurance Company-New York", 19 in. wide.   S-30.00
Stocking darner & needle holder, "Ashbrop/Germany".   D-8.50
Therometer, for Brown-Formans Kentucky Whiskey, 14 in. long.   D-85.00
Urn, aluminum, "Trixy Specific Exhalant/Concord, NH".   D-8.50

AFRICAN ART

Bowl, handcarved wood, oval, 5 x 8¼ inches.   D-25.00
Charm, boar tusk, suspension hole, lightly carved, 2¾ in. long.   D-35.00
Crocodile, hardwood with movable jaws, export item, 11 in. long.   D-14.00
Ebony bust of woman.   A-20.00
Elephant-hair bracelet, well-woven.   D-15.00
Fly-whisk, Zebra tailhair, wood handle, recent export item.   D-40.00
Gourd figure, natural-shape rind painted to resemble animal.   D-30.00
Horn chess set, brown and light pieces, inlaid wooden box.   D-90.00
Horn drinking vessel, 13 in. long.   A-40.00
Ivory pacifier box, 2¼ in. high.   A-30.00

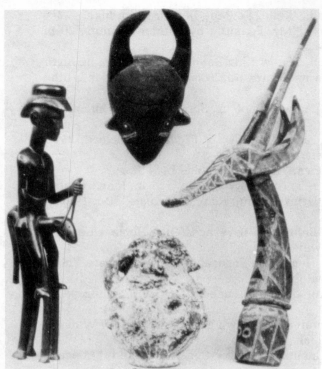

Left, **African wood sculpture of man on horse,** early 20th century, 30 in. high.
A/120

Bot. center, **African Baule tribe pottery animal-form vessel,** 15½ in. high.
A/50

Top center, **African carved wood mask** in form of water buffalo.
A/40

Right, **West African Krumba antelope headdress,** polychrome decorated.
A/100

Courtesy Adam A. Weschler & Son, Washington, D.C.; photograph by Breger & Associates.

Ivory tusk, swirling panel of various game, fish and birds, and crouching human-figure finial, 16 in. long.	**A-110.00**
Masks, carved wood and polychromed, pair.	**A-70.00**
Paddle, carved hardwood, dark, two open panels in blade, 35 in. long.	**D-90.00**
Saltbox, rectangular, carved wood, lidded, 5 in. long.	**D-35.00**
Shield, covered with cape(?) buffalo hide, lion-mane fringes, oblong, man-size.	**D-225.00**
Spear, 19 in. steel blade, carved hardwood handle, 47 in. overall.	**D-110.00**
Stabbing sword, hardwood handle, 18½ in. long.	**D-70.00**
Wood bust of woman, probably Makonde Tribe.	**A-170.00**
Wood and steel-blade axe, overall length 25 inches.	**A-30.00**

ALUMINUM TABLEWARE

This is a growing area of acquisition, but not yet one with wide collector interest. One wonders what the values will be ten years from now.

Admiration: Bowl, ruffled, leaf scroll, 14 inches. — D-5.00

Arthur Armor: Tray, pines and mountains, 9 x 11½ inches. — D-10.00

Brillianton: Dish, basket, wild rose, 8 inches. — D-2.50

Buenilum: Bowl, flower and loaf, 9 inches. — D-3.00

Buenilum: Casserole holder, handled, lid, 9½ inches. — D-3.00

Canterbury Arts: Ashtray, autumn bouquet, 5¼ inches. — D-2.00

Caldwell Silver Co.: Plate, iris, 13½ inches. — D-4.00

Designed Aluminum: Tray, flying ducks, 9 x 13½ inches. — D-3.50

Continental: Server, two-tier, acorns, 17¼ inches. — D-8.00

Continental: Lazy Susan, chrysanthemum, 18 inches. — D-7.00

Continental: Bread tray, chrysanthemum, 7½ x 13 inches. — D-8.00

Cromwell: Dish, fruits and flowers, hexagonal, 10 inches. — D-3.00

Crown: Dish, ruffled, roses, 13½ inches. — D-4.00

Everlast: Bowl, dogwood, 11 inches. — D-3.50

Farber & Shlevin: Dish, holly, scalloped, 7½ inches. — D-2.50

Farberware: Tray, rose, 13 inches. — D-3.50

Federal Silver Co.: Lazy Susan, glass insert, 14½ inches. — D-5.50

Hammercraft: Ice Bucket, plain, covered, insulated. — D-7.50

Hand-finished Aluminum: Tray, 7 x 11¾ inches. — D-3.00

Hand-finished Aluminum: Candy dish, covered, on tray, 7 inches. — D-5.00

Hand-wrought Aluminum: Dish, 20 inches. — D-6.50

Keystone: Tray, "Keystoneware Aluminum Hand Hammered", 16½ inches. — D-5.50

Lehman: Bowl, bouquet and bow, 13½ inches. — D-4.50

Hodney Kent: Coasters, tulip, seven in holder. — D-3.00

Hodney Kent: Lazy Susan, 18 inches. — D-6.00

Hodney Kent: Candy container, footed, blossom and bow. — D-4.00

Hodney Kent: Tray, tulip, handled, 11 x 16 inches. — D-45.00

Unidentified Aluminum: Coasters, ducks, set of eleven.   **D-5.00**

Unidentified Aluminum: Tray, dogwood, 5½ x 11 inches.   **D-3.00**

Wrought Aluminum: Serving plate, dish insert, 16½ inches.   **D-6.00**

AMERICAN INDIAN ARTIFACTS AND ART-WORKS [See also Eskimo]

Collecting artistic objects of the Native American groups has risen greatly in popularity in the past few years. Items of quality decorate fine homes, and have appeared in prestigeous exhibitions, in U.S. Embassies abroad. Basket, jewelry, pot or rug, the pieces exist in a range to match nearly every taste and budget. Good Indian art compares favorably as an investment with more traditional collectibles.

American Indian—*Baskets*

Passamaquoddy, 6¾ in. diameter.
C/25-30

Lidded basket, woven of thin splint and sweetgrass, Northeastern Indian-made, 4 in. diameter.
C/20-30

Photos courtesy Judy Morehead, Creative Photography, Lancaster, Ohio.

Penobscot, 3½ in. diameter.
C/10-12

Papago basket, Man-in-the Maze, 14 inches, ca. early 1900.   **A-100.00**

Achomawi basket, flying geese, 4½ x 6 inches, ca. 1884.   **A-120.00**

Apache-San Carlos tray, 3 x 12 inches, ca. 1898.   **A-350.00**

Hupa basket-bowl, Mt. Shasta pattern, 7 in. high, ca. 1911.   A-250.00

Inyokern basket, 9 x 11½ inches, caterpiller motif, ca. 1904.   A-175.00

Maidu coiled-bowl basket, 5½ in. high, stairway pattern, ca. 1889.   A-300.00

Miwok-Washoe basket, 9 x 15½ inches, storage bowl, ca. 1889.   A-275.00

Paiute-Washoe conical basket, 6½ x 8 inches, ca. 1902.   A-55.00

Panamint and Mission bottleneck basket, 6 x 9 inches, ca. 1892.   A-225.00

Panamint basket, 3½ x 5 x 8 inches, ca. 1911.   A-350.00

Pima basket, 7½ in. high, geometric "windows", ca. 1900.   A-80.00

Pomo gambling tray, 12 in. diameter, ca. 1891.   A-175.00

Salish embricated basket, 12 x 12 inches, ca. 1893.   A-300.00

Tlinglit basketry-covered inkwell, 2 x 3 inches, ca. 1893.   A-55.00

Tulare-Yokut basket, 5 x 12 inches, Adams Collection, ca. 1888.   A-350.00

Wappo basket, rare redbud, 2 x 2½ inches, ca. 1861.   A-180.00

Yokut basket, snake pattern, 3½ x 11 inches, ca. 1907.   A-375.00

American Indian—*Northwest Coast*

Bella Coola pipe with cooper bowl, contemporary, 11½ in. long.   A-180.00

Ceremonial copper knife, inlaid wooden handle, contemporary.   A-275.00

Haida ceremonial silver spoon, 6 in. long, hand-carved.   A-30.00

Haida potlatch pattern bowl, contemporary, wooden kneeling frog.   A-80.00

Kwakiutl carved sacred rattle, with frog, human and raven.   A-375.00

NW Coast basketry cap, 5 in. diameter, ca. 1879.   A-15.00

NW Coast wood beaver bookends, 3½ x 6 inches, ca. 1910-30.   A-60.00

NW Coast totem, carved walrus tusk 8½ in. long, ca. 1898.   A-100.00

Two small **lidded baskets.** On left, larger basket is 6 in. diameter, of reed and sweetgrass, fine condition. This is a recent Eastern U.S. item.   D/15
Smaller basket, woven from thin reed splints, is about 4 in. in diameter, also recent.   D/10

NW Coast totem pole, 14½ in. high, wood, ca. 1910.   **A-25.00**
NW Coast wooden bow, carved and inlaid, 36 in. long, early.   **A-350.00**
Tlinglit carved horn spoon, 6½ in. long. ca. 1888.   **A-105.00**

American Indian—*Plains Material*

Apache charm pouch, cross-pattern beadwork, ca. 1890.   **A-45.00**
Apache flint-and-steel bag, 3 x 4½ in., ca. 1875.   **A-110.00**
Arapahoe-Plains moccasins, 11in. long, ca. 1875.   **A-125.00**
Blackfoot beaded cape, dentillium, beads and bells. ca. 1877.   **A-750.00**
Blackfoot knife sheath, U.S. flag on rawhide, 15 in. long.   **A-125.00**
Cheyenne beaded armbands, buckskin with cloth liners, ca. 1916.   **A-110.00**
Cheyenne moccasins, quilled, beaded trim, ca. 1898.   **A-85.00**
Cheyenne umbilical fetish, lizard, 8 in. long, ca. 1890.   **A-150.00**
Dakota pipestone pipe, elaborate serpent, 24½ in. long.   **A-600.00**
Northern Ute ammunition pouch, 3 x 4½ inches, ca. 1888.   **A-120.00**
Plains Indian gambling sticks, various sizes, ca. 1885.   **A-125.00**

Shoshone beaded peace medal pouch, 3½ inches, ca. 1890. — A-160.00

Sioux beaded doctor's bag, 8 x 16 inches, fully beaded. — A-725.00

Sioux cradleboard, 36 in. high, from Montana Collection, ca. 1892. — A-1450.00

Ute belt pouch, buckskin, 6 in. long, beaded both sides, ca. 1889. — A-100.00

Ute warshirt, beading and ghost medicine paintwork, ca. 1890. — A-650.00

Oglalla Sioux **women's boots,** sinew sewn and fully beaded front and sides. The high tops make this pair a distinctive collector item; ca. 1920-25.

D/165

Photo courtesy Crazy Crow Trading Post, Denison, Texas.

Small Delaware **beaded purse,** 6 in. in diameter, with nicely balanced floral design on front. About 100 years old, it is ca. 1870-80. D/150

Photo courtesy Winona Trading Post, Santa Fe - Pierre & Sylvia Bovis.

American Indian—*Pottery*

Acoma Pueblo pot, 2 inches, geometric pattern. — A-25.00

Acoma pottery canteen, 7¾ in. high, geometric polychrome. — A-55.00

Acoma Pueblo effigy quail, 3 x 6 inches, signed "G. Lewis". — A-40.00

Black pottery, 5 in. high, early Marie and signed. — A-450.00

Cliff-dweller black-on-white ladle, 6 in. long, ca. AD 900. — A-45.00

Cochiti Pueblo pot, 3 x 3 inches, signed, Frog Devil spirit.　　　　　A-15.00

Cochiti Pueblo Storyteller doll, 4 inches, signed "Felipa".　　　　　A-20.00

Hopi bottleneck bowl, Tewa Pueblo, ca. 1950.　　　　A-100.00

Hopi jar, 11½ in. high, old-pattern Rainbirds, ca. 1830.　　　　　A-150.00

Mimbres prehistoric bowl, 6½ x 11 inches, repaired kill-hole.　　　　　A-110.00

Miniature pot, 2 inches, Acoma, by Lucy Lewis.　　A-35.00

San Juan Pueblo ceremonial plate, 15 in. diameter.　A-20.00

Santa Clara pottery, 4½ x 7 inches, signed "Betty & Lee Tafoya".　　　　　A-300.00

Santa Clara vase, 7 x 10½ inches, signed "Margaret Tafoya".　　　　　A-550.00

Zia Pueblo bowl, 9 in. high, signed "Seferina Pino".　A-135.00

Zia Pueblo turtle effigy, 5½ inches, signed "Kathy Pino".　　　　　A-18.00

AMERICAN INDIAN—
Silver and Turquoise

Trade silver brooch, 2 in. in diameter, and with elliptical and circular cutouts, scalloped rim, and touchmarked "DE". Sheet silver, and perfect condition.
C/Above 250

Photo courtesy Bob Coddington, Illinois.

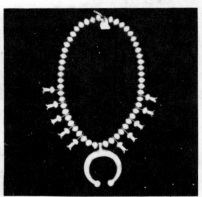

Heavy Navajo man's old **silver squash blossom necklace,** made with U.S. and Canadian dimes. No sets; fastened, necklace is 15 in. long and Naja is 4 in. wide. Has abalone piece tied to top. Sandcast Naja. This is a pawn piece from Teec Nos Pos Trading Post, Navajo reservation and ca. 1915.
C/600

S.W. Kernaghan photo; Marguerite Kernoghan Collection.

Bola tie, 3 x 6 inches, inlaid snake dancer, ca. 1950.　A-625.00

Navajo buckle, 3½ x 5 inches, single stone in silver, signed.　　　　　A-200.00

Navajo concho belt, signed, six 4 x 6 in. handtooled plates.　　　　　A-325.00

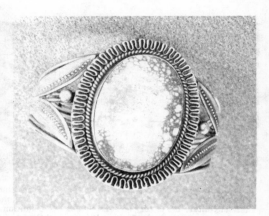

Old Navajo silver and turquoise bracelet, with circumference of bracelet 6¼ in. and stone measures 1¾ in. thick, 1¼ in. wide. A very fancy silver setting surrounds the turquoise, the stone along the edges gives an appearance of being spotted, with dark blue and a lighter blue. At bottom of bracelet back are etched two words, "Joann" and "Becent". Outstanding workstyle and in excellent condition, the piece is ca. 1920's.
C/650

Courtesy Hugo Poisson, photographer; Edmunds of Yarmouth, Inc: West Yarmouth, Massachusetts.

Navajo flask, handmade sterling, with 1922 silver dollar.   A-80.00

Navajo "Old Pawn" ring, 2 inches, one turquoise, signed.   A-25.00

Navajo "Pawn" bowguard, 3 x 4 inches, sandcast, ca. 1930.   A-150.00

Navajo silver ash tray, 4 x 6½ inches, turquoise centerpiece.   A-85.00

Navajo Squashblossom necklace, 15 in. worn length, ca. 1915.   A-225.00

Navajo-Zuni concho belt, eight plaques, heartline jet bears with coral, Taos Collection.   A-750.00

Silver Padre cross, 4 x 5½ inches with approx. 100 carats of Nevada spiderweb turquoise.   A-800.00

Zuni bracelet, 52 turquoise stones, sunburst, ca. 1930-40.   A-100.00

Zuni channel-work necklace, 15½ in. length worn, ca. 1937.   A-580.00

Zuni heartline fetish, 4½ x 8 inches, coral inlay with jet.   A-110.00

Zuni "Old Pawn" bracelet, cluster turquoise in silver, ca. 1930-50.   A-200.00

Zuni "Old Pawn" bracelet, natural turquoise clusterwork, ca. 1920-30.   A-125.00

AMERICAN INDIAN—*Weavings*

Chief's parade blanket, Germantown, 26 x 27 inches, ca. 1910.   A-150.00

Chimayo on Rio Grande striped blanket, 41½ x 49 inches.   A-100.00

Classic **Chevron/Terrace chief's blanket**, black, orange, pink and gray. Has eye-dazzler center, and is very soft. Excellent condition, and 54½ in. by 77½ in. It is ca. 1875-85.

C/1750

Photo courtesy Rob Swan Town-shende, California

Transitional diamond pattern blanket, tight weave, in white orangeish, and brown. Fair condition, and 47 in. by 62 in. Ca 1890-1900. C/650

Photo courtesy Rob Swan Town-shende, California

Eastern Woodlands belt pouch, 3½ x 5 inches, ca. 1850-60. **A-70.00**

Hopi ceremonial sash, handwoven, fringed, 72 in. long. **A-50.00**

Navajo Ganado-Hubbell picture rug, 48 x 74 inches, classic. **A-1100.00**

Navajo Ganado Spirit rug, 41 x 63 inches, classic red, ca. 1890. **A-900.00**

Navajo Germantown eye-dazzler, 25 x 64 inches, ca. 1890. **A-200.00**

Navajo rug, classic Crystal, 4.2 x 7.8 ft., five colors and cross-feather-fishhook motifs. Ca. 1920-29. **A-1600.00**

Navajo rug, Two Grey Hills, vegetal dye and home-spun. McCormick Collection; 5.2 x 8 feet, ca. pre-1940. **A-2250.00**

Navajo Teec-Nos-Pos, a masterpiece. Vegetal dyes, 6 ft. x 8 ft. 2 in., winner of over 200 blue ribbons. Ca. 1915-30. **A-11,000.00**

Navajo-Ute vegetal-dye weaving, 2.2 x 5.6 feet, ca. 1956. **A-475.00**

Navajo wedding rug, Window Rock origin, 3 x 5 feet. **A-125.00**

Tuba City Storm Pattern, 33 x 51 inches, fine weave. **A-275.00**

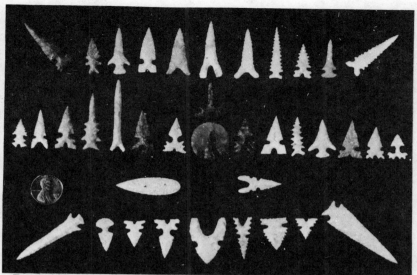

Frame of fine **birdpoints**, gem quality, all from Greene County, Missouri. Some forms would be drills, the balance arrowheads. Note the serrated edges on many, and the wide variety of forms. Items found by Lynn Denby, Earnest Giboney and Harley Israel.

Photo courtesy of Lynn W. Denby,
Rogersville, Missouri.

Each C/5-35

French trade pipe, historic, from Ontario, Canada. Piece is 2 in. high and 2 in. long, quite well made and in fine condition.
C/25

Photo courtesy Robert C. Calvert, London, Ontario, Canada.

Slate birdstone, from Victoria County, Ontario, Canada. This is a fine popeyed specimen, and measures 4-1/8 in. in length. Piece is drilled on bottom ridges and is in perfect condition.
C/1200-1500
Photo courtesy Robert C. Calvert, London, Ontario, Canada.

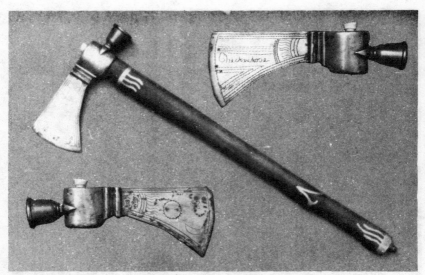

Cheek-cah-kose (Little Crane) presentation grade pipe **tomahawk**. Little Crane was a Chief of the Pottawattomie, with a village at the headwaters of the Tippecanoe River in northern Indiana. Three views: Left and right sides of the head; and a full view. Head is of engraved pewter, with a brass screw-out bowl. The blade is hallmarked (DV) over a coronet. Presentation pieces of this quality are rare. CA 1767.

C/1800

Photo courtesy Bob Coddington, Illinois.

Left

Fine **three-quarters grooved axe**, 7½ in. long, 3¼ in. wide below notch. Very good condition, some polish. Franklin County, Ohio. Archaic period; axe is made of a compact brownish material.

Private collection.   C/70

Right

Unusual **three-quarters grooved axe**, from Franklin County, Ohio, and 6-7/8 in. long, 3-5/8 in. wide. Made of grayish quartzite material.

Private collection.   C/60

Lure box, Northwest Coastal Indian-made, incised decorations, used to hold fishing gear. Made of spruce, 12 in. wide.
C/85-110

Photo courtesy Judy Morehead, Creative Photography, Lancaster, Ohio.

ANIMATION CELS

"Cels" are artists' figures done on transparent film to illustrate each movement of the story feature. Collecting cels began in the early 1930's, and some limited-edition reproductions are being made today.

Alice, Carpenter and Oyster (ALICE IN WONDERLAND), full figures, some minor paint chips. **D-135.00**
Bongo (FUN AND FANCY FREE), full sheet and figure. **D-165.00**
Donald Duck, with ten-gallon hat and sheriff badge. **D-95.00**
Donald Duck, wearing safari hat and with rifle on shoulder. **D-60.00**
Donald's Nephew holding axe, full figure, matted. **D-40.00**
Girl, (CASEY BATS AGAIN), sitting, holding flower. **D-90.00**
The Green Fairy, (SLEEPING BEAUTY), full "good fairy" attire, cut-out image. **D-65.00**
Greta Garbo and Edward G. Robinson, (MOTHER GOOSE GOES HOLLYWOOD). Attractive airbrushed background, both on seesaw. Gold leaf Disney stamp; 1938. **D-425.00**
Ichabod, large image from waist up, with pointer and book in hands. Professionally matted, oval cut. **D-120.00**
Lady (LADY AND THE TRAMP), full figure side view. **D-70.00**
Lambert the Sheepish Lion, full figure, clinging to crate top. **D-90.00**
Pluto, large side view, full figure, early 1950's. **D-85.00**

ANTIQUITIES

Axhead, Hittite, copper, incised decoration, 7 in. long. **A-50.00**
Bottle, Phoenician, tear-drop glass. **A-60.00**
Bottle, Roman, flare-neck, glass, ca. 2nd C. AD, 3½ in. high. **A-150.00**
Cover, Egyptian, terracotta, in form of sphinx head, with polychrome decoration. **A-225.00**
Cup, unknown source, red clay with handle, incised decoration. **A-10.00**
Dagger, Roman, bronze with cast hilt, 9½ in. long. **A-120.00**
Ewer, Roman, bronze, ca. 1st C. AD, 6 in. high. **A-150.00**

Attic Black glaze kylix, 6
in. high, prob. 5th
Century BC.
A/250

Attic Black glaze kylix. 5¼ in.
high, prob. 5th Century BC.
A/250

Attic red figure amphora,
7½ in. high, prob. 500
BC.
A/600

Courtesy Adam A.
Weschler & Son, Wash-
ington, D.C.; photograph
by Breger & Associates.

Figure, Greek, seated, terracotta, 3½ in. high.   A-75.00
Figures, Egyptian, bronze, of Horus and Isis, taller
4¾ in. high.   A-180.00
Flask and cup, Greek, two pieces, terracotta.   A-90.00
Fragments, Greek, marble, of capital tops, ca. 1st C.
BC, 7 to 8 in. high.   A-50.00
Glass, Phoenician, three pieces; beaker, vase, and
bowl, from 3 to 5 in. high.   A-210.00
Glass, Phoenician, four pieces, three vases and
bowl, 3½ to 5½ in. high.   A-140.00
God, Egyptian, baboon, of basalt.   A-80.00
Head, Greek, terracotta, of bearded man; ca. 2nd C.
BC, 4½ in. high.   A-300.00
Jars, Egyptian, alabaster, unguent type, late 18th
Dynasty, ca. 1400 BC; 10 in. high.   A-175.00
Lamp, Cypriot, oil, ca. 400 BC, 6½ in. high.   A-75.00
Lamps, Cypriot, pottery, oil, ca. 300 BC, 3 to 4 in.
high.   A-125.00
Lamp, Roman, bronze, circular, 1st C. BC, 3 in.
diameter.   A-75.00
Mask, mummy, Egyptian, polychrome, 8 in. high.   A-275.00
Necklaces, and ibis, Egyptian, jackal, faience ibis.   A-70.00
Osiris, statue, Egyptian, polychromed wood, 16½ in.
high.   A-120.00
Pin, Scythian, cloak, 2¼ in. long, of bronze wire.   A-45.00

Pitcher, Roman, greenish glass, 3rd to 4th C. AD, 4¼ in. high.   A-200.00

Scarabs and wax seal, Egyptian, three scarabs.   A-160.00

Scarabs and wax seals, total of eight.   A-190.00

Torso, Greek, marble, of man, 10 in. high.   A-550.00

Ushibdi, standing, Egyptian, basalt.   A-130.00

Ushibdis, Egyptian, three, faience.   A-80.00

Vase, source unknown, tomb, stone.   A-110.00

ART DECO

Box, ruby, hinged top; 18-K yellow gold engine-turned, decorated. Set with approx. 320 French cut rubies, averaging .05 carats each, and ruby thumb push clasp. Rubies total weight approx. 16 carats, box 103.5 pennyweight.   A-2,050.00

Lamp, table, art-glass and brass. Geometric honeycomb caramel glass shade supported by trumpet base, 26 in. high.   A-325.00

Lamp, onyx, with champleve enamel mounts, 23 in. high.   A-110.00

Torcheres, table; bronzed, pair. Three nude males supporting cylinder-shaped mica shade on round base raised on bun feet. By Oscar B. Bach Studios, 1st Qtr. 20th Century, 24 in. high.   A-325.00

Vase, iridescent glass; copper color with white ribbing. Signed Dominique Labino, 5 in. high.   A-60.00

Art Deco and Art Nouveau Works of Art: Bot. left and 6 pcs. bot. right, **Tiffany favrile glass seven-piece liqueur set,** inscribed "L.C.T.".

A/500

Top left, **Tiffany favrile glass vase,** 5 in. high.

A/225

Top right, **Tiffany favrile glass trumpet-form bud vase,** irridescent pale green-to-yellow, 6 in. high.

A/250

Bot. center, **blue iridescent glass lily-form** vase, 5½ in. high.

A/250

Courtesy Adam A. Weschler & Son,

26

ART NOUVEAU

Bracelet, unmarked sterling, leaf concentrics and Victorian lady's head, oval medallion 1½ in. long. **D-35.00**

Chandelier, brass and frosted crystal; eight etched crystal fan-shaped panels, floral staffs, blue mirrored ground, 30 in. high. **A-375.00**

Clock, figural relief, gilted white metal, "Germany", 6½ in. high. **D-32.50**

Cyclist's cup, polished brass, collapsable, head and shoulders of Victorian lady in raised relief. **D-14.50**

Figure, bronze, of a maiden, inscribed Clio Bracken, (American). **A-350.00**

Lamp, bronzed, interior-painted glass shade, inscribed Bradley & Hubbard, four floral panels, ribbed exterior, 20 in. high. **A-225.00**

Lamp, bronze and art-glass, pierced silhouetted arbor and sunset coloration glass shade, pine needle rim, on stylized tree trunk stem on round base. Overall height, 24 inches. **A-875.00**

Lamp, bronzed and art-glass, octagonal shade, overall height 26 inches. **A-130.00**

Lamp, gilt-metal and art-glass shade, domed six caramel colored glass tapered panels on hexagonal base, 21 in. high. **A-175.00**

Lamp, desk, hammered copper and art-glass, by Handel, 14 in. high. **A-400.00**

Lamp, floor, bronze, cut green glass melon-form inset, 57 in. high. **A-90.00**

Lamp, table, bronze and frosted glass shade with four painted landscapes, 21 in. diameter, 26 in. high. **A-475.00**

Lamp, table, clear crystal, signed "Val St. Lambert", 25½ in. high. **A-140.00**

Lamp, table, gilted metal and caramel glass, ca. 1908, 24 in. high. **A-200.00**

Lamp, table, bronzed and art-glass, geometric and floral shade, 29 in. high. **A-550.00**

Torcheres, table, pair; French satinglass cone-shaped shades, "Roby/Paris", fitted in tulip leafage. **A-325.00**

Vase, molded green glass, six maidens supporting grape arbor, 5 in. high. **A-80.00**

Vase, molded green glass, three maidens supporting trumpet-shape vase, 8¾ in. high. A-90.00

Vase, porcelain, three-handled, yellow colors, signed, 6 in. high. D-15.00

Above left.
Stained glass window.   200

Above right, top.
Belt buckle, gold.   175-200

Above right, center.
Match safe, silver.   75-100

Above right, lower.
Cigarette case, silver.   75-100

Art Nouveau. **Stained glass window.**

250

Art Nouveau leaded glass lamp, 19½ in. diameter, overall height 26 inches. Domed leaded glass shade on bronze base with acanthus leaf stem on shaped base with reeded border. CA. 1900.

A/850

Courtesy Adam A. Weschler & Son, Washington, D.C.; photograph by Breger & Associates.

Art Nouveau mirror, sterling silver.

C/25-35

Art Nouveau manicure, sterling silver handle.

C/10-15

Lar Hothem photo.

ARTISTS' ORIGINALS — *Icons*
(Religious-motif paintings)

Mother and child, on wood panel. Brass rizza and
titled in Cryillic, 7 x 9 inches; Russian. A-125.00

St. George, gilded rizza, 19th Century, 9 x 11 inches. A-275.00

St. Peter and St. Paul, 18th Century, Russian, 10 x 12
inches. A-275.00

St. Stephanos, on wood panel, Russian, 8 x 11
inches. A-145.00

Set, two: Of St. Nicholas, and of a Deisis group, late
19th Century, each with silvered brass rizzas; 5½ x
7 inches. A-525.00

ARTISTS' ORIGINALS — *Miniatures on Ivory*

Child with blue eyes, trimmed in blue ribbon. Some
water damage and brass case needs repair, 1¾ in.
high. A-105.00

Gentleman, small oval gold case, 1½ in. high. A-135.00

Gentleman, in rectangular gold case, 2½ in. high. A-235.00

Gentleman, in ornate oval brass case, base with
minor repair, 2½ in. high. A-115.00

Gentleman with brown coat, and curly hair, embossed brass on wood frame, 2¾ x 3½ inches. A-155.00

Gentleman with curly red hair, window in back with
scrap of orig. swatch of cloth from subject's coat,
2-7/8 inches. A-375.00

Gentleman with white powdered hair, gold case
with lens in back holding brown swatch of subject's
coat, 3 in. high. A-135.00

Gentleman with white hair, wearing red uniform,
unframed, 2½ in. high. A-125.00

Lady with red beads and purple dress, ornate oval
gilt brass case with empty window in back, 2¾ in.
high. A-145.00

Lady with ruffled cap, rectangular gold case. Window in back shows two dates on ivory back, 1791
and 1832, 2½ x 3-1/8 inches. A-145.00

Young man, flowing hair, ivory frame. A-90.00

Young woman in short dark hair, watercolor, 2½ in.
high. A-95.00

Portrait Miniatures:
Top center, **Lord Wellington.** French, late 18th-early 19th Century.
A/160
Bot. left, **Marcihal Ney.** French, 19th Century, signed "P. Roitz".
A/250
Bot. right, **Princess Pauline Bonaparte.** Watercolor on ivory. French, ca.
1810, signed "R. Mayer".
A/325

Courtesy Adam A. Weschler & Son, Washington, D.C.; photograph by
Breger & Associates.

ARTISTS' ORIGINALS — *Multi-Media*

Acrylic on canvas, by George Henry Duquet (Canadian 19th/20th C.), "Un Matin de Septembre", signed and dated " '22", 28 x 40 inches. A-450.00

Charcoal drawing, unknown, "View on the Hudson", sidewheeler steamboat and porch with vines, 22¼ x 28¼ inches. A-165.00

Charcoal drawing, unknown, of young girl with fruit, old curly maple frame, 12½ x 16¾ inches. A-65.00

Oil on board, by R. Wogerer or R. Wogertt, (Aus. 19th-20th C.), "Alpine Landscape With Chalet". Signed, 10 x 15 inches.

A/450

Courtesy Adam A. Weschler & Son, Washington, D.C.; photograph by Breger & Associates.

Oil on panel, by Hermanus Koekoek (Dutch 1836-1895), "Coastal Shipping". Signed, 7 x 9½ in.

A/750

Courtesy Adam A. Weschler & Son, Washington, D.C.; photograph by Breger & Associates.

Charcoal on paper drawing, unknown, of bearded gentleman, old pine frame partially stripped, 10¼ x 11½ inches. **A-25.00**

Charcoal portrait of child, grained frame, 9½ x 11½ inches. **A-30.00**

Crayon on paper, English 20th Century school, still life with vase of flowers, 9½ x 13 inches. **A-60.00**

Engraving, handcolored, "Gooseander, Male", unframed, matted size 25 x 30¾ inches. **A-85.00**

Etching and drypoint, James Abbot MacNeil Whistler (American 1834-1903), "Eagle Wharf", signed in plate, dated 1859, 5½ x 8½ inches. **A-450.00**

Ink and pencil drawing, profile of gentleman, Michigan; old pine frame, 5½ x 6½ inches. **A-125.00**

Mixed media on paper, Eugene Berman (Russian, 1899 -), "Ballet Roma Angel", signed on monogram, dated 1955, 9 x 11½ inches. **A-160.00**

Oil on board, May Ames (American, died 1934), "A Country Road", signed and dated 1933, 3¼ x 5 inches.   A-100.00

Oil on board, attrib. to Julian Alden Weir (American, 1852-1919), "New York Street Scene", signed 8½ x 13 inches.   A-375.00

Oil on board, primitive, Georgia, framed, 19 x 26½ inches.   A-52.50

Oil on cradled panels, in the manner of Francois Boucher (French, 18th Century), "Muses With Amori", 13½ x 19 inches. Pair.   A-700.00

Oil on masonite, David Burliuk, Jr., (Russian-American, 1922-1967), "Girl With Yellow Babushka . . .", signed, 9½ x 12 inches.   A-300.00

Oil on panel, attrib. to Bernard De Hood (Dutch, 1867-1943), "Farm Girl", signed with initials, 7 x 9 inches.   A-375.00

Oil on panel, school of Joseph Israels (Dutch, 19th Century), "Woman Seated Beside Window Mending", apocryphal signature, 13 x 17 inches.   A-525.00

Oil on panel, attrib. to Jacob Maris (Dutch, 1837-1899), "Windmill Near Dordrecht", signed, 9¼ x 11½ inches.   A-425.00

Oil on panels, pair; primitive portraits of man and woman, Hall-Northway, Ohio. Unframed, 20¾ x 28½ inches.   A-2,000.00

Oil on tin, Dutch 19th Century school, "The Young Cavalrymen", 8½ x 10 inches.   A-300.00

Oil on wood, Dutch 18th Century school, "Portrait Of Young Man", 7 x 8½ inches.   A-700.00

Oil on wood panel, portrait of young child in red, minor touch-up needed, 15 x 18 inches.   A-450.00

Oil on wood panel, primitive, scene of goat in farmyard with white picket fence. Signed and dated 1837, old frame, 11 x 11¼ inches.   A-125.00

Opaque watercolor on paper, painting of sailing ship, minor paper damage. Framed, 21½ x 22½ inches.   A-55.00

Pastel on canvas, portrait on young girl wearing grey dress with white collar, red and black background. Old grained frame, 15½ x 19¾ inches.   A-320.00

Pencil drawing, of leopard, primitive, framed, 4½ x 5¼ inches.   A-26.00

Pen and ink, drawing of bird, Spencerian, signed and dated 1883. Purple and brown ink, old pine frame.   **A-40.00**

Pen and ink watercolor map, of New Hampshire, pine frame, 12¼ x 15 inches.   **A-40.00**

Pencil drawing, of farm building, dated 1888, framed, 11½ x 17 inches.   **A-32.50**

Pencil drawing, primitive, of lady in fancy lace hat. Date(?) 1830 on back, curly maple frame, 10 x 12 inches.   **A-80.00**

Pencil and watercolor drawing, of basket of flowers in soft colors. Old gilt frame, 13 x 16¼ inches.   **A-95.00**

Penmanship drawing with watercolor, with maps, verse, floral decoration, signed, dated 1818. Tears in paper, frame is yellow with brown graining, 16 x 18 inches.   **A-280.00**

Reverse painting on glass, oval frame, 14 x 24 inches.   **D-125.00**

Reverse painting on glass, "Martin Van Buren" very minor wear. Old pine frame painted black, 15¼ x 17¼ inches.   **A-575.00**

Theorem on paper, yellow finch in cherry tree, old gilt frame, 12 x 15½ inches.   **A-75.00**

Theorem on velvet, primitive basket of flowers in yellow, blue, green and pink. Old gilt frame, 12½ x 13 inches.   **A-200.00**

Theorem on velvet, bird in fanciful cage, 20th Century. Framed, 21¼ x 23¼ inches.   **A-300.00**

Watercolor, basket of fruit, old gold-gilt frame, 14¾ x 15¾ inches.   **A-180.00**

Watercolor, bird, red and dark brownish green. Walnut frame, 7 x 8¼ inches.   **A-85.00**

Watercolor, carnation, old frame with alligatored varnish, 9 x 10¾ inches.   **A-75.00**

Watercolor drawing, girl and cat on bench, "My Kitten", old pine frame, 10¼ x 12¾ inches.   **A-200.00**

Watercolor on paper, basket of flowers, old gilt frame, 13 x 16½ inches.   **A-220.00**

Watercolor on paper, William Rickarby Miller, (American, 1850-1923), "Stream By Rocky Cliff". Signed, dated 1880, 9 x 12 inches.   **A-300.00**

Watercolor on paper, drawing of a hawk, "Falco, Tinnunculus/A. F. 1804". Good detail, framed, 13½ x 15½ inches.   **A-355.00**

Watercolor painting, primitive, of farmstead, vegetables and corn growing in patches. Paper with old repairs, modern frame and matt, 23¼ x 31¼ inches.   **A-515.00**

Watercolor, primitive, of crowned Goddess of Harvest with cornucopia and bouquet of flowers. Old frame with black paint, 11½ x 13½ inches.   **A-165.00**

Watercolor on paper bookplate, red, green and yellow vining border, owner's name and date, 1800. Old veneer frame, 6½ x 9½ inches.   **A-550.00**

Watercolor and pencil, drawing of flowers, 13 x 15½ inches.   **A-85.00**

White chalk on blue paper, Dutch 18th Century school, military engagement, 3½ x 11½ inches.   **A-225.00**

ARTISTS' ORIGINALS—*Oil on Canvas*

American 20th Century primitive school, portrait of man and wife, two paintings. Each signed "Oscar", unframed, 13¼ x 17¼ inches.   **A-250.00**

American, 20th Century school, "Landscape With Winding Path", signed and dated 1930, 9 x 12 inches.   **A-60.00**

After Thomas Gainsborough, 18th-19th Century, "Mother With Child" 39 x 60 inches.   **A-450.00**

After Thomas Gainsborough, 19th Century, portrait of a young girl, 24 x 29 inches.   **A-175.00**

Attrib. to Edmond Darch Lewis, (American, 1837-1910), "Sun Rising In Mountain Landscape", 14 x 34 inches.   **A-525.00**

Brydall, Robert; (Scottish, 19th Century), "The Douglas Tragedy", signed, 30 x 38 inches.   **A-950.00**

Oil on canvas, mounted on aluminum, by G. P. Ohlgart (English, 19th century), "Sheep Grazing by Stream". Signed, and 22 x 34 inches.

A/575

Courtesy Adam A. Weschler & Son, Washington, D.C.; photograph by Breger & Associates.

35

Oil on canvas, "Still Life of Snipes", by William H. Machen, American, 1832-1911. Signed; 14 x 18 inches.
A/650

Courtesy Adam A. Weschler & Son, Washington, D.C.; photograph by Breger & Associates.

Burliuk, David, Jr.; (Russian-American, 1922-1967), "Farmyard Scene In Florida", signed and dated 1946, 18 x 22 inches.   A-550.00

Carmiencke, Johan-Herman; (American, 1810-1867), "Hyde Park From Eastern Shore...". Signed and dated 1888, 7 x 10 inches.   A-725.00

"Death And The Wind", signed, titled and dated on reverse, 1930, 30 x 36 inches.   A-190.00

Dutch 18th-19th Century School, pair of paintings, "Still Life With Urn of Flowers", each 29 x 34 inches.   A-975.00

Dutch 19th Century school, "Still Life With Vase of Flowers", 24 x 30 inches.   A-250.00

English 19th Century school, sporting scene of fox-hunt, 20 x 27 inches. — A-275.00

European 19th Century school, portrait of bearded gentleman with fur hat, round, 12 in. diameter. — A-375.00

Forbes, John Colin; (Canadian 1846-1925), sailboats in harbor, signed, 13½ x 17½ inches. — A-500.00

Foster, J.; (English 19th-20th Centuries), portrait of three-masted square rigger, signed, 24 x 36 inches. — A-100.00

"Fountains At The New York World's Fair, 1939", unsigned, 32 x 39 inches. — A-350.00

French 17th Century school, herdsman resting on patch with other figures, 47 x 57 inches. — A-375.00

Frost, George Albert; (American, born 1843), Arctic scene with three dogsleds, 20 x 25 inches. — A-750.00

German 19th Century school, "Der Gasthof", signed with initials, 20 x 25 inches. — A-1,400.00

Graves, Abbott Fuller; (American, 1859-1934), coastal view with breakers, signed, 28 x 49 inches. — A-800.00

Howard, Cortile; (American, 20th Century), view of Paris, signed, 15½ x 19½ inches. — A-150.00

Inness, George; (American, 1825-1894), oil landscape signed and dated 1881, 15½ x 20 inches. — A-1,425.00

Jensen, Leif Rabn; (American, 20th Century), setter flushing quail. Signed and dated 1969, 24 x 35 inches. — A-190.00

Key, John Ross; (American, 1832-1920), harbor scene. Signed and dated 1877, 10 x 16 inches. (Son of Francis Scott Key who wrote the "Star Spangled Banner".) — A-1,150.00

Landscape, fancy gilt frame, 10 x 13 inches. — A-320.00

Landscape, sunset over wooded lake, dark, crazed surface. Fancy gilt frame, 15½ x 17½ inches. — A-245.00

"Le Rocher des Mouettes"; (Gull Rock), "...painted at New York, 1909", 34 x 36 inches. — A-575.00

"Little Bermudian Girls'; signed and dated on reverse, "Bermuda/1910", 29 x 30 inches. — A-800.00

Luks, George Benjamin; (American, 1867-1933), Royal Canadian Mounty, signed, 24½ x 34 inches. — A-4,000

Lewis, Narcissa; painting of farm ca. 1882, pine frame, 27 x 34½ inches. — A-220.00

Martin, Thomas Mower; (Canadian, 1838-1934), wooded landscape in Massachusetts, signed and dated 1893, 8 x 13 inches. — A-325.00

Mira, Alfred S.; impressionist street scene in the rain, signed, 11¾ x 16 inches. This was a 20th Century American artist. A-325.00

Muller, August; (German, 1836-1885), "The Cello Maker", signed, 8 x 10 inches. A-1,700.00

"Music At Evening", signed, titled and dated on reverse, 1938, 30 x 40 inches. A-100.00

New Orleans 19th Century portrait school, gentleman standing, leaning on rock. ca. 1840, 19 x 23 inches. A-400.00

"Northern Lights", signed, titled and dated on reverse, 1937, 23 x 30 inches. A-90.00

Opennser, A.; (Contemporary), "Hong Kong Harbor", signed, oil on canvas mounted on board, 18 x 27 inches. A-150.00

Oil on canvas, portrait of gentleman, inscription on back: "Painted...by Waldo in the year 1790". Old gilt frame missing some plaster detail, 33 x 38 inches. A-500.00

Oil on canvas portraits, pair; man and woman, late 19th Century. Framed, 26 x 31 inches. A-300.00

Oil on canvas primitive, portrait of two children, good rich colors, drapery background. Orig. condition with one small patch. Attrib. to Horace Bundy, Vermont; unframed, 24¼ x 28¼ inches. A-950.00

Primitive portrait, of gentleman, red drapery background. Some restoration necessary, framed, 29 x 34 inches. A-600.00

Primitive portrait, of young woman, back with inscription and date "July, 1846". One gilt frame, 29½ x 34¾ inches. A-360.00

Primitive portrait, gentleman, two small repairs, orig. condition including stretcher, unframed, 24 x 29 inches. A-300.00

Primitive portrait, old woman in white bonnet, old poplar frame, 22 x 24 inches. A-165.00

Scene, of Union Army encampment, reported to be Kings Mountain. Rebacked, cleaned and repaired, unframed, 24 x 28 inches. A-550.00

Still life, painting of fruit, rich old colors. Two small old tears, pine frame, 17 x 21 inches. A-280.00

Verny, Jos.; (European, 20th Century), barnyard scene with sheep. Signed, 12 x 24 inches. A-170.00

Zeebroek, L. Van (Dutch, 1822-1890), skaters on the canal. Signed and dated 1849, 23½ x 29 inches. A-450.00

ARTISTS' ORIGINALS—*Silhouettes*

Cut sil. of gentleman, inscription on back, 4¼ x 5¼ inches.   A-55.00

Cut silhouette, grained frame, signature, 12¼ x 16¼ inches.   A-425.00

Hollow-cut silhouette, marked "Peale Museum", 7 x 8¼ inches.   A-150.00

Hollow-cut sil. of boy, old wood frame, 4½ x 4¾ inches.   A-75.00

Hollow-cut sil. of child, full-figure, old frame, 6 x 8 inches.   A-65.00

Hollow-cut sil. of old woman, elaborate hat, 4-5/8 x 5½ inches.   A-70.00

Hollow-cut sil. of young girls, pair; pencil highlights, turned wooden frames painted black, 5¼ in. diameter.   A-240.00

Ink sil. of gentleman, gold highlights, "1813", 5¾ x 6¾ inches.   A-145.00

Ink on paper sil. of gentleman, brass-trimmed frame, 4¾ x 5½ inches.   A-77.50

Portrait of **woman reading** by an anonymous 19th Century silhouette.
C/175

A rendering of **Arthur Middleton,** signer of the Declaration of Independence, by an unknown 19th Century American silhouettist.
C/225

AUTOGRAPHS

The collecting of signed names—of the famous, the great, even the notorious—has long been a popular field. Such signatures may exist by themselves or may be placed in books or be on photographs or documents. All are eagerly sought today.

Note that the word "autograph" means self-writing and can be more than a signed name. An unsigned, handwritten letter is still an autograph. Signed, it would be an autograph letter with signature. Value determinants for autographs include clarity and condition of the work, importance of the communication or document, if any, and the fame or lasting importance of the personage.

Rarity is also usually a factor, meaning how many other autographs by that person are believed to exist.

Abbot, Charles Greeley. American astro-physicist, signed letter, 1958. **D-15.00**

Agnew, Spiro T. U.S. Vice-President under Nixon. Signed 4¾ x 6½ in. color photo. **D-30.00**

Allen, Woody. American writer and entertainer. Signed 8 x 10 photo. **D-35.00**

Andrews, Roy Chapman, (1884-1960). American naturalist, explorer and author, signed quotation. **D-10.00**

(Atomic bomb). Group photo, 8 x 10, of nine men with bomber, "Enola Gay". Signed by **Paul W. Tibbets**, pilot. **D-25.00**

Astor, Lady Nancy, (1879-1964). First woman to sit in the British Parliament. Signed letter, London, 1923. **D-12.50**

Bankhead, Tullulah, (1844-1923). Stage and screen actress. Signed 5 x 7 photo. **D-15.00**

Barnum, Phineas T. (1810-91). American showman. One-page signed letter, 1853. **D-22.50**

Baruch, Bernard M. (1870-1965). American businessman and Presidential adviser. Signature. **D-10.00**

Beatrice, Princess (1857-1944). Daughter of Queen Victoria. Signature. **D-10.00**

Begin, Menachem. Israeli Prime Minister. Four-page printed speech, signed "M. Begin, Jerusalem". **D-65.00**

Bunche, Ralph J. (1904-71). American diplomat, winner of Nobel Peace Prize. Signed letter. **D-12.00**

Cahn, Sammy. American composer. Quotes five lines from his famous song, "I'll Walk Alone". Signed letter. **D-25.00**

Carnegie, Andrew (1835-1919). Industrialist and humanitarian. Signed one-page letter, 1887. **D-80.00**

Carter, Lillian. President Carter's mother. Signed 8 x 10 color photo. **D-40.00**

Chadwick, Florence. First woman to swim the English Channel both ways. Signed 1962 letter. **D-12.00**

Chagall, Marc. Russian Impressionist and Cubist painter. Signed reproduction of the color painting "Bella". **D-75.00**

(Civil War—Confederate). Group of eighteen letters of William Browning Co. I, 9th Texas Infantry. Concerns battles, leaders, etc. Some original envelopes, stamps removed. Texas Civil War material, and rare. **D-375.00**

(Civil War—Union). Augustus W. Bradford (1806-81). War Governor of Maryland. Bank check issued and signed, 1864. **D-15.00**

(Civil War—Union). James C. Rice, Union General, killed in action, Spotsylvania, 1864. Signed document. **D-30.00**

Parrish, Maxfield, ALS "Dad" 3½ pp., Windsor, May 12, 1942, re: life at home during WW II.
D/235

_____, TLS, Windsor, VT., Sept. 24, 1924, re: his prints, w/orig. env.
A/30

_____, LS, 1p., Windsor, Jun. 10, 1953, re; his painting, Giant and Soldier.
D/150

Sandburg, Carl, TMsS, about ½ p., poem "Lost" inscribed and signed, 1961.
C/40

Crosby, Bing (1901-77). American singer and actor. Signed photo inscribed to "Duane".   **D-100.00**

Davis, Bette. American actress. Signed 8 x 10 photo.   **D-30.00**

Dean, Dizzy (1911-74). Baseball pitcher; member of Baseball Hall of Fame. Signature.   **D-10.00**

Dempsey, Jack. World heavyweight boxing champion. Signed 8 x 10 photo, plastic tape attached.   **D-15.00**

Dietrich, Marlene. German singer-actress in America. Signed 8 x 10 photo.   **D-40.00**

Doyle, Sir A. Conan (1859-1930). Creator of Sherlock Holmes. Signature.   **D-38.50**

Durbin, Deanna. Canadian singer and actress. Signed 8 x 10 photo.   **D-17.50**

Edison, Thomas A. (1847-1931). American inventor. Signed 5 x 7 photo, 1921.   **D-90.00**

Ford, Gerald R. President of the U.S. Printed 3 x 5 picture of Nixon; signed as Minority Leader.   **D-40.00**

Garibaldi, Giuseppe (1807-82). Italian leader and patriot. Signature.   **D-35.00**

Glenn, Jr., John H. First American astronaut to orbit the earth. Signed 1962 **Project Mercury** First Day Cover.   **D-17.50**

Goethals, George W. (1858-1928). American general and engineer, of Panama Canal fame. Signed letter.   **D-65.00**

Hoover, J. Edgar (1895-1972). American criminologist, F.B.I. Director. Signature.   **D-10.00**

Houdini, Harry (1874-1926). American magician. Signed 1925 letter.   **D-130.00**

Hunt, H. LaFayette. Texas millionaire and food manufacturer. Signed one-page letter.   **D-17.50**

Jay, John (1745-1829). First Chief Justice of the U.S. Supreme Court. Signature.   **D-90.00**

Johnston, Joseph E. (1807-91). American Confederate general. Autograph 1877 signed letter.   **D-75.00**

Kantor, MacKinlay (1904-77). American author and Pulitzer Prize winner. Signed 1963 Civil War Centennial Battle of Gettysburg First Day Cover.   **D-12.50**

Kipling, Rudyard (1865-1936). Great English writer. Signature.   **D-22.50**

Lindbergh, Charles A. (1902-74). American aviator, first non-stop solo Atlantic flight. Signed one-page letter on personal stationery, 1930.   **D-350.00**

Longfellow, Henry Wadsworth (1807-82). American poet. Signature.   **D-25.00**

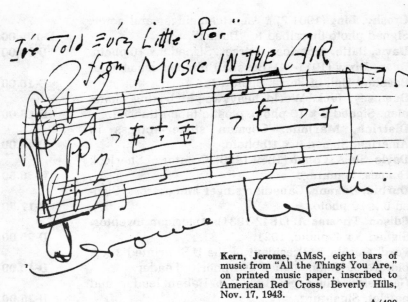

I've Told Ev'ry Little Star" from MUSIC IN THE AIR

Kern, Jerome, AMsS, eight bars of music from "All the Things You Are," on printed music paper, inscribed to American Red Cross, Beverly Hills, Nov. 17, 1943.

A/400

Louis, Joe. World Heavyweight boxing champion. Signature. **D-15.00**

MacArthur, Douglas (1880-1964). American general, WW-II and Korean War. One-page signed letter, 1957. **D-28.50**

Marshall, Thurgood. Associate Justice of U.S. Supreme Court. Signed 5 x 7 photo. **D-20.00**

Monroe, Marilyn (1926-1962). American motion-picture superstar. Signed two-page agent contract, 1949. **D-350.00**

Moses, Grandma. American primitive painter. Signed 1948 "100 Years of Progress of Women" First Day Cover. **D-85.00**

Nast, Thomas (1840-1902). Pioneer political cartoonist. Signature. **D-8.50**

Oakley, Annie (1860-1926). American Markswoman. Autograph note, signed, no date. **D-450.00**

Rockwell, Lincoln. Assassinated leader of the American Nazi Party. Signed bank check. **D-40.00**

Rogers, Will (1879-1935). American humorist and actor. Signature. **D-85.00**

Roosevelt, Theodore. President of the U.S. Signed one-page letter, 1902. **D-70.00**

Spock, Benjamin. American pediatrician. Signed
one-page letter, 1967.   **D-15.00**
Stein, Gertrude (1974-1946). American writer.
Autograph signed two-page letter, no date.   **D-500.00**
Streisand, Barbra. American signer and actress.
Signed 8 x 10 photo.   **D-40.00**
Truman, Bess W. Former First Lady. Signature.   **D-10.00**
Washington, Booker T. (1856-1915). American Black
educator. One-page signed letter, 1911.   **D-65.00**
West, Mae. American leading lady of the Thirties.
Signed 8 x 10 photo.   **D-25.00**
Wilson, Woodrow. President of the U.S. Engraved
military commission, signed, 1916.   **D-110.00**
Winkler, Henry. American actor of TV fame. Signed
8 x 10 photo.   **D-37.50**

AUTOMOBILIA AND RELATED ITEMS

Ashtray, "Pratt Chuck Mufflers", copper.   **D-4.00**
Auto hood ornament, early 1950's Pontiac.   **D-35.00**
Automobile folding running board luggage rack, to
60 in. long.   **D-29.50**
Calendar, print with 1923 Chevy and two Flappers.   **D-14.00**
Car part, Boyce Motometer, Ford part, temperature
gauge.   **D-15.00**
Car part, G. & E. Motometer, nickle over brass, early
'30's.   **D-12.50**

Running light, kerosene, all brass, clear
front. With red rear and side lens,
"Neverout / Insulated Kerosene Safety
Lamp", by Rose. Mfg. Co., and cast iron
mount, 9¾ in. high.   C/60-85

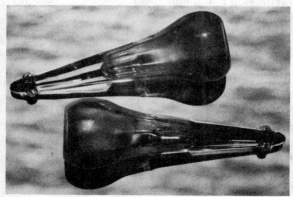

Left,
**Automobile flower hold-
ers,** matched pair, per-
fect condition, clear and
carnival-type glass crys-
tal-cased.
C/60-85

Lar Hothem photo.

Clock, "AC Spark Plugs", electric, light up. **D-75.00**

Driving lamp, "New York/USA", pat'd 1897, 11½ in. high. **D-49.50**

Driving lamp, brass, copper, tin and iron, 5 in. diameter. **D-55.00**

Gasoline sign, "FLYING A ETHEL", porcelain, 12 in. square. **D-50.00**

Gasoline sign, "SHAMROCK GASOLINE", porcelain, 12 in. square. **D-25.00**

Automobilia. Top and bottom, wooden gas tank **depth-measuring sticks.** Half of one side, "For Ford Cars Only", Firestone Tires and local shop ads on other. Each: C/10-15 **Center,** all-brass **oil-changing pump,** 12½ in. long. C/13-17

Gas pump globe, "CHAMPLIN PRESTO", all glass. **D—150.00**

Gas pump blobe, "GULF", all glass, one side blank. **D-115.00**

Gas pump globe, "STANDARD/GOLD CROWN". **D-175.00**

Gas pump lens, "CONOCO". **D-35.00**

Gas pump lens, "SKELLY KEOTANE/4 STARS". **D-40.00**

Gas pump lens, "TEXACO ETHYL", pair. **D-90.00**

Gas pump sign, "ETHYL", 1930's, 8 in. diameter. **D-25.00**

Gas pump sign, "INDIAN/GASOLINE", Zuni, 12 x 18 inches. **D-45.00**

Gas pump sign, "TEXACO SKY CHIEF", porcelain, 8 x 12 inches. **D-30.00**

Light-up sign, "Trailers & Cabins", 1930's, 14 in. square. **D-50.00**

Medal, Ford; silver-dollar size, with 1933 Ford radiator. **D-12.50**

Motor oil can, "WHITE STAR", one gallon size. **A-7.00**

Name plate from car grill, Buick, enamel. **D-18.00**

Name plate, script, Ford, Metal. **D-8.00**

Radiator cap, brass ca. 1920, Chevrolet; dented. **D-20.00**

Radiator cap, brass, ca. 1920, Ford. **D-25.00**

Rim spreader, cast iron, "Reliable No. 502 Rim Tool". **D-12.50**

Road sign, "Public Telephone", porcelain, 7 in. diameter. **D-28.00**

Salesman's sample advertisement, Ford and woman, 1928. **D-25.00**

Tire Gauge, "BALLOON TIRES", Schrader Universal. **D-10.00**

Tire sign, "FISK TIRES", heavy paper, 28 x 48 inches. **D-75.00**

BADGES

Auxiliary police, Mt. Vernon, New York.   D-16.00

Board of Health inspector, Winthrop, Mass., raised seal.   D-15.00

Building Inspector, enameled crest of Commonwealth of Mass.   D-15.00

Cap badge, brakeman, C. & O. Railway.   D-22.00

Cap badge, control room New Hampshire State Prison   D-15.00

Cap badge, steward, C. N. Railroad.   D-22.00

Citizen's Military Training Camps, National Defense.   D-8.00

Consultant Dept. of Public Works, Mass., enameled crest.   D-16.50

Fire Department, embossed center with fire equipment.   D-25.00

Fire Lieutenant, Mass., enameled seal.   D-21.00

Fireman's, enameled lettering, raised state seal.   D-20.00

Fireman's, gold-plated, Peoria Heights, Illinois.   D-15.00

Fire Warden's, New Hampshire Forest; round, ca. 1870.   D-20.00

GAR, 38th National Encampment, 1904, extra fine.   D-12.00

Governor's Commission, Boating Advisory, relief crest.   D-18.00

Mayor's Office, city seal enameled to center, gold plated.   D-16.00

Old Guard, Civil War Veterans, 1891, Wash. D.C.   D-10.00

Security Guard, enameled seal of state of North Carolina.   D-15.00

Star Security, security police.   D-12.50

Badge collection, fire and police.
C/Unlisted

Lar Hothem photo.

BANKS—*Mechanical*

Big Moon, Chein, cast iron, orig. paint, 10 inches. **A-110.00**
Bulldog, cast iron; jaw missing. **A-12.50**
Elephant, Chein, tin; missing bottom. **D-40.00**
Monkey, Chein, tin. **D-40.00**
Novelty mechanical bank, cast iron, automobile, 6½
inches. **A-90.00**
Parking meter bank, metal, boxed, ca. 1940's. **D-22.00**
"Tammany" bank, about mint paint; no coin door in
base. **D-105.00**
"Zoo" bank, "Press the Monkey No. 134", cast iron,
orig. paint. **A-320.00**

Baseball. 400+

Jonah & the Whale.
500+

Indian & bear. 300+

47

BANKS—*Still*

Atlas canning jar, glass with zinc top, 3¾ inches. A-20.00
Bank building, cast iron, 4 inches. A-15.00
Barrel-shape, "Chein's Happy Days", all good paint. D-7.50
Barrel bank, clear glass, embossed staves and bands. D-6.00

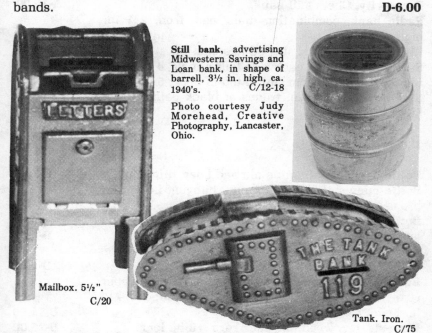

Still bank, advertising Midwestern Savings and Loan bank, in shape of barrell, 3½ in. high, ca. 1940's. C/12-18

Photo courtesy Judy Morehead, Creative Photography, Lancaster, Ohio.

Mailbox. 5½".
C/20

Tank. Iron.
C/75

Chrysler car, grey metal, white rubber wheels, 9 inches. A-40.00
Clown, cast iron, yellow and brown suit, ca. 1880. D-62.00
Coin-deposit bank, cast iron, combination lock, 6 inches. A-22.50
Cube bank, glass, 1939 World's Fair, 5½ inches. D-25.00
Dandy self-registering nickel bank, orig. paint, 5¼ inches. A-12.50
DeSoto car, 1950, beige metal, black rubber wheels, 8 inches. A-37.50
Dime register bank, "Gem Eagle". D-12.50
Donkey with saddle, cast iron, 7¼ in. high. A-85.00
Horse bank, "Black Beauty", ca. 1888; 5 in. long. D-58.00
House bank, Cape Cod style, of celluloid. D-3.50
Kewpie candy container, glass bank, "Borgfeldt & Co./NY". D-85.00

Lion, standing, cast iron, orig. gold paint, 5 inches. A-12.50
Lion, cast iron, 3½ in. high. S-47.00
Mickey Mouse, glass, 6 in. high. A-37.50
Nash bank, automobile, glass. A-5.00
Pig-bank, sponge spatterware, 3¾ in. high. A-60.00
Postal letterbox, cast iron, 50% orig. paint. S-25.00
Prosperity, Chein still bank. A-15.00
Radio bank, combination dials, cast iron, 2¾ in. high. A-80.00
Rival Dogfood bank, shaped like can, tin. D-5.00
Safe Deposit bank, each side four panels, 4 in. high. D-27.50
Sheep, cast iron, coin slot in top of neck, 5 in. long. S-45.00
Stag bank, oval base, traces of black paint, 10 in. high. A-67.50

BAR ITEMS

Bottle opener, Ballantine ale and beer, 4 in. long. D-3.50
Bottle opener, fishhead-shaped, hanging holes and brass grommet. D-4.50
Bottle opener, "G. Dextraze/Liquor Dealer", round and square holes. D-2.50
Bottle opener, "Schaffer—America's Oldest Lager Beer", metal. D-1.50
Bucket, beer, copper with tin bail ears and copper rivets; trio of concentric circles around outside, 7¼ in. high. D-55.00
Bung-starter, wood, for beer kegs, 18 in. long. D-25.00
Funnel, beer, copper; brass thumblift to close strainer part, strap handle, 9½ in. high. D-49.50
Funnel, brewer's; copper, "Eastern Bottlers Supply Co.", rolled seam edges, 9¼ in. diameter, 11 in. high. D-48.00
Ice shaver, bartender's, all copper, steel blade. Heavy, 9½ in. long. D-35.00
Jug, liquor; two-gallon, advertises a registered wholesale liquor dealer, stoneware. D-29.50
Lunch box, brewery worker's, tin, ca. 1920. Belonged to worker in a New Hampshire brewery of ale, 10 in. long. D-8.50
Poster, beer; "Try Puritan Malt", ca. 1940's, 15 x 30½ inches. D-2.00
Sign, ale; "Mule Head Ale", full color, stand-up. D-8.00
Sign, beer; tin, stand-up, "Holihans Beer & Ale", 9 x 13 inches. D-7.00

Tank, beer; copper, "Eldridge Brewing Co.", brass
faucet, 17 in. diameter, 19½ in. high.   **D-295.00**
Tankard, tin, ca. 1860, 6 in. high.   **D-10.00**
Tankard, copper, double-handled, tapering waist,
tin-lined, very early American, 4½ in. top diameter.   **D-145.00**
Serving tray, "Columbia Brew", 12 in. square.   **D-25.00**
Thermometer, beer, brass-faced.   **D-20.00**

Schlitz. **Beer tap.** Metal.
C/22

BASKETS

One of the more popular collecting fields, baskets have risen
dramatically in value in recent years. Among the most valuable are
woven splint baskets, made of thin strips of hardwood. Other
varieties in demand are made of willow lengths, and those handmade of unusual materials. Early factory-made baskets are also
now being sought.

Apple-gathering basket, carved double handles,
11½ in. high.   **D-85.00**
Apple basket, nailed rim, wire-bale handles, 7 in.
high.   **D-10.00**
Apple basket, handmade notched handles, ½ bushel
size.   **D-75.00**
Apple basket, dark splint, "New Hampshire" type,
20 in. diameter.   **D-98.50**
Covered barrel basket, for storage, square base,
rounded body, 58½ in. top diameter, 30. in. high.   **D-165.00**
Basket, bobbin holder, 5 x 7½ x 13 inches.   **A-25.00**
Bread basket, folding handle, 12½ x 20x 29½ in-
ches.   **D-175.00**

Baskets. Largest is 11¾ in. high. All in perfect condition.
Left, **buttocks basket**. C/55-75
Lower, **cylindrical**, of willow. C/10-15
Right, **Cherokee** or Great Lakes Indian. C/75-95
Private collection.

Basket, peeled willow, lidded, 18 in. high.
C/70-95
Photo courtesy Judy Morehead, Creative Photography, Lancaster, Ohio.

Buttocks basket, splint, 3½ x 6 x 7 inches.	A-75.00
Egg basket, willow wicker, five colors, 13 in. high.	D-75.00
Egg basket, splint, child-size, 8 in. to handle top.	D-85.00
Flax basket, woven splint, wood handle, 6½ in. diameter.	A-40.00
Fruit gathering basket, two-handled, 9½ in. diameter.	D-49.50
Gathering basket, mustard paint, 12 in. diameter.	D-35.00
Gleaner's basket, woven splint, 31 x 45 inches.	A-100.00
"Go-to-market" basket, rigid handle, unwrapped rim, 8 x 16¼ inches.	D-60.00
Kitchen storage basket, splint, beet-dyed, 8¼ in. square.	D-39.50
Kitchen storage basket, splint, vegetable dye, 10 in. square.	D-49.50
Lunch basket, splint, wooden top cover, 7 x 7¾ x 12 inches.	D-22.50
Market basket, nailed rim, bentwood arched handle, 23½ in. long.	D-40.00
Melon-type basket, twisted, peeled-twig handle, 22 in. long.	S-90.00
Nantucket basket, 3½ x 7½ inches.	A-120.00
Picnic basket, double-hinged lid, 7½ x 11½ x 17½ inches.	D-69.50
Produce basket, elongated, splint, higher back, 18 in. long.	S-40.00
Rib-type buttocks basket, 12 x 18 inches.	S-62.00
Ryestraw basket, 4 in. high, 11 in. diameter.	A-35.00
Sifter basket, splint, bottom holes, 8½ x 13 inches.	D-50.00

51

Splint basket, rectangular, 6 x 8½ x 13 inches.	**D-49.50**
Storage basket, swing handles, 4½ x 9 x 12 inches.	**D-85.00**
Trinket basket, sweetgrass, hinged top, loop clasp.	**D-22.50**
Vegetable basket, splint, handled, 12 in. square base, 13 in. high.	**D-95.00**
Wicker basket, oval, 9 x 12½ x 17 inches.	**D-39.50**
Wicker basket, lidded, handles, 15 x 20 inches.	**A-42.50**
Winnowing basket, woven split, 16½ x 18 inches.	**A-22.50**
Wood basket, splint, good old color, 10 x 21 x 26½ inches.	**A-65.00**
Woven splint basket, three colors, round rim, 5 in. diameter.	**A-12.00**
Woven splint basket, minor damage, 24½ x 37½ inches.	**A-125.00**
Woven splint basket, bentwood rim and handles, 13½ in. diameter.	**A-70.00**
Woven splint basket, 8 x 10¾ x 18 inches.	**A-27.50**

BELLS

Bells, brass, set of eight in modern wood frame 29½ in. long.	**A-85.00**
Cow bell, iron, on strap.	**D-10.00**
Cow bell, sheet iron with orig. cast clapper, 6 in. high.	**D-15.00**
Cow bell, brass, cast iron clapper, 4½ in. high.	**D-15.00**

Livestock bells, sheet iron, handmade, central bell 8 in. high.
Left: C/9-12
Center: C/20-25
Right: C/10-15

Photo courtesy Judy Morehead, Creative Photography, Lancaster, Ohio.

Fire bell, mounted on wooden platform, bell 10½ in. diameter at mouth.	**D-175.00**
School bell, with wooden handle, bell metal, 9 in. high.	**A-65.00**
School bell, brass, 6½ in. high.	**D-40.00**
School bell, brass, 7-5/8 in. high.	**A-50.00**
Sleigh bells, set of 14, new strap 59 in. long.	**A-90.00**

Summons bell, used to call servant, one of set, on platform, rung with long cord from appropriate room.   **D-30.00**

Bells, wood and brass, patina untouched. Scale, first bell is 8¾ in. high.
Top.   C/45-60
Lower right.   C/45-60
Bottom center.   C/30-40
Bottom left.   C/35-45
Left center.   C/100-125
Private collection.
By permission of **The Antiques Journal** September, 1979.

BICENTENNIAL—CENTENNIAL, ETC.

Advertising tin, "John McCann Oatmeal", with yellow litho. coin medallion with certification of the 1876 U.S. Centennial Commission; 6 in. diameter, 6¾ in. high.   **D-45.00**

Belt buckle, Centennial, thermo-plastic, "1776-1876", shields, brass fittings, two-piece, 2 x 3½ inches.   **D-50.00**

Broadside, 1876 Jaffrey Centennial Programme, listing schedule of the day, 6 x 14½ inches.   **D-12.00**

Biscuit box, "Jacob & Co. Biscuits", British Empire Exhibition, Centennial, 2 in. high.   **D-9.50**

Coin, Sesquicentennial, brass, 34mm, Philadelphia, 1926.   **D-8.00**

Compact, Sesquicentennial, celluloid top, incised and with set stones, 2 x 2¾ inches.   **D-15.00**

Fan, hand, folding advertising, 1876, Philadelphia, opens to 22 inches.   **D-46.00**

Kerchief, "Centennial/1776-1876", picture of Memorial Hall Art Gallery and eagle, 20 x 24 inches.   **D-59.00**

Medal, Bi-Centennial, 39mm, "1 Troy Ounce", 1776-1976.   **D-10.00**

Medal, gilt, Centennial, 13mm, "Independence Hall/Liberty Bell", with ribbon.   **D-6.00**

Medal, pewter, Washington taking oath as first President, "1783-1883", with connecting brass eagle; 1½ in. diameter.   **D-27.50**

Souvenir, Sesquicentennial, 1¼ in. cello with 1½ in. suspended metal bell; Philadelphia, 1776-1926. **D-25.00**

Ticket set, Centennial, four varieties of the official 1876 tickets. **D-20.00**

Trade card, Centennial, postcard size, for 1876 International Exhibition, Philadelphia; mint cond. **D-6.00**

Trade card, Centennial, for 1876 German Collection Exhibition of Jewelry and Silverware. **D-3.50**

BOTTLES *[See also* **Flasks***]*

Ale, "Hanley & Peerless Ale", with orig. label, amber color. **D-2.50**

Blown, clear, pewter and cork ring stopper, 6¼ in. high. **A-55.00**

Blown, whittled mold, olive-yellow, "ladies leg" neck, 9½ in. high. **A-16.00**

Bitters, "Atwoods Jaundice" (not **Formerly**), 6 in. high. **D-5.00**

Bitters, "Formerly Made by Moses Atwood", aqua, 12-sided. **D-3.00**

Bitters, square, amber, "Dr. Jostetter's Stomach Bitters, 9 in. high. **D-9.00**

Case gin, whittled mold, applied blob-top, olive green, 9½ in. high. **D-14.00**

Caster, three-part mold, clear, blown, without stopper; 4¼ in. high. **A-32.50**

Corker, clear, "The Worcester Flask", 8¼ in. high. **D-3.50**

Left,
Davids Writing Fluid. **Ink.**
Cobalt blue w/label.
C/15-20

Right,
Louisville Glass Works.
Flask. Aqua.
C/65-85

Left, Dr. Harters Iron Tonic. **Medicine.** Amber w/label.
C/12-15

Right,
E. E. Hall. **Bitters.** Amber.
C/85-100

Cure-all, label intact, "Burnett's Standard Jamaica Ginger", 6½ in. high.   D-8.50

Decanter, blown, copper wheel engraving, 11 in. high.   A-37.50

Demijohn, green, four-part mold with applied sloping lip and 17 in. high; moulded "9" at shoulder.   A-27.50

Medicine, "Paines Celery Compound", amber, 9¾ in. high.   D-4.50

Milk, "Farmer's Dairy/Mishawaka, Indiana", embossed.   D-3.00

Perfume, clear, "...Spiehler/Perfumer...", stopper present.   D-4.00

Pickle, aqua, cathedral-shaped, bubble-glass, 7½ in. high.   D-7.50

Purse, mini-rounded flask shape; ca. 1890, 1¼ x 1¾ inches.   D-7.50

Quart, Schlitz ruby red, textured body, "Duraglass Royal Ruby".   D-8.50

Quart, black-glass, graphite pontil, ca. 1830, 10½ in. high.   D-21.50

Quart, wire neck and porcelain cap, "Wood-Dunnells Co.".   D-3.50

Shaker, "Anodyne/Enfield, N.H.", aqua, embossed, 4 in. high.   D-36.50

Shaker, "Tomato Ketchup/Put Up By The Shakers/East Canterbury, N.H.", white with red lettering, corker, 95% label intact.   D-35.00

Soda, neck wire and porcelain cap, 9½ in. high.   D-3.00

Spirits, black glass, blown, 10 in. high, 3¼ in. neck.   D-22.50

Torpedo, aqua, round bottom, corker, 9½ in. high.   D-4.00

Whiskey, amber quart embossed "Paul Jones/Louisville, Ky.".   D-4.50

Whiskey, "The Duffy Malt Whiskey Co.", embossed, pat'd. 1886.   D-4.00

Wine, olive green, 9 in. high.   A-11.00

BOXES

General-purpose and specialized containers are made of many materials, hardwood, softwood, metal, papiermache, cardboard and so forth. Some collectors keep to the narrower fields of hatboxes, storage containers, spice boxes and document boxes.

Tramp art **trinket box,** 6¼ in. wide.
C/30-40

Bentwood box, (bottom shown) with stenciled name, "S. Hawke" and carved initials; 6 in. diameter.

C/20-30

Lar Hothem photo.

Shaker bentwood box, left; 1½ in. high, 4¼ in long.
C/40-60

Tinderbox, right, tin, with orig. steel **striker** (center) for flint. These are also called strike-a-lights.
Pair. C/55-75

Wooden box, salt fish, 12 lb. size.
C/5.50

Lar Hothem photo.

Apple box, turned wood, 4¼ in. high.	**A-16.00**
Bibelot box, birdseye maple top, brass-studded, 5 in. high.	**D-55.00**
Bible box, pine, rose-head nails and chip-carving, 7½ in. high.	**A-210.00**
Box, walnut, inlaid escutcheons, signed on lid bottom.	**A-45.00**
Box, mahogany, rosewood, brass inlay, 9½ in. high.	**A-27.50**
Box, pine, chip-carved lid top, old leather hinges.	**A-45.00**
Box, basswood, orig. red paint, 8¼ in. high.	**A-80.00**
Box, pine, orig. red and black graining, 4 in. high.	**A-45.00**
Box, poplar, stenciled and decorated in five colors, 3¼ in. high.	**A-85.00**

Box, two drawers and shallow well' 9¼ x 11½ x 17 inches. A-80.00

Butter box, orig. old blue paint, bentwood, 14½ in. diameter. D-35.00

Cardboard box, wallpaper covered, round, 4½ in. diameter. A-30.00

Cardboard box, floral wallpaper, cylindrical, 16 in. high. D-40.00

Chip-carved box, six-board pine, 4¾ x 6 x 11 inches. A-20.00

Collection box, walnut, circular, long wood handle. A-67.50

Decorated box, flame graining, brass bail handle, worn paint. A-22.50

Document box, copper, tin lining, 4½ x 10½ x 12 inches. D-89.50

Document box, tin, "black" tin and early seaming; 6½ in. high. D-45.00

Deed box, orig. orange-red paint, 6 x 6 x 9½ inches. A-30.00

Dome-top box, red and black graining, poplar wood. A-30.00

Dome-top box, pine, orig. blue-grey paint, 10¼ in. high. A-115.00

Dome-top box, poplar, orig. brass bail handle, 10 in. high. A-47.50

Dovetailed box, pine, till and wooden lock, 8½ in. high. A-60.00

Dovetailed box, pine, 4¼ x 4¼ x 9½ inches. A-65.00

Dovetailed box, pine, small till, lid decorated with compass star. Orig. red paint with dark brown grained stripes, 6¾ in. high. A-285.00

Dovetailed box, poplar, compartmentalized, 20 in. long. A-35.00

Dovetailed box, inlaid checkerboard on top, 9½ in. square. A-102.50

Dovetailed box, basswood, floral decorations, 19¾ in. wide. A-195.00

Dust box, double-hinged lids, maple, 7½ in. high. A-50.00

Fish box, "Bone Out Codfish", 4 x 5 inches. S-6.50

Figural boxes, pair; tops have ladies in folk costumes. A-65.00

Gift box, inscribed "When you see/Think of me", pine. A-60.00

Hat box, oval, lined with 1809 Mass. newspaper, 5½ in. long. D-65.00

Jewelry box, wood, burned designs, 5 x 30 inches. A-23.50

Kindling box, old, copper lining, old blue paint. A-155.00

Octagonal box, attributed to the Dunkards, 9 in. diameter.   **A-85.00**
Pantry box, straight lap, grey, 9 in. diameter.   **S-34.00**
Pantry box, straight lap, large; 15 in. diameter.   **S-78.00**
Pantry box, sturdy early construction, 12½ in. diameter.   **D-50.00**
Papiermache box, yellow circle and band, 2 in. diameter.   **A-35.00**
Pipe box, front board with slight curve, 18½ in. high.   **A-100.00**
Secret compartment box, pine, 7½ x 7½ x 9½ inches.   **A-47.50**
Storage box, round, red paint, 9¼ in. diameter.   **A-30.00**
Storage box, tin, oval, 7 x 9 x 13 inches.   **A-27.50**
Storage box, bentwood, lid inside dated 1765.   **A-175.00**
Storage box, round, old green paint, 8 in. diameter.   **A-45.00**
Storage box, round, worn blue-grey paint, 13¼ in. diameter.   **A-50.00**
Wallpaper-covered cardboard box, yellow and red printed paper with jungle scenes, swans on lid; 11 x 12 x 13½ inches.   **A-320.00**
Writing box, pine and poplar, 10 in. high.   **A-90.00**
Writing box, black graining over red, 7½ x 10¾ x 16 inches.   **A-45.00**
Writing box, cherry and maple, 4¼ x 8¼ x 12 inches.   **A-35.00**
Writing box, pine, early dovetailing, slant top, lift lid.   **A-425.00**

BRASS COLLECTIBLES

Anvil, miniature, solid brass, early 3 in. long.   **D-22.00**
Basin, sheet brass, polished, 18 in. diameter.   **A-40.00**
Bucket, spun brass, iron handle, 16½ in. high.   **D-55.00**
Bucket, spun brass, wrought iron handle, 14 in. high.   **D-45.00**
Can, oil, for steam engine cylinder oil, 9 in. long.   **D-24.00**
Can, oil filler, strap handle, rolled edge, 4½ in. high.   **D-55.00**

Scoop, brass, lapped joins, tubular handle, 7 in. long.
C/30-45

Photo courtesy Judy Morehead, Creative Photography, Lancaster, Ohio.

Oiler, for steam engine, one replaced glass tube, solid brass and brass parts, 10½ in. high.

C/55-80

Sprinkler, 10 in. high, "Rain King Model D". Item consists of two cast iron sections and 14 separate brass pieces, cast and drawn.

C/25-35

Photos courtesy Judy Morehead, Creative Photography, Lancaster, Ohio.

Check protector, mechanical, pat. 1912, 3 in. diameter.	**D-9.50**
Cup, folding, five segments, finger-loop handle, 3 in. high.	**D-12.50**
Finial, flag, eagle, presentation name, and "Post No. 285/G.A.R.".	**A-55.00**
Finial, flag, eagle, 8½ in. high.	**A-40.00**
Hatchet, all-brass head, break at end of one nail claw.	**D-22.00**
Kettle, candle, dents and small break, 14 in. top diameter.	**D-45.00**
Kettle, cast brass, 12½ in. diameter.	**A-40.00**
Kettle, spun brass, stationary iron handle, 13¼ in. diameter.	**A-35.00**
Kettle, spun brass, iron handle, 15 in. diameter, top.	**D-65.00**
Kettle, spun brass, maker stamp on bottom, 15 in. high.	**D-100.00**
Opium burner, cage-like cover over burner, 6 in. high.	**A-25.00**
Pail, spun brass, 9 in. diameter.	**A-35.00**
Pail, spun brass, wrought iron handle, "signed", 8¼ in. high.	**A-55.00**
Parrot, cast brass, worn polychrome paint, 2½ in. high.	**A-42.50**
Parrot, cast brass, worn polychrome paint, 3 in. high.	**A-50.00**
Pan, spun brass, single slant iron handle, cover, 7 in. diameter.	**D-30.00**

Left, **call bell**, brass.
15-20

Center, **Teacher's bell**,
brass w/wood handle.
40-50

Right, **team bell**, brass.
10-15

Pan, spun brass, iron slant handle, no cover, 9¼ in.
diameter.   **D-22.50**

Tray, serving, rectangular, handled, scalloped edge,
7 x 14½ inches.   **D-42.50**

BRONZE FIGURES AND SCULPTURES

Aeschlus, figure, late 19th Century, 9 in. high.   **A-70.00**

The Bronco Buster, by Federic Remington
(American, 1861-1909). Inscribed on base and
underside, dark patina, 20½ in. high.   **A-7,000.00**

Cossack Embracing A Woman, Russian bronze
group, inscribed on base. Bronze 12 in. long and 12
in. high.   **A-2,600.00**

Crouching panther, on rocky plinth. French, 19th
Century, 7½ in. high, 15 in. long.   **A-150.00**

Greyhound, by Emmanuel Fremiet (French, 1824-
1910). Orig. bronze casting by the artist on shaped
molded-edge oblong base. Piece 9 in. high and 10 in.
long.   **A-900.00**

Left, French **bronze figure of pointer with hare,** inscribed "F. Pautrot", 20th
Century. Height, 12 inches.
C/550

Right, French **bronze figure of retreiver,** inscribed "P. J. Mene", 20th Century.
Height, 8 inches.
C/400

Courtesy Adam A. Weschler & Son, Washington, D.C.; photograph by Breger &
Associates.

Bronze figure of seated athlete on rocky plinth. Italian, 19th C. school, 20 in. high, base 18 inches.

A/650

Bronze figure of Napoleon standing with folded arms. Probably French and 19th century.

A/175

Courtesy Adam A. Weschler & Son, Washington, D.C.; photograph by Breger & Associates.

Illinois Black Earth, Gary Jameson (contemporary American). Sculpture on step wood base, signed and dated on the bronze, 12 in. long. A-100.00

Indian On A Horse, by Charles H. Humphriss (American, 1867-1934). Warrior with brown patina from the Roman Bronze Works, New York. Mounted on oval black-veined marble step base, 16 in. high. A-2,900.00

Olympian Holding Wreath, figure, on black slate base. Piece is 20th Century, 14½ in. overall height. A-125.00

Pointer, figure, stamped "Kayser" on bottom, German. Bronze is 19th Century, 4¾ in. long. A-60.00

Quail, on round wooden base, 4½ in. high. A-155.00

Reclining Lion With Gazelle, after Louis Antione, 19th Century. On molded marble plinth and 10 in. long. A-210.00

Reclining Mountain Lion on rocky plinth, after Louis Antione, 19th Century. On shaped molded marble plinth, 9½ in. long.   **A-225.00**

Borzoi, (Russian Wolf Hound), black patina, 9 in. long.   **D-200.00**

Seated Indian Medicine Man, after Carl Kauba, 19th Century. On shaped green marble molded base, 5½ in. high.   **A-175.00**

Seated Negro Boy, by John K. Daniels (American, 1895-1948). Exhibitions at Minneapolis Institute of Art, and Chicago Art Institute, 1921-1928.   **A-175.00**

Bronze figural group of German police dogs. On mottled green marble base; 11 in. high, 15 in. long. Inscribed "A. Varnier / Salon des Beaux Arts". French, 19th Century.

A/650

Courtesy Adam A. Weschler & Son, Washington, D.C.; photograph by Breger & Associates.

Shenandoah Valley Fence Post, by Gary Jameson (contemporary American). Sculpture mounted on step wooden base, signed and dated on the bronze, 10½ in. long.   **A-100.00**

Standing Russian Wolf Hound, attrib. to Paul Troubetsky, (Russian, 1866-1938). Gorham Foundry, 5¼ in. high.   **A-150.00**

Standing man, drinking from canteen, inscribed Kriesch Nagy. Hungarian, 19th Century, 15½ in. high.   **A-325.00**

Two Whippets With Ball, after P. J. Mene, patinated bronze. On oval base, 6 in. high.   **A-350.00**

Vases, pair; inscribed Ruff Bessereich, French, 19th Century. Each has tapered body with relief sculpture of dancing figures, 11 in. high.   **A-310.00**

BUTTER—*Related Items (See also* **Kitchen***)*

Butter box, bentwood, covered, wire handle, 9½ in. diameter. **D-42.50**

Churn, redware, with handles; base has clear glaze, 11½ in. high. **A-55.00**

Churn, glass one-gallon size, geared metal top, wood paddle. **D-35.00**

Churn, glass, one-gal. size, metal top, perfect condition. **S-40.00**

Churn, tin, cylindrical, tin dasher, bail handle, 25 in. high. **D-165.00**

Churn, stave-construction, break in bottom metal band. **A-50.00**

Churn, oval, wooden, swings in tubular frame, 28 in. high. **A-20.00**

Churn, crank handle, barrel-type, on brace legs, 27 in. high. **D-85.00**

Ladle, wood, handle hooked at end, 7½ in. long. **S-9.00**

Ladle, curved, square handle, 9 in. long. **S-12.00**

Butter mold, rectangular, dovetailed corners, plunger print with floral motif.

C/40-55

Lar Hothem photo.

Butter tool, one of a pair of "Scotch hands", with ridged inner surface used to make butter balls.

C/9-12

Photo courtesy Judy Morehead, Creative Photography, Lancaster, Ohio.

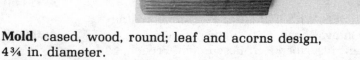

Mold, cased, wood, round; leaf and acorns design, 4¾ in. diameter. **A-35.00**

Mold, rectangular one-lb. size, dovetailed corners. **D-22.50**

Mold, rectangular, one-lb., press plunger, 4½ in. high. **D-18.50**

Paddle, pine, handmade, small size.   **D-4.50**
Paddle, ridged for patterning, 7 in. long.   **S-8.00**
Paddle, wood, carved one-piece construction, 9 in. long.   **A-45.00**
Paddles, pair; corrugated flats for molding.   **S-15.00**
Pats, ironstone, unmarked white.   **D-1.25**

Butter pats, very early, glazed and decorated.   Each C/3-5

Lar Hothem photo.

Print, pineapple-like flower, round, 4¼ in. diameter.   **A-30.00**
Print, wood, three leaves, 2 in. diameter.   **A-25.00**
Print, one surface, flowers, other checkerboard, 5 in. diameter.   **A-47.50**
Print, cased, round, 4½ in. diameter.   **A-15.00**
Print, round, flower and leaves design, 4¼ in. diameter.   **A-25.00**
Print, round, sheaf of wheat design, 5½ in. high.   **A-35.00**
Print, cased, round, swan design, 4¾ in. diameter.   **A-32.50**
Print, rectangular, 2 x 3½ x 4 inches.   **A-15.00**
Print, rectangular, two sheaves of wheat design, 4¼ in. long.   **A-17.50**
Print, miniature, wood, thistle design, 1¼ in. diameter.   **A-31.00**
Scoop, wooden, handle with old initials, 9 in. long.   **A-10.00**
Scoop, wooden, carved one-piece, 8 in. long.   **A-12.50**
Scoop, burlwood, rare; 8 in. long.   **A-205.00**
Scoop, curly maple, minor crack in bowl, 10½ in. long.   **A-60.00**
"Scotch Hands", corrugated paddles for butter balls, pair.   **S-14.50**
Smoother, one-piece wood, 4 in. length.   **A-7.50**
Spade, wood, well-shaped, ca. 1890, 9 in. long.   **D-8.50**
Stamp, leaf pattern, wood, 2 in. diameter.   **S-33.00**

CANDLESTICKS—(See also **Lamps** and **Lighting Devices**)

Baluster-shape, pair; brass, octagonal step base, 8¾ in. high.　　　　　　　　　　　　　　　　　　**A-85.00**

Brass, pair; 20th Century, 7 in. high.　　　　　**A-45.00**

Brass, pair; Persian hurricane shades, ruby and gilt decorations, faceted clear crystal prisms. Overall, 19½ in. high.　　　　　　　　　　　　　　　　**A-110.00**

Brass, with pushup, "The Diamond Princess", 10¾ in. high.　　　　　　　　　　　　　　　　　　**A-62.50**

Brass, pair; plunger type, octagonal base, 10 in. high.　　　　　　　　　　　　　　　　　　　**A-70.00**

Brass, pair; stamped out, weighted bases, reeded stem, 6 in. high.　　　　　　　　　　　　　　**A-40.00**

Candlesticks, brass.
C/50-180

Candlestick & snuffer w/tray, silver.
C/85-150

Candle-holders, all brass, center example 6 in. high without candle.
Left, (finger ring missing).　　　C/35-50
Center.　　　　　　　　　　　　　C/65-90
Right　　　　　　　　　　　　　　C/65-90

Candle-holders, pair; tin, finger loop, "1913", 5 in. diameter.　　　　　　　　　　　　　　　**D-35.00**

Capstan, brass, upper flange bent, 6 in. high, 4½ in. diameter.　　　　　　　　　　　　　　**A-125.00**

Capstan, pair; copper, worn bronze color, 6 in. high.　　　　　　　　　　　　　　　　　**A-45.00**

Capstan, brass, old flange-base repair, 4 in. high. **A-115.00**
Drum-base, brass, 5 in. diameter, 4-3/8 in. high. **A-170.00**
Flint glass, clear, pair; Pittsburg, 9¾ in. high. **A-60.00**
Hogscraper, iron, with pushup and lip hanger, 6 in. high. **A-37.50**
Hogscraper, iron, pushup and lip hanger, 5 in. high. **A-50.00**
Hogscraper, iron, pushup and hanger, 7½ in. high. **A-110.00**
Middrip, brass, 9¾ in. high. **A-85.00**
Middrip, pair; iron, minor edge damage to one, 9¼ in. high. **A-65.00**
Sheffield, pair; weighted bases, both with minor repairs. **A-40.00**
Octagonal-base, brass, 5 in. high. **A-57.50**
Tin, weighted, cone base, crimped ring, drip pan, 5 in. high. **A-130.00**
Tin, pair; weighted bases, applied floral decorations, 9½ in. high. **A-175.00**
Tin, pushup with saucer base, loop handle, 3½ in. high. **D-45.00**
Victorian, pair; brass, 6 in. high. **A-62.50**
Victorian, pair, brass, one with split in flange, 6¼ in. high. **A-50.00**
Victorian, pair; brass, with pushups, 10¾ in. high. **A-105.00**
Wooden, three inset cutout feet, tin drip pan. Old green paint, 6½ in. high. **A-187.50**

CAP GUNS—*[See also* **Toys***]*

Often the playthings of recent yesteryear are the collectibles of today. Toy cap guns of most kinds now command attention at auctions and shows. Metal types in good condition with maker's mark or identification with movie or television heros are in demand.

Cap Guns—*Detective, Etc.*

Acme-45. Sheet metal, small, black. **D-8.00**
Army-45. Black, white handles, Hubley. **D-6.00**
Buck Rogers. Painted gold, rough. **D-25.00**
Champ Army-45. Maroon handles, silver, medium. **D-5.00**
Dandy-Hubley. Police .38, silver, small, hammer missing. **D-15.00**
Dick-45. Silver handles, metal "H" in circle, medium. **D-8.00**

Dick Tracy. Pull-trigger siren on side, red, black metal.   **D-35.00**

Flash. Pat'd, dark, .38-type sawed-off barrel.   **D-15.00**

Luger. Automatic 9mm, black, Hongkong, large.   **D-4.00**

Police Automatic. Dark blue metal, policeman's head.   **D-5.00**

Presto. Light maroon handles, silver, no center section.   **D-4.00**

Spitfire-45. White airplane handles, silver, metal.   **D-10.00**

Terror. Silver color, small, no hammer.   **D-10.00**

Trooper. Hubley, silver, medium-size, .38 type.   **D-4.00**

UNXLD. Army .45, sheet metal, silver, large.   **D-8.00**

Cap Guns—*Holster Sets and Boxed*

The Detective. Holster and gun, black handles, Robert Taylor.   **D-15.00**

The Deputy. Two Bronco pistols; Henry Fonda and Allen Case.   **D-15.00**

Gene Autry. Two pistols in silver, holsters medium-fancy.   **D-35.00**

Gene Autry Ranch Outfit. Horse-head pistols, leather holsters.   **D-35.00**

Gunsmoke. Halco, brown and white handles and holsters.   **D-20.00**

Have Gun Will Travel. Derringer and holster, cards.   **D-15.00**

Lone Ranger Official Outfit. Belt, keys, badge, mask, on card.   **D-20.00**

Matt Dillon. White and brown handles, silver, large.   **D-8.00**

Nevadan. Silver and mercury, clear plastic, board holder.   **D-15.00**

Paladin. Two holsters, one gun, Paladin emblem.   **D-15.00**

Purple Sage Box. Pistols, 1942, silver, Lone Ranger.   **D-30.00**

Roy Rogers. Pistol and holster.   **D-15.00**

Sheriff and Ranger Accessories. Badge and keys on card.   **D-4.00**

Wyatt Earp. Holster and gun.   **D-15.00**

Young Buffalo Bill Box. Wild Bill Hickok pistols, bronze color, fancy holsters.   **D-25.00**

Cap Guns—*Western*

Bang-O. Cowboy and horsehead handles, silver, missing pieces. **D-6.00**

Big Chief. Cast iron, 3¾ in. long. **A-5.00**

Big Horn. Marroon handles, metal "K" in circles. **D-15.00**

Big Scout. Cowboy and horsehead handles, silver, small. **D-6.00**

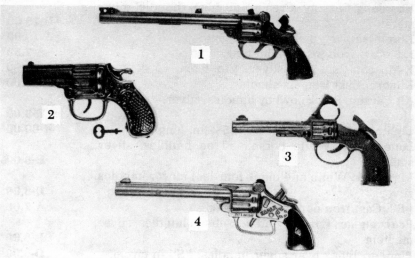

Revolver type pistols. 1. "FOUR WAY" c. 1928, cast iron combination pistol that will shoot a cap, rubber band and pea simultaneously. **C/20**

2. "AIM TO SAVE" c. 1909, steel dime bank in shape of a pistol. Pressing the trigger causes an arm to extend from the barrel to receive the coin. **C/150**

3. "SNAPPY JACK" c. 1935, cast iron cap shooter made in England shown with cap holder raised, ready to load. **C/40**

4. "EAGLE" c. 1940, a typical cast iron single shot pistol of the period. **C/30**

Buck. Stag black handles, silver, metal "K" in circle, small. **D-6.00**

Buck'N Bronc. BB white handles, silver, George Schmidt. **D-8.00**

Buffalo Bill. White cowboy and horeshead handles, silver. **D-10.00**

Cheyenne Shooter. No handles, silver, Hamilton Line. **D-5.00**

Cowboy King. Pearl color handles, silver, "S" in circle. **D-8.00**

Dale Evans. Black horse handles, gold, medium. **D-10.00**

Echo. Silver metal, small, split barrel. **D-10.00**

Gene Autry. White horse head handle, silver, medium. | D-10.00

Gene Autry. Repeating, cast iron, Kenton in orig. box. | A-15.00

Gray Ghost. Gray handles, silver metal, medium size. | D-12.00

Gunsmoke. Bronze steer head handles, silver color. | D-12.00

Hero. Cowboy and buffalo handles, silver metal, small. | D-25.00

Hopalong Cassidy. Cream and black handle, silver metal. | D-15.00

King. Cast iron pistol, 4½ in. long. | A-10.00

K-6. Cast iron pistol, 7 in. long. | A-7.50

K-Mascot. Cast iron, silver, 4 in. long. | A-4.00

Kilgore. Cast iron six-shooter. | A-10.00

Kit Carson. Black cowboy handles, silver, "K" in circle. | D-8.00

Lightning Express. Cast iron, 5¼ in. long. | A-80.00

Lone Rider. White horsehead on handles, silver, small. | D-6.00

Maverick. White and black four-leaf clover handles, silver. | D-8.00

"P". Cast iron cap pistol 5 in. long. | A-7.00

Peacemaker. Cowboy and horsehead handles, silver, medium. | D-8.00

Pioneer. Black over silver handles, "S" in circle. | D-6.00

Red Ranger. Black horsehead and horseshoe handles, gold. | D-25.00

Roy Rogers. Gray flowered handle, silver color, large. | D-10.00

The Sheriff. White cowboy and horsehead handles, silver. | D-8.00

Sportsman. Cast iron cap pistol 8 in. long. | A-17.50

Texas Ranger. White horsehead handle, silver metal. | D-6.00

W & S. Silver color, sawed-off barrel, blank shooter, small. | D-15.00

Westerner. No handles, silver, large, Hamilton Line. | D-5.00

Wild Bill Hickok. White horse handles, silver color, medium. | D-10.00

CELLULOID—*Dresser and Personal Items*

Celluloid—also known as "French Ivory"—is the term applied to the many small dresser accessories and personal aids manufactured in the early part of the 20th Century. Most are in surprisingly good condition and the color has gentled to a pleasing yellow-amber. One day these items will undoubtedly be in much demand, not only for their attractiveness, but as predecessors of modern molded plastics. Some pieces are marked on outside bottoms, or elsewhere.

Comb, heavy, 8-5/8 in. long.	**D-3.50**
Cream jar and cover, glass liner, 1-1/8 in. high.	**D-2.50**
Cuticle tool, handled.	**D-1.50**
Dresser tray, 6 in. x 10 inches.	**D-4.50**
Hair brush, good bristles.	**D-3.00**
Hair receiver, three-piece.	**D-3.50**
Hand mirror, silver with light spots.	**D-4.50**
Holder, partitioned, 4 in. diameter.	**D-1.50**
Nail buffer and cover, chamois mint, 6 in. long.	**D-3.50**
Powder box, with cover, 2 in. high, 4 in. diameter.	**D-2.50**
Powder box, with cover, 3½ in. diameter.	**A-2.00**
Rouge jar with cover, glass liner, 1½ in. high	**D-2.50**
Shoe horn.	**D-1.50**

CHESTS

Blanket chest, cherry six-board, 16½ x 41 inches.	**A-265.00**
Blanket chest, turned feet and till, 18¼ x 22 x 27 inches.	**A-110.00**
Blanket chest, dovetailed, poplar; turned legs, 43 in. wide.	**A-350.00**
Blanket chest, till and iron strap hinges, 51¾ in. wide.	**A-200.00**
Blanket chest, one dovetailed drawer, six-board construction.	**A-290.00**
Bride's chest, orig. paint and lining, 23½ in. long.	**D-89.50**
Chest, with till; orig. yellow paint, 13 x 15 x 28 inches.	**A-220.00**
Chest, dovetailed pine, old blue paint, 23 in. high.	**A-525.00**
Chest on frame, pine, staple hinges, 39½ in. wide.	**A-500.00**
Chest, oak, English; 18 x 28 x 35½ inches.	**A-75.00**
Chest, poplar, red paint, 14¾ x 19½ x 37 inches.	**A-115.00**

Chest, pine, grained, salmon color; 22 x 28½ x 42 inches.   A-750.00

Chest, dovetailed pine, bracket feet, 18 x 24 x48 inches.   A-350.00

Chest, dovetailed pine, blue paint, 17½ in. high.   A-105.00

Chest, incomplete "beartrap" lock, 18 x 22½ x 45 in. wide.   A-360.00

Mule chest, two dovetailed drawers, 18½ x 42 x 43½ inches.   A-350.00

Mule chest, two overlapping drawers, 17 x 37 x 37¾ inches.   .A-525.00

Pennsylvania dower chest, ca. 1840, 22 x 27 x 50 inches.   A-500.00

Philadelphia dower chest, ca. 1875, 22 x 27½ x 51 inches.   A-525.00

CHILDRENS' BOOKS

The Adventures Of Paddy The Beaver, by T.W. Burgess, 1922.   D-6.50

Beloved Lindy, Raggedy Ann series, Negro theme, by J. Gruelle, hardcover, 1916.   D-18.50

Chatter Box, dust jacket, eight color plates, 1926.   D-12.50

The Circus Comes To Town, by L. Mitchell, color plates, first edition, 1921.   D-7.50

Doings Of Little Bear, F. Margaret Fox, 14 color plates, 1915.   D-15.00

The Joy Book For Little People, color front plate, 1916.   D-7.50

Knowledge Primer Games, with 79 childrens' games to play, each with illustration and story, 1923.   D-8.50

The Little Keepsake, prose, woodblock cuts, ca. 1850.   D-6.50

Little Red Riding Hood, linen, four color plates, 7½ x 9 inches.   D-8.50

Little Red Riding Hood, Father Tucks Nursery Friends Series, two color plates, 5¼ x 9¼ inches.   D-12.50

Mother Goose Nursery Rhymes, by R. Allyn, color plates, 5 x 9 inches.   D-10.00

The Tea Party, early, four color plates and color cover.   D-10.00

The Teddy Bears, one color plate, dust jacket, hardcover, 1907.   D-17.50

The Three Bears, frontispiece color plate of bears, 6¼ x 8½ inches. D-7.50

Tom Thumb, Kriss Kringle Series, four color plates, 1897. D-14.50

The Traveling Bears Across The Sea, color cover, illustrated, hardcover, 1916. D-20.00

Uncle Wiggiliy's Adventures, by Garis, hardcover, 1912. D-7.50

Uncle Wiggiliy And The Pirates, illus. by Lang Campbell, hardcover. D-7.50

Waltz Songs Against Evil, prose and morals, color cover, ca. 1870. D-8.50

Wise Mr. Turtle, by E. Rosencrans, hardcover, ca. 1920. D-4.50

The Poetical Present, b&w engravings, cat theme, 3¾ x 4½ inches. D-12.50

Raggedy Andy Stories, artist-signed color plates, hardcover, 1920. D-15.00

The Robber Kitten, 22 color illus., cat theme, hardcover. D-6.50

Roy Rogers And The Ghost Of Mystery Rancho, 250 pages. D-2.00

The Santa Claus Book, Santa writing in Christmas ledger. D-12.00

The Story Of Little Black Sambo/The Story of Topsy From Uncle Tom's Cabin, two books in one binding, 1908, by Bannerman. D-16.50

Sunnycrest Farmyard, by F.R. Buchanan, color illus., 1925. D-7.50

The Tale Of Benny Badger, color plates, by A.S. Bailey, 1919. D-4.50

CHILDRENS' PLAYTHINGS *(See also* **Toys)**

Collecting the entertainment devices of children includes the early primitive hand- and homemade objects, as well as later factory-made pieces. A plaything can be used indoors or outdoors, and for stimulating imagination, for whiling away hours, for education, or for exercise. The field as covered here includes a range of non-toy items.

Building blocks, solid walnut (a few replacements), approx. 130 individual pieces. In orig. box with dovetailed corners; missing lid. Box measures 4-7/8 x 10 x 12½ inches.

C/125-175

Child's armchair rocker, oak, bentwood armrests, some split damage to back center, 28 in. high.
Lar Hothem photo.   C/35-45

Baby carriage, doll-size, wooden wheels and frame. Orig. brown paint with orange striping, folding top, "leatherized" cloth covering, 34 in. long.   **A-145.00**

Baby rattle, pewter, wood handle, three-piece construction. Handpainted red stripes, finial at end, ca. 1840's, 10¼ in. long.   **D-75.00**

Baby rattle, tin, lacy cutout concentrics, hinged hatch at end. Whistle built into handle; ca. 1850, 5½ in. long.   **D-60.00**

Baby rattle, tin, handle-whistle, old paint, 7 in. long.   **S-18.00**

Baby rattle, drum end, lithographed silver against blue; handle with whistle and porcelain mouthpiece, 6 in. long.   **D-65.00**

Baby walker, primitive, pine; worn green paint, 14 in. high.   **A-20.00**

Block, wood, with picture of elephant, 3½ x 4 inches.   **D-8.50**

Blocks, four-sided, set of 24 to make 9 x 11 in. pictures.   **D-62.00**

Blocks, picture; set of 12 to make six pictures, each 5 x 7 inches.   **D-32.50**

Building blocks, set of six, paper-covered, each with soldier, ea. ½ x 3 inches.   **A-37.50**

Chair sled or "seat-ski", for winter sport. Ca. late 1800's, bottom runner 31 in. long. Private collection. C/50-75

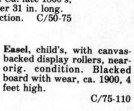

Easel, child's, with canvas-backed display rollers, near-orig. condition. Blacked board with wear, ca. 1900, 4 feet high.
C/75-110

Cookie roller, corrugated surface, one-piece maple, 11 in. long.	**D-18.50**
Cookie cutters, aluminized tin, set of four, flowers, 1 in. high.	**D-8.00**
Cupboard, doll-size, two drawers and double doors, 11½ x 22½ x 32¼ inches.	**A-115.00**
Dining room table, orig. finish, pine, 9 x 10 x 15 inches.	**D-45.00**
Dinner set, 25-piece, with 8 x 10 in. tray plus plates, cups, saucers, etc. Motif, child bride, groom, license, etc.	**D-29.00**
Drop-leaf table, swivel-top; may be chestnut wood. Top of 7½ x 16½ inches opens to 16½ x 18½ inches, 12 in. high.	**D-150.00**
Egg beater, child-size, two tin blades, turned wooden handle, 5¼ in. high.	**S-11.00**
Flatiron trivet, child's, lacy cast iron.	**D-12.50**
Flatware, six-piece group of spoons, knives and one fork, of white metal. Ca. 1880.	**D-6.50**
Handcuffs, with catch releases for each shackle, ca. 1930's.	**D-4.50**
Horse, wooden, Appaloosa with saddle and harness. Paint has flaked and mane missing, modern frosted plexiglass base; overall height 19 inches.	**A-300.00**
Kitchen, early tin, set of 40 pieces.	**D-185.00**
Kitchen range, cast iron, tin chimney, with coal skuttle and boiling pot. Door missing, 6½ x 11 x 12 inches.	**A-32.50**

Iron, "Lady Dover", cast iron sole, tin frame and wood handle.   D-10.00

Irons, with removable wood handles, individual lengths: 3½, 3¾, and 5 inches long.   A-35.00

Ironing board, child-size, wood, 18½ in. high.   D-19.00

Masher, kitchen; 4½ in. long, and rolling pin 8½ in. long.   A-10.00

Noise-maker, tin, lithographed. Wooden-handled, "Made in USA/Brooklyn", ca. 1920's.   D-2.50

Pail, wood, stave-constructed. Orig. paint and stenciling, "Good Boy", stars, flags and horses; 4¼ in. high.   D-47.50

Piano, upright, "International Pitch Symphony", 17 keyboard, 8½ x 11¼ x 18½ inches.   D-62.00

Pip-squeak chicken, in cage. Drawer missing and base with glued repair, 7 in. high.   D-10.00

Rocking horse, worn black, red and white paint, 38 in. long.   A-90.00

Rocking horse, carved wood, black and white fabric, 36 in. long.   D-175.00

Sand "sleeper", oak-cased, glass-covered. "The Sandman", gravity flow of sand makes figure twirl on tree branch. Lithographed forest background, lines of poetry, beadwork florals, 5¼ x 11 inches.   D-425.00

Sewing machine, German, works good, ca. 1940.   D-13.50

Sewing machine, hand-turned, 11 in. long.   D-37.50

Sled, orig. red paint, hand-forged iron runners, 8¼ x 28 inches, 4¼ in. high.   D-39.50

Sled, iron frame, curved runners, wooden top. Worn red and green paint with hellow striping and simple stencil.   A-105.00

Sleigh, child's, iron-bound runners, orig. red paint, 37 in. long.   A-110.00

Sleigh, push-type; wicker body, iron runners, trailing handle for adult control, 45 in. long.   D-150.00

Stove, tin, electric; element in oven heats stovetop; 6 x 8 x 10 inches.   D-18.00

Stove, cast and sheet iron, "Home" on door. Complete with top utensils; 10 in. high.   A-50.00

Swings, wooden, pair; each with boat-shaped swings with passengers. Polychromed, 3 in. high, 3½ in. wide.   A-55.00

Tableware, fork and knife, "For A Good Boy".   S-22.50

Velocipede, (Irish mail velocipede), wire wheels, steering bar, 22 in. high. 36 in. long. D-350.00

Wagon, wooden, rubber tires, orig. stencil "Red Racer". "Auto Wheel/1930", 43 in. long with 29 in. pull handle wood. D-53.00

Wagon, wood, 14 in. high, body 30 in. long, wood tongue and wheels. S-125.00

Washer, stave-constructed tub with wringer, 9 in. high. A-62.50

Washing set, "Peerless", table (11 in. high), wringer, tub, wash-board and two buckets, ca. late-1800's. A-62.50

Wash tub, tin, ca. 1870, 4 x 6 x 8¼ inches. D-85.00

Wheelbarrow, old red paint, 38 in. long. A-40.00

A) **Auction.** These are the top-bid, realized prices from recent auctions.

C) **Collector.** A few listings came from people who have kept up with market conditions for their collecting area(s).

D) **Dealer.** These represent antiques listings from top dealers.

S) **Shows.** A few listings are from important antiques exhibitions and sales.

CHINESE COLLECTIBLES—[See also Oriental]

There has long been an interest in quality Chinese antiques and art objects in the United States of America. With the recent thawing of relations between the two super-powers, and the inevitable increase in travel and trade, there will no doubt be a resurgence of collector attention to this field.

Altar, teak, simulated bamboo edge and legs, bamboo and vine skirt; mid-19th Century, 18 x 36 x 71 inches. **A-850.00**

Altar, teak, carved and pierced with brown marble inset top; 19th Century, 20 x 33 x 36 inches. **A-575.00**

Bottle, Ch'ing flambe glaze, long-neck, 16 in. high on teak stand. **A-300.00**

Chinese famille jaune barrel-shaped garden seat. Good Luck seals within wide banding, poly-chrome floral decorations within raised beaded studdings. Mid-19th Century. A/650

Courtesy Adam A. Weschler & Son, Washington, D.C.; photograph by Breger & Associates.

Top left, **Chinese carved agate figural group of reclining sow and piglets,** 6 in. long. A/550

Top right, **Chinese carved smokey quartz bottle,** with agate stopper. A/75

Bot. left, **Chinese carved carnelian leaf-form dish,** 3¼ in. long. A/40

Bot. center, **Chinese carved carnelian lotus-form bowl,** 3½ in. long. A/80

Bot. right, **Chinese carved agate lotus-form bowl,** 4 in. long, late 19th Century. A/80

Bowl, Ming, blue and white, decorated with lotus scrolls on blue wash ground. Ca. 16th-17th Centuries, 4¼ in. diameter. **A-150.00**

Bowl, blue and white, exterior with coffee enamel glaze, 12 in. diameter. **A-100.00**

Bowl, 19th Century, cream color with stylized flowers, 4 in. diameter. **D-90.00**

Box, tobacco; cloisonne cylinder-shape, foo dog finial, ca. 1900, 7 in. high. A-85.00

Buddha, iron, polychrome, seated on carved and pierced shaped teak base, overall 14 in. high. A-185.00

Cabinet, display; mandarin, carved, red lacquer with gilt high-lighted panels. Ca. 1880, 22 x 62 x 87 inches. A-1,200.00

Cabinet, two-part; coromandel, each with double doors of family scenes, brass mounts, 20 x 34 x 34 inches. A-550.00

Candleholder, iron, two small sockets, 14th Century, 18½ in. high. A-250.00

Candlesticks, pair; brass and pewter, equestrian forms, each on mythical horned horses on lotus bases, 24½ in. high. A-550.00

Case, jewel; traveler's, teak, 8 x 10 x 13 inches. A-100.00

Chairs, pair; mandarin Ming-style rosewood, 19th Century. Serpentine and pierced crestrail above circular carved and pierced splat. A-800.00

Charger, porcelain, polychrome; green underglazed phoenix bird, leafage and blossom border. Ca. 1850, 12 in. diameter. A-175.00

Charger, cloisonne, phoenix bird medallion on light blue ground, 19 in. diameter. A-300.00

Chest, miniature; gold and black lacquered, 15 in. wide. A-110.00

Dish, warming covered, pewter, duck-form, 15 in. long. A-110.00

Garniture, three-piece, blue and white, ca. 1820, covered vase 11 in. high. A-400.00

Hanging, wall; brocaded silk, segmented dragon medallions, 53 x 61 inches. A-200.00

Jars, rose, pair; porcelain, enamel-decorated, ca. 1820, 12½ in. high. A-350.00

Jardiniere, enamel, jewelled tree in Peking, approx. 19 in. high. A-250.00

Jardiniere, Jewel tree, rose quartz and soapstone, on wood stand. A-110.00

Kettle, bronze, animal-form, removable pierced top, 7 in. high. A-220.00

Lanterns, hanging; multicolored semi-precious hardstone, coral and Peking glass flowers and leaves in vermeil filigree basket with blue enamel decoration. Height, 17 inches, pair. A-500.00

Plate, Canton, blue and white, mounted in carved and pierced wood screen. Early 19th Century, plate diameter 9½ inches.   A-275.00

Pedestal, teak, carved, Mid-19th Century, 33 in. high.   A-300.00

Plaque, relief; carved hardstone, five vased flowers with ivory calligraphy, 24½ x 55 inches.   A-275.00

Pot, water; peach bloom, K'ang Hsi mark, 3½ in. high.   A-150.00

Robe, mandarin, embroidered silk, dragon vignettes over wavy sea.   A-225.00

Rug, sculptured, 8.10 x 11.7 feet.   A-850.00

Top   **Chinese flambe-glazed bowl,** 7 in. diameter, 17th-18th Century.   A/250

Lower   **Chinese flambe-glaze celadon interior rimmed bowl,** 10 in. diameter, 6 in. high. Period 17th-18th Century.   A/300

Courtesy Adam A. Weschler & Son, Washington, D.C.; photograph by Breger & Associates.

Chinese flambe-glaze baluster shape vase, 16 in. high, glaze of brilliant lavender-purple streaking. Period 17th-18th Century.   A/400

Screen, altar; eight-fold, straw panels with paper cut-outs of dieties, in bright colors. Ca. 19th Century, 19 x 40 inches.   A-120.00

Screen, three-fold, teak, 45 in. high.   A-225.00

Screen, floor; four-fold, coromandel, continuous interior scenes of family life with table-top vignettes above and bird vignettes below. Mid-19th Century, 72 in. high.   A-800.00

Screen, floor; four-fold, four paintings of mountain scenes, 67½ in. high.   A-175.00

Screen, table; four-fold, reverse painting on glass, 20 in. high.   A-70.00

Tables, lamp; pair, teak, saddle-shape top on cabriole legs and joined by central shelf, 32 in. high.　　A-250.00

Tabouret, rosewood, round beaded molded edge top with mottled rouge marble inset.　　A-275.00

Vase, flambe glaze, pomegranate form, 8 in. high.　　A-35.00

Vase, porcelain, flared-top, blue and white, 18 in. high.　　A-350.00

Vases, pair; porcelain, trumpet, enamel decoration of archaic vessels and calligraphy. Ca. 1820, 17 in. high.　　A-625.00

Washer, brush; ox-blood red, shallow circular-form covered with pinkish glaze. Late 19th Century, 4¾ in. diameter.　　A-75.00

Watercolor on paper, philosopher and his student in mountainous background. Makemono, 20 x 44 inches.　　A-125.00

Watercolor on paper, cat pursuing spider beneath flowering tree amidst two birds in flowering tree. Kakemono, two pieces.　　A-35.00

Watercolor on rice paper, six; family life scenes, ea. 4½ x 6½ inches.　　A-120.00

Watercolor on silk, Chinese mid-19th Century school, parrot in flowering tree. Kakemono, 19 37½ inches.　　A-225.00

CHINESE EXPORT COLLECTIBLES

Basket and undertray, with polychrome relief floral decoration. Ca. 1800, undertray 10½ in. long.　　A-425.00

Bowl, grisaille swag and floral decoration, ca. 1800, 10 in. diameter.　　A-200.00

Bowl, footed, elaborate polychrome scenes of family life, landscape, etc. Early 19th Century, 9½ in. diameter.　　A-250.00

Bowls and saucers, tea; set of five. Four with grisaille decorations, one polychrome, ca. 1800, ten pieces.　　A-225.00

Cabinet pieces, four; tea caddy, covered pot-de-creme, mug, and saucer. Ca. 1800.　　A-100.00

Cups, two pair, ca. 1820.　　A-50.00

Jugs, milk; pear-shape, two, height of taller 5 inches.　　A-60.00

Mug, painted blue and white borders with interlaced handles and polychrome armorial crest, 6 in. high.　　A-275.00

Plates, two, one with Neptune in the sea, other of farmers. Ca. 1790, 9 in. diameter.   **A-225.00**

Salts, pair, blue and white, open; with traces of gold. Ca. 1800.   **A-125.00**

Tables, nest of three; decorated black lacquer. Tops with birds and flowers, lyre shape trestle supports, mid-19th Century.   **A-275.00**

Teapot, straight spout with interlaced handle and fruit finial with blue decoration. Ca. 1800, 5½ in. high.   **A-275.00**

Teapots, two, straight-spout; each with polychrome figural and landscape decoration. Ca. 1820, taller 6 in. high.   **A-175.00**

Vase, Nanking export, baluster-shape having blue and white decorations with gold highlights. Mounted as lamp, vase 10 in. high.   **A-200.00**

Vases, covered pair, baluster-shape; basketweave and gilted decoration with foo dog finials. Ca. 1800, 11 in. high.   **A-325.00**

CHRISTMAS COLLECTIBLES—*Tree*

Ball, blue, embossed brass hanger, 5½ in. long.   **A-70.00**

Ball, silver color, brass hanger, large; 7 in. diameter.   **A-90.00**

Ball, green, embossed brass hanger, 3¾ in. high.   **A-50.00**

Balls, lot of two, gold and green, brass caps, 4 in. diameter.   **A-45.00**

Balls, lot of two, green and gold, also 4 in. diameter.   **A-55.00**

Balls, lot of three, green, gold and blue, 4 in. diameter.   **A-75.00**

Bulbs, tree, electric, socketed, handpainted milk glass. Earliest made ca. 1910.

    Bulldog, (clear glass), 3 in. high.   **D-15.00**

    Cat and fiddle, 3 in. high.   **D-15.00**

    Clown, 2½ in. high.   **D-20.00**

    Japanese lantern, 4 in. high.   **D-17.00**

    Parakeet, 4 in. high.   **D-12.00**

    Santa Claus, 3 in. high.   **D-17.00**

    Snow man, 2½ in. high.   **D-17.00**

    Snow-covered cottage, 2 in. high.   **D-15.00**

    Snow-covered lantern, 2 in. high.   **D-12.00**

    Star, w/moon imprint, 3 in. high.   **D-17.00**

Clamp, tin, candle-holder, miniature cylinder at one end, 1½ in. long.   **D-3.00**

Light, opalescent pale blue, quilted pattern, 4 in. high. **A-65.00**

Light, opalescent pale green hobnail, glass, 4 in. high. **A-60.00**

Light, purple, blown in quilted mould, 3¼ in. high. **A-42.50**

Railing, used around 19th Century Christmas trees, wood. Pieces 10¼ in. high, and 48 and 62½ in. long. **A-77.50**

Stand, for tree, cast iron, has three adjustable clamps, 13 in. high. **D-55.00**

CLOCKS—*[See also* **Tiffany***]*

Alarm, "Cyclone" by Waterbury, pat. 1907 & 1911, overwound. **D-10.00**

Banjo, mahogany, by New Haven Clock Co., eagle pediment above circular dial, eglomise paneled throat flanked by pierced brass mounts, hinged glazed door viewing pendulum. Ca. 1900, approx. 45 in. high. **A-425.00**

Bracket, chiming; Victorian, walnut. Brass and tole dial within gilt-medal and embossed frame, domed top with urn finials on moulded base. By Ungens, ca. 1890, 12 x 22 in. high. **A-300.00**

Seth Thomas. Nickel. Artist Lever.
70-75

Seth Thomas. Albany. Black Walnut. Ht. 20 in., 6 in. dial.

120-130

Left, oak **wall clock.**
225-275
Above, oak, **kitchen clock.**
175-200
Right, oak **mission Grand-father clock.**
450-500

Left, oak **Kitchen clock.**
125-150

Right, oak **Wall clock.**
300-350

Grandfather's, pine case with old reddish-orange paint, ogee feet and reeded quarter-columns. Bonnet with free-standing reeded front columns; painted metal face with basket of flowers and bird, marked "Simon Forest/Kirkfield Bank", calendar movement, 86 in. high. — A-775.00

Grandfather's case; pine and poplar, shelves in pendulum area, 81 in. high. — A-95.00

Mantel, Louis XV style, gilt metal and crystal, by Ansonia, N.Y. White painted Roman numeral dial, open escapement, urn pediment, 15½ in. high. — A-225.00

Mantel, Victorian, onyx, classical case with ormolu mounts and centering a female mask pediment, by Japy Fries & Co. Height, 10½ inches. — A-125.00

Mantel, Seth Thomas eight-day, bell on half hour, chimes on hour, mahogany. Porcelain face, ca. 1880, 11¼ in. high. — D-95.00

Regulator wall, German, Walnut, late 19th Century. Enamelled-over-brass Roman numeral dial within arched glazed door flanked by fluted pilasters, 17 x 50 inches. — A-275.00

Shelf, American eight-day, by Chauncey Jerome, New Haven, Conn. Mahogany case enclosing painted Roman numeral dial, 17 x 30 inches. — A-150.00

Shelf, Federal mahogany, painted black and white Roman numeral dial with hinged door with eglomise panel. Ca. 1840, 15½ x 26 inches. — A-130.00

Shelf, Victorian slate, "Agnew & Son/spects", black classical-form slate with dial with Roman numerals, sides with bas relief panels of after-the-hunt scenes. Ca. 1880, 10 x 19 in. high. — A-300.00

Shelf, mahogany, by Jerome Clock Co., eight-day. Brass works, bezel, and Roman numeral face. Orig. clock paper intact, 5 x 9½ x 14¼ in. high. — D-165.00

Tall case, English mahogany, chiming, early 20th Century. Silvered brass engraved dial with copper numerals within cathedral arched case flanked by free-standing columns ending on bun feet; nine chiming tubes and pendulum, 80 in. high. — A-1,100.00

Tall case, American knotty pine, ca. 1820. Swan's neck bonnet-top centering brass eagle and orb finial housing replaced movement, 84 in. high. — A-250.00

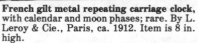

French gilt metal repeating carriage clock, with calendar and moon phases; rare. By L. Leroy & Cie., Paris, ca. 1912. Item is 8 in. high.

A/8500

Courtesy Adam A. Weschler & Son, Washington, D.C.; photograph by Breger & Associates.

Tall case clock, English Chippendale, inlaid mahogany. Height, 90 inches; ca. 1800.

A/1500

Courtesy Adam A. Weschler & Son, Washington, D.C.; photograph by Breger & Associates.

Tall case, Hepplewhite mahogany, by Joakin Hill, Flemington, N.J., ca. 1795. Bonnet hood with molded swan's neck cresting into satinwod inlaid rosette and fluted urn finials, French bracket feet. White painted dial with phases of moon, 84 in. high.　　**A-3,300.00**

Tall case, American Chippendale, walnut, ca. 1800. Painted dial with black Roman numerals with floral bouquet pediment within arched swan's neck scrolling bonnet. Height, 100 inches.　　**A-1,550.00**

Wall, weight-driven, ca. 1840. Similar to Ansonia, brass works, spiral spring chime strike, key, veneered case, orig. glass, ca. 1840. Clock 4¼ x 15 x 25½ in. high.　　**D-250.00**

Wall, wooden works, ca. 1830. By Terry & Andrews, eight-day time & strike, eight-driven, solid mahogany. Restored, furniture finish, wooden face with Roman numerals, sectioned door with lower half an old mirror.　　**D-575.00**

CLOTHING AND ACCESSORIES

Baby shoes, pair, homespun lined, dark ribbon laces, 5¼ in. long.　　**A-10.00**

Beaver top hat, in orig. box, ca. 1870, 6¾ in. high.　　**D-50.00**

Boots, man-size, leather with wood-pegged soles, pair.　　**S-30.00**

Boots, childs' copper toe plated Pat'd. 1859, 10 in. high.　　**A-25.00**

Button hook, ivory-handled.　　**D-6.50**

Button hook, Victorian, "French Ivory" handle.　　**D-5.00**

Brass buttons, set of ten, plain, smooth surfaces.　　**A-16.00**

Cane, dog-head handle, brass ground-tip; 34½ in. long.　　**D-15.00**

Evening bag, silver thread, silver clasp, chain strap.　　**D-10.00**

Evening bag, gold sequins frame and chain, ca. 1940's.　　**D-12.50**

Evening gloves, ladies, soft grey material, early 1900's.　　**D-18.00**

Flapper's beads, Twenties, four strands glass beads, 20 in. long.　　**D-15.00**

Granny glasses, oblong lenses, wire frame.　　**D-5.00**

Hand fan, vegetable ivory struts, white satin, spans 22½ inches.　　**D-4.50**

Hatpin, Victorian, ball head gold or gold-gilt filled.   D-7.50
Hatpin, Victorian, figural head of roaring tiger, 6½
in. long.   D-10.00
Ladies bonnet, folding, with accordian pleats, forest
green.   D-25.00
Shawl, paisley, 19th century, 77 x 80 inches.   A-250.00
Straw hat, black.   A-10.00
Vest, child's brown woven wool on linen homespun,
14 in. long.   A-45.00

COCA-COLA *(All items marked)*

Advertisements, from backs of National Geographic
magazines, years 1933-1949. Each: D-2.50
Advertisement, framed, porter pushing lady at
seaside resort, from 1908 Cosmopolitan magazine.   D-20.00
Baseball cap, Giants' Willie Mays.   D-2.50
Blotter, ink, lithographed in color, unused, year
1956.   D-4.50
Bottle, miniature gold Cola-Cola.   D-3.00
Button, "Vote The Party Favorite", small size, 1972.   D-1.00
Calendar, 1972 misprints, with August 12th missing.   D-3.00
Calendar, framed under glass, pictures WAC, 1943.   D-60.00
Carriers, bottles, retractable strap handle, Coca-
Cola logo, aluminum, room for twelve bottles.   D-16.50
Commemorative bottle, 75th Anniversary of Coca-
Cola, capped, full contents.   D-6.50
Clock, electric, "Things Go Better With Coke",
1960's, 14 in. square.   D-60.00
Fountain glass, ca. 1930's, marked.   D-5.00
Ice chest, red, "Drink Coca-Cola" on both sides and
end, with attached opener, 1942, 6½ x 17 inches.   D-25.00
Ice pick, ca. 1930's, fine condition.   D-15.00
Lighter, cigarette, miniature Coke bottle, ca. 1946.   D-10.00
Magazine, Coca-Cola "Pause For Living".   D-2.50
Medals, "Great Olympic Moments", orig. envelope,
cards, medals and pamphlet.   D-10.00
Negro Comics, Golden Legacy Vol. 1, "The Saga of
Toussaint L'Ouverture and The Birth of Haiti, 1966.   D-3.00
Negro Comics, Vol. 10, Joseph Cinque and the
Amistad Meeting, 1970.   D-5.00
Negro Comics, Vol. 11, Men of Action, Wilkins and
Marshall, 1970.   D—3.50

1914. "Betty".   C/50-100   1937.   C/15-25

Opener, bottle, metal, "Drink Coca-Cola In Bottles",
3½ in. long.   **D-4.00**
Opener, wire hand type.   **D-.50**
Pamphlet, "Discover America" Teacher's Guide, 18
pages, 1962.   **D-5.00**
Pamphlet, "Teacher's Guide To Elementary Science
Laboratory/Weather", 16 pages, small size.   **D-4.00**
Pamphlet, "Teacher's Guide to Communication by
Sound and Light".   **D-4.00**
Pinback button, "Courtesy of Coca-Cola", for high
school athletic teams, 2¼ in. diameter. Ca. 1940's.   **D-4.50**
Poster, "Lumber", 1943 litho. by Forbes, color, 11 x
16 inches.   **D-15.00**
Poster, "Our American Cotton No. 3", 22 x 32 in-
ches.   **D-35.00**
Poster, "Our American Glass, No. 2", methods of
mfgr., 22 x 32.   **D-35.00**
Poster, "Our American Lumber, No. 4", the future.   **D-35.00**
Plate, tole-decorated, the Coca-Cola Girl, framed.   **A-55.00**
Sign, porcelain, 1942, "Drink Coca-Cola", 18 x 30 in-
ches.   **D-15.00**
Sign, tin, 10 in. diameter, picturing bottle.   **D-35.00**
Sign, tin, company logo, bottle-shape, white on red,
25 in. high.   **D-35.00**

Sign, double-sided, tin, "6 Bottles 25¢", dated 1933, 8½ x 18 inches.　　　　　　　　　　　　　　**D-55.00**

Sign, cardboard, people drinking Coke from cooler, "Enjoy The Friendly Circle", dated 1954, 20 x 30 inches.　　　　　　　　　　　　　　　　　　　　　**D-25.00**

Sign, tin, bottle-shaped, Christmas bottle, 1923, 36 in. high.　　　　　　　　　　　　　　　**D-100.00**

Tag, first hand-on tag for 602 Cokes, light green.　　**D-1.00**

Thermometer, figural bottle-shaped, tin, dated 1953, fine condition, 17 in. high.　　　　　　　　　**D-20.00**

Thermometer, oval shape, "Sign Of Good Taste", 27 in. high.　　　　　　　　　　　　　　　　**D-45.00**

Thermometer, two bottles, dated 1942, 7 x 15 inches.　　　　　　　　　　　　　　　　　　**D-65.00**

Thermometer, bottle-shaped, fine condition, 27 in. high.　　　　　　　　　　　　　　　　　**D-45.00**

Toy truck. Tin. 1925.　　　C/60-75

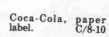

Coca-Cola, paper label.　　C/8-10

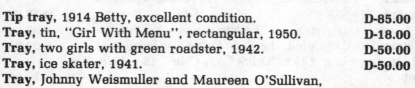

Coca-Cola, combination icepick and bottle opener, wooden handle with logo, 9 in. long. C/9-15

Tip tray, 1914 Betty, excellent condition.　　　　**D-85.00**
Tray, tin, "Girl With Menu", rectangular, 1950.　　**D-18.00**
Tray, two girls with green roadster, 1942.　　　　**D-50.00**
Tray, ice skater, 1941.　　　　　　　　　　　**D-50.00**
Tray, Johnny Weismuller and Maureen O'Sullivan, 1934.　　　　　　　　　　　　　　　　**D-275.00**
Tray, sailor girl, 1940.　　　　　　　　　　　**D-40.00**
Tray, springboard girl, 1939.　　　　　　　　**D-45.00**

COIN-OPERATED DEVICES

Items in this category are marked with the unique "C/D" designation, meaning many of the pieces are from a major collection, and offered by a dealer. The Coin-Operated section is taken from the Limited Edition Catalogue including over one hundred different items from the Carl Jensen Collection.

The material is used here courtesy, and by special permission of, American International Galleries, of Irvine, California. See Directory for complete information on A.I.G.

Cigarette machine, Select-A-Pack, circular red metal cabinet. Scarce, operates, 6½ x 18 x 27 in. high. **C/D-129.00**

Claw machine, by Exhibit Supply Co., ca. 1930's. Amusement park device manipulated to pick up toys, coins, etc. Two-tone wood cabinet, excellent operating condition, 25 x 25½ x 67½ in. high. **C/D-1,195.00**

Coin scoop, "Steam Shovel", by Chicago Coin, electrically-operated. Arcade item from 1930's/40's, wood and glass cabinet, 67¾ in. high. **C/D-549.00**

Jukebox, Rocola Rhythm King, ca. 1937, 12 selectional Three independent coin slots, requires refinishing and restoration. **C/D-549.00**

Jukebox, Seeburg 100 Select-o-Matic, 45 rpm, 100 selections. Wood cabinet, painted grain surface, choice unrestored condition, 4 ft. 6 in. high. **C/D-475.00**

Jukebox, Wurlitzer Model 1200, very nice and plays. Some additional work to have it operating perfectly, 4 ft. 9½ in. high. **C/D-1,495.00**

Jukebox, Wurlitzer Style 1600, late-style 78 rpm, 48 selections. Nice, unrestored condition, 4 ft. 7 in. high. **C/D-595.00**

Metal stamper, arcade, table-top model, by Autotic Stamping Machine Co., prints on aluminum discs. Nice operational condition, 22 x 24 x 31½ in. high. **C/D-995.00**

Nickelodeon piano, Peerless; richly figured quartered oak case, with three colorful art-glass panels. Uses ten-tune "A" roll, plays somewhat, would benefit from full restoration. From Peerless' "Golden Age", 2 ft. 7 in. x 5 ft. 6 in. x 4 ft. 10 in. **C/D-3,950.00**

Nickelodeon piano, Philipps; unrestored, electric, ca. 1920's. Upright style, attractive oak case, 2 ft. 7 in. x 5 ft. x 4 ft. 7 in. high.   **C/D-1,995.00**

Peep-show machine, Mutoscope, arcade, 1920's. Sheet metal cabinet painted blue, angle-iron base, uses nickels; 14 x 21 x 6 ft. 3½ in. high.   **C/D-795.00**

Pinball machine, "Auto Race" by Gottlieb, with bumpers and flippers. Push-button, orig. condition, works well, 26¼ x 55 x 66 in. high.   **C/D-695.00**

Pinball machine, Bally Dude Ranch, brightly colored back panel and interior. Operates, 26¾ x 55½ x 70½ in. high.   **C/D-379.00**

Race-Horse piano, "Derby", by Western Electric Piano Company, ca. 1924. Quartered oak case, front door replaced with clear glass so mechanism can be seen, some repairs needed. Rare example. 26½ x 35¾ x 51½ in. high.   **C/D-7,995.00**

Scale, 1900 patent date, cast iron, by Automatic Vending Company. Painted ivory, gold trim, "Your Correct Weight/One Cent". Ornate, rare, 5 ft. 11½ in. high.   **C/D-895.00**

Skill game, Whirl-a-Ball, air-propelled, operates, 21½ in. high.   **C/D-195.00**

Slot machine, Jennings Dutchess, clean unrestored condition, in a popular style.   **C/D-895.00**

Slot machine, Mills "Bursting Cherry" dime-operated. Old repaint, clean unrestored condition, 15 x 16 x 15½ in. high.   **C/D-1,195.00**

Slot machine, Mills "Silent Mystery", early 1930's. Ornate cast front, three-reel type, nickel-operated. Completely restored, 15¼ x 16 x 25½ inches.   **C/D-1,695.00**

Slot machine, poker, displays "hand" of five cards, oak case. Good unrestored condition, needs refinishing, table-top model.   **C/D-595.00**

Stamp vendor, ca. 1921, by United States Vending Machine Company, for 1 cent and 2 cents stamps. Beveled glass sides, 10¼ x 11¾ x 10¾ in. high.   **C/D-345.00**

Target skill arcade game, mechanical, five shots for 1 cent, "Big Game Hunter". Early 1930's, ornate cast-metal backplate, 10½ x 27 x 18 in. high.   **C/D-325.00**

Trade stimulator, "Free Play", nickel-operated, pays off in free plays, 9 x 9¾ x 12¼ in. high.   **C/D-329.00**

COPPER COLLECTIBLES—*[See also* **Kitchen***]*

Apple butter kettle, wrought iron bail, 25 in. diameter. **A-200.00**

Basin, 15 in. diameter. **D-40.00**

Bee smoker, polished, wooden bellows, 9¼ in. long. **D-85.00**

Boiler, oval, handled, brass cap; 12 x 18 x 22 inches. **A-75.00**

Cooking pan, tin-lined, Greek stamp, 19 in. diameter, 2 in. high. **A-47.50**

Cooking vessel, for stage coach inn. Ca. 1830, 19 in. wrought iron handle, copper rivets, 14½ in. diameter, 9 in. deep. **D-325.00**

Candy dish, square, fluted edge, 6 in. square, 1 in. deep. **D-24.00**

Dish, shell-shaped, oval, signed "Roycraft", 1 x 3½ x 5½. **D-24.00**

Dipper, early seaming, 6¼ in. handle, bowl 8 in. top diameter. **D-65.00**

Funnel, thumb-lever valve, for filling bottles, 6½ in. diameter. **A-15.00**

Glue pot, polished, early seaming, 2¾ in. diameter, 3¼ in. high. **D-30.00**

Heater, for hot-dog vending, boiler bottom, brass faucet, 15 in. high. **D-125.00**

Hot-dog steamer, "W. B. Berry Co./Boston, Mass", two compartments; 7 x 9¾ x 21½ inches. **D-89.00**

Kettle, blackened, iron handle, 18 in. high. **A-90.00**

Kettle, iron handle, 22 in. diameter. **D-195.00**

Lather dispensing urn, barber's; three-gal. capacity, 2½ in. side spout, ca. 1880, 17 in. high. **D-125.00**

A) **Auction.** These are the top-bid, realized prices from recent auctions.

C) **Collector.** A few listings came from people who have kept up with market conditions for their collecting area(s).

D) **Dealer.** These represent antiques listings from top dealers.

S) **Shows.** A few listings are from important antiques exhibitions and sales.

Lather dispensing urn, barber's ; two-gal. capacity, 2 in. base spout, 14½ in. high.   **D-100.00**

Measure, four arched side-windows, handle and spout, 9 in. high.   **A-55.00**

Pan, dovetail construction, iron handle, 17 in. diameter.   **A-55.00**

Sauce pan, wooden handle, interior tin-washed, 6 in. diameter.   **A-22.50**

Sink, Pat'd. 1885, Philadelphia, 7 x 14½ x 20 inches. Rare.   **D-180.00**

Step-pot, with cover; bilateral side handles, 10¼ in. base diameter, 12½ in. high.   **D-95.00**

Still unit, with copper spout for tubing, 30 in. high. **D-125.00**

Still, complete, with copper coils, three-gal. capacity. Side handles, 9½ in. diameter, 16 in. high.   **D-165.00**

Strawberry pail, folding wireware handle, 6¼ in. diameter, 5 in. deep.   **D-49.50**

Sundial, ornamental garden; five paint colors, 21 in. high.   **A-80.00**

Teakettle, dovetailed construction, spout-flap gone, 5 in. high.   **A-95.00**

Wash bain, 14 in. diameter, 4½ in. high.   **D-38.00**

COUNTRY STORE COLLECTIBLES

The days of penny candy and cracker barrels are past, but interest in country or general stores remains high. There are many thousand items that could have been, or once were, sold from these establishments. The field for collectors has two aspects. One would be the goods actually inventoried, and the other area concerns country store fixtures of all kinds, from string holders to biscuit boxes, coffee bins to advertising signs.

Flour barrel, thick pine wood, 26 in. high, ca. 1870. **D-85.00**

Food slicer, countertop, "Arcadia Mfg. Co.", adjustable.   **D-85.00**

Fly catcher, sticky ribbon, "Holco Fly Catcher", unused.   **D-2.50**

Hat brush, maple, store item; 13 in. long.   **D-12.50**

Ice cream freezer, "Snow Peak", two qts., with scoop.   **D-45.00**

Ice cream scoop, brass bowl and body, hardwood handle.   **S-30.00**

Coffee can, about 2-pound size, Dwinell - Wright & Co. / Boston Roasted Coffees".
C/20-30

Photo courtesy Judy Morehead, Creative Photography, Lancaster, Ohio.

Shot cabinet, for dispensing lead pellets of various sizes. These came in various sizes and numbers of compartments, with this piece about 14 in. high. Shot-cabinets were sometimes country store items.
A/150-225

Lar Hothem photo.

Store-size coffee mill, "National / Elgin". Some decorative paint lines remaining; 27 in. high, wheel diameter 19½ inches. Private collection.
C/250-325

Key box, drawer type with 200 assorted keys, brass trim. **D-35.00**

Linen marker, "Gorham", four-footed, with orig. instructions. **D-11.00**

Penny candy scoop, "Germany", early aluminum. **D-6.00**

Rack for selling glass lamp chimneys, wood, 48 in. high. **A-85.00**

Seed-packet display frame, folding, opened halves, 26 in. high. **D-50.00**

Shoe forms, pair, wooden, orig. paint, each with lacquered handle. **D-6.00**

Spool cabinet on legs, ten pull-drawers, slanted top. **D-285.00**

Spool cabinet, walnut, three-drawer, 12 in. high. **S-250.00**

String holder, cast iron ball, pierced sides, ca. 1880. **D-25.00**

Barrel, for cider jelly, with orig. paper labels, small size. **D-24.50**

Bottle, cure-all, full label, for "nerve pain", etc. **D-3.50**

Box, tin, "Walter Baker Co./Breakfast Cocoa", some stain. **D-3.50**

Box, wood, for "Gloucester Style Codfish", 2 x 4 x 6 inches. **D-5.00**

Candy scoop, tin, holds 8 oz., early seaming on tin. **D-6.50**

Carpet-tacker, professional, fulcrum hammer, 65 in. handle. — D-45.00

Coffee bin, worn red paint, 13½ x 18 x 24 inches. — A-65.00

Coffee bin, "V.T. Hills and Co./Delaware, O.", 32 in. high. — A-155.00

Coffee storebox, slant top, old red paint, 28 in. high. — S-60.00

Chocolate pot, polished copper with copper chocolate well. — D-95.00

Counter-top desk, slant top, unusual iron hinges; 24 in. long. — D-125.00

Dipper, tin, never used, orig. tin plating, 11 in. long. — D-8.50

Display bin for candy, lithographed, 8 x 10 x 11 inches. — D-39.00

Display rack for buggy whips, cast iron, 14½ in. diameter. — D-55.00

Display rack, "Queen Anne/Fresh Nuts", wireware folding rack. — D-25.00

Display stand, for watches, "Ingersoll", 19 in. high. — D-35.00

Display stand, for candy, brass, 8 in. diameter, 7¼ in. high. — D-49.50

Display stand, for candy, brass, 14 in. diameter, 8 in. high. — D-75.00

Store container, biscuit, tin; sheet brass front with clear window, 15 in. high.

C/45-60

Photo courtesy Judy Morehead, Creative Photography, Lancaster, Ohio.

Tea bin, bulk leaves, "Finest Family Tea", 9¾ in. high. — D-77.50

Tea container, tin, "Chase & Sanborn's", half-pound, pull-top. — D-10.00

Tea container, large, bulk leaves, floral and oriental figures. — D-45.00

Thread box, cardboard, full label, ca. 1870. — D-5.00

Tin, "Mica Axle Grease", one pound size. — D-4.25

Tin, "Reed...Jamaica Ginger", one-quarter pound size. — D-5.00

Tin, "Penn Mar/5 lbs./Golden Syrup", 5 in. diameter.   **D-5.00**
Tin, "Excelsor Metal Polish", 2½ in. high.   **D-6.00**
Tongs, ornate, for removing pickled herring from keg, 12 in. long.   **D-45.00**

DECOYS AND SHOREBIRDS

Decoy-collecting is no longer confined to the hunter-sportsperson, and the better examples are avidly sought on today's market. Value factors include age, condition, material, replaced parts, paint, and manufacture skill.

Also to be considered are the absence or presence of a maker's stamp, date, locale and signature. Especially desired by some collectors are the early, wooden primitively carved decoy types.

DECOYS—*Named Varieties*

Black duck, carved feather detail, initialed, 14½ in. long.   **A-57.50**
Black duck, early example by Bill Finkel, Mich.; branded, paint worn, 17 in. long.   **A-50.00**
Black duck, hollow, worn working repaint, 14¾ in. long.   **A-45.00**
Bluebill drake, carved wood, orig. paint, tack eyes, 11½ in. long.   **A-85.00**
Bluebill drake, from Maryland, early wooden. Glass eyes, underside of bill branded "P.H.", 14½ in. long.   **A-55.00**
Brant, unused condition, circular label with swimming duck in center, glass eyes, 16¼ in. long.   **A-100.00**
Brant sleeping, primitive, repairs to neck and head 13¼ in. long.   **A-215.00**
Brant sleeping, primitive, orig. worn paint.   **A-75.00**
Brant, carved wood, old split in head, 13 in. long.   **A-35.00**
Brant, carved wood, traces of black paint, 16 in. long.   **A-150.00**
Canadian goose, wood and wire frame with canvas cover; from Swan Island Club, N.C., 21 in. long.   **A-75.00**
Canadian goose, hollow, wood, old repairs, worn paint, 29½ in. long.   **A-95.00**

Male Mallard.
C/200

Old Redhead.
C/35-50

Blue Wing Teal.   C/40-50

Canadian goose, carved wood, primitive, preening. Carved wing details, old weathered paint, cracks in block, 14 in. high.   **A-390.00**

Canvasback, Mason's wooden, worn orig. paint, glass eyes, 16¼ in. long.   **A-57.50**

Canvasback, oversize, with lead anchor. Working repaint, 24 in. long.   **A-32.50**

Canvasback, primitive, carved wood, some wear, 13 in. long.   **A-25.00**

Canvasback drake, carved wood, by Capt. Harry Jobes, Md., 13½ in. long.   **A-75.00**

Canvasback drake, by Robert Michels, Mich., 15¼ in. long.   **A-27.50**

Canvasback drake, splits in block, carved wood. Maker's mark brand "C. Klopping", Ohio, 13¾ in. long.   **A-80.00**

Canvasback drake, sentry duck, neck loose, 16 in. long.   **A-60.00**

Canvasback hen, alert head, from Green Bay, Wisc. Shot holes in head, minor water damage on back, 16½ in. long.   **A-45.00**

Coot, hollow, carved wood. Rare, branded "C.W.", 10¾ in. long.   A-75.00

Goldeneye drake, carved wood, orig. paint, brandmark, 13¼ in. long.   A-100.00

Goose, wooden, worn black and white paint, 19 in. long.   A-35.00

Goose, canvas over framework, 22½ in. long.   A-65.00

Heron, on driftwood base, carved wood. Bill broken at joint and glued. By Hurley Conklin, 27 in. long.   A-235.00

Hooded merganser, carved wood, unused condition, Maine, 12 in. long.   A-110.00

Lesser scaup, carved wood, Long Island, 11 in. long.   A-60.00

Mallard hen, carved wood, New Jersey ca. 1861-1920, 11 in. long.   A-205.00

Mallard hen, carved hollow decoy, lead weight, from Merrymeeting Bay, 16½ in. long.   A-55.00

Mallard hen, carved wood, by Miles Smith, Mich., 18¾ in. long.   A-75.00

Mallard hen, turned head, carved wood, Michigan, 14¼ in. long.   A-95.00

Merganser, carved wood, old worn paint; plastic wood repairs, 18¼ in. long.   A-82.50

Merganser drake, branded "R.C.W.", carved wood, 15½ in. long.   A-50.00

Merganser, worn paint, primitive wood carved, repaired bill.   A-35.00

Pintail, repainted Victor, glass eyes, 17¼ in. long.   A-27.50

Pintail drake, carved wood, by Madison Mitchell, 17 in. long.   A-95.00

Pintail hen, carved wood, Backbay, Va., 17½ in. long.   A-70.00

Redhead, mismatched head and repaired bill, 15½ in. long.   A-25.00

Redhead, primitive carving, old paint, tack eyes, Lake Ontario 14 in. long.   A-35.00

Redhead hen, one glass eye missing, 14¼ in. long.   A-30.00

Scaup drake, factory decoy, Mason's' weathered paint, 13¼ in. long.   A-55.00

Swan, carved wood, old white paint, black bill, 18½ in. high.   A-295.00

Whistler, carved wood, from Connecticut, 12 in. long.   A-25.00

White-winged scooter, wooden shadow decoy, old black and white paint, 44 in. long.   A-22.50

DECOYS—*Related Types*

Confidence bird, carved wood seagull, no stand, 12¼ in. long.   A-35.00

Confidence decoy, canvas-covered swan, unused, 28 in. long.   A-255.00

Crow decoy, wood, old black paint, 14½ in. long.   A-35.00

Decoy, Victor factory-made, 14 in. long.   A-25.00

Decoy, primitive carving, details crude, 14 in. long.   A-37.50

Decoy, balsa body, orig. paint good, 14½ in. long.   A-120.00

Duck decoy, old black and white paint, 14 in. long.   A-52.50

Duck decoy, one glass eye missing, carved wood, 15 in. long.   A-77.50

Duck decoy, carved wood, old paint, 12½ in. long.   A-52.50

Duck decoy, orig. paint good, carved wood, 14¼ in. long.   A-90.00

Field decoy, sheet iron stick-up, 16 in. long.   A-25.00

Goose decoy, wood head only, 6½ in. high.   A-15.00

DECOYS—*Shorebirds*

Shorebird, repaired neck, no rod or stand, 13 in. wide.   A-20.00

Shorebird, modern metal base, 11½ in. high.   A-45.00

Shorebird primitively carved, 12 in. high.   A-45.00

Shorebird carved from ½ in. wood, 7½ in. high.   A-50.00

Shorebird, unusual, made from redware with grey applied color. Back damaged; 8 in. wide, 11 in. high.   A-60.00

Shorebird, carved wood, 20th Century, 9 in. high.   A-65.00

Shorebird, root head, carved wing detail. Head split, modern metal stand, 10½ in. high.   A-70.00

Shorebird, tip of bill incomplete, minor putty repair, 10¼ in. high.   A-75.00

Shorebird, old worn paint, modern stand, 9¼ in. wide.   A-85.00

Shorebird, small, old dark paint, modern stand, 6 in. high.   A-100.00

Shorebird, dark brown with white spots, carved wood base resembles rockpile; 8 in. wide, 9 in. high.   A-125.00

Shorebirds on driftwood base, five, Long Island
sandpipers. Tallest bird 11 in. high.   A-155.00
Shorebird, backward-turned head, birch base, 13½
in. high.   A-190.00
Shorebird, long wooden beak, carved wood. Orig.
black and white paint with spots. Modern wooden
stand; 9½ in. wide, 13 in. high.   A-230.00

DISNEY MEMORABILIA

Album, two-record, 78rpm, "Lady And The Tramp",
and color booklet.   D-9.50
Bank, figural, Pinocchio, composition, ca. 1939.   D-14.00
Beach ball, Mickey Mouse, boxed, 1950's.   D-5.00
Beanie, child's, Mickey Mouse, illustrated, ca. 1933.   D-8.00
Book, "Adventures Of Mickey Mouse/Book I", soft-
bound, McKay, 1931.   D-85.00
Book, "Mickey Mouse Stories", softcover, McKay,
1934.   D-45.00
Book, linen, "Pluto The Pup", in color, 1937.   D-70.00
Bow and arrow set, Mickey Mouse Club, with orig.
box, 1956.   D-9.50
Ceramic figurine, Flower and Skunk, American Pot-
tery, small size.   D-12.50
Ceramic tile, Bambi, Kemper-Thomas, 1949.   D-8.50
Charm, sterling, figural, Peter Pan, ca. 1960.   D-14.00
Creamer, Mickey Mouse, figural, Lusterware, ca.
1933.   D-32.00
Doll, bisque, Doc, 3¼ inches.   D-16.00
Doll, Bubble-Blower, Donald Duck, boxed, 1950's   D-10.00
Doll, Mouseketeer, girl Puppette, boxed, 1950's   D-17.50
Doll, stuffed, large, Bambi, orig. label, 1940's   D-38.00
Doll, stuffed, Timothy Mouse from Dumbo, 1942, 17
inches.   D-125.00
Drawing set, electric, Disney, boxed, 1965.   D-15.00
Drinking glass, "1939/All Star Parade", featuring
Goofy.   D-22.00
Drinking glass, Pinocchio, red variety, 1939.   D-12.00
Drinking straws, Mickey Mouse, boxed, Herz,
1950's.   D-4.50
Easter egg transfers, Mickey Mouse, complete
package, 1937.   D-18.00
Fancard, Peter Pan, full color, 1960's.   D-3.50

Fancard, color, Walt Disney surrounded by six characters. — D-4.00

Figural scenes, set of six, Ludwig Von Drake, each boxed, 1961. — D-25.00

Figure, wood, Pluto, missing tail, 1934, 3 inches. — D-24.00

Film, "Donald Gets Ducked", with box; 8mm B&W, 50 feet, 1936. — D-15.00

Film, "Donald's Trained Seals", with box; 8mm B&W, 50 feet, 1937. — D-15.00

Guidebook, Disneyland, 1974. — D-3.00

Inlay puzzle, "Snow White and the Seven Dwarfs", Jaymar, 1950. — D-4.50

Jigsaw puzzle, "Cinderella", frame tray, Jaymar, 1950. — D-5.00

Key chain, Sword in the Stone, on orig. card. — D-4.00

Paper napkins, Donald Duck, pkg. of 25, 1950's. — D-12.00

Pencil box, Disney, hardcover, 1950's. — D-10.00

Pillowcase, Minnie Mouse powdering nose, color, ca. 1932, 16 in. square. — D-35.00

Pressbook, Robin Hood. — D-2.50

Print, color, Sleeping Beauty, heavy stock, 8 x 10 inches. — D-4.50

Ring, child's, metal, Mickey Mouse in relief, 1940's. — D-12.00

Scrapbook, "Snow White's Scrapbook", color covers, unused, 1938, 10 x 15 inches. — D-23.00

Soap figure, Jiminy Cricket, 1938, 4 inches. — D-7.00

Spoon, Mickey Mouse, silverplate, Branford, ca. 1935. — D-10.00

Squeeze toy, rubber, Sleeping Beauty, with animals. — D-12.00

Store poster, J.C. Penney's, Mickey Mouse, ca. 1935, 19 x 26 inches. — D-95.00

Tablecloth, Mickey and Minnie, color, ca. 1931, 38 x 72 inches. — D-90.00

Theatre standup, heavy cardboard, "One Little Indian", 4 ft. high. — D-17.50

Thermos bottle, Zorro. — D-7.00

Toon-A-Vision, Mickey Mouse Club, 1950's. — D-15.00

DOLLHOUSE FURNISHINGS

Armchair, ladderback, rocker, maple, ca. 1890, 5¾ in. high. — D-29.50

Bench, park; slatted back, plank seat, pine, ca. 1930. — D-12.50

Bootjack, miniature, wood, 1 in. long. — D-3.00

Bottle, amber glass, contents intact, "Pepsi Cola", 1½ in. high. — D-7.50

Bowl and tumbler, wood, ¾ in. high, pair. — D-2.00

Carpenter's tools, brass, ca. 1930's, six-piece set, average 1½ in. long. — D-5.00

Bugle, cast metal, 1¼ in. long. — D-1.50

Candlesticks, brass, classical form, 1½ in. high, pair. — D-15.00

Cauldron, copper, bail handle, 1½ in. high. — D-5.00

Cradle, pine, hooded, natural finish, 2¾ in. long. — D-12.50

Creamer and sugar, porcelain, floral decoration, 1 in. high. — D-5.00

Dinner set, plates and flatware, pot metal, 1 to 1¼ in. diameter, 14 pieces. — D-10.00

Dollhouse doll, boy, clothed, composition extremities, 3¼ in. high. — D-18.50

Dollhouse doll, girl, clothed, wired limbs, 3½ in. high. — D-18.50

Dollhouse doll, clothed, mama-doll type, 5 in. high. — D-15.00

Dustpan, pressed tin, 2¼ in. edge, 2 in. handle. — D-3.50

Fireplace, wooden, hearth opening 2 x 2 inches, 3 in. high. — D-22.50

Flatirons, not antique, ¾ x 1 in. long. — D-.75

Frypan, cast iron, pouring lip, 2¼ in. diameter. — D-6.50

Frypan, aluminum, looped to hang, 2 in. diameter. — D-2.50

Frypan, 1 in. diameter, with ¾ in. handle. — D-5.00

Jars, apothecary, blown glass with labels and corks, 1½ in. high. Pair. — D-8.50

Napkin rings, set of three, white embossed metal, ¾ in. diameter. — D-18.50

Pitcher, glass, cobalt blue, ruffled top, 1¼ in. high. — D-10.00

Purse, ribbed fabric, brass handle, 2½ in. long. — D-8.50

Rug, hooked; six basic colors, rayon on cotton, 5 in. diameter. — D-12.50

Rug, needlepoint; house and barn country scenes, 3¼ in. dia. — D-12.50

Scissors, brass, 1½ in. long. — D-1.50

Sewing machine, cast metal, "Singer", on stand, 1¼ in. high. — D-5.00

Spoons, set of four, white metal, 1-7/8 in. long. — D-7.50

Stove, cast iron, burner lids missing, 3¼ x 3¼ x 5 inches. — D-25.00

Table, end; turned legs, top 1 x 2¼ inches, 1½ in. high. — D-8.00

Table, lamp; top 1½ in. square, 1¼ in. high. — D-7.50

Table and two chairs, table 2 x 2½, chairs 1-7/8 in. high. — D-13.50

Table, cast iron, rectangular top, 1½ in. high. — D-7.50

Teapot, ironstone porcelain, white, covered, 2 in. high. — D-4.50

Teapot, tin, painted, brown, 1¾ in. high. — D-4.00

Toys, cast metal, set of four, ½ to 1 in. long. — D-4.00

Tray, oval, cast metal, open-handled, floral motif, 1¾ in. long. — D-4.50

Tumbler, or spooner, porcelain, pedestaled, 1-3/8 x 1¾ inches. — D-6.50

Vase, cast metal, embossed decoration one side, 1½ in. high. — D-8.00

Wicker loveseat, done with thin wire, unusual, 2¼ in. long. — D-17.00

DOLL ITEMS—*[See also* **Miniatures***]*

Bed, walnut, spool-turned posts, 12 x 17 inches. — A-40.00

Bed, Victorian, 11¼ x 20 inches. — A-40.00

Bed, rope, spool-turned, 19 in. long. — A-42.50

Bottle, nursing, glass, dog embossed on one side, 3 in. high. — D-6.00

Chest-of-drawers, three, pine, ca. 1870, 7¾ in. high. — D-45.00

Cradle, pine, with rockers, blue and white coverlet, 22 in. long. — A-45.00

Cradle, wooden, primitive, 10 x 18 inches. — D-65.00

Cradle, pine, dovetailed, velvet padding, ca. 1880, 18 in. long. — D-85.00

Desk, slant top, four compartments below, two full-length drawers underneath; 5 in. high. — D-18.50

Display case, glass front, 10½ x 14¼ inches. — A-25.00

Rattle, handpainted ivory, 2½ in. long. — D-19.00

Shoes, honey-color leather, ankle straps, rust bows, 4 in. size. — D-25.00

Stand, Queen Anne type, walnut, 1-7/8 in. high. — D-9.00

Trunk, cardboard, brass latch, 14 in. long. — A-17.50

Top, toy, painted, turned wood, 1¼ in. high. — D-6.00

Tumbler, pattern glass, table accessory, 2 in. high. — D-6.00

Tumblers, set of three, pewter, 1¾ in. high. — D-18.00

Three miniatures:
Sheraton carved **tiger maple tester doll bedstead**, 19½ in. long. Prob. New
England, ca. 1820.   A/275
Top right, **Queen Anne transitional walnut miniature chest-on-frame**, 10 in.
high. Late 19th - Early 20th Century.   A/75
Bot. right, **Queen Anne mahogany miniature tip-top tea table**, 9¾ in. high.
Late 18th Century.   A/375

Courtesy Adam A. Weschler & Son, Washington, D.C.

Table, wood, rectangular top, straight legs, 13 in.
high.   D-12.00
Table, wood, dresser style with metal mirror, 16½
in. high.   D-16.00
Teakettle, painted tin, white and red, 3 in. diameter.   D-10.00
Teapot, ceramic, crack in lid, flowers decaled on
side.   D-8.00
Wash boiler and wash board, tin, boiler 6¾ in. long.   A-17.50
Baby boy doll, with moving extremities, blue jumper
suit, "Germany", blond molded hair, handpainted
features; 6 inches.   D-20.00
Bisque doll, handpainted features, hair in Buster
Brown cut, "Made in USA", no clothing; 5½ in. high.   D-29.50
Bisque piano baby, sitting position, handpainted in
blue and yellow, artist mark on bottom. Girl, head to
one side, out-stretched hands, 5½ in. high.   D-72.00
Boy rag doll, printed cloth face, orig. blue jumper
suit. Ca. 1890, 13 in. high.   D-25.00
Bride and groom dolls, pair; full wedding attire.
Movable limbs, prob. Germany, ca. 1880, each 4¼
in. high.   D-69.50
Cat rag doll, printed cloth, human clothing, blue
eyes, ca. 1920's.   D-17.50

Doll body, composition arms and legs, orig. paper
label "Fabrication Francas", needs head.   D-200.00

Miniature doll, Frozen Charlotte, Black, outstretch-
ed hands, rich glaze. Ca. 1890, 2-1/8 in. high.   D-22.50

Papa doll, composition head, hands and feet, wired
limbs to assume any position, pants missing, 5¼ in.
high.   D-17.50

Penny doll, bisque, blond molded hair, extremities
wired to move, 2¼ in. high.   D-20.00

Penny doll, blonde-haired girl, moving extremities,
glazed bisque, handpainted features, marked
"280-30½", 2¼ in. high.   D-22.50

Penny doll, boy, bisque with brown molded hair, extremities wired to move, 2-3/8 in. high.   D-20.00

Penny doll, bisque, movable arms, molded hair,
handpainted features.   D-17.50

ESKIMO

Adz, stone blade, long-handled, oogruk (seal-gut)
hafting.   A-60.00

Basket, lidded, plant fiber, coil-weave, 4 in.
diameter.   D-90.00

Boots, sealskin, man-size, thigh-length, waterproof
seams.   C-275.00

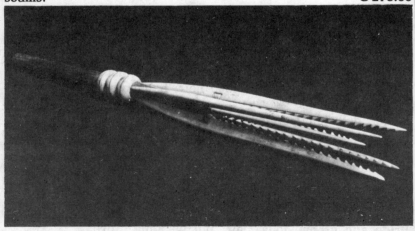

Ivory spear point, Eskimo, 9¾ in. (25 cm) long. C/Unlisted

Photo and item courtesy Walrus Gallery, Kennebunkport,
Maine.

Bracelet, contemporary, of fossilized ivory.	**A-40.00**
Carving, soapstone, large Billiken over 4 in. high. ca. early 1900's.	**A-35.00**
Carving, seal hunter poised with harpoon and seal coming up for air. Whalebone base, ivory figures.	**D-125.00**
Carving, fish, soapstone, done by Tom Mayac, contemporary.	**A-35.00**
Cribbage board, walrus ivory, ca. 1930.	**A-90.00**
Factory-kayak, sealskin covered. Holds two smaller kayaks, and many small implements.	**D-650.00**
Hunter's belt, suspensions of teeth, beads and cartridge cases; 248 sets of caribou front teeth.	**A-1,100.00**
Ivory carving, snowy owl, walrus tooth, uncertain age.	**A-30.00**
Mask, whalebone (by Alex Frankson, Point Hope, Alaska), with ivory teeth and eyes.	**A-95.00**
Mittens, leather, with thumb extension, 14½ in. long.	**C-65.00**
Napkin ring, walrus tooth, in polar bear head effigy form, ca. 1890. 2 x 2½ inches.	**A-100.00**
Soapstone carving, old, of walrus, 3 in. long.	**A-25.00**
Yo-yo, of braided sealskin with baleen handle.	**A-20.00**

Eskimo doll, from coastal Alaska, about 13 in. long. Item made of tanned skin, tradecloth, sealgut sinew and black thread. Rare.

C/150-200

Lar Hothem photo.

EXPOSITIONS

Badge, souvenir, Panama Pacific Expo., 1915.	**D-30.00**
Badge, two-piece, brass, Trans-Mississippi Expo., Omaha, 1898.	**D-12.00**
Book, "Paris International Exposition Series #3", 1937.	**D-8.00**

Bookmark, aluminum, buffalo and flowers, Pan American Expo. ... **D-12.00**

Button, Panama-Pacific International Expo., San Francisco, 1915. ... **D-10.00**

Calendar, perpetual; brass, rotating, dollar-size, Columbian Expo. ... **D-50.00**

Coin, brass, building and water scene, 27mm, Columbian Expo. ... **D-10.00**

Coin, brass, 33mm, Cotton States Exposition, 1895. ... **D-25.00**

Coin, brass, dollar-size, Trans-Mississippi Expo, 1898. ... **D-15.00**

Coin, brass, dollar-size, Jamestown Expo., 1907. ... **D-20.00**

Coin, Exposition Universelle D'Anuers, Antwerpen, 1885. ... **D-12.50**

Coin, silver, 38mm, Panama Pacific Expo., 1915. ... **D-35.00**

Coin, Sixth Annual Industrial Expo., Spokane, 1899. ... **D-5.00**

Corkscrew, chrome casing, 2¾ in. long, Columbian Expo. ... **D-10.00**

Elongated cent, electric tower, Pan American Expo, 1901. ... **D-7.00**

Elongated cent, Amour Lard, Pan American Expo., 1901. ... **D-8.00**

Encased cent, lucky; Pan American Expo., 1901. ... **D-7.00**

Fan, opens to 25 inches, multi-colored, Columbian Expo., 1893. ... **D-50.00**

Fob, gold-filled "Exposition/Chicago/1893", Columbian Expo. ... **D-35.00**

Letter-opener, brass, 6¼ in. long, tip snapped, Pan American Exposition. ... **D-12.00**

Map, color, Panoramic View of the World's Columbian Expo. ... **D-10.00**

Match safe, engraved aluminum, Pan American Expo., 1901. ... **D-25.00**

Medal, aluminum, 45mm, Admin. Bldg./Ferris Wheel, Columbian Expo. ... **D-20.00**

Medal, brass, 28mm, "The Ludwig Piano/Pan American Expo.", 1901. ... **D-12.00**

Medal, bronze, 32mm, "Arbetet Adlar", Panama Pacific Expo, 1915. ... **D-10.00**

Medal, bust and birdseye view, gilt, 50mm, Columbian Expo. ... **D-60.00**

Medal, Trans-Mississippi and Internal Expo., Omaha, 1898. ... **D-10.00**

THE FERRIS WHEEL,
MIDWAY PLAISANCE,
WORLD'S COLUMBIAN EXPOSITION,
CHICAGO, 1893.

Chicago World's Exposition Postcard.   C/12

Paperweight, mourning McKinley, Pan American Exposition.   **D-20.00**

Pendant, brass, 1¼ in. diameter, Pan-American Expo., 1901.   **D-10.00**

Plate, aluminum, 6¼ in. diameter, landing scene, Columbian Expo.   **D-10.00**

Playing cards, 52 plus Joker; worn, orig. box, Columbian Expo.   **D-50.00**

Postcard, picturing "Torpedo Fleet", Jamestown Official Expo., 1907.   **D-7.50**

Spoon, sterling, 5½ in. long, gold-wash bowl, Columbian Expo.   **D-25.00**

Spoon, 6 in. long, plate, head of Columbus, Columbian Expo. 1893.   **D-8.50**

Spoons, set of four; Columbian Exposition.   **D-20.00**

Stud, bronze, 7/8 in. diameter, Paris Exposition, 1900.   **D-8.00**

Tray, Pavilion of Canada, Expo 67, Montreal.   **D-5.00**

FARM COLLECTIBLES (See also Primitives and Tools)

Baling hook, for hay bales, hand-forged wrought iron.   **D-4.50**

Barn heater-lamp, kerosene, all tin, 10¾ in. high.   **D-24.50**

Barrel spigot, wooden, early, 8½ in. long.   **D-3.50**

Bee box, pine, old square hand-made nails, tin exit port.   **D-35.00**

Bit, horse; chain-type, new condition.   **D-5.00**

Bit, horse' for racing, 14 in. long.   **D-10.00**

Blueberry pail, polished copper with iron ears, 6 in. diameter.   **D-49.50**

Boring machine, with top framework to be angled two ways.   **D-55.00**

Boring machine, "Millers Falls" maker, can be angled.   **D-68.00**

Boring machine, stationary, 90-degree angle only.   **D-47.00**

Buck saw, small, wooden frame, 16 in. long.   **A-27.50**

Calf yoke, bentwood with pine crossbar.   **D-6.50**

Cheese ladder, old, wood pegged and mortised.   **D-25.00**

Cheese sieve, heart-shaped punched tin, 6 x 7½ inches.   **A-82.50**

Food press, primitive design. Three separate pieces of tin make up the press container, with innermost perforated. Long handle is oak, pressboard of solid walnut; it stands 39 in. high.

C/85-150

Lar Hothem photo.

109

Upper left, **Grain measures**, left and central items both single measures. Example at right is a rare double measure of about peck/half-peck volume, orig. paint. Example on left is 9-5/8 in. high.
Left.   C/40-55   Lower center.   C/20-30   Right.   C/75-100

Lower left, **barn lantern** or **lamp holder**, tin, orig. green paint, electrified. New England area, scarce, 23½ in. high.   C/150-200
Private collection.

Lar Hothem photo.   Upper right, **wagon jack**, all wood, wrought position bar.   C/20-25

Cheese strainer, woven splint, old paint, 13 in. diameter.   A-305.00

Chick-watering bottle, pottery, black glaze, 8¼ in. high.   A-15.00

Corn-cutting knife, "Parkers Clipper, Pat. Sept. 9, 1874". Strapped to leg; heavy blade 11 in. long.   D-100.00

Corn-sheller, "Pennsylvania", handcranked, 34 in. high.   A-25.00

Corn-sheller, metal hand-twist type, 6 in. long.   D-65.00

Cream funnel, tin, 6 in. high with ½ in. botton opening.   D-4.50

Cream pail, copper, iron ears, wire bail handle, wood grip.   D-49.50

Cream separator, wooden legs, tin body, brass on/off spigot.   C-90.00

Drinking mug, tin, handled, dark gray color.   D-5.00

Fencing tool, "Stetler, 1-2-1900", 17 in. long.   D-28.00

Filtering funnel, copper-plated tin, Pat'd. 21 Mar 1911.   D-15.00

Glue pot, double-boiler, cast iron, 5 in. diameter.   D-8.00

Grain grinder, "#4", handle on wheel, 15 in. high.   D-17.00

Grain cleaner, "Eureka Mill/1870", incomplete, 44 in. high.   A-40.00

Grain scoop, wood, leather and strap metal; handled.   D-22.50

Above, **melting ladle,** three-spouted, cast iron with maker-mark on handle.
C/9-15

Right, **lead-melting pot,** cast iron, wire-bale handle, 6 in. diameter.
C/12-20

Lar Hothem photos.

Harness hanger, "Bubier & Co., Boston", 8 in. high. **A-22.50**

Harness hook, board-mounted, 3½ in. long and wide. **D-6.00**

Hatchel, (flax comb), wrought iron nails, 6¾ x 15¼ inches. **A-65.00**

Hay knife, spade-type blade, long wooden shaft/handle. **D-37.50**

Hewing dog, iron, spiked ends for holding log, 13½ in. long. **D-9.00**

Hog scraper, metal ring with central wooden handle. **A-4.00**

Hog scraper, tin, circular blade, 6½ in. high. **D-6.50**

Horse tether-weight, cast iron, hemispheric, 18 pounds. **D-22.50**

Husking pegs, collection of ten, all different sizes. **D-20.00**

Ice auger, hand-forged, for testing ice thickness, 40 in. long. **D-18.50**

Ice axe, "Underhill Edge & Tool Co.", pick end, lightweight. **D-39.50**

Ice chisel, with original wood handle, blade 17 in. long. **D-30.00**

Ice tool, handforged pick, for moving ice blocks, 15 in. handle. **D-16.50**

Keg, stave-constructed with wooden bands, 8½ in. high. **A-55.00**

Kettle stand, iron, openwork top, 13 in. high. **A-45.00**

Keg, 2½ gal. size, for shipping paint. "B.A. Rahnestock / Estab. 1844", copper label, oak staves.

C/20-30

Double grain measure, scarce if not rare, in softwood with wire hoops, 15 in. high. Capacities, peck and half-peck.

C/80-125

Harness hames, brass knobs. C/25-35

Stoneware churn.
C/40-75

Wagon seat, spring.
C/40-50

Milk can, metal.
C/10-15

Egg crate.
C/20-35

Ladle, hand-hammered brass, copper rivets, iron handle. Early. **D-110.00**

Lard press, ash, with galvanized, handled pan. **A-50.00**

Leather-riveting tool, harness-maker's, iron, lever action. **D-6.50**

Leather-workers vise, iron sawtooth ratchet; 40 in. high. **A-35.00**

Lunch pail, loop and bail handle, covered, 4½ x 6 inches. **D-12.50**

Maiden yoke with chains and hooks, red paint, 37 in. long. **A-22.50**

Mail box, cast iron, orig. red paint, 12 in. long. **A-35.00**

Maple sugar bucket, orig. label "Pure Maple Sugar", 6 in. diameter. **D-30.00**

Maple sugar form, "Vermont Machinery Co.", 200 tin molds. **D-75.00**

Maple sugar stirrer, wood, holed to hang, 16 in. long. **D-8.50**

Maple sugar strainer, tin, 11½ in. overall length. **D-12.50**

Measure, wood, round stave-constructed type, 6½ in. high. **A-22.50**

Measure, quart size, reinforced with tin band, 4 in. high. **D-27.50**

Measure, grain; stenciled "4 quart dry measure" on outside. **D-24.50**

Measure, grain; prob. cut-down from larger example, 7 in. diameter. **D-13.00**

Measures, unusual set; three nestled sizes, tin sides, wood bottoms. Quart, half-gal. and gallon volumes. **D-45.00**

Meat press, "Wilder's", tin, wood pressure plate. **D-35.00**

Milk can with lid, 15-gallon size. **A-9.00**

Milk container, "12-Qt. Liquid", with cap and metal ball. **S-18.00**

Milk pan, for cooling-down milk, 12 in. diameter. Tin. **D-6.50**

Milk skimmer, perforated tin, holed for hangup, ca. 1880's. **D-10.00**

Milk skimmer, used to remove debris from milk. **A-7.00**

Milk strainer. fine mesh, 12 in. diameter. **D-6.00**

Nail holder and guide, "Never Pound Your Thumb Again". **D-6.00**

Pitcher pump, cast iron, orig. red paint, complete. **D-25.00**

Poultry-killing tool, cast brass, steel blade, 6½ in. long. **D-30.00**

Reaping hook, "T.W. Shaws Co./Globe Works", 19
in. long.   D-20.00
Rope-making outfit, metal, handle-turned holed disc.   A-20.00
Sap yoke (maiden yoke), one-piece wood, for maple
sap buckets.   D-35.00
Sausage filler, "Sargent & Co., N.Y.", iron and tin.   D-24.00
Seeder, "Tiron", handcranked at waist to space
seed.   D-17.50
Sickle, replaced socket handle, old.   S-8.00
Singletree, wood and iron, fastened behind horse,
14½ in. long.   C-10.00
Skimmer, brass, delicate punched design in bowl,
wrought handle.   D-110.00
Skimmer, brass, riveted with copper to iron handle,
16 in. long.   D-95.00
Skimmer, copper, punched bowl, wrought-iron handle.   D-90.00
Skimmer, wooden, 4 in. bowl with 3½ in. handle.   D-29.50
Slaw cutter, walnut, heart cut-out, 7¼ x 18 inches.   A-27.50
Sleigh bells, 24 graduated-size bells, strapped.   A-65.00
Snow knocker-hammer, to tap snow from horses'
hooves.   D-20.00
Strawberry huller, tin, "Nip-It".   D-3.00
Surveyor's reel, early, 7¾ x 18 inches.   D-8.50
Tractor box, raised lettering, "Richard Mfg. Co.",
for tools.   D-14.50
Wagon jack, lever action, cast iron, 25 in. high.   D-21.50
Wire stretcher and splicer, "Hayes", 18 in. long.   S-40.00
Wool carder, wood, worn metal teeth.   A-15.00
Wrench, buggy; brass double-headed, 8½ in. long.   S-12.00

FIREARMS—*Revolvers and Pistols [See also War Weapons]*

Allen & Thurber pepperbox pistol, six-section barrel.   A-195.00
Belgian folding-dagger pistol, center hammer, 9 in.
long.   A-130.00
Colt revolver, pearl-handled, chrome, .22 caliber.   A-85.00
Colt pistol, "Woodsman", .22 caliber, 6½ in. barrel.   A-115.00
Colt pistol, "Match Target", .22 caliber.   A-175.00
Colt revolver, Army .44 caliber, checkered grip,
Mod. 1860.   A-300.00
Colt revolver, six-shot double-action, .38 caliber,
1894.   A-65.00

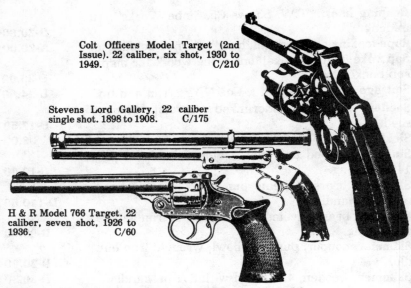

Colt Officers Model Target (2nd Issue). 22 caliber, six shot, 1930 to 1949. C/210

Stevens Lord Gallery, 22 caliber single shot. 1898 to 1908. C/175

H & R Model 766 Target. 22 caliber, seven shot, 1926 to 1936. C/60

Colt revolver, six-shot double-action, .45 caliber, 1878.   **A-185.00**

Colt revolver, Mod. 1917, .45 caliber, with leather holster.   **A-185.00**

Colt pistol, semi-auto., .32 caliber rimless.   **A-95.00**

"Defender" revolver, .22 caliber, spur trigger; incomplete.   **A-20.00**

English pinfire revolver, six-shot, .35 caliber.   **A-25.00**

English silver-plated revolver, six-shot transition piece.   **A-150.00**

H. & R. revolver, double-action, .38 caliber, 3¼ in. barrel.   **A-35.00**

H. & R. .22 single-shot target pistol, checkered grips.   **A-175.00**

Iver Johnson revolver, .38 five-shot, with holster.   **A-45.00**

Marlin revolver, five-shot, "Standard" Mod. 1875, chrome.   **A-50.00**

Mauser pistol, Mod. 1910, .32 semi-auto. with holster.   **A-105.00**

"Muff" pistol, flintlock, "South Hall/London", 6 in. long.   **A-135.00**

Pepperbox pistol, six-section barrel, percussion ignition.   **A-155.00**

Pinfire revolver, .30 caliber, six-shot, hinge trigger.   **A-25.00**

Pistol, saloon, percussion, .17 caliber.   **A-25.00**

Prescott revolver, .35 caliber, 6 in. octagonal barrel.   **A-105.00**

Remington Elliot derringer. .32 caliber, four-barrel.	**A-185.00**
Remington revolver, percussion five-shot, Beal's patent.	**A-220.00**
Revolver, "Robin Hood No. 1", seven shot, .22 caliber.	**A-30.00**
Revolver, nine-shot, folding trigger, European proofmarks.	**A-35.00**
Ruger pistol, .22 caliber semi-automatic, 6 in. barrel.	**A-95.00**
Ruger pistol, Super Single-Six convertible, both cylinders.	**A-105.00**
Russian revolver, .38 caliber chrome.	**A-30.00**
Russian revolver, .32 caliber, dated 1912.	**A-55.00**
"Sash" pistol, flintlock, raised, carved stock, 8½ in. long.	**A-175.00**
Sharps pepperbox pistol, four-section square barrel.	**A-255.00**
Smith & Wesson revolver, .32 caliber Army No. 2, custom grips.	**A-95.00**
Smith & Wesson revolver, six-shot revolver, .32 caliber.	**A-50.00**
Walther pistol, Model 4, .32 caliber semi-auto. with holster.	**A-85.00**
Waters flintlock conversion pistol, Model 1838, dated 1844.	**A-220.00**

FIREARMS—*Rifles*

British flintlock musket, Brown Bess, 37¼ in. barrel.	**A-410.00**
German rifle-shotgun, 7.8-57 and 16-gauge, telescope mounts.	**A-170.00**
Kentucky rifle, full stock, converted, brass patch box.	**A-260.00**
Kentucky rifle, full stock, curley maple, .45 caliber, 40 in. long.	**D-345.00**
Kentucky rifle, full stock, signed "George Biddle", 42 in. barrel.	**A-675.00**
Kentucky rifle, half stock, brass patchbox, Ger.-silver thimble.	**A-325.00**
Kentucky rifle, half stock, signed owner and maker, fancy box.	**C-550.00**
Marlin rifle, lever-action, .38 caliber, octagonal barrel.	**A-100.00**
Marlin rifle, .45-90 caliber, Model 1895, octagonal barrel.	**A-120.00**

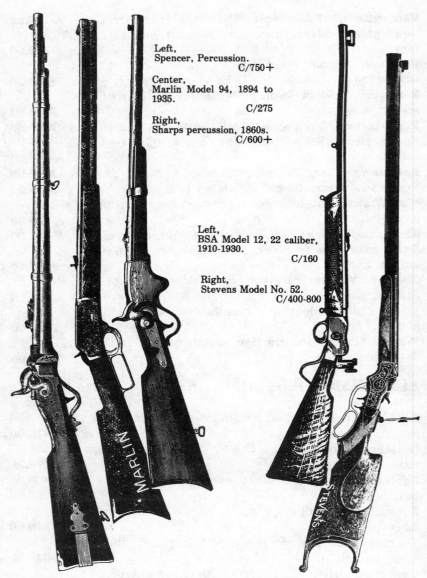

Left,
Spencer, Percussion.
C/750+

Center,
Marlin Model 94, 1894 to
1935.
C/275

Right,
Sharps percussion, 1860s.
C/600+

Left,
BSA Model 12, 22 caliber,
1910-1930.
C/160

Right,
Stevens Model No. 52.
C/400-800

Mauser rifle, sporter 8 x 60 norm. caliber, walnut stock.   A-340.00

Maynard sporting rifle, .40 caliber, percussion; incomplete.   A-155.00

Meriden single-shot rifle, Model 10, .22 caliber, 20¾ in. barrel.   A-35.00

Mossberg rifle, Palomino model 402, .22 caliber, level-action.   A-65.00

Over & under percussion rifle, .44 and 12-gauge, "H. S. Miles".　　A-175.00

Quackenbush rifle, .22 caliber single shot, swinging breech.　　A-45.00

Remington take-down rifle, Model 4, .32 rimfire.　　A-55.00

Remington rolling-block rifle, .44 caliber, with leather sling.　　A-85.00

Remington rifle, .22 long rifle, pump-action.　　A-95.00

Remington rifle, Model 4, .32 caliber, single shot.　　A-55.00

Savage rifle, Model 1905, bolt action .22 caliber.　　A-60.00

Savage rifle, Mod. 29, .22 caliber pump-action.　　A-55.00

Schutzen target rifle, 7.6mm, drop-block action. Marked "E. Schmidt & Habermann", receiver with ornately engraved hunting scenes.　　A-325.00

Springfield rifle, .45-70 Trapdoor, missing hammer.　　A-120.00

Springfield rifle, .45-70, Model 1884, missing ramrod.　　A-175.00

Stevens rifle, lever-action, .22 caliber.　　A-115.00

Stevens over and under rifle-shotgun, .22 and .410 calibers.　　A-55.00

U.S. Remington rifle, P-17, .30-06 caliber, with sling.　　A-110.00

U.S. Remington rifle, .30-06 caliber, semi-pistol grip.　　A-90.00

Wesson, Frank; two-trigger rifle. Pat. 1862, .32 cal. rimfire.　　A-85.00

Winchester rifle, Model 1873, .22 caliber.　　A-105.00

Winchester rifle, .30-40 Model '73, octagonal barrel.　　A-155.00

Winchester rifle, .32-20 Model '73, octagonal barrel.　　A-130.00

Winchester rifle, .22 long rifle, Model 1890, pump-action.　　A-195.00

Winchester rifle, .38-56 lever action, full octagonal barrel.　　A-130.00

Winchester rifle, sporting, .30-06 caliber, lever action.　　A-185.00

Winchester rifle, .30-30, Mod. '94, tang peep sight.　　A-165.00

Winchester rifle, .38-56 Model 1886, lever-action, oct. barrel.　　A-200.00

FIREARMS—*Shotguns*

"American" 12-gauge, Hyde Shatcuck & Co., 30¼ in. barrel.　　A-70.00

Blunderbuss, flintlock coach gun, brass hardware, 14 in. barrel. — A-350.00

"Champion" 12-gauge, fair condition, 30 in. barrel. — A-15.00

Single-barrel 12-gauge, Crescent Fire Arms Company. — A-25.00

Double-barrel percussion, fine locks, oakleaf-carved wrist. — A-190.00

Double-barrel hammer, 12-gauge, "New Baker, Batavia, N.Y.". — A-45.00

Double-barrel percussion, London mfgr., 12-gauge. — A-115.00

Double-barrel percussion, German mfgr., intricate carvings and patchbox with engraved lion; inlaid barrel. — A-600.00

H. & R. 12-guage, "Topper M-48", 30-1/8 in. barrel. — A-25.00

Le Fever Arms Co. 12-guage, double-barreled. — A-75.00

Richards 12-guage, Belgain mfgr., double barreled. — A-35.00

Stevens 16-guage, Model 94-C, 28 in. barrel. — A-35.00

Stevens 16-guage, hammerless pump-action, full choke. — A-55.00

Stevens double-barrel, 16-gauge, Model 311. — A-75.00

Whitmore patent 12-gauge, double barrels 26 in. long. — A-85.00

Winchester 12-gauge, double-barrel percussion, Class B engraving. — A-215.00

FIREFIGHTING

Axes, wooden, pair; old brownish red paint with worn striping and gilt, 44 in. long. — A-105.00

Badge, "Field Day—Alert Fire Dept./1907", 1¼ in. diameter. — A-12.00

Badge, fireman's gilt bar and border, blue ribbon below, 1¼ in. diameter. — A-15.00

Belt, fireman's, leather, red, white and black, with silver-metal band with embossed fireman and child, 38 in. long. — A-85.00

Certificate, fireman's, appointment to force. "Binghamton Fire Department, 1856", 14½ x 17½ inches. — A-70.00

Fire extinguisher, brass, "Fyr-fyter", with bracket, 18 in. high. — D-21.50

Fire extinguisher, "Pyrene", brass, 17 in. high. — D-16.50

Fire extinguisher, copper, hanging, small size. — A-20.00

Fire bucket, leather, miniature, 3¼ in. high. — A-40.00

Fire bucket, leather, painted black with arm on side, holding sheaf of wheat. Bucket 16 in. high.

D/250

Lar Hothem photo.

Glass slide, full color, closeup of horsedrawn fire engine and helmeted firemen. Ca. 1909, 3¼ x 4 inches.   D-12.50

Horn, fireman's, silver-plated, floral engraving and typical fireman-related decoration. "Harmony Hose/Co. No. 6", 22½ in. long.   A-550.00

Hose nozzel, fire, brass, 12 in. long.   A-17.50

Hose nozzel, brass, petcock thumbscrew, "Fairy", 6 in. long.   D-15.00

Lantern, fireman's, brass, copper-wheel engraving "Essex 4", burner missing, 13 in. high.   A-235.00

Lantern, fireman's, brass, clear blown globe with copper wheel engraving, "R. A. Snyder/1 Hose", 13 in. high.   A-225.00

FIREPLACE Tools And Accessories
(See also **Kitchen** and **Household**)

The large room with the big fireplace was once the center of every early home. And some of the best-made objects of the times went to improve or decorate this first "family room".

Some of the collectibles, like andirons and bellows, had to do with the fire itself. Others utilized the heat as a cooking source, placing the food in the embers, in front of the fire, or over the flames. Some items held the food, still other objects served to hold the containers themselves.

Please note that some items listed here could well have been placed in the **Kitchen** section. However, in the opinion of the

Upper Left, **fire screen**, folding, brass & iron.   C/75-125
Center, **andiron**, brass, pr.   C/75-125
Right. **poker, tongs, shovel & holder**, brass.   C/90-100
Lower right, **bellows**, fireplace, maker-marked in top wood. Good leather, tin air-spout, 16 in. long.
                                                              C/30-40

writer, each has a characteristic—such as a fork's handle-length—that would indicate likely hearth, rather than kitchen, usage. Age was also a strong factor here.

Either way, fireplace and fireroom objects remain one of the largest and most varied collecting fields.

Andirons, pair; brass, 18th Century, 17 in. deep, 12½ in. high.   **A-135.00**

Andirons, balltop, pair; brass, claw feet, "firedog" posts match fronts, 19 in. long, 20½ in. high.   **A-300.00**

Andirons, brass, pair; early, brass with dents, 18 in. deep, 19½ in. high.   **A-75.00**

Andirons, brass, pair; 14½ in. both deep and high.   **A-85.00**

Andirons, brass pair; 19th Century, 18½ in. high.   **A-105.00**

Andirons, Chippendale, pair; ca. 1800, spool finials and ring-turned ball, spool plinths, scrolled supports, 26 in. high.   **A-350.00**

Andirons, Chippendale, pair; cannonball finial, baluster standard, spurred arched supports, 17 in. high.   **C-275.00**

Andirons, cast iron, brass cannonball finials, polished.   **D-85.00**

Andirons, handforged iron, gooseneck styling, ca. 1850 or before; 19 in. log rest, 19 in. high.   **D-45.00**

Andirons, knifeblade, simple finials, 12½ in. deep, 13 in. high.   **A-32.50**

Andirons, pair; wrought iron and bar, 31 in. high.   **A-125.00**

Andirons, wrought iron, pair, brass finials, 28 in. high.   **A-87.50**

Bellows, decorated; yellow ground with stenciled pears and leaves, professionally releathered.   **A-45.00**

Bellows, decorated; yellow ground with stenciled and freehand fruit and foliage, brass tip, 17½ in. long.   **A-37.50**

Bellows, poplar, copper nozzle, carved initials, 18 in. long.   **A-17.50**

Bellows, turtle-back, free-hand painting of basket of flowers, worn paint.   **A-65.00**

Bellows, turtle-back, free-hand fruit and flowers, old leather deteriorated, 17 in. long.   **A-45.00**

Bellows, turtle-back, yellow ground with pot of flowers in four colors, leather deteriorated, 18½ in. long.   **A-135.00**

Bellows, turtle-back, dark orig. paint, stenciled foliage and shell in gold, brass nozzle, professionally releathered.   **A-175.00**

Bellows, wooden, iron nozzle, deteriorated leather, 20 in. long.   **A-15.00**

Bread peel, hand-forged iron, mushroom knob, 50 in. long.   **D-65.00**

Broiler, wrought iron, 19 in. long.   **A-30.00**

Broiler, rotary; wrought iron, late, 10¼ in. diameter, 25¼ in. long.   **A-65.00**

Brioler, revolving; wrought iron, needs minor repairs, 11½ in. diameter, 27 in. long.   **A-90.00**

Broiler, stationary; wrought iron, well-made handle, 18 in. long.   **A-50.00**

Broiler-grill, eleven viaduct juice channels, cast iron, one-piece.   **D-20.00**

Cooking pan, sheet metal, welded iron frame and fireplace hook, 21 in. diameter, 18 in. high.   **A-42.50**

Crane, fireplace; hand-forged, ca. 1790, 29 in. long.   **D-42.50**

Crane, fireplace; hand-forged, large, ca. 1750, 38½ in. long.   **D-75.00**

Crane, fireplace; wrought iron, 54 in. high, 28½ in. long. **A-25.00**

Crane-plate, footed, for hanging or sitting on hearth. Iron, 18 in. high, 13¾ in. diameter. **D-90.00**

Dipper, brass and iron, handle signed and dated 1848, 18 in. long. **A-160.00**

Dipper, iron and brass, handle signed and dated 1844, 19 in. long. **A-140.00**

Ember tongs, wrought iron, 18½ in. long. **A-10.00**

Ember tongs, cast brass, 14 in. long. **D-17.00**

Doughnut kettle, cast iron, iron handle 10½ x 4¼ in. deep. **D-16.50**

Doughnut kettle, cast iron, rattailed bail handle, 10¼ x 4¼ in. deep. **D-20.00**

Fire-back, Victorian, cast iron. Relief of dogs and cattails, 21 x 27 inches. **A-110.00**

Fire fender, English, pierced brass, late 19th Century, 45 in. wide. **A-150.00**

Fire fender, American, wire, ca. 1800, 37 in. long. **A-80.00**

Fire fender, English, brass, 48 in. long. **A-80.00**

Fire fender, English, brass, shell feet, ca. 1900, 47 in. wide. **A-140.00**

Fire fender, brass, on three scrolling wrought-iron feet, 50 in. wide. **A-125.00**

Fire fender, brass, paw feet, small, 7 x 12 inches. **A-95.00**

Fire fender and tools, brass, Chippendale style fire tools, fender 33 in. long. **A-110.00**

Fireboard, walnut, three raised panels, 35¾ x 49 inches. **A-110.00**

Fire kindler, composition head, clay, wire handle 11 in. long. **D-10.00**

Fire kindler set, clay 2 in. ball encased in wire, wire handle, in cast iron pot 4 in. high, with lid, opening in lid. **S-35.00**

Fire lighter, metal, "Lutz Patent Fire Lighter", orig. directions for use, 8 in. long. **A-35.00**

Fireplace set, three pieces, brass (poker, shovel, sweeper), with stand, 16 in. high. **D-67.50**

Fireplace set, brass and wrought iron, tripod base with turned finial, three tools, 41 in. high. **A-150.00**

Fireside bench, pine, old greenish-grey paint. Early, bottom edge of backboards scorched, 12½ x 48 x 65 inches. **A-625.00**

Firetool dogs, brass, 8 in. high. **A-100.00**

Above
Lantern, D. & H. RR, Adlake-Kero.
C/50-65

Above
Plunger churn, stave-constructed,
iron hoops. Body 21 in. high, basal
diameter 11 inches.   C/125-175

Above
Candle-holders, all brass, center example 6 in.
high without candle.
    Left, (finger ring missing).   C/35-50
    Center.   C/65-90
    Right   C/65-90

Above
Two Grey Hills Weaving, 2 ft.
6 in. by 4 ft. 6 in. Contemporary, fine weave, and all
natural wools.   D-3600

Photo courtesy Jackson David
Co. / Toh-Atin Trading Co.;
Durango, Colorado.

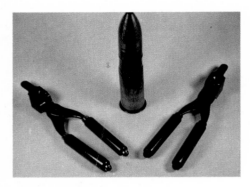

Above
Winchester; marked. Left and right, bullet molds (calibers, respectively, .38-255 and .25-20). Of steel, walnut and brass, factory information.
C/25-40

Complete **37mm shell,** with both casing and projectile marked on brass.　　　　C/15-20

Below
Jelly cupboard, pine and ash, two-shelved. Top drawer with orig. pulls, 17 x 40 x 49½ in. high.　　C/325-400

Above
Candlesticks, turned wood, prob. mahogany, center example 8¾ in. high.　　　　Each: C/18-28

Left
Model train **passenger / observation car**, metal, Lionel, 11 in. long.
C/40-55

Right
Railroad collectibles.

Top, **lock and chain** with copper dated (26) nail; rare. Brass lock, "C & M V RR", no key.
C/55-65

Bot. right, **lock**, brass hasp, "H.V.R.R. Co.", for section shanty, no key.
C/30-40

Badge, "Pennsylvania / 1921", Keystone mark.
C/15-20

Cap badge, "Brakeman", passenger car brakeman's. C/10-13

Key, (left), solid brass, caboose, "Adlake".
C/14-19

Key, (right), C & N, by "Fraim", for switch lock
C/8-12

Left
Bible stand, walnut, tilted top, tripod legs. Turned column, 34 in. high.
C/100-150

Below
Winter scene, "Copyright 1897 / J. Hoover & Son / Philad'a". Gold-leaf frame, 26½ x 31 inches.
C/75-100

Above
Rocker, needlepoint seat and back with hip rests. Walnut with burl walnut insets, oak siderungs. On tin seat bottom, "Patented 1872 / H. Closterman / Cincinnati", 34¾ in. high at back.
C/225-300

Above
Erickson glass. Left and right, **candle bases**, matched pair, purple encased in clear crystal, pair:
C/90-125

Pitcher, center, amber with clear crystal attached handle, clear spaced-bubble "paperweight" base.
C/150-200

Above
Brakeman's lantern, "H.V.Ry", on globe and stamped on lantern top; wick adjusts from bottom center of base; rare.
C/150-200

Above
Kitchen churn, unused condition, 14 in. high. C/25-35

Left
Candy mold, consisting of eight 5-bear white-metal units within rectangular metal frame. All units can be removed, total measures 10½ x 19¼ inches.
Private collection.   C/30-45

Right
Grain measures, left and central items both single measures. Example at right is a rare double measure of about peck/half-peck volume, orig. paint. Example on left is 9 5/8 in. high.

Left.	C/40-55
Lower center.	C/20-30
Right.	C/60-85

Private collection.

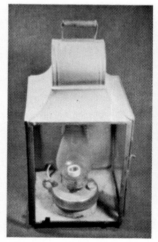

Above
Kettle, copper, known as apple-butter kettle in the Midwest. Excellent condition, wrought iron handle, 23¾ in. diameter, top.
Private collection.   C/225-295

Above
Barn lantern or **lamp holder,** tin, orig. green paint, electrified. New England area, scarce, 23½ in. high.
Private collection   C/150-200

Right
Bakery box, with additional label inside lid in pristine condition. Slight damage to lid corner, right; 10 x 14 x 22¾ inches.
Private collection.   C/35-55

Left
Unknown furnishing. Golden oak with small projecting piece at bottom. Complete, and never attached to anything else. Various persons have suggested this is a sheet-music holder, spice rack or plate shelf; 12 x 25¾ inches.
Private collection.   C/45-75

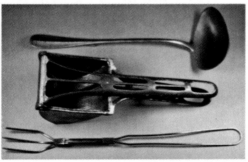

Left
Kitchen implements.
   Ladle (Germany.   C/4-6
   Fruit press.   C/10-14
   Fork.   C/3-5

Right
Canning items.
   Fruit jar holders, wireware, each.   C/9-12
   Jar filler, clear glass. C/4-6
   Canning jar, ½ gal., Atlas, each.   C/10-13

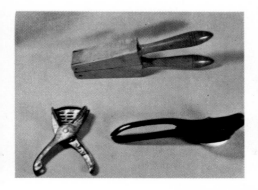

Left
Lemon squeezers, three varieties.
Top, all-wood, turned handles.
          C/30-45
Left, white metal, spring handle
opener   C/10-15
Right, japanned cast iron, removable ceramic insert.
Private collection.   C/25-35

Right
Restaurant creamers, full set (24), matched, in orig. wire frame; ea. one oz. size.
Private collection.   C/35-45

Left
Cream whipper, tin, by Fries, 9½ in. high.
Private collection.   C/40-55

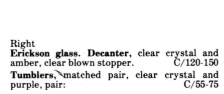

Right
Erickson glass. Decanter, clear crystal and amber, clear blown stopper.   C/120-150
Tumblers, matched pair, clear crystal and purple, pair: C/55-75

Above
Railroad collectibles.
Postcards, "L.S. & M.S.", and, "N.Y.C. & H.R.", all postmarked 1916. Each: C/7-10
Key, for switch, brass, "T. & O.C.RR", maker's mark. C/15-20
Identification tag, baggage, brass, "C. & M.V. P.C. & S.L. - Penn - N.C.". Via Dresden. C/15-20
Pencil, "Pennsylvania Railroad / Work in Safety". C/2-4
Ledger book, Hocking Valley RR, 300 pages, 11½ x 17 inches. C/40-50

Above
WW-I shell, deactivated 37mm souvenir. Markings are floral design on brass case, plus "Verdun / 1918". C/25-35

Above
Spice cabinet, with orig. drawer pulls, 10 in. wide. Note, back is a later addition, attached for hanging purposes, 17 in. high. C/60-85

Above
Master engraver's samples, script, monogram and etched building (landmarks). All done on silver, sealed custom case. C/150-200

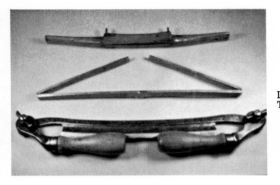

Left
Tools, woodworking.
Top, **spokeshave.** C/15-20
Rule, folding, brasshound.
C/9-13
Drawknife, folding handles.
C/25-35

Right
Cut glass.
  Knife rest, 5½ in. long.
C/60-75
Toothpick holder. C/35-40
Shakers, pair. C/30-40

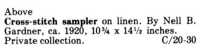

Above
Cross-stitch sampler on linen. By Nell B.
Gardner, ca. 1920, 10¾ x 14½ inches.
Private collection. C/20-30

Above
Dressing table items.
  Large **mirror**, beveled glass, cast iron
  frame. C/90-125
  Comb. & brush, set. C/20-25

Right
Enamelware.
  Coffee pot.   C/15-19
  Cream can, missing lid.
                               C/14-18

Above
Ballot box, late 1800's, brass hinges, oak,
15 in. long.   C/60-85

Above
Lamps, kerosene, left to right:
  Miniature, orig. shade, replaced globe.
                               C/25-35
  Lamp, old but not orig. chimney.
                               C/35-45
  Miniature, frosted base, acorn wick
  knob.   C/25-35

Left
Tobacco items.
  Tiger tobacco lunch pail.   C/30-45
  Cigar mold, 25 holes.   C/25-40

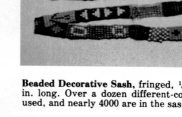

Beaded Decorative Sash, fringed, ½ in. wide and 45 in. long. Over a dozen different-colored beads were used, and nearly 4000 are in the sash. Good condition. C/22.50

Candle Lantern, Paul Revere type, tin, punched designs, 16" high. C/75-95

Bandolier or Shoulder Bag, 17½ in. by 17½ in. This is not a true bag, but a flat "apron" type with no openings. Worn by males as decoration; piece is exquisitely and solidly beaded on entire surface. Chippewa, and ca. 1900-25. C/500-750

Spool Cabinet, oak ca. 1910.
700
Canvas Goose Decoy, ca. 1920.
65
Photo John Barry, Calif.

Photo courtesy Harvey and Rose King, Muskogee, Oklahoma.

Left
Tintypes, Victorian period, each: C/6-9

Right
Iron.
   Ladle, cast iron, maker's mark, pat. 1871.   C/13-17
   Fork-spatula combination, wrought iron, decorative handle grooves, 15½ in. long. Very rare. C/300-450
   Ladle, cast iron, handle attached later.   C/12-16

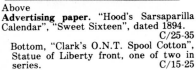

Above
Advertising paper. "Hood's Sarsaparilla Calendar", "Sweet Sixteen", dated 1894.
C/25-35
   Bottom, "Clark's O.N.T. Spool Cotton", Statue of Liberty front, one of two in series.   C/15-25

Above
Gold watch and chain, by Rockford, hunter case. Made in Rockford, Illinois, case by C.W.C. Company.   C/115-140

Firetool stand (only), pair; four scrolling legs, 9 in. high. **A-60.00**

Fork, wrought iron, simple tooling, 20½ in. long. **A-20.00**

Fork, wrought iron, handle signed "J. Schmidt/1842", 17½ in. long. **A-135.00**

Fork, wrought iron, 14 in. long. **A-15.00**

Fork, iron, with cast handle, 15 in. long. **A-10.00**

Fork, two-tined sheet medal, wood handle, copper rivets. **D-10.00**

Fork, wrought iron, 19 in. long. **A-15.00**

Griddle, floor; cast iron, footed, straight handle, 22½ in. long. **D-115.00**

Gypsy kettle, cast iron, wrought handle 9 in. diameter. **A-17.50**

Gypsy kettle, cast iron, three legs, two handles, 24 in. diameter. **A-65.00**

Gyspy kettle, cast bronze, iron handle, 7 in. diameter. **A-22.50**

Hearth brush, painted decorations, 28 in. high. **D-70.00**

Hearth cooker, inn-size, hinged top, tubular steam vent. Brass dovetailing each side, rolled edges. Rectangular, fitted into open hearth architecture; 18½ x 20¼ x 22 inches. **D-295.00**

Hearth kettle, brass, hand wrought iron handle, rim diameter 14 in. Copper rivets, ca. 1860, 9¼ in. deep. **D-150.00**

Hearth peel, hand-forged iron, bun handle end, 5 in. wide blade, 22½ in. long with handle. **D-39.50**

Hearth peel, wrought iron, 29½ in. long. **D-60.00**

Hearth plaque, bronzed bas relief, embossed interior scene, 22½ x 25 inches. **A-125.00**

Hearth shovel, wrought iron, scoop 5¾ in. wide, 18 in. long. **D-25.00**

Hearth shovel, "pancake" end, wrought iron, 34 in. long. **D-29.00**

Kettle, bellmetal brass, wrought rattail handle. Brass ears, 10 in. top diameter, 10¾ in. high. **D-160.00**

Kettle, wrought iron, handled, 10¾ in. diameter. **D-26.00**

Kettle, cast iron, 5 in. diameter, 4½ in. deep. Mfgr. mark. **D-15.00**

Kettle, copper, "tulip" handles, attached link chain for crane, dovetailed brass side and bottom, 9½ in. diameter, 5¾ in. deep. **D-160.00**

Kettle shelf, iron with brass rod, 9 x 16½ inches. **A-17.50**

Kettle tilter, wrought iron, 18th Century, graceful. **D-265.00**

Ladle, wrought iron, double pouring lips, 4 in. diameter bowl, 22½ in. handle.   **D-60.00**

Ladle, wrought iron, 21 in. long.   **A-27.50**

Ladle, wrought iron, 24-3/8 in. long, fancy handle.   **D-45.00**

Ladle, wrought iron, 19 in. handle with wooden end grip.   **D-35.00.**

Log tongs, Victorian, cast iron, fancy finial.   **D-10.00**

Peel, wrought iron, minor rust damage, 41½ in. long.   **A-35.00**

Peel, wood, baking; 78 in. long.   **A-20.00**

Peel, wrought iron, ram's horn finial, 41 in. long.   **A-55.00**

Poker, wrought, loop handle, 23 in. long.   **D-14.50**

Popcorn popper, tin, slide cover, handle, 3½ x 7¼ x 10.   **D-18.50**

Reflector oven, tin, center divider, 8 x 13 x 14 inches.   **D-42.00**

Reflector oven, folding handles, Maine, 10½ x 19½ inches.   **D-45.00**

Skewers, set of four; eagle finials, silver plate, 5 in. long.   **A-40.00**

Skillet, cast iron, on short feet, 11 in. diameter.   **A-22.50**

Skimmer ladle, copper, punched holes in 6 in. diameter bowl, 17¾ wrought iron handle.   **D-125.00**

Skimmer ladle, brass, punched bowl, wrought handle, 19 in. long.   **D-45.00**

Skimmer ladle, brass bowl, copper rivets, 18 in. handle.   **S-55.00**

Spatula, brass and wrought iron, 15½ in. long.   **A-45.00**

Spatula, wrought iron, unusual shape, 18 in. long.   **A-30.00**

Spatual, wrought iron, stamped handle name, 15½ in. long.   **A-75.00**

Spider, iron, sheet iron pan, wrought legs and handle, 8¾ in. diameter.   **A-25.00**

Spider, spun brass pan, wrought iron feet and handle, 6 in. diameter, 6½ in. high.   **A-50.00**

Strainer, brass and iron, stamped mfgr. name, 1886, 16 in. long.   **A-70.00**

Strainer, wrought iron and brass, handle stamped with name and date, 1848; 20 in. long.   **A-180.00**

Toaster, wrought iron, shaped handle with initials, 13½ x 18 inches.   **D-175.00**

Tongs, fireplace; wrought iron, mushroom top, 24 in. long.   **D-22.50**

Tongs, fireplace; 17½ in. long.   **A-12.50**

Tongs, fireplace; wrought iron, scrolls and twisting, 31 in. long. **A-35.00**

Tongs, pair; wrought iron, 12 in. long. **A-17.50**

Tongs, wrought iron, 26 in. long. **A-25.00**

Tongs, wrought iron, one end can be used as poker, 28 in. long. **A-60.00**

Trammel, wrought iron, adjustable, 31 in. long. **A-27.50**

Trammel, short hook, adjusts (closest) to 18 inches. **D-115.00**

Trammel, (chain and pothook), wrought iron, sixteen 3- to 4-in. loops, ca. 1830, 80 in. long. **D-150.00**

Trammel, sawtooth; adjustable, wrought iron, 30 in. long. **A-35.00**

Trivet, cast iron, 6½ in. diameter, three-footed. **D-22.50**

Trivet, cast iron, "New England Butt Co.". **A-17.50**

Trivet, kettle-shelf; brass and iron, removable wood handle, 15½ in. long. **A-50.00**

Trivet, wrought iron, heart-shaped, 9½ in. long. **A-145.00**

Utensil hook, wrought iron, three-pronged, looped to hang. **D-6.50**

Utensil rack, wrought iron, 16½ in. long. **A-15.00**

Wafer iron, round design with roosters, iron, 28 in. long. **A-85.00**

Wafer iron, wrought iron, cast waffle pattern, 24 in. long. **A-22.50**

Waffle iron, wrought iron, 25 in. long. **A-15.00**

Waffle iron, wrought and cast iron, head design, 23 in. long. **A-55.00**

Waffle iron, wrought iron, cast pattern, 25½ in. long. **D-49.00**

FLASKS

Flask and cover, pewter, 6½ in. high. **A-20.00**

One-half pint, embossed "Patent/Stoddard", amber glass, polished pontil, ca. 1850. **D-22.50**

One-half pint, likely Stoddard, honey-amber, 6¼ in. high. **D-12.50**

Flask, brown glass wrapped in split willow, pint or more, 9 in. high. **D-25.00**

Flask, leather-covered, silver-plated top, 7 in. high. **D-24.00**

Flask, bubbly dark amber, 6¾ in. high. **D-20.00**

Half-quart, Civil War era, bottom half covered with leather. **D-25.00**

Pocket flask, glass and sterling, lizardskin and silver cap, two touchmarks, 3/8 pint. D-48.00

Pocket flask, glass with stainless steel bottom, monogrammed. D-14.00

FLOOR COVERINGS—*[See also* **Rugs***]*

Carpeting, rag rug, black and white stripes with colorful bands of various shades of red that run length. Never used, 33 x 38 inches. A-360.00

Rug, hooked, rag and yarn, red and black, white stag and polychrome flowers, 25½ x 44 inches. A-127.50

Rug, hooked on homespun linen. Earliest variety, geometric pattern, muted colors, 25½ x 51 inches. D-90.00

Rug, hooked, checkerboard pattern with brown and floral squares, minor edge wear, 25½ x 33 inches. A-35.00

Rug, hooked, oval, leaf pattern in grey and browns, edge wear, 35 x 40 inches. A-35.00

Rug, hooked, yarn, six floral squares, 21½ x 34 inches. A-22.50

Rug, hooked, sculptured, Waldoboro type. Floral pattern with dark brown ground and sheared flowers in three colors. Rug is 18¾ x 39 inches. A-300.00

Rug, hooked, wool, American eagle with shamrocks, flowering thistle and roses in talons. Made in 1912. A-135.00

Rug, hooked, rag, three kittens on checkerboard floor, 25 x 49 inches. A-115.00

Rug, hooked, rectangular, grey and white sawtooth borders, 34 x 38 inches. A-40.00

Rug, wool felt, hexagonal, colorful, some wear, 39 in. diameter. A-55.00

Rug, woven, rag, unusual stencil decoration, red and green floral design, 3 x 10 feet. A-105.00

Runner, hooked rag, stair-tread size rugs stitched together in colorful floral patterns, 20 inches x 11 feet. A-105.00

FOLK ART

Box, decorated, done in old brown with yellow, simple striping on outside. Inside cover had five-pointed star, center divider; pine, 5¾ x 7 x 10¼ in. wide. D-65.00

Carving, of country character with whiskers, plinth base, well done, Ca. 1890, 2¼ in. high. D-8.50

Carving, of monkey eating coconut, 9¾ in. high.　　A-90.00
Elephant, primitive style, 3 x 5½ inches.　　D-26.00
Figure, of bearded man, primitive details, 20th Century, 12½ in. high.　　A-30.00
Figure, made from tree fork, jointed arms and legs. Tree-bark trousers, button eyes, fur mustache and eyebrows. Hair missing, 60 in. high.　　A-710.00
Lid, from grain bin, pine with orig. red paint and stenciled black horses and hearts, 20½ x 37 inches.　　A-195.00
Rooster, carved from fork in tree branch, recent, 3 in. high.　　C-8.00
Swizzle stick, carved, four graduated hoops, spun between hands.　　D-45.00

FRAKTUR

Birth certificate, in German, dated 1810. Colorful border with heart and flowers in five colors, framed, 6¼ x 9¼ inches.　　A-210.00
Birth certificate, stylized figural form, dated 1801, from Connecticut, old black painted frame, 9 in. wide.　　A-270.00
Birth and baptismal certificate, German text. In four colors, and with tape stains, unframed, 7 x 8½ inches.　　A-110.00
Certificate, dated 1842, enclosed in rose garlands held by angel at bottom and pair of birds at top. Paper stained, good colors, framed, 15½ x 16¼ inches.　　A-365.00
Cut-out, circular design bordered by yellow with heart, compass stars and circles. Unframed, 7¾ x 9¾ inches.　　A-110.00
Family record, old red frame, family begins in late 1700's.　　A-105.00
Family record, birth/death years 1796 to 1855. Old gilt frame, 19¼ x 23¼ inches.　　A-95.00
Family record, in German, hand-drawn with border design. Old pine frame painted black, 11¾ x 16½ inches.　　A-125.00
Hand-drawn, dated 1819, in four colors, framed, 10 x 13¼ inches.　　A-135.00
Late fraktur, on lined paper, dated 1884, framed, 16¾ x 20¼ inches.　　A-45.00

Printed, recording births in Pennsylvania, 1818. Modern painted frame, 16½ x 19¼ inches.   **A-100.00**

Printed, form done in 1843, hand-colored, modern painted frame, 17 x 20 inches.   **A-55.00**

Printed, Pennsylvania, hand-colored in green and yellow, modern frame in dark green, 16 x 19 inches.   **A-215.00**

Printed, hand-colored, recording 1897 Pennsylvania birth.   **A-25.00**

Valentine, folding cut-out fraktur, circular. Water-colored birds and stars, unframed, 14 in. diameter.   **A-155.00**

Vorschrift, hearts and vining tulips border, central passage ends with alphabet and date, 1799. Hand-drawn and colored in three shades; faded colors. Old black frame, 16½ x 19½ inches.   **A-485.00**

FRAMES

Beveled pine, old red paint and old mirror glass, 6½ x 9½.   **A-35.00**

Cherry, with square edge and inset bevel, 13¼ x 25 inches.   **A-17.50**

Easel frames, pair; fancy pierced scrollwork, brass-plated, gilded, ea. 8¾ x 11¾ inches.   **D-40.00**

Gold-gilded softwood, with unsigned painting, 20 x 42 inches.   **A-20.00**

Mahogany-pine, with beaded edge, 17½ x 18¼ inches.   **A-15.00**

Mahogany veneer, beveled, 11¼ x 14¼ inches.   **A-17.50**

Mahogany veneer, beveled, 14¼ x 18½ inches.   **A-20.00**

Oak, two-inch quarter-sawed, 9½ x 15½ inches.   **S-25.00**

Painted frame, mortised and pinned corners, 11½ x 13¼.   **A-17.50**

Pennsylvania Dutch chip-carved frame, 14 x 18 inches.   **S-45.00**

Pine, diagonal cutting, panel only, 10½ x 36 inches.   **A-11.00**

Pine, old black paint, two-flame veneer, 16½ x 19½ inches.   **A-20.00**

Pine, molded ridging, 14 x 21¼ inches.   **D-22.00**

Walnut frame, chip-carved, 9¾ x 14¾ inches.   **A-60.00**

Walnut, clear finish, 9½ x 16 inches.   **S-18.00**

Walnut, oval with gold liner, wood backed, 11 x 13 inches.   **D-60.00**

Walnut, glass-covered front, 15¼ x 23½ inches.   **A-35.00**

FURNITURE—*Chairs*

Armchair, arrowback, turned legs, plank seat, scrolled arms. **A-65.00**

Armchair, arrowback, plank seat, American, ca. 1830. ..... **A-75.00**

Armchair, bannisterback, turned posts and finials with nicely shaped crest. Old black paint with striping and floral painting. **A-550.00**

Armchair, bowback, English, Windsor, good turnings, yew wood seat. **A-105.00**

Armchair, comb back, English, Windsor, arms repaired, has old metal brace. **A-155.00**

Above left, **Set of twenty [20] Chippendale style ribbon ladder-back dining chairs.** Upholstered seats; 18 side, 2 arm. Set A/4000

Courtesy Adam A. Weschler & Son, Washington, D.C.; photograph by Breger & Associates.

Above right, **chair,** one of six, chair parts of mixed woods including maple. Set: C/250-350

Photo courtesy Judy Morehead, Creative Photography, Lancaster, Ohio.

center, **New England cherry corner chair,** with horseshoe backrest with chamfered edge and shaped cresting on turned baluster supports. Ca. 1770. A/900

Queen Anne turned armchair, with spooned back centering a baluster splat, the shaped arms on ring-and-vase turned supports. Ca. 1750. A/800

Courtesy Adam A. Weschler & Son, Washington, D.C.; photograph by Breger & Associates.

Oak stool.
C/110-130

Oak rocker.
C/90-105

Oak desk chair.
C/80-95

Oak rocker.
C/100-125

Set of four.
C/180-200

Oak, set of four.
C/180-200

Armchair, Chippendale mahogany "Martha Washington", ca. 1800. **A-250.00**

Armchair, open, Chippendale-style "Martha Washington", Biggs & Co., Richmond, Virginia. **A-200.00**

Armchair, open, Chippendale mahogany and yew wood; pierced ribbon ladderback continuing to outward scrolling arms, ca. 1760. **A-400.00**

Armchair, hoopback, American Windsor, late 18th Century. **A-525.00**

Armchair, ladderback, turned backposts, good finials, four graduated slats, woven splint seat, linsey-woolsey cushion.   A-475.00

Armchair, ladderback, sausage turnings, worn black paint with traces of gold striping, new woven cane seat.   A-400.00

Armchair, ladderback, hickory, rush seat, ca. 1850.   A-100.00

Armchair, ladderback, child's, very worn red and black paint.   A-45.00

Armchair, ladderback, good finials and shaped top slat. Worn old red finish, sausage turnings, splint seat with black cloth cover.   A-545.00

Armchair, New England, maple, rush seat, hickory stretcher, ca. 1760.   A-250.00

Armchair, Country Queen Anne; turned legs with bulbous front stretcher, boldly shaped scrolled arms, shaped splat and crest.   A-425.00

Armchair, Windsor bowback, seat splits, green over white paint.   A-495.00

Armchair, Windsor bowback, carved knuckle arms, old refinishing with signs of black and green paint; papers with chair show it was made in 1796, Massachusetts.   A-875.00

Armchair, Windsor continuous-arm, child's; bamboo turnings with bar to hold child in place; pin to fasten base to hole in floor. Worn orig. dark brown paint, 19 in. high.   A-750.00

Armchair, Windsor bowback, shaped seat, turned legs, seven spindles in back, "H" stretcher.   A-375.00

Chair, Windsor, continuous arm braceback. Bulbous turnings in base and arm supports, shaped seat, simply shaped arms, one arm support with old break; seat height 18 inches.   A-2,250.00

Captain's chair, country, bowback Windsor eight-spindle back. Good turnings and scrolled arms, old repairs, old black paint.   A-800.00

Corner chair, country, simple turnings, shaped slats, maple.   A-250.00

Sidechair, bannisterback, turned legs, posts and stretchers, shaped crest, good finials.   A-355.00

Sidechair, bannisterback, old worn finish, new cane seat.   A-100.00

Sidechair, bannisterback, delicate turnings, well-shaped crest.   A-110.00

Sidechair, bannisterback, from Salem, Massachusetts. A-150.00

Sidechair, Boston, birch, turned front legs with bulbous stretcher, striped upholstery, old worn finish. A-475.00

Sidechair, Chippendale mahogany, "H" stretcher, ca. 1770. A-175.00

Sidechair, Hepplewhite mahogany, early 19th Century. A-60.00

Sidechair, Hitchcock, dark brown graining. A-60.00

Sidechair, ladderback, turned posts and finials, four slats. A-220.00

Sidechair, ladderback, turned posts with good finials, old red paint. A-210.00

Sidechair, ladderback, four-slat back with sausage turnings and well-turned finials, new rush seat, old red paint. A-280.00

Sidechair, ladderback, ash; duck feet, turned front stretcher. A-45.00

Sidechair, ladderback, sausage turnings with good finials, three graduated slats, rush seat. A-210.00

Sidechair, plank seat, bamboo turnings, orig. dark brown paint. A-115.00

Sidechair, country Queen Anne, turned legs and front stretcher. Shaped splat and crest rail, old rush seat. A-220.00

Sidechair, country Queen Anne, refinished, new paper rush seat. A-210.00

Sidechair, unusual, turned legs and posts, only one slat. A-125.00

Sidechair, Windsor bowback, seven spindles, shaped seat, old paint. A-240.00

Sidechair, Windsor bowback, seven-spindle back, shaped seat. A-100.00

Sidechair, Windsor bowback, nine-spindle back, shaped seat, old dark finish. A-220.00

Sidechair, Windsor chickencoop, dished-out seat, bamboo turnings. A-135.00

Wing chair, Hepplewhite-style, exposed frame with "H" stretcher in walnut; upholstered in gold plush. A-400.00

Wing chair frame, made up of old parts, ball and claw feet. A-155.00

Wing chair and footstool, Queen Anne style, mahogany, covered in tortoise-shell leather. A-275.00

Wing chair, Queen Anne style, mahogany, lounge-type, upholstered.   A-300.00

FURNITURE—*Chair Sets*

Side, arrowback, pair; refinished.   A-110.00

Side, Chippendale, mahogany, pair; refinishing necessary.   A-230.00

Side, Chippendale, mahogany, pair; arms once added, upholstered.   A-150.00

Side, Hitchcock, stencil-decorated, pair; ca. 1830.   A-130.00

Side, rabbit-ear, plank seat, pair; refinished.   A-50.00

Armchairs, pair; and ottoman, three pieces. Rosewood chairs and ottoman upholstered in lime velvet.   A-450.00

Side, American Victorian, walnut, pair; late 1800's.   A-70.00

Side, arrowback country, set of four, refinished.   A-220.00

Side, balloonback, set of six. Orig. brown ground with yellow and black striping, gold stenciled flowers and fruit.   A-630.00

Side, maple, new cane bottoms, good condition, set of five.   A-125.00

Side, Federal shieldbacks, set of six; "H" stretcher bases, square tapered legs, pierced and carved splats. Upholstered seats, minor repairs, refinished.   A-750.00

Side and (1) arm, Hitchcock, six side, set of seven. Orig. decoration, red and black graining with yellow striping and gold stenciling. Old rush seats on four, others have replaced paper rush.   A-1,190.00

Side, plank seat, decorated, set of six; ground color is olive brown with black and yellow striping.   A-330.00

Side, plank seat, set of six; orig. painted decoration brown feather graining with white striping and leaf-like painting on crests.   A-660.00

Side, plank seat, decorated, set of six; orig. brown paint with yellow striping, stenciled floral designs on crest.   A-450.00

Side, Queen Anne curley maple, set of six; button feet, bulbous turned front stretcher, slender turned posts and shaped splat and crest. Old rush seats with worn white paint, maple with good curl throughout set, excellent color.   A-7,650.00

Side, decorated, set of ten; orig. white paint with decorations in three shades of green, rush seats.   A-600.00

Side, spindleback, decorated, set of six; orig. brown paint with black and yellow striping and stenciled polychrome fruit on crest. **A-450.00**

Stools, set of six; made like chair bases with woven cane seats; Old alligatored red paint shows black beneath, 16½ in. high. **A-520.0**

Side, Victorian, walnut, set of five; three with pierced crestrail and splat, serpentine front seats, ca. 1870. **A-175.00**

Side, plank seat, Windsor, set of four. Set of three arrowback and one four-spindle back; Pennsylvania, ca. 1820-30. **A-250.00**

Side, Windsor, set of six; plank seats, with bamboo turning in legs and five-spindle backs, refinished. **A-840.00**

FURNITURE—General

Bench, child's bootjack ends, low back, pine, 39½ in. long. **A-90.00**

Bench, deacon's, three-chair back, scrolling crestrail, straight splat and bannister stiles. Pennsylvania, ca. 1820. **A-350.00**

Bench, fireside, shaped ends and raised panel back, early construction. Wide pine boards, worn red paint over orig. white, 22 x 47¼ x 60 in. high. **A-2,600.00**

Bench, pine, legs mortised into top, old blue paint, 17¾ in. high. **A-235.00**

Bench, pine, cut-out legs mortised through top, 12 x 87 x 18 in. high. **A-95.00**

Bench, pine, splayed legs and old grey paint, 49 x 19 in. high **A-50.00**

Bench, pine, worn old dark green paint, 9½ x 70 x 17 in. high. **A-95.00**

Bench, mammies, rocking; holes for two baby guards, back spindle replaced, repairs to feet, 72 in. long. **A-200.00**

Bench, settle, Windsor, bamboo turnings and whittled arrow spindles. Holes for baby guard, refinished, 55½ in. long. **A-400.00**

Bench, settle, turned legs and spindles, 9 feet long. **A-170.00**

Bench, settle, country Sheraton, good turnings, shaped crest. Old repaint with flower and thistle decorations, 82 in. long. **A-420.00**

American Chippendale pine chest of drawers, 40 in. wide and 41 in. high. Molded edge and dove-tailed top about five graduated drawers on molded edge base ending on bracket feet. Ca. 1820.

A/650

Chest of drawers, bow-front; New England Salem cherry and bird's-eye maple, and ca. 1810. Piece is 44 in. wide, 22 in. deep, 42 in. high.

A/475

Massachusetts Chippendale carved mahogany serpentine front chest of drawers, 32 in. high. Ca. 1790.

A/4100

Courtesy Adam A. Weschler & Son, Washington, D.C.; photograph by Breger & Associates.

Bench, spindleback, with scrolled arms. Refinished with traces of old red paint, iron rod braces in arms, 72 in. long.　　　　　　　　　　　　　　　　A-425.00

Bench, Windsor, bamboo turnings and spectacular arms. One end of seat indicates bench may have been longer; feet clipped. Seat height 14½ in., 86½ in. long.　　　　　　　　　　　　　　　A-1,800.00

Bookcase, Victorian rosewood double-glazed door; with four adjustable shelves. Ca. 1870, 16 x 58 x 100 in. high.　　　　　　　　　　　　　　　　A-325.00

Bookcase-secretary, American Federal, mahogany, in two parts. Upper has three shelves, lower with slanting writing flap above two convex and two long drawers; 22 x 46 x 74 in. high.　　　　　　　A-425.00

Cabinet, corner, country, pine; in two parts. Upper with two doors concealing three shelves, lower with two doors, one shelf. Flush base, 24 x 46 x 79 in. high.　　　　　　　　　　　　　　　　A-450.00

Victorian chestnut **dresser**, carved handles, ca. 1880.
700

Walnut dresser, ca. 1880.
400

Spool cabinet, oak, ca. 1910.　　700

Canvas goose **decoy**, ca. 1920.　　65

Photos by John Barry

Cabinet, label, pine; paneled door with orig. thumb latch, interior divided into 144 pigeonholes. Piece is 62½ in. high.　　　　　　　　　　　　　A-225.00

Cabinet, pewter, oak, leaded glass windows at top, ca. 1875, 83 in. high.　　　　　　　　　　D-745.00

Cabinet, side, Italian, walnut; 18th Century, 11 x 28 x 37 in. high.　　　　　　　　　　　　　A-350.00

Oak china cabinet.
500-600

Oak kitchen cabinet.
325-375

Oak buffet (side-
board) 425-475

Oak china cabinet.
800-1100

Oak corner china buffet
with leaded glass front
& beveled mirror in
back.
900-1000

Oak china cabinet.
500-800

Oak buffet (sideboard).
Leaded glass doors.
425-475

Candlestand, adjustable, sides mortised through "X"-base, wooden ratchet and rectangular top, gallery with applied moulding. Old worn red paint, top 9¾ x 12 inches, 24 to 28 in. high. **A-985.00**

Candlestand, American, cherry, ca. 1790, 28½ in. high. **A-70.00**

Candlestand, American, Sheraton, walnut, 17 x 18 x 29 in. high. **A-110.00**

Candlestand, birch, rectangular top, 12½ x 13¾ x 26¼ inches. **A-275.00**

Candlestand, delicate proportions, turned column with legs mortised into hexagonal base. Old black paint over red, 25 in. high. **A-320.00**

Candlestand, country, cherry spider-legs, curly maple column, and cherry two-board top. Refinished, 27¼ in. high. **A-270.00**

Candlestand, maple and birch, round top, turned column, 26 in. high. **A-175.00**

Candlestand, Queen Anne, country, round dish top. Rectangular bird-cage with turned posts, tripod base, worn orig. reddish-brown paint. One leg an early replacement, 27 in. high. **A-700.00**

Candlestand, tilt-top, cherry, tripod base, 30½ in. high. **A-60.00**

Candlestand, tip-top, New England, cherry, with oval top tilting on turned standard. Ca. 1790, 13 x 24 x 28 in. high. **A-325.00**

Candlestands, pair. Tilt-top bird-cage, curly maple, handmade reproductions. Both 15½ x 22 x 29 in. high. **A-420.00**

Chest-on-chest, Pennsylvania transitional, cherry; in two parts. Upper, flat molded cornice top above three aligned drawers and four graduated drawers, lower with two graduated drawers on French Feet. Ca. 1790, 21½ x 42½ x 71 in. high. **A-3,500.00**

Chest, bow-front, American Sheraton mahogany, with four drawers. Ca. 1810, 23 x 41 x 41 in. high. **A-325.00**

Chest-of-drawers, oak, eight drawers, 4 feet high, ca. 1890. **D-190.00**

Chest-of-drawers, cherry, short turned feet, reeded pilasters, four dovetailed cockbeaded drawers, 20½ x 45 x 46 in. high. **A-500.00**

Chest-of-drawers, Chippendale, mahogany, bracket feet, dovetailed drawers, replaced brasses. Back edge of top has repair. — A-370.00

Chest-of-drawers, Chippendale, mahogany, English. Back feet replaced, 22 x 45½ x 36 in. high. — A-210.00

Chest-of-drawers, country, pine; dovetailed bracket feet, six dovetailed drawers with orig. wooden knobs, 51½ in. high. — A-500.00

Chest-of-drawers, country Chippendale, pine; five dovetailed drawers, feet and top moulding partially replaced, new brass hardware, 40 in. high. — A-650.00

Chest-of-drawers, country Empire, poplar, 48 in. high. — A-170.00

Chest-of-drawers, country Empire, walnut, 31½ in. high. — A-120.00

Chest-of-drawers, country Sheraton, cherry; turned legs, 44¾ in. high. — A-305.00

Chest-of-drawers, George III campaign, walnut, in two parts. Top above two aligned drawers and one long, lower two long drawers on cannonball feet. Ca. 1800-10, 39½ in. high. — A-700.00

Chest-of-drawers, Hepplewhite, cherry; French feet, four dovetailed overlapping drawers. Replaced hardware, refinished, 18¼ x 35¾ x 36¾ in. high. — A-850.00

Chest-of-drawers, Hepplewhite, New England, bass wood with fine orig. grained decoration, brown over natural wood ground. High feet, dovetailed drawers, scalloped apron, orig. brasses; 21 x 30 x 37½ in. high. — A-4,600.00

Chest-of-drawers, poplar, five drawers, moulding, 25 in. high. — A-90.00

Chest-on-frame, Queen Anne, walnut; flat molded cornice top above one square drawer centered by four drawers and continuing above four thumbmolded and graduated drawers; 43 x 25 x 66 in. high. — A-2,000.00

Clothes press, two-part, applewood; scalloped apron and three overlapping dovetailed drawers, considerable restoration, but good color, 18 x 43 x 77¾ inches. — A-500.00

Couch, country, spool turnings with scalloped apron, old brown paint. Removable upholstered ecru cushions, 74 in. long. — A-505.00

Couch, country; turned wooden legs, mustard yellow hopsack upholstery with wear, 68 in. long. — A-320.00

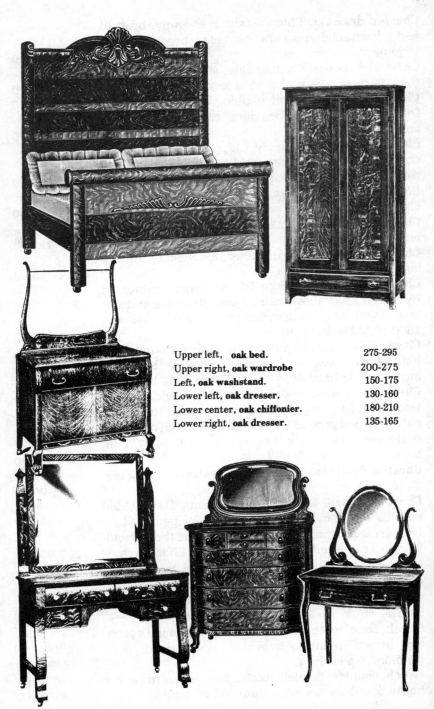

Upper left, **oak bed**. 275-295
Upper right, **oak wardrobe** 200-275
Left, **oak washstand**. 150-175
Lower left, **oak dresser**. 130-160
Lower center, **oak chiffonier**. 180-210
Lower right, **oak dresser**. 135-165

Couch, fainting, country Empire. Dark brown paint, 74 in. long. **A-175.00**

Cupboard, corner, cherry, very large size. **D-875.00**

Cupboard, corner, poplar; bottom door with two panels, top door four. Refinished, added wooden knobs, 19½ x 40 x 77 in. high. **A-475.00**

Cupboard, corner, one-piece, butternut; paneled doors, simple moulded cornice, 48 in. wide, 91 in. high. **A-310.00**

Cupboard, corner, two-piece, pine; scalloped base, paneled doors, moulded cornice. Orig. cast iron latches, 42 x 87 in. high. **A-675.00**

Cupboard, corner, solid cherry, 7 feet high. **D-650.00**

Cupboard, corner, architectural, pine; door in base with double raised panels, continuous moulding from base to moulded keystone. Three butterfly shelves in top, worn blue-grey paint with darker blue beneath, 18½ x 46 x 85 in. high. **A-1,525.00**

Cupboard, corner, two-piece, pine; orig. red graining over yellow ground. Turned feet, paneled doors, single dovetailed drawer flanked by two false drawers. Single 12-pane top door, old glass, with arched top lights, 41½ in. wide, 84 in. high. **A-3,400.00**

Cupboard, corner, country Irish, pine; 44 x 76¼ in. high. **A-450.00**

Cupboard, corner, one-piece pine. Raised panel doors with single base door, double above doors, 46 in. wide, 85 in. high. **A-575.00**

Cupboard, jelly, walnut; paneled doors and two dovetailed drawers. Refinished, low back crest, 17 x 43 x 46 in. high. **A-330.00**

Cupboard, jelly or pie, pine; 16 x 66½ x 61½ in. high. **A-105.00**

Cupboard, jelly, country Sheraton, turned feet, paneled doors and two dovetailed drawers. Knobs replaced, 20½ x 44¼ x 49 in. high. **A-425.00**

Cupboard, jelly, pine; with turned feet, paneled doors and good cornice, 20½ x 40½ x 55¾ in. high. **A-375.00**

Cupboard, jelly, pine; scalloped base, board and batten door and moulding around base. Refinished, 50½ in. wide, 51 in. high. **A-470.00**

Cupboard, hanging, pine; white interior, dark varnish finish, 36 in. high. **A-65.00**

Cupboard, hanging, corner, nicely scalloped top and bottom brackets, dark red with four-color decorations, 12 x 17½ x 24 in. high.   A-210.00

Cupboard, pewter, pine, open one-piece. Shoe feet, paneled door, moulded cornice, worn paint, 17½ x 50 x 77¼ in. high.   A-920.00

Cupboard, pewter, open, pine; one-piece with shoe feet and room for pewter chargers in base. Orange-brown paint, 16 x 54 x 76½ in. high.   A-660.00

Cupboard, top, poplar, 14 x 42 x 33 in. high.   A-85.00

Cupboard, wall, one-piece, pine; open shelves, board and batten door, old grey paint, 23 x 46½ x 82 in. high.   A-400.00

Cupboard, wall, two-piece, walnut; bracket feet, scalloped apron, paneled doors below, twin six-pane doors with old glass above. Chamfered corners, 21 x 64 x 88¾ inches.   A-900.00

Cupboard, wall, one-piece, walnut; two deep drawers, bracket feet replaced, 24 x 48 x 83 in. high.   A-530.00

Cupboard, wall, walnut, six orig. glass panes at top, bottom with two drawers and two doors, 8 feet high.   A-350.00

Cupboard, wall, one-piece, poplar. Raised-panel doors, reeded edges, base with three shelves, top with four, 80 in. high.   A-475.00

Cupboard, wall, one-piece, pine; base has paneled door, twelve glass panes in top door, old worn yellowish green paint over red. One end of cornice replaced, 20¾ x 35¼ x 85½ in. high.   A-950.00

Cupboard, one-piece wall, pine primitive, single-board door in base, double six-pane doors above. Base door an old replacement, 19½ x 37½ x 68½ in. high.   A-550.00

Dental cabinet, 24 drawers, dated 1919, fine wood, five ft. high.   D-850.00

Desk, accountant's, American, walnut, ca. 1850, 58 in. high.   A-200.00

Desk, box, table-top, primitive, pine; 19½ x 19¾ x 13½ in. high.   A-70.00

Desk, fall-front, Chippendale, cherry, New England. Central open compartment flanked by four pigeon-holes above six drawers, case having four graduated drawers on molded edge base. Ca. 1780-90, 20 x 41 x 41.   A-700.00

George III mahogany pedestal desk, 48 in. wide, 28 in. deep, 29 in. high. Tooled leather inset top above three cockbeaded and aligned drawers. Ca. 1810-20.   A/750
Courtesy Adam A. Weschler & Son, Washington, D.C.; photograph by Breger & Associates.

Walnut flattop office desk. Ca. 1900.   600
Photo courtesy John W. Barry

Desk, Chippendale, English, mahogany on pine, overlapping dovetailed drawers, interior with pigeonholes and six dovetailed drawers. Some veneer repair, 19½ x 48 x 42 in. high.   A-500.00

Desk, Chippendale-style, walnut, 75 in. high, slant writing surface.   D-375.00

Desk, curly maple, ogee feet, overlapping dovetailed drawers, dovetailed case and slant top, interior with dovetailed drawers, eight pigeonholes and two letter drawers. Refinished, 18 x 34¾ x 40¾ inches.   A-2,400.00

Desk, lap, rosewood, dated 1855, 20 in. high.   A-150.00

Desk, Larkin-type, fold-down writing surface, oak, 42 in. high.   D-195.00

Desk, mahogany, dovetailed, lid with figural veneer, fitted interior with pigeonholes and drawers, 30-in. writing height.   A-325.00

Desk, Sheraton, two-piece, mahogany; Cambour top, turned and reeded legs. Top with pigeonholes and small drawers, 46¼ in. high.   A-1,550.00

Desk, slant-top, country; turned legs, paneled doors and one dovetailed drawer, interior with four drawers, 38¾ in. high.   A-520.00

144

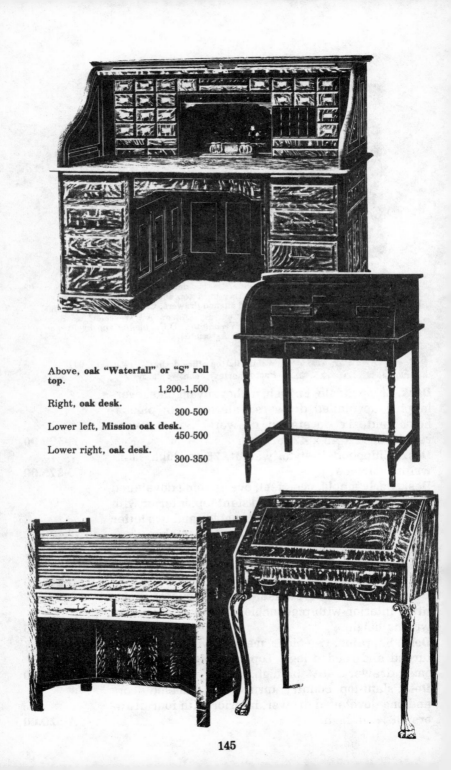

Above, oak "Waterfall" or "S" roll top.
1,200-1,500

Right, oak desk.
300-500

Lower left, Mission oak desk.
450-500

Lower right, oak desk.
300-350

Desk, oxbow, Chippendale-style, mahogany; ogee feet, dovetailed drawers and fitted interior. Some replacements, 23 x 42 x 43 in. high, 32¼ in. writing height. **A-725.00**

Desk, pine, simple scalloped base, three drawers, refinished; 21½ x 33 x 36½ in. high. **A-230.00**

Desk, plantation, country Hepplewhite, cherry; tapered square legs, one drawer and fold-down writing surface in base. Pigeonholed interior, 20½ x 33 x 65 in. high. **A-700.00**

Desk, rolltop, child's, 32 in. high. **D-125.00**

Desk, schoolmaster's, cherry; square tapered legs, slant front, interior with pigeonholes, refinished, 32½ in. high. **A-320.00**

Desk, schoolmaster's, walnut; slant top 31¾ in. high. **S-175.00**

Desk, tabletop, six interior drawers in stepback arrangement, fold-down lid missing. Shows transition from bible to desk-box, 16 x 25½ x 21¼ in. high. **A-650.00**

Desk, tabletop, box, oak with pine bottom and backboards, 10¾ in. high. **A-475.00**

Dresser, child's, play; three drawers, late 1800's, 13 in. high. **D-35.00**

Dresser, marble-top, maple burl, 28 in. high. **S-195.00**

Dresser, vanity, butternut wood, three mirrors. **D-235.00**

Dresser, vanity, oak, two drawers, ca. 1890. **D-245.00**

Dresser, Victorian, oak, ca. 1890, 77 in. high. **D-265.00**

Half-commode, drawer at top, oak, door in base, 20 in. high. **A-55.00**

Harpsichord converted to desk, Federal, inlaid mahogany, 25 x 66 x 34 in. high. **A-120.00**

Highboy, Queen Anne, maple; banty feet with nicely scrolled apron, dovetailed overlapping drawers with bottom drawer divided. Replaced brasses, refinished, 19 x 36 x 78½ in. high. **A-3,100.00**

Highboy base used as lowboy, Queen Anne, cherry. Cabriole legs with duck feet, one long drawer at top, three below, 36½ in. high. **A-650.00**

Huntboard, cherry, turned and reeded legs, three dovetailed drawers, lift lid with shallow well. Extensive alterations, refinished, 21½ x 39½ x 38 in. high. **A-725.00**

Huntboard, Hepplewhite, inlaid walnut; rectangular top above central panelled door compartment flanked by two drawers and raised on tapered legs. Virginia, ca. 1800, 20 x 46 x 45 in. high. — A-1,800.00

Hutch, table, early pine; shoe feet, boldly scalloped cutouts and lift lid in base. Three-board top, yellow over blue paint. Top rods and left part of scroll at base are replacements. — A-6,750.00

Nightstand, child's, Sheraton-style, cherry, one-drawer, 24 in. high. — D-65.00

Nightstand, American Sheraton cherry, walnut and pine, 28 in. high. Ca. 1830. — A-80.00

Pedestal, pine, octagonal, old worn brown paint, 29 in. high. — A-75.00

Pole screen, Hepplewhite, mahogany. Tripod base, shield-shaped frame, needlework on silk floral embroidery, 61 in. high. — A-180.00

Rocker, arrowback, scrolled seat, stenciling on crest and seat. — A-60.00

Rocker, arrowback, painted, crestrail with fruit-leaf decoration, ca. 1820. — A-90.00

Rocker, child's, arrowback, tan graining on white ground. — A-65.00

Rocker, arrowcomb-back, American Windsor. — A-180.00

Rocker, Boston, decorated, orig. worn dark paint with stenciled floral decoration, yellow striping, grained seat. — A-205.00

Rocker, captain's, child-size, orig. paint brown with yellow. — A-105.00

Rocker, child's, old paint in good condition, 18 in. high. — D-55.00

Rocker, decorated, turned legs and arm supports, scrolled seat. — A-130.00

Rocker, ladderback, turned front legs with sausage turned backposts. — A-135.00

Rocker, ladderback, arm, turned finials and woven grass seat. — A-125.00

Rocker, platform, oak; plain form in low rectangular frame, held by wire and spring catchments. — D-200.00

Rocker, pressedback, oak, good condition. — A-90.00

Rocker, spindleback, scrolled seat and arms, worn graining. — A-95.00

Rocker, spindleback (double), cane seat, oak, fine condition. — A-145.00

Rocker, swivel, spindleback, cane seat, walnut wood.   A-140.00

Safe, pie, cherry; turned legs and two dovetailed drawers. Eight punched tin panels in pinwheel design, refinished, 17¾ x 40¾ x 46¼ in. high.   A-410.00

Safe, kitchen, Pennsylvania, cherry and pine, two pierced tole doors above long drawer, 84 in. high.   A-225.00

Secretary-bookcase, American, walnut, in two parts. Ca. 1870, four shelves plus pigeonholes and drawers, 98 in. high.   A-750.00

Secretary-bookcase, Federal, mahogany, in two parts. Probably from Virginia, ca. 1840, 24 x 43 x 53 in. high.   A-500.00

Server, American, pine, shaped top above one long drawer and shaped niche flanked by square drawers. Ca. 1840, 18 x 36 x 36 inches.   A-425.00

Settee, Victorian, rosewood, exposed molded frame, floral tapestry upholstery. Ca. 1870, 43 in. high.   A-400.00

Sideboard, American Federal, mahogany, ca. 1840, 52 in. high.   A-100.00

Sideboard, American, cabinet-made, pine, 22 x 63 x 34 in. high.   A-200.00

Sideboard, Hepplewhite, mahogany, with top center drawer opening out into desk fitted with pigeonholes and eight dovetailed drawers. Oval brasses replacements, 30¾ x 72 x 42½ inches.   A-1,600.00

Sideboard, pine turned legs, paneled doors and three dovetailed drawers in base. Grained, 18½ x 51 x 55 in. high.   A-210.00

Sofa, American Victorian, walnut, carved and molded exposed frame continuing to serpentine front raised on shaped legs, 67 in. long.   A-275.00

Sofa, camelback, Chippendale-style, mahogany, 20th Century. Scroll arms raised on eight legs joined by stretcher, striped silk upholstery, 36 in. high.   A-700.00

Sofa, Sheraton mahogany, ca. 1840, 79 in. long, 35 in. high.   A-800.00

Sofa, Sheraton-style, mahogany, upholstered in striped and floral satin damask. By Biggs & Co., Richmond, Va.; 77 in. long.   A-1,025.00

Sofa, Victorian, walnut, molded exposed frame cresting on scrolling pediment, upholstered. Ca. 1865, 64 in. long.   A-300.00

Stool, pine, oval top, four turned legs, 7½ in. high.   A-35.00

Stool, pine, scalloped apron with cutout feet, 7¼ in. high.   **A-60.00**

Stool, pine, cutout feet and wide side aprons, 7¼ in. high.   **A-27.50**

Stool, wooden, legs go from pencilpost to round, orig. dark green paint is worn, 24 in. high.   **A-105.00**

Washstand, American, mahogany; shaped splashboard and three round cup cut-outs. Ca. 1800, 17 x 24 x 38 inches.   **A-160.00**

Washstand, corner, country, pine; one drawer and dovetailed gallery. Old red paint, back foot repaired, 38½ in. high.   **A-180.00**

Washstand, drop-leaf, Sheraton, walnut; breadboard end top supporting hinged "D"-shaped leaves. Ca. 1840, 19 x 21 x 33 inches.   **A-400.00**

Washstand with splashboard, poplar, two drawers.   **A-120.00**

Washstand, one drawer at top, twin doors at bottom, oak.   **A-85.00**

Water bench, oak, old blue paint, 27 in. high.   **D-175.00**

Water bench, pine, stripped of paint, 11 x 33 x 29½ in. high.   **A-115.00**

Water bench, walnut and cherry, two shelves, 42 in. high.   **S-325.00**

FURNITURE—*Stands*

Stand, country Sheraton, birch, turned and reeded legs, 29 in. high.   **A-180.00**

Stands, fern, Sheraton-style mahogany, pair; molded trifoil top with ram's-head corbel supports, 43½ in. high.   **A-325.00**

Stand, drop-leaf, cherry; low, square tapered legs, two dovetailed drawers, 23 in. high.   **A-160.00**

Stand, mahogany, Empire tilt-top; tripod base, turned column, 28 in. high.   **A-115.00**

Stand, marble-top, brown, walnut.   **A-165.00**

Stand, marble-top, oak, four legs, 30 in. high.   **A-150.00**

Stand, pine, one-drawer, 24 x 25 in. top, 29 in. high.   **A-250.00**

Stand, plant, turned legs, applied column turnings, 35 in. high.   **A-40.00**

Stand, primitive, wrought iron tripod base, turned column, 25¾ in. high.   **A-85.00**

Stand, spider-leg, tilt-top, walnut; tripod base, chip-carved column, octagonal top, 28 in. high. A-100.00

Stand, tilt-top, turned column, rectangular top, 27½ in. high. A-425.00

Stand, unusual, base a square hickory post split in fours, maple top, 26 in. high. A-160.00

Stand, walnut, turned legs, dovetailed drawer, 29 in. high. A-170.00

Stand, bedside, birch, turned legs, dovetailed drawer, 26¾ in. high. A-120.00

Stand, bedside, cherry and curley maple, two dovetailed drawers, 29½ in. high. A-265.00

Stand, bedside, cherry, turned legs, two drawers, 29 in. high. A-185.00

Stand, bedside, cherry, one drawer, 29 in. high. A-120.00

Stand, bedside, cherry, turned legs, two drawers, 29 in. high. A-155.00

Stand, bedside, country, one drawer, one-board top, birch with orig. dark red paint, 27¾ in. high. A-400.00

Stand, bedside, country Hepplewhite, cherry, one cockbeaded drawer. A-165.00

Stand, bedside, pine, one drawer, turned legs, 28½ in. high. A-45.00

Stand, bedside, pine and poplar, turned legs, 31 in. high. A-120.00

Stand, cherry, turned legs, one drawer, refinished, 29 in. high. A-170.00

Stand, circular walnut, round shelf on base, 25½ in. high. A-65.00

Stand, birch, country Hepplewhite, one drawer, 28¾ in. high. A-150.00

Stand, cherry, country Hepplewhite, dovetailed drawer, 25 in. high. A-200.00

Stand, country Hepplewhite, pine, tapered hardwood legs, 25½ in. high. A-115.00

Stand, country Hepplewhite, one drawer, unpainted maple and birch. A-175.00

FURNITURE—*Tables*

Banquet, Sheraton, three-part, set; turned and rope-carved legs, flame veneer aprons and solid cherry tops. Extends to 130 in., 43¾ in. wide, 30 in. high. A-750.00

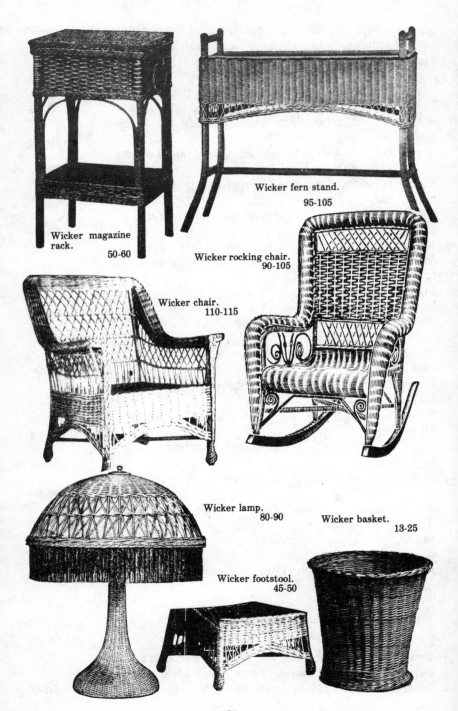

Wicker magazine rack.
50-60

Wicker fern stand.
95-105

Wicker rocking chair.
90-105

Wicker chair.
110-115

Wicker lamp.
80-90

Wicker basket.
13-25

Wicker footstool.
45-50

Breakfast, drop-leaf, cherry, American Sheraton style, 46 x 52 (extended) x 28 in. high. — A-300.00

Card, country; square tapered legs, old red paint, 32 (open) x 36½ x 28½ in. high. — A-425.00

Card, country Hepplewhite, square tapered legs with bowed front and conforming top, dovetailed drawer. Old red and black graining in good condition, 28½ in. high. — A-1,700.00

Center, turtle-shape, Victorian mahogany, rectangular mottled marble top. Ca. 1855, 31 in. high. — A-250.00

Center, Pennsylvania, walnut, oblong top above two drawers raised on turned, tapered legs. Table 35 x 56½ x 30 in. high. — A-475.00

Clerk's, pine, turned legs and dovetailed drawer, 34½ in. high. — A-115.00

Country Hepplewhite, pine, one-drawer and one-board top, 17½ x 25½ x 28¼ in. high. — A-260.00

Dish tip-top, tea, George III, mahogany, circular top. Ca. 1800, 27 in. high. — A-275.00

Dressing, country Hepplewhite, pine and poplar; square tapering legs, 28½ in. high. — A-110.00

Dining, Federal mahogany drop-leaf, rectangular top flanked by rounded drop-leaves, 42 x 53 x 29 in. high. — A-220.00

Eight-leg, New England, maple, drop-leaf top of later period, ca. 1740, 25 in. high. — A-275.00

Game, fold-top, American Hepplewhite, mahogany, with shaped top and apron with satinwood line inlay. Ca. 1810, 29 in. high. — A-525.00

Harvest, pine, Pennsylvania, rectangular top with drop-leaves raised on square tapered legs. Ca. 1830, 29 in. high. — A-450.00

Hepplewhite Pembroke, birch, top with oval cut-out corners. Replaced dovetailed drawer, 29 in. high. — A-150.00

Hutch, pine and birch, mortised construction, one dovetailed drawer and shelf under seat. Table 33 x 36 x 28½ in. high. — A-510.00 '

Hutch, round-top, birch, maple and pine. Turned legs, mortised stretcher base, three-board pine top, traces of old red paint; 48 in. diameter, 27½ in. high. — A-675.00

Hutch, pine, round top, mortised and pinned construction in base. Refinished, good color, 48 in. diameter, 28 in. high. — A-875.00

Upper right, **Queen Anne walnut dining table,** 27½ in. high, and ca. 1740.

A/625

Above left. American furniture: **William and Mary white oak hutch table.** Piece 57 in. wide, 30½ in deep, 30 in. high. Poss. Rhode Island, and ca. 1700-20.   A/700

Photos courtesy Adam A. Weschler & Son, Washington, D.C.; photograph by Breger & Associates.

Above right, **stand,** bedside, poplar stained as cherry, one-drawer, all walnut, 33 in. high.

C/100-150

Lower right, **washstand,** bedside, one-drawer, all walnut, 33 in. high.   C/195-235

Photos courtesy Judy Morehead, Creative Photography, Lancaster, Ohio.

Upper left, **Philadelphia Federal carved mahogany card table**, "D"-shape top which folds and pivots above apron with applied bronze and satin-wood inlay panel. Piece 35 in. wide, 17½ in. deep, 29½ in high. Ca. 1810.   A/550

Right, **Sheraton mahogany tip-top candlestand**, 28½ in. high, top down. Ca. 1810.   A/230

Lower left, **American Sheraton mahogany corner wash stand**, 33½ in. high, ca. 1820.   A/450

Lower right, **table**, American Salem mahogany and stain-wood Pembroke, 28 in. high and ca. 1820.   A/550

Photos courtesy Adam A. Weschler & Son

Chippendale mahogany fold-top game table, 33 in. wide, 16 in. deep, 28½ in. high. Shaped top above apron with one thumb-molded edge frieze drawer, pierced bail handle, raised on cabriole legs ending in distinctive claw and ball feet. Ca. 1760.   A/900

Courtesy Adam A. Weschler & Son

Right, **Oak round table.**
                    350-400

Lower left, **Oak round table.**
                    450-550

Lower right, **Oak library table.**
                    150-195

Lamp and smoker, walnut, with marble top, 32 in. high. — D-145.00

Occasional, rectangular top, 30 in. high. — A-47.50

Pier, formal, Empire, carved gilded paw and leaf feet. Figured mahogany veneer or pine with white marble pillars, white marble top delicately figured with black, 20 x 42 x 37½ inches high. — A-1,300.00

Pembroke, cherry, 18½ x 35 x 26¾ in. high. — A-145.00

Sawbuck, oak, square legs with chamfered upper corners. Old finish, 17½ x 36 x 27 in. high. — A-180.00

Side, American Hepplewhite, mahogany, ca. 1815, 27 in. high. — A-120.00

Side, commode, Hepplewhite, mahogany, 19th Century, 32 in. high. — A-350.00

Six-leg, drop-leaf, country Hepplewhite, cherry; square tapering legs, single-board top and leaves, refinished, 28¾ in. high. — A-350.00

Splay-leg, country Hepplewhite, one dovetailed drawer and replaced birdseye maple top, 25 x 28 x 30 in. high. — A-300.00

Swing-leg, Hepplewhite, mahogany; square tapered legs, 28½ in. high. — A-425.00

Table, dressing, Empire, mahogany and cherry, turned legs, ogee dovetailed drawers in base, 35½ in. high. — A-250.00

Table, drop-leaf, birch, well-turned legs, figured wood, 28½ in. high. — A-140.00

Table, drop-leaf, turned legs, wide boards, 29 in. high. — A-110.00

Table, drop-leaf, mahogany, one dovetailed drawer, 28¾ in. high. — A-170.00

Table, Chippendale walnut eight-leg drop-leaf, square legs, plain apron, two sets of swing legs. With birch and ash, 27¾ in. high. — A-425.00

Table, cherry drop-leaf with square tapered curly maple legs, refinished in good color. 18 (with 11-in. leaves) x 45 x 27½ in. high. — A-625.00

Table, country drop-leaf, poplar with old red paint, 27½ in. high. — A-105.00

Table, country Queen Anne swing-leg drop-leaf, cabriole legs with narrow ankles, maple. Orig. dark brown paint on base, unpainted top 14¾ (unextended) x 48 x 27 in. high. — A-1,500.00

Table, drop-leaf, walnut, refinished, 29 in. high. — **A-115.00**

Table, country Hepplewhite drop-leaf, maple with some curl in top, 26¾ in. high. — **A-200.00**

Table, drum, walnut top with two concealed drawers, 27 in. high. — **A-100.00**

Tavern, country Queen Anne, turned maple legs with pine aprons and pine two-board top. Refinished, with traces of brown paint. Table 25 x 36 x 25½ in. high. — **A-775.00**

Tavern, country Queen Anne, sturdy, pine, and poplar legs. Splayed legs terminate in duck feet, wide apron with one-board removeable top. Old finish, 23½ x 34¾ x 30 in. high. — **A-975.00**

Tavern, pine, folding base and removeable octagonal three-board top. Table 27½ x 41½ x 26¼ in. high. — **A-240.00**

Tavern, splay-leg country Queen Anne, birch base, breadboard top, dovetailed drawer, 28½ in. high. — **A-600.00**

Tavern, splay-leg, turned legs, mortised and pinned stretcher and apron. One-board top is old replacement, 24 in. high. — **A-610.00**

Tavern, oval-top, maple base with turned legs and mortised stretcher. One-board pine top has old split, old refinishing, 20½ x 29 x 24 in. high. — **A-1,100.00**

Tavern, Queen Anne country style, turned legs, stretcher base, good replaced feet, oval pine one-board top. Table 32 in. high. — **A-1,050.00**

Tea, tip-top pie-crust Chippendale, mahogany, circular top on boxed and fluted standard, acanthus leaf knees ending in egg and claw feet. Ca. 1780, 28½ in. high. — **A-1,500.00**

Tea, New England tilt-top, cherry and pine, round top. Ca. 1800, 24 in. diameter, 27 in. high. — **A-350.00**

Tea, tip-top, Queen Anne, cherry, circular three-board top raised on turned and baluster standard. Late 18th Century, 27 in. high. — **A-375.00**

Tea, Queen Anne, mahogany, small size with well-proportioned cabriole legs with duck feet. Oval top replaced, 24½ in. high. — **A-475.00**

Walnut table, turned legs, one drawer, refinished, 29 in. high. — **A-90.00**

Work, one-drawer, turned legs with mortised stretcher, dovetailed overlapping drawer with orig. wooden knob. One-board pine top, old black paint with orig. red underneath, 26½ x 48½ x 26¾ in. high.   **A-2,200.00**

Work, square tapered legs with braces to apron, one dovetailed drawer, two-board pine top, 34 x 46½ x 29 in. high.   **A-270.00**

Work, two-drawer, simple turned legs, removeable top, dark finish, 32½ x 40 x 29 in. high.   **A-250.00**

Work, turned legs, dovetailed drawer, two-board curly maple top. Orig old red paint, replaced largest top board, 27 x 43½ x 28 in. high.   **A-595.00**

Work, American Hepplewhite, walnut, ca. 1800, 29½ in. high.   **A-170.00**

Work, American Sheraton, pine, ca. 1840, 30 in. high.   **A-120.00**

Work, Federal, walnut, 14 x 15 x 30 in. high.   **A-275.00**

Work, country Hepplewhite, square tapered legs, dovetailed overlapping drawer, pine two-board breadboard top. Birch base, 31½ x 43¼ x 27¾ inches.   **A-390.00**

Work, New England Sheraton, mahogany and maple, ca. 1840, 29 in. high.   **A-130.00**

Work, pine, one dovetailed drawer, refinished, 30¼ in. high.   **A-255.00**

Work, Sheraton, walnut, two drawers, ca. 1840, 29 in. high.   **A-280.00**

GLASS—*Cambridge*

Apple Blossom Amber comport, 7 in. high.   **D-25.00**

Caprice Clear four-footed bowl, ruffled, 5¼ x 12 inches.   **D-12.00**

Caprice Clear three-part relish, black sticker, 7½ inches.   **D-12.00**

Caprice Pink four-footed bowl, 11 inches.   **D-29.00**

Caprice Blue handled bowl, footed, 7½ inches.   **D-12.00**

Caprice Blue torte plate, 14 inches.   **D-15.00**

Chintz Clear sandwich server, center handle.   **D-9.50**

Crown Tuscan three-part dish, gold trim, 8 inches.   **D-24.00**

Decagon Amber bowl, open, handled, 10 inches.   **D-5.50**

Farber Chrome Amber decanter, clear stopper, 12 inches.   **D-19.00**

Farber Chrome Amethyst shaker, handled, 2¾ inches. **D-3.00**

Farber Chrome Cobalt basket dish, handled, 5-3/8 inches. **D-12.00**

Farber Chrome Forest Green creamer/covered dish. **D-14.00**

Honeycomb Amber compote, 5-1/8 x 7 inches. **D-18.00**

Lightning Ebony creamer/sugar, footed. **D-11.00**

Martha Washington Clear candy and lid, inner rim flake. **D-7.50**

Number 933 cup, pink, #520 etch. **D-3.75**

Number 3130 Shape tall sherbet, #731 etch. **D-4.00**

Number 3400 Line tilt jug, ebony, ice lip. **D-40.00**

Rosepoint tumbler, footed, 7 inches. **D-20.00**

Round Shape (signed) plate, amber, 8 inches. **D-3.00**

Square Scalloped Shape butter bottom, pink, handled. **D-11**

Rosepoint tumbler, footed, 7 inches. **D-20.00**

Round Shape (signed) plate, amber, 8 inches. **D-3.00**

Square Scalloped Shape butter bottom, pink, handled. **D-11.00**

GLASS—*Carnival*

Amethyst and Purple

Acorn flat dish, 7½ inches.	**D-27.50**
Age Herald plate, 9½ inches.	**D-1,225.00**
Beaded Cable Rose Bowl.	**D-100.00**
Captive Rose flared bowl, 9 inches.	**D-50.00**
Coin Spot ribbon-edge bowl, 7¾ inches.	**D-27.50**
Daisy and Drape three-footed vase, 6½ inches.	**D-175.00**
Feathered Serpent flared bowl, 10 inches.	**D-60.00**
Field Flowers water set, seven pieces.	**D-1,000.00**
G. & C. Berry set, seven pieces.	**D-550.00**
G. & C. Powder jar, chip on lid.	**D-150.00**
G. & C. Sweetmeat with lid.	**D-200.00**
G. & C. Perfume bottle.	**D-500.00**
Heavy Grape chop plate, 11½ inches.	**D-500.00**
Leaf and Beads rose bowl, three-footed.	**D-100.00**
Maple Leaf ice cream set, seven pieces.	**D-375.00**
Oriental Poppy water set, seven pieces.	**D-1,300.00**
Peacock Lamp, complete.	**D-350.00**
Question Mark stemmed bonbon.	**D-32.50**
Single Flower candy dish.	**D-25.00**

Three Fruits plate (Millersburg), 9½ inches.	**D-175.00**
Windflower bowl, 8½ inches.	**D-50.00**

Aqua

Fine rib vase, 9½ inches.	**D-35.00**
Holly Carnival bowl, 8¾ inches.	**D-75.00**

Aqua Opalescent

Beaded Cable rose bowl.	**D-150.00**
Fine-cut and Roses candy dish.	**D-150.00**
Hearts and Flowers compote, 6 x 6 inches.	**D-200.00**
Rose Show bowl, 8¾ inches.	**D-300.00**
Three Fruits bowl, 8¾ inches.	**D-175.00**

Blue

Blackberry Spray hat shape, 6 inches.	**D-37.50**
Good Luck bowl, tiny chip, 8½ inches.	**D-125.00**
Holly Carnival ruffled bowl, 9 inches.	**D-65.00**
Horse Medallian footed bowl, 7½ inches.	**D-125.00**
Rambling Rose water set, seven pieces.	**D-700.00**
Two Fruits divided bonbon, 8 inches.	**D-85.00**

Clambroth/Off White

Frosty Block plate, 9½ inches.	**D-50.00**
Luster and Clear sherbet set, six pieces.	**D-50.00**
Open Rose bowl, 8 inches.	**D-20.00**
Scroll Embossed bowl, 7¾ inches.	**D-60.00**

Cranberry

Shriners St. Paul goblet, 1908.	**D-160.00**

Green

Coin Dot rose bowl, 5¼ inches.	**D-38.50**
Diamond Ribbed vase, 11 inches.	**D-25.00**
G. & C. stemmed ice cream dish, 4½ inches.	**D-36.50**
Hollywhirl bowl (Millersburg), 9½ inches.	**D-47.50**
Little Barrel, 3¾ in. high.	**D-80.00**

Ruffled Ribs pastel bowl, 9½ inches.   D-35.00
Singing Birds water set, seven pieces.   D-650.00
Sunflower bowl, heat line, 8½ inches.   D-65.00
Two Flowers footed bowl, 7½ inches.   D-60.00

Ice Blue

Concave Diamond tumbler.   D-45.00
Double Dolphin fan-shaped vase.   D-125.00
Grape Arbor tanker pitcher.   D-1,000.00
G. & C. orange bowl, footed, 11 inches.   D-450.00

Ice Green

Acorn Burr punch set, eight pieces.   D-2,300.00
G. & C. three-footed bowl, 8¾ inches.   D-190.00
Peacock on Fence plate, 9 inches.   D-250.00

Lavendar

Millersburg Courthouse.   D-600.00
Stippled Ray flared dish, 6 inches.   D-30.00

Peach Opalescent

Bells and Beads low bowl, 7 inches.   D-40.00
Dragon and Lotus bowl, 8¾ inches.   D-125.00
Fanciful ruffled plate, 8½ inches.   D-80.00
Folded Fan stemmed compote.   D-65.00
Question Mark compote, 3 x 6½ inches.   D-50.00
Six Petals bowl, 8 inches.   D-40.00
Ski Star flared bowl, 11 inches.   D-90.00

Pearl

Grape and Gothic Arches table set, four pieces.   D-1,500.00
Grape and Gothic Arches sugar and lid.   D-375.00
G. & C. punch bowl base, only.   D-250.00

Pink

Brocaded Palms center bowl, 12 inches.   D-125.00
Swan master salt.   D-30.00
Winged heavy shell, rare.   D-200.00

Shriners

1908 St. Paul, cranberry, chip.   D-95.00
1909 Louisville, KY, white.   D-175.00
1910 New Orleans, LA, white   D-175.00

Smokey

Floral and Optic three-footed bowl, 9 inches.   D-25.00
Melon Rib relish dish, 8½ inches.   D-35.00
Wide Panels collar-based bowl, 9½ inches.   D-35.00
Imperial Jewel basket, 10½ in. high.   D-90.00

White

Appleblossom Twig bowl, 8¾ inches.   D-125.00
Brocaded Palms bonbon, 7 inches.   D-85.00
Cherry Circles flared bowl, 10½ inches.   D-125.00
Garden Path varient bowl, 10 inches.   D-195.00
Imperial Jewel pedestal-based bowl, 10 inches.   D-75.00
Lined Lattice vase, 9½ inches.   D-65.00
Orange Tree punch set, eight pieces.   D-550.00
Palm Beach butter dish and cover.   D-450.00
Peacock at Fountain spooner.   D-150.00
Seaweed and Constellation compote.   D-90.00
Strawberry flared bowl, 10 inches.   D-150.00
Wishbone footed flared bowl, 8½ inches.   D-125.00

GLASS—*Crystal*

Centerpiece, inscribed "Steuben", round body raised on four scrolling feet, 10½ in. diameter.   A-100.00
Champagne flutes, set of ten; signed "Baccarat",
9¼ in. high.   A-210.00
Decanter, French, molded; multi-lobed long neck
continuing to bulbous body. Signed "W. Fritche", 12
in. high.   A-125.00
Decanter, Dutch, inscribed "Belegevan", with
silver, 11 in. high.   A-85.00
Goblets, set of ten; inscribed in monogram, "S" for
Steuben, tear-drop stems, 8¼ in. high.   A-270.00
Spoon holder, 6 in. high.   A-38.00
Supremes, silver-banded, with liners, set of twelve.   A-70.00
Vase, tapered, Steuben, 7 in. high.   A-80.00

GLASS—*Cut Crystal*

Bowl, monogrammed Taylor Brothers Co., Inc., Philadelphia, in daisy and butterfly pattern, 8 in. diameter.   **A-100.00**

Bowl, 3½ in. high, 8 in. diameter.   **A-90.00**

Bowl, deep, 4 in. high, 9 in. diameter.   **A-130.00**

Bowl, 3½ in. high, 8 in. diameter.   **A-120.00**

Candelabras, European, pair; 20th Century, 19 in. high.   **A-200.00**

Above photo, left and right, pair of **crystal covered urns,** 17 in. high. Waterford, 19th Century.

(pair) A/240

Center, pair of **cut crystal three-light candelabra,** 22 in. high. Waterford, mid-19th Century.

A/525

Cut glass. Courtesy Adam A. Weschler & Son

Knife rest, 5½ in. long.   C/60-75

Toothpick holder.   C/35-40

Shakers, pair.   C/30-40

Carafe, 10 in. high.   **A-80.00**

Carafe, water, pinwheel and pineapple design on rayed base, 7½ in. high.   **A-50.00**

Centerpiece, European, on trifid scroll feet, 12 in. diameter.   **A-50.00**

Decanters, pair; panel-cut club-form, double ring neck and hexagonal stopper, 10 in. high.   **A-70.00**

Dish, celery; leaf monogram, Maple City Glass Co., Honesdale, Penn., 12 in. long.   **A-100.00**

Dish, ice cream; pineapple and scalloped edge centering starburst bottom, 14½ in. long.   **A-110.00**

Dish, relish; 11½ in. long.   **D-80.00**

Dish, sweetmeat; four-compartment, two-handled.   **A-110.00**

Lamp, table; converted from covered jam jar, overall 19½ in. high.   **A-125.00**

Left, **cut crystal bowl**, prob. Libbey, 9 in. diameter, 4½ in. high. A/425

Bot center, **American cut crystal squat vase**, 8 in. high. A/325

Top center, **American cut crystal trumpet-shape vase**. Signed "Hawkes", 11½ in. high. A/130

Right, **American cut crystal deep bowl**. Signed, "Libbey", 9½ in. diameter. A/140

Courtesy Adam A. Weschler & Son

Pitcher, 11 in. high.	S-125.00
Pitcher, water; stenciled "Libbey", 13 in. high.	A-220.00
Pitcher and four tumblers, pitcher 9 in. high.	A-125.00
Serving pieces, two; round shallow dish and plate, diameters 8 and 7 inches, respectively.	A-70.00
Vase, fluted body, stenciled "Libbey", 9½ in. high.	A-80.00
Vase, American, 14 in. high.	A-90.00
Vase, flared foliate-shape, 16 in. high.	A-230.00
Vase, long-neck, daisy and leaf cut body, 14 in. high.	A-35.00
Vase, ribbed body with slant base and flared top, 15 in. high.	A-80.00
Vase, trumpet-shaped, 14 in. high.	A-80.00

GLASS—*Etched Crystal*

Candlesticks, European, pair; baluster form on round pinwheel bases, etched designs, 10 in. high.	A-70.00
Compote, grape and vine pattern on round base, 5 in. high, 10 in. diameter.	A-80.00
Lemonade set, seven-piece; covered pitcher and six matching tumblers with handles having engraved florals, pitcher 10 in. high.	A-110.00
Vase, with German silver, late 19th Century, 20 in. high.	A-150.00

GLASS—Depression

Adam Green footed tumbler,base rim flake.	D-3.50
Adam Pink candy and lid.	D-25.00
Akro Octagonal Opaque plate, green, 4½ inches.	D-2.50
Akro Concentric Ring Opaque cup, green.	D-2.00
Akro Stacked Disc Opaque creamer, white, 1¼ inches.	D-2.50
American Sweetheart Monax plate, 8 inches.	D-3.00
American Sweetheart Pink salver, 12 inches.	D-4.50
Anniversary Clear butter top.	D-11.00
Ashtray scuttle, green, 3 inches.	D-2.75
Bamboo Optic (Liberty) creamer, green.	D-1.00
Black Amethyst bowl vase, 4 x 6¼ inches.	D-12.00
Block Clear pitcher, 6½ inches.	D-3.40
Block Green creamer, straight.	D-2.75
Block Pink tumbler, 3-7/8 inches.	D-3.50
Block Topaz cup.	D-2.50
Bowknot Green flat tumbler, 5 inches.	D-4.00
Bubble Blue cup and saucer.	D-2.50
Bubble Clear sugar.	D-2.00
Cameo Green pitcher, 6 inches.	D-23.00
Candlewick Clear hollow stem sherbet, 4½ inches.	D-2.75
Charade Pink bowl, 11 inches.	D-8.00
Cherryberry strawberry compote, pink, 5½ inches.	D-7.00
Cherry Delfite handled bowl, 9 inches.	D-10.00
Chinex Classic floral plate, 6¼ inches.	D-1.75
Circle goblet, green, 6 inches.	D-4.50
Cloverleaf candy bottom, green.	D-10.00
Colonial Clear butter and lid.	D-20.00
Colonial Green whiskey, 1½ oz., 2½ inches.	D-5.00
Columbia Clear plate, 9 inches.	D-2.00
Corded Optic tumbler, green, 5 inches.	D-3.25
Coronation Ruby bowl, 8 inches.	D-6.00
Crowsfoot cream soup, ruby.	D-7.00
Cubist Clear handled tray, 7½ inches.	D-2.00
Cubist Pink creamer/sugar, 2 inches.	D-3.00
Daisy three-part relish, clear, 7 inches.	D-1.75
Diamond Quilted Pink bowl, 5½ inches.	D-1.50
Diana demi-cup and saucer, clear.	D-3.00
Doric Pink plate, 9 inches.	D-3.50
Duncan Miller Carribbean cheese and cracker insert.	D-7.50

Depression ware, sherbet, rare
pattern, Roxana-yellow.
C/7-10

Depression ware.
Salt and pepper, matched, 6 in. high.
"Poinsetta", pink, by Jeanette Glass Company.
Pair: C/25-35

Depression ware.
Above left, mixing cup with missing top, green
Depware.   C/6-9
Above right, measuring cup, green Depware.
C/7-10
Lower right, Depression ware covered butter
dish, Madrid-amber, mint condition.   C/35-45

Cookie-jar, Depression ware,
Patrician pattern, amber, perfect
condition.   C/40-55

Doric and Pansy handled sandwich.	D-4.75
English Hobnail Clear footed creamer, 4 inches.	D-4.25
Fiesta eggcup, turquoise.	D-12.00
Fiesta coffeepot, cobalt, without lid.	D-20.00
Feather Cobalt tumbler.	D-5.00
Federal wheelcut vase, clear, 6¾ inches.	D-3.00
Fine Ribbed Clear ice-lip pitcher, 80 oz.	D-9.00
Fireking Carnival swirled bowl, 8 inches.	D-1.80
Fireking Custard three-part children's dish.	D-5.00
Fireking Plain Jadeite mixing bowl, 7¾ inches.	D-2.00
Fireking Madonna Blue handled casserole stand, 8¼ in.	D-5.00
Fireking White pheasant bowl, 5 inches.	D-.75
Flaners Pink goblet, 7 inches.	D-12.00
Floragold tray, no indent, 13½ inches.	D-7.00
Floral Sterling shaker.	D-7.00
Florentine #1 Clear Creamer.	D-3.00
Florentine #2 footed cocktail, clear, 3½ inches.	D-3.50
Forest Green ice-lip pitcher, 7¾ inches.	D-12.00
Fostoria American olive, 8½ inches.	D-3.50
Fostoria Baroque Clear cnadlesticks, pair, 4 inches.	D-11.00
Fostoria Beverly Amber plate, 8-5/8 inches.	D-3.00
Fostoria Fairfax footed sugar, ebony.	D-3.50
Fostoria Heirloom Vaseline bowl, 6 x 10 inches.	D-25.00
Fostoria Mayfair plate, green, 8 inches.	D-2.50
Fostoria #766 Optic goblet, green, 6½ inches.	D-5.00
Fostoria #2329 Rose centerpiece, 13½ inches.	D-14.00
Fostoria Seville Amber plate, 8½ inches.	D-3.25
Fostoria Versaille Pink footed tumbler.	D-16.00
Frigidaire Frosted Green ice bucket, block pattern.	D-4.00
Georgian Line W215 Ruby tumbler, 4¾ inches.	D-3.50
Georgian Lovebirds Green plate, 8 inches.	D-2.00
Grape (Standard) W46 Clear tumbler, 3-7/8 inches.	D-2.00
Harlequin casserole and lid, yellow.	D-10.00
Harlequin platter, gray, 11 inches.	D-4.00
Hazel Atlas Clear punch bowl and plastic ladle.	D-8.00
Hazel Atlas Green crimped vase, 6¾ inches.	D-3.50
Hazel Atlas White vase, crimped top, 6¾ inches.	D-3.00
Hobnail Clear cologne bottle, ground stopper.	D-9.50
Hocking Prescut sugar, clear with ruby lid.	D-3.00
Homespun Pink plate, 6 inches.	D-1.25
Honeycomb Green tankard pitcher, 8-3/8 inches.	D-13.00
Imperial Optic Rib Iridescent bowl, 7¾ inches.	D-3.00
Iris Clear ruffled bowl, 12 inches.	D-4.00

Lancaster plate, openwork pansy etch, 9 inches.   **D-3.75**
Laurel McKee W238 French Ivory cup.   **D-4.75**
Lenox Clear goblet, 6½ inches.   **D-3.00**
Lorain Clear cup.   **D-2.00**
MacBeth-Evans Clear MacHob tumbler, 5 oz. juice.   **D-2.50**
Madrid Amber platter.   **D-4.30**
Madrid Sunburst console bowl, 11 inches.   **D-8.00**
Manhattan handled plate, clear, 14 inches.   **D-2.00**
Mayfair Clear pitcher, 6 inches.   **D-6.50**
Miss America Clear 12-oz. chopper top.   **D-1.00**
Moderntone creamer/sugar.   **D-5.50**
Molly (Imperial) handled bowl, green, 5 inches.   **D-6.50**
Moondrops metal-stem goblet, ruby, 5¼ inches.   **D-7.00**
Mt. Pleasant handled plate, black, 7 inches.   **D-7.00**
New Century (Ovide) console bowl, pink, 13 inches.   **D-5.50**
New Martinsville creamer, cobalt, scalloped, footed.   **D-7.00**
Newport cream soup, burgandy.   **D-4.50**
Normandie Sunburst bowl, 8½ inches.   **D-6.00**
Old Cafe mint tray, ruby.   **D-4.75**
Oyster and Pearl console bowl, clear, 10½ inches.   **D-6.00**
Patrician Amber sugar and lid.   **D-15.00**
Penny goblet, ruby, 4-5/8 inches.   **D-6.00**
Petalware monax cup and saucer, gold trim.   **D-4.00**
Pineapple and Floral sugar, amber.   **D-3.50**
Pretzel creamer/sugar.   **D-4.75**
Princess frosted butter bottom, pink.   **D-4.50**
Ring Clear decanter and stopper, red stripes.   **D-7.00**
Ring Green flat tumbler, 5 inches.   **D-2.40**
Rock Crystal footed goblet, clear, 6¾ inches.   **D-8.50**
Riviera sugar, yellow.   **D-2.30**
Rosemark plate, pink, 9½ inches.   **D-2.80**
Royal Lace saucer, green.   **D-2.90**
Royal Ruby Coolidge vase, 6-3/8 inches.   **D-2.50**
"S" Pattern flat tumbler, clear, 4¾ inches.   **D-3.50**
Sandwich Hocking Clear oval bowl, 8¼ inches.   **D-3.25**
Sandwich Indiana plate, clear, 10½ inches.   **D-4.50**
Seneca Clear tumbler, black foot, 4¼ inches.   **D-2.80**
Sharon bowl, amber, 8½ inches.   **D-2.50**
Shell Pink oval footed bowl, 10 inches.   **D-12.00**
Sierra Green bowl, point chip, 8 inches.   **D-2.50**
L.E. Smith Black vase, silver decoration, 8½ inches.   **D-12.00**
L.E. Smith Blue oval dish, four-footed, 4 x 6 inches.   **D-5.00**
Spindle (MacBeth-Evans) Clear pitcher.   **D-4.25**
Spiray plate, green, 8 inches.   **D-1.25**

Spiral Block tumbler, olive, 5 inches.   **D-1.00**
Sportsman Series Blue Foxhunt cocktail shaker and
top.   **D-11.00**
Sunflower Pink tumbler, footed.   **D-5.00**
Swirl Pink creamer/sugar set.   **D-7.00**
Swirl Ultra plate, rim bubble, 12¾ inches.   **D-5.00**
Sylvan Green butter bottom.   **D-21.00**
Teardrops Clear nut dish, two-part.   **D-4.50**
Tearoom heavy sugar, pink.   **D-3.75**
Tendril Green plate, 8¼ inches.   **D-1.80**
Twisted Optic bowl, green, 9 inches.   **D-3.50**

Above left, **Vinegars,** left and right, mint condition.   Each: C/10-15
Mustard container, glass dispenser, individual size, pressed glass.   C/6-10

Above right, **salt,** individual, clear pressed glass, 1½ in. long.   C/5-8

Left, **Rose bowl,** pressed glass, clear, 6 in. high.
    C/15-25

Left, **Celery dish,** clear pressed glass.
    C/12-18

Glass—*Early American Pattern*

Actress cheese cover	D-50.00
Almond Thumbprint wine glass	D-11.00
Amazon champagne glass	D-21.00
Arched Ovals water pitcher, 11 in.	D-19.00
Argus spill, flint	D-42.50
Ashburton double egg cup	D-115.00
Atlas jelly compote, 4¼ x 4¼ in.	D-14.50
Aurora tray, etched. 10 in.	D-15.00
Automobile vase, yellow	D-15.00
Baby Thumbprint champagne, flint	D-70.00
Balder pitcher, 9½ in.	D-35.00
Ball and Swirl Band footed sauce	D-5.00
Banded Buckle egg cup	D-21.50
Barberry goblet	D-18.00
Barley relish, 5 x 9½ in.	D-9.00
Barred Ovals flat-base celery	D-14.00
Beaded Grape Medallion goblet	D-17.50
Beaded Swirl creamer, three-footed	D-15.00
Beatty Rib sauce, opal, 4½ in.	D-14.00
Bellflower open sugar, flint	D-25.00
Bent Buckle mug, gilt trim	D-11.00
Bigler goblet, flint	D-30.00
Bird at Fountain goblet	D-35.00
Bird and Strawberry oval bowl	D-12.50
Birds and Roses etched goblet	D-19.50
Bleeding Heart sauce, 4 in.	D-12.00
Block and Fan celery	D-16.00
Bradford Blackberry tumbler, flint	D-85.00
Broken Column carafe, column chip	D-26.00
Bridle Rosettes wineglass	D-7.00
Bulls-Eye and Daisy goblet, green eye	D-17.00
Bulls-Eye and Fan creamer, 3½ in.	D-7.50
Button Arches salt and pepper, souvenir, ruby-stained	D-17.50
Cane toddy plate, tiny imperfection	D-8.00
Cardinal Bird covered sugar, small chip	D-25.00
Cathedral wineglass, blue	D-39.50
Centennial goblet	D-35.00
Chain goblet	D-18.00
Chain and Shield goblet, base nick	D-7.00
Champion punch cup	D-5.00

Checkerboard creamer, 4 in.	D-9.50
Clematis goblet	D-22.00
Clear Ribbon footed butter base	D-6.00
Colonial goblet, flint	D-45.00
Colorado sauce, green, gilt trim, 4½ in.	D-12.50
Comet bar tumbler, flint	D-75.00
Crossed Disks creamer, etched	D-12.00
Crowsfoot sauce, 5½ in.	D-6.50
Cube Square Stem goblet, etched	D-14.50
Cupid and Venus compote, low standard, 8 in.	D-14.50
Cut Log compote, 5¼ x 7 in.	D-16.00
Cut and Panels goblet	D-21.50
D & B with Almond Band goblet	D-11.00
D & M #42 Creamer	D-10.00
Dahlia goblet, etched	D-11.00
Dakota footed sauce, 3½ in.	D-11.00
Deer and Dog square bowl goblet	D-49.50
Deer and Pine tree goblet	D-30.00
Delaware octagonal bowl, gilt trim, 9 in.	D-24.50
Dew and Raindrop creamer, 4 in.	D-25.00
Dewdrops and Flowers sauce, 4¼ in.	D-4.50
Dewey covered butter, two nicks, yellow	D-22.00
Diagonal Band with Fan champagne	D-17.00
Diagnoal Medallion covered butter	D-19.50
Diagonal Quilted footed sauce, 4½ in.	D-8.00
Diagonal Sawtooth Band wineglass	D-20.00
Diamond Point goblet, flint	D-39.50
Diamond Thumbprint honey, flint	D-12.00
Dickinson goblet, flint	D-24.00
Draped Red Block bowl, 7 in.	D-12.00
Drapery open sugar	D-14.00
Duncan Block egg cup	D-24.50
Egg in Sand goblet, base nick	D-19.00
Egyptian compote with Sphinx, 5¼ in.	D-59.50
Eugenie goblet, flint, tiny imperfection	D-29.50
Excelsior pint bar bottle, flint	D-34.50
Eyewinker salt shaker	D-18.00
Feather covered sugar	D-27.50
Fernland miniature creamer	D-7.00
Festoon water tray, 10 in.	D-18.00
Fickle Block wineglass, gilt trim	D-6.00
Fishscale plate, 8 in.	D-18.00
Flamingo Habitat egg cup	D-22.00
Fleur-de-Lis and Drape tray, 11½ in.	D-17.50

Fluted Icicle goblet, flint	D-25.00
Row Honeycomb footed tumbler, flint	D-12.50
Frosted Leaf spooner, flint	D-65.00
Frosted Ribbon goblet	D-12.50
Frosted Roman Key open sugar, flint	D-22.50
Galloway covered sugar	D-19.50
Gothic open sugar, flint	D-22.50
Girl with Fan goblet	D-37.50
Grape and Festoon egg cup	D-17.00
Grasshopper flared bowl, 10 in.	D-12.00
Hamilton egg cup, flint	D-28.00
Hairpin bowl, flint, 7½ in.	D-12.50
Hartley footed sauce, amber, 4 in.	D-12.00
Henry Clay cup plate, flint	D-14.00
Herringbone Band goblet	D-13.00
Herringbone goblet, green	D-29.50
Hickman punch cup	D-5.50
Hidalgo goblet, etched	D-13.00
Higbee master salt, footed	D-5.00
High Hob saucer	D-4.00
Hinoto goblet, flint	D-35.00
Hobnail mug, 3¼ in.	D-7.50
Honeycomb high standard compote, 7½ in.	D-10.00
Horn of Plenty spill, flint	D-37.50
Horsehead Medallion celery	D-27.50
Hotel Thumbprint goblet	D-12.00
Huber egg cup, flint	D-13.50
Hummingbird tumbler, amber	D-40.00
Iconoclast goblet, flint	D-37.50
Independence Hall champagne	D-27.50
Interlocking Hearts covered sugar	D-17.50
Jeweled Heart water pitcher	D-18.00
Kentucky sauce, blue, 4 in.	D-11.50
Kings Crown open sugar	D-11.00
Knight goblet	D-15.00
Knights of Labor mug	D-30.00
Kokomo salt shaker	D-9.50
Krom goblet, flint	D-35.00
Lacy Valance salt shaker, blue	D-17.00
Laminated Petals wineglass, flint	D-35.00
Lattice and Oval Panels honey 3¼ in.	D-9.00
Laverne water pitcher, applied handle	D-37.50
Liberty wineglass	D-10.00
Liberty Bell covered sugar, tiny imperf.	D-69.50

Lily of the Valley goblet	D-35.00
Lincoln Drape goblet, flint	D-57.50
Lion in Jungle goblet, etched	D-82.50
Lobular Loops goblet	D-12.00
Loganberry and Grape footed sauce	D-6.00
Loop wineglass	D-11.00
Loop and Dart egg cup	D-17.50
Loop and Moose Eye spooner, flint	D-19.50
Lotus relish, 5¼ x 9½ in.	D-11.00
Maidens Blush goblet	D-70.00
Marquisette goblet	D-18.00
Mascotte creamer, etched	D-26.50
Master Argus goblet, flint	D-45.00
Mellor creamer, 5½ in.	D-14.50
Melrose goblet	D-16.00
Michigan finger bowl	D-15.00
Minerva round plate, handled, 10 in.	D-57.50
Mioton goblet ruby-stained	D-20.00
Monkey Climber etched goblet	D-82.50
Moon and Star footed sauce, 4 in.	D-11.00
Nailhead plate, 9 in.	D-14.50
New York Honeycomb open sugar	D-9.50
Northeast Pineapple egg cub, flint	D-39.50
Oaken Bucket toothpick, blue, 2 in.	D-7.00
One-O-One plate, 7 in.	D-13.50
Opposing Pyramids wineglass	D-9.50
Oval and Fine Pleat goblet, flint	D-17.50
Oval Mitre open sugar, flint	D-17.50
Oval Panels goblet, amber	D-21.00
Overshot water pitcher, flint, 8 in.	D-79.50
Panelled Cane mug, cobalt, 2¼ in.	D-17.50
Panelled Fern creamer, handle check	D-17.50
Panelled Julep goblet	D-17.50
Panelled Nightshade goblet	D-20.00
Parrot goblet	D-25.00
Pathfinder tumbler	D-8.50
Pavonia tumbler, ruby-stained	D-26.50
Peacock Feather compote, low standard	D-13.50
Pecorah goblet	D-10.00
Peerless celery	D-14.50
Pillar and Bulls-Eye goblet, flint	D-45.00
Plain Sunburst goblet	D-13.00
Pleat and Panel footed sauce, 3½ in.	D-6.00
Pleating water pitcher, ruby-stained	D-65.00

Plume sauce, flint, 4 in.   **D-8.00**
Primrose sauce, blue, 4-7/8 in.   **D-7.00**
Prism goblet, flint   **D-17.50**
Prism & Block Band mug, etched, 3 in.   **D-12.50**
Prism and Sawtooth goblet, flint   **D-24.50**
Proxy Ashburton goblet, flint   **D-37.50**
Powder and Shot creamer   **D-95.00**
Princess Feather spooner   **D-17.50**
Pyramid Flute goblet, flint   **D-14.50**
Quantico goblet   **D-27.50**
Quihote celery   **D-15.00**
Rail Fence Band goblet   **D-12.50**
Recessed Ovals champagne   **D-18.00**
Red Block covered sugar, ex. fine   **D-59.50**
Red Riding Hood punch cup, milkglass   **D-21.50**
Reticulated Cord sauce, 4½ in.   **D-6.00**
Reverse 44 goblet, amethyst-stain   **D-18.50**
Reverse Torpedo pitcher, etched, 11½ in.   **D-38.00**
Ribbed Ivy bar tumbler, flint   **D-75.00**
Ribbed Leaves mug   **D-10.00**
Ribbed Palm goblet, flint   **D-28.00**
Richardson large salt shaker   **D-12.00**
Rose Sprig oval compote, amber   **D-35.00**
Rose in Snow plate, 7 in.   **D-12.00**
Rosette and Palm plate, 10 in.   **D-9.00**
Roanoke sauce, ruby-stained edge, 4¾ in.   **D-7.00**
Row Honeycomb goblet, flint   **D-11.50**
Royal Crystal sauce, ruby-stained, 4 in.   **D-16.50**
Ruby Thumbpoint toothpick, ruby-stained, etched   **D-25.00**
Sandwich Star quart bar bottle, flint   **D-60.00**
Sawtooth creamer, applied handle   **D-27.50**
Scalloped Diamond Point relish, cobalt   **D-20.00**
Sheaf of Wheat goblet   **D-26.50**
Shoshone cakestand, green, 8¾ in.   **D-22.50**
Shrine goblet   **D-32.00**
Shuttle punch cup   **D-6.00**
Slashed Swirl sauce, footed, 3¼ in.   **D-5.50**
Smocking creamer, small, flint   **D-85.00**
Snail banana stand   **D-75.00**
Spearpoint jelly compote, 4 x 4¼ in.   **D-12.00**
Spirea Band compote, low standard, 7½ in.   **D-18.00**
Squirrel sauce, 4½ in.   **D-14.50**
Star Rosetted relish, 5 x 9½ in.   **D-6.00**
Stars and Stripes wineglass   **D-9.50**

Stedman goblet, flint	D-24.00
Stippled Ivy egg cup	D-15.00
Sunburst relish, 5 x 10¼ in.	D-6.00
Sunk Honeycomb creamer, ruby-stained, 4½ in.	D-24.00
Swan handled mug, blue, 2-5/8 in.	D-9.00
Tappan miniature creamer	D-8.00
Thousand Eye square plate, amber, 8 in.	D-19.00
Three Panel compote, low standard, 8½ in.	D-17.50
Three Stories covered butter	D-17.50
Tile Band jelly compote	D-12.50
Tiny Lion water pitcher	D-27.50
Tody footed master salt	D-15.00
Tree sauce, ruby-stained, 4 in.	D-12.50
Tree of Life bowl, 10 in.	D-9.00
Triple Band Mioton egg cup	D-9.00
Triangular Prisms ladies goblet	D-15.00
Triple Triangle goblet, ruby-stained	D-35.00
Truncated Cube creamer, ruby-stained, 3 in.	D-24.00
Tulip with Ribs creamer, applied handle	D-62.50
Two Giraffes goblet, etched	D-82.50
Two Tigers goblet, etched	D-82.50
Vermont basket, 6½ in.	D-18.50
Viking footed sauce, 4 in.	D-11.00
Waffle compote, high standard, 9½ in.	D-35.00
Washboard rectangular bowl, yellow	D-18.00
Washington pitcher, handle check, 9¼ in.	D-45.00
Wheat and Barley covered butter	D-21.00
Wildflower goblet	D-18.00
Willow Oak open sugar	D-17.50
Worchester ale glass, flint	D-47.50
Wyoming compote, 5¼ x 7¾ in.	D-15.00
Zipper pitcher, yellow, 7¾ in.	D-37.50

GLASS—Erickson

This high-quality blown and freehand glass was made in the post WW-II years (1944-1960) by Carl Erickson and his workers at Bremen, Ohio. Each piece was handmade, but with individual differences.

Ashtray, green, crystal-cased, spaced bubbles, 7 in. across.	D-47.50
Ashtray, amethyst, crystal-cased, spaced bubbles, clear applied rests cigar-size, 6-3/8 in. across.	C-60.00

Above left
Low dish, Erickson, in smoke, with clear crystal spaced-bubble "paperweight" center, 9 in. diameter.   C/65-90
Photo courtesy Judy Morehead, Creative Photography, Lancaster, Ohio.

Above right
Erickson glass. Decanter, clear crystal and amethyst, clear blown stopper.   C/120-150
Tumblers, matched pair, clear crystal and amethyst.   Pair: C/55-75

Above
Erickson glass. Left and right, **candle bases**, matched pair, amethyst encased in clear crystal, pair: C/90-125
Pitcher, center, amethyst with clear crystal attached handle, clear spaced-bubble "paperweight" base.   C/150-200

Ashtray, red, crystal-cased, spaced bubbles, 5 in. across.   **S-40.00**

Bowl, free-form, clear crystal glass, 8 inches.   **D-50.00**

Bud vase, red, solid spaced-bubble base, 9 in. high, signed.   **D-45.00**

Cologne, smoke, clear stopper, 9½ in. high.   **D-65.00**

Compote, red, top 8 in. across, crystal, "paperweight" foot with spaced bubbles.   **S-145.00**

Cruet, crystal, ground stopper, 9½ in. high.   **D-60.00**

Cruet, crystal, hand-ground stopper, heavy-base hourglass shape, 8 in. high.   **D-55.00**

Decanter, spirits, green, ground clear stopper, 14 in. high.   **S-85.00**

Decanter, flame, blown stopper with bubble, 16 in. high.   **S-115.00**

Perfume, green, clear stopper, 7 in. high.   **S-40.00**

Pitcher, smoke, applied clear handle, with heavy bottom, 13 in. high.   **D-95.00**

Tumbler, aqua, 3¼ in. high.   **D-20.00**

Vase, red, with clear space-bubble base in paperweight size, 15 in. high.   **D-135.00**

GLASS—*Flint (Clear)*

Flint or crystal glass was ordinary glass mix (sand, potash, etc.) but with the addition of a quantity of lead. This greatlly improved the quality. Flint glass has been made since American Colonial times.

Bowl, footed, eight panels, scalloped rim, base-flakes, 6¼ in. high. — **A-22.50**

Candlestick, double-cup, folded-rim base, applied socket and pan, 7¼ in. high. — **A-90.00**

Candlestick, pressed step base, blown socket, separated by three wafers, 8 in. high. — **A-160.00**

Compote, frosted bowl with round and oval depressions, 5 in. high. — **A-25.00**

Goblet, Argus, bruise on rim, 6½ in. high. — **A-9.00**

Goblet, Ashburton variant, 6¼ in. high. — **A-25.00**

Goblet, Bellflower, 5-7/8 in. high. — **A-25.00**

Goblet, Frosted Greek Key, 6 in. high. — **A-22.50**

Goblet, Thumbprint, 5¾ in. high. — **A-18.00**

Goblets, (two); Thumbprint, 5 in. diameter, 6 in. high. — **A-36.00**

Lamp, hexagonal base, loop font, pewter collar, 9¼ in. high. — **A-50.00**

Spooners (two); similar, but not paired, Thumbprint, 5¼ in. high. — **A-46.00**

Syllabub, cut panels in bowl base, 4 in. high. — **A-5.00**

Tumblers, (pair), Thumbprint, 3¾ in. high. — **A-56.00**

Wineglass, Inverted Palm, 4 in. high. — **A-2.00**

Wineglass, narrow-cut stem with cut panels in bowl, 4½ in. high. — **A-5.00**

Wineglass, Rib and Palm 4 in. high. — **A-8.00**

GLASS—*HEISEY (Signed unless noted)*

Crystolite clear punch cup. — **A-4.50**

Chrystolite Clear plate, unmarked, 11 inches. — **D-9.00**

Empress Pink plate, 4½ inches. — **D-3.75**

Empress Pink footed sugar. — **D-10.00**

Empress Pink three-handled sugar, dolphin-footed. — **D-12.00**

Ipswich Clear goblet, 10 oz. — **D-12.00**

Moongleam Green plate, pinpoint rim nick, 8¾ inches. — **D-4.50**

Oceanic Clear bowl, unsigned, 2 x 12 inches. — **D-18.00**

Orchid Etch Clear cocktail.	D-10.00
Orchid Etch Clear salad bowl, 12 inches.	D-35.00
Orchid Etch Clear open candy, footed	D-28.00
Orchid Etch Clear creamer/sugar.	D-36.00
Orchid Etch three-part relish, 11 inches.	D-30.00
Puritan Clear goblet, 6 oz., 4-3/8 inches.	D-10.00
Ridgeleigh Clear centerpiece, 8 inches.	D-15.00
Ridgeleigh Clear nut dish, individual, handled, 3 inches.	D-5.50
Ridgeleigh Clear punch cup.	D-7.00
Twist Pink creamer, footed.	D-11.00
Unidentified Clear nearcut hair receiver.	D-28.00
Unidentified Clear bowl, footed, 3½ x 11 inches.	D-33.00
Unidentified Pink saucer, 5 inches.	D-2.50
Unidentified Pink flared bowl, octagonal, 2 x 12 inches.	D-40.00

GLASS—*Ruby Flashware*

Cream pitcher, dated 1901, engraved "Agnes", zipper pattern, 3 in. wide, 4½ in. high.	C-50.00
Cream pitcher, dated 1907, engraved "R. M. Riffle", thumbprint pattern, 3 in. wide, 4¾ in. high.	C-60.00
Cream pitcher, dated 1914, engraved "Laurie", slight chip on lip, 4¼ in. high.	S-40.00
Mug, miniature souvenir, engraved "Rhoda", dated 1911, 1½ in. wide, 2 in. high.	C-27.50
Mug, miniature souvenir, engraved "Amanda", dated 1898, 1¼ in. wide, 1¾ in. high.	C-36.00
Punch cup, no inscription or date, thumbprint pattern, 3½ in. wide, 2¼ in. high.	C-22.00

Left, **Glass,** ruby, 3½ in. high.   C/8-12

Right, **Ruby flashware.**
Tumblers, matched pair, sawtooth pattern, 2½ in. high.   C/55-70
Bud-vase, center, inscribed "Mrs. W. G. Freese / 1907 / Jamestown", 8 in. high.
C/80-100

Punch cup, "Wilber", dated 1909, 2-3/8 in. high.	**D-25.00**
Shaker, engraved "Elizabeth", dated 1910, sawtooth pattern, 3 in. high.	**C-30.00**
Shakers, salt and pepper, matched pair; both dated 1933, one with "Hettie", other with "Snow". Each 3 in. high; pair.	**C-45.00**
Spooner, engraved "Edgar", dated 1911, internal crack that does not reach interior/exterior surfaces; daisy and button pattern, 3-7/8 in. high.	**C-35.00**
Toothpick holder, engraved "Julia and Pete", dated 1944, 1-7/8 in wide, 2-1/8 in. high.	**C-25.00**
Toothpick holder, engraved "Soldiers Home/Dayton, O.", sawtooth pattern, 2¼ in. high.	**C-32.50**

GLASS—*STRETCH*

Black Amethyst bowl, flared, 9½ inches.	**D-20.00**
Black Amethyst base, holds 2½ in. bottom.	**D-7.00**
Black Amethyst three-footed base, holds 4-3/8 in. bottom.	**D-10.00**
Blue Amethyst compote, collar bottom, 1½ x 11 inches.	**D-25.00**
Blue Amethyst dish, footed, 5½ x 7½ inches.	**D-25.00**
Blue Amethyst plate, twelve-paneled, 11 inches.	**D-30.00**
Blue Amethyst vase, trumpet-shape, 5 x 8 inches.	**D-30.00**
Blue bowl, 10 inches.	**D-30.00**
Blue Opaque bowl, pedestaled, 3 x 8½ inches.	**D-40.00**
Blue Opaque compote, 3½ x 8½ inches.	**D-35.00**
Charcoal Gray sandwich server, center handle, 10½ inches.	**D-30.00**
Clear cheese and cracker set.	**D-22.00**
Clear fruit server, orange rainbow irid., 10 inches.	**D-35.00**
Clear Iridescent bowl, 2-1/8 x 10¼ inches.	**D-28.00**
Cobalt bowl, 3 x 10 inches.	**D-25.00**
Cobalt candlesticks, 9¾ in. high, pair.	**D-35.00**
Cobalt cheese stand, for cracker/cheese set.	**D-12.00**
Cobalt console bowl, 1¾ x 12 inches.	**D-25.00**
Cobalt mint dish, treebark footed, 3¼ x 6 inches.	**D-25.00**
Custard Opaque bowl, 3¼ x 10 inches.	**D-70.00**
Green bowl, fifteen-ribbed, 2-5/8 x 6¼ inches.	**D-20.00**
Green candy and lid, 9½ in. high.	**D-30.00**
Green fan vase, ribbed, 5¼ x 5½ inches.	**D-20.00**

Green Opaque bowl, turned-in edge, footed, 4 in. high.	**D-40.00**
Ice Blue compote, bead stem, 6 x 6¾ inches.	**D-35.00**
Olive bowl, collar bottom, 3½ x 9½ inches.	**D-25.00**
Olive candlesticks, 8½ in. high.	**D-60.00**
Orange compote, 3 x 8½ inches.	**D-30.00**
Pale Blue-Gray compote, Imperial, 8½ in. high.	**D-50.00**
Pink bud vase, 11¾ in. high.	**D-25.00**
Pink cigarette container, footed.	**D-55.00**
Pink rose bowl, melon-ribbed, 3½ x 5 inches.	**D-30.00**
Pink vase, 6 x 6 inches.	**D-25.00**
Purple bowl, fluted, 3½ x 9 inches.	**D-35.00**
Purple plate, polished bottom, 8 in. diameter.	**D-12.00**
Red sherbet, Amberina, footed, 3-3/8 x 4 inches.	**D-50.00**
Red vase, Amberina, Imperial, 5-7/8 x 8½ inches.	**D-150.00**
Smokey Blue bowl, paneled, 3½ x 8¼ inches.	**D-25.00**
Teal Blue vase, rim flares, 4½ x 5 inches.	**D-19.00**
Teal Blue vase, scalloped flared rim, 14½ in. high.	**D-55.00**
Topaz bowl, flared, 3½ x 13 inches.	**D-22.00**
Vaseline bowl, rolled-in edge, 3¼ x 6½ inches.	**D-20.00**
Vaseline tray, treebark feet, 3¼ x 5¾ inches.	**D-25.00**
Vaseline vase, flared shape, 5 x 5½ inches.	**D-35.00**
White basket, 10¼ in. high.	**D-100.00**
White candlesticks, Colonial, 10½ in. high, pair.	**D-225.00**

Egg, blown milk glass, handpainted, 8 in. long. C/35-55

Vase, orange-red iridescent, old Imperial glass bottom-mark, 7 in. high.   C/70-90

Eye-cup, cobalt blue, 2½ in. high.   C/7-10

Photos courtesy Judy Morehead, Creative Photography, Lancaster, Ohio.

GRANITEWARE (Also called Enamelware)

In recent years there has been an upswing of interest in collecting the enameled sheet-iron utensils commonly called "Graniteware". Various colors may have different regional names, but all refer to items made by the same process of manufacture. Collectors look for unusual utensils, and those in near-perfect condition.

Basting spoon, white, large, slotted to hang.   **D-4.50**

Bean pot, gray, covered, graniteware handles, 7 in. diameter.   **D-15.00**

Candlestick, white, ring loop handle, "Germany", 5 in. diameter.   **D-22.50**

Chicken roaster, gray, covered, oval, 8¾ x 13¾ inches.   **D-20.00**

Coffee boiler, gray, bail handle and wood grip, 10 in. high.   **D-29.50**

Coffee boiler, 12-cup size, mottled gray, graniteware lid.   **D-22.50**

Coffee boiler, tin top, gray, 9 in. high.   **D-24.50**

Coffee pot, gray, bail handle, wooden grip, "L & G. Mfg. Co.", 11 in. high.   **D-45.00**

Coffee pot, gray, gooseneck spout, tin top, 9½ in. high.   **D-24.50**

Coffee pot, chuck-wagon size, gray, bail handle, wood grip, 12 in. high.   **D-45.00**

Cooking pot, three-fingered side handles, gray, covered, near-black gray, 10½ in. diameter.   **D-16.50**

Cookpot, gray, handle holed to hang, 5 in. deep, 7½ in. handle.   **D-6.50**

Above
Enamelware coffee pot.   C/15-19
Cream can, missing lid.   C/14-18

Right
Coffeepot, enamelware, black trim, green wooden lid-knob, 10 in. high.   C/8-13

| Water filter (11 qts.). | 30-55 | Square lunch box. | 35-45 |

Lipped preserving kettles.   10-12

Collander.   8-11

Upper center
Tea kettle.   15-18

Above right
Coffee boilers.   18-25

Dish pan, blue & white agateware, 3½ in. deep, 12½ in. diameter.   **D-8.50**

Frying pan, gray, 6¼ in. bottom diameter, 8 in. handle.   **D-14.50**

Graniteware set, three pieces: Dishpan, draining pan, pudding pan, all somewhat damaged.   **D-10.00**

Kettle, gray, wire handle, large, partial label.   **D-12.50**

Layer cake pan, gray, mottled, 1 in. deep, 9 in. top diameter.   **D-6.50**

Mixing bowl, navy blue and white, speckled, 8 in. top diameter.   **D-14.50**

Pie plate, dark gray, minor damage, 9¾ in. diameter. **D-4.50**

Pie plate, gray, mottled, excellent condition, 9 in. diameter. **D-6.50**

Pie plate, cobalt blue and white, 1½ in. deep, 10 in. top diameter. **D-8.50**

Pitcher, blue and white speckled, marked "Geuder, Paeshke & Frey Co./U.S.N.", 9½ in. high. May be WW-I. **D-35.00**

Pitcher, cobalt blue and white "spongeware", white interior, black handle and lip trim, 10½ in. high. **D-40.00**

Preserve kettle, tin lid, gray, 13 in. deep, bail ears, 18 in. top diameter. **D-29.50**

Pudding bowl, blue and white, rim damage. **D-11.50**

Pudding pan, marbleized blue, lavender and white, 12 in. diameter. **D-12.50**

Roasting pan, covered, gray, orig. label, "Nesco". **D-15.00**

Utility pan, gray, 3½ in. deep, 12 in. top diameter. **D-6.50**

Wash basin, navy blue and white speckled, part of orig. label, "Enameled Steelware/Newark, N.Y.", holed to hang. **D-16.50**

Wash basin, blue and white "spongeware", 11 in. diameter. **D-8.50**

Wash basin, cobalt blue and white "agateware", 9¾ in. diameter. **D-10.00**

HOME ENTERTAINMENT (See also Childrens' Playthings)

Before the days of television and electronic entertainments, a number of diverting activities were possible. Many were family oriented, and could be enjoyed on a rainy afternoon or during long winter evenings. Games of many sorts were possible, and most families had scenic viewers; a few had the more expensive magic lanterns.

"American Logs", 328-piece set; in machine-dovetailed wood box with color 12 x 15 in. label. Wood logs, box measures 5 x 17 x 20 inches. **D-89.00**

Book of Parlor Games, Victorian, illustrated, parties, etc. **D-8.50**

Building stones, set; "Richter's/Anchor Box", metal corners, instructions. **D-20.00**

Lone Star Dominoes, 1890s.
7-11
Bataan, 1940s.   4-6
Game of the States, 1930s.
5-7

Children's book, "Painting Plays for Rainy Days",
ca. 1880.   **D-7.00**
Card game, "Old Maid", complete, boxed.   **S-5.00**
Card game, "The Game of Grand Slam", boxed, in-
structions.   **D-7.50**
Checkerboard, folding; hinged wood, red and black
squares, 15½ in. square.   **D-58.00**
Checkerboard, wood, black and white, 12¾ in.
squares.   **D-33.00**
Chinese checkers game, complete with colored
marbles.   **S-13.00**
Game, "The Fairies' Cauldron Tiddley Winks",
Parker Bros.   **D-17.50**
Game, "Humpty-Dumpty", orig. container, litho., ca.
1930.   **D-6.50**
Game, "Peter Cuddle/His Latest Trip to New York",
cards.   **D-15.00**
Game, "The International Speedway Auto Race",
Parker, 1920's.   **D-22.00**
Game, "Lindy/New York To Paris", map, two com-
peting planes.   **D-25.00**
Game, "Lotto", markers, color litho. box, directions,
Milton Bradley Co.   **D-10.00**
Game, "The Magnetic Fish Pond", boxed, Spear's,
ca. 1910.   **D-15.00**

Game, "Ring Scaling", The Martin Co., boxed, 7 in.
square.   **D-11.00**

Game, "Roulette Baseball Game", complete, Wm.
Bartholomae.   **D-15.00**

Game, "Round Game of Tiddley Winks", McLoughlin
Bros., 1890.   **D-12.50**

Game, "Three-In-One Rolaweel", Rosebud Art Co.,
N.Y., 1920's.   **D-5.00**

Game, "Tiddly Winks", boxed, complete, with instructions.   **D-8.00**

Game, "Tinkle Bell Tiddly Winks", Parker Bros.,
complete.   **D-12.50**

Game, "Touring", card game, Parker Bros./Mass.,
ca. 1920's.   **D-20.00**

Game board, "Uncle Wiggily", Milton Bradley Co.,
incomplete.   **D-10.00**

Jig saw puzzle, "Puppy Sam—The Banjo Man",
Barbello, 1920's.   **D-3.00**

Jig saw puzzle, "Mother Goose", complete, by
Playtime House.   **D-2.75**

Magic lanter, kerosene-fired, six long and six round
glass slides.   **D-145.00**

Magic lantern, kerosene, tin, periscoping lens, 7 in.
high.   **D-55.00**

Magic lantern, boxed, black and yellow finish, with
12 slides, ea. 2 x 7¼ inches.   **D-145.00**

Magic lantern slides, boxed set of 36 different 2 x 7
slides.   **D-85.00**

Magic lantern slides, cardboard box of 12, 2 x 5½
in. each.   **D-15.00**

Marbles, lot of 200, old clay types.   **D-10.00**

Parlor croquet set, mallets, balls, guide-sets, complete.   **S-40.00**

Spelling game, cardboard, circular disc with animal
sketches.   **D-30.00**

Stereoptican viewer, walnut, eye hood replaced.   **D-24.00**

Stereoptican viewer, leather eyepiece, velvet trim,
"Keystone".   **D-41.00**

Viewer, scenes pass in box opening decorated like
stage; 2¼ x 5 x 8 inches.   **A-125.00**

HOUSEHOLD ITEMS—[See also Furniture & Kitchen]

Ant trap, redware, glazed interior, 6½ x 2¾ in. high.   A-45.00

Bed, high headboard, American Victorian, walnut; ca. 1879, 60 in. wide, 78 in. long.   A-800.00

Bed, pencil post, with lamb's tongue at base of chamfer, and posts with old brown paint. Some replacements, 55 x 75 inches.   A-600.00

Bed, rope, turned posts and orig. rails. Unusual turnings, 50½ x 76½ in., 49 in. high.   A-210.00

Bed, rope, curly maple, turned posts; inverted bell finials, 53 x 77 inches.   A-160.00

Bed, rope, tall legs, maple posts and pine headboard; refinished, 44¼ x 81 inches.   A-135.00

Bed, rope, hired man's, turned legs, 28 x 65 x 16 in. high.   A-55.00

Bed, rope, poplar, turned posts with high feet and tulip finials, 53 x 77½ x 43 in. high.   A-100.00

Bed, single, American, maple; turned posts with nailhead finials, ca. 1840.   A-325.00

Bed, tall-post, all pine with poplar head board, orig. rails with turned knobs for rope and orig. canopy rails. Refinished 58½ x 80½ x 78 in. high.   A-950.00

Bed, three-quarter size, American, maple. Turned posts with cannonball finials, curly maple headboard, ca. 1840.   A-325.00

Bed, trundle, poplar, turned posts with finials, 16½ in. high.   A-135.00

Bed, tester, Sheraton carved walnut and knotty pine, having shaped arched headboard and turned head, reeded footboards with canopy. Virginia(?), ca. 1800, 51 x 74½ x 60 inches.   A-2,300.00

Bed, walnut, hired-man size, refinished.   A-135.00

Bed-smoother, old worn paint, dated 1886, 21 in. long.   A-37.50

Bed-smoother, handcarved, holed to hang.   D-36.00

Bed-smoother, wood, carved hearts and hex signs with handle a two-headed horse. Dated 1832, 25 in. long.   A-205.00

Bed-warmer, brass, round, baluster-turned walnut handle, brass cover, ca. 1820.   A-160.00

Bed-warmer, brass, treen handle, Pennsylvania, ca. 1820.   A-225.00

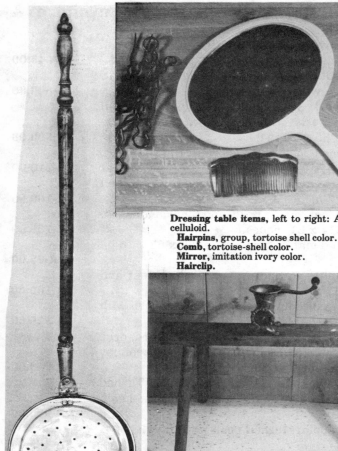

Dressing table items, left to right: All of early celluloid.

    Hairpins, group, tortoise shell color.   C/4-6
    Comb, tortoise-shell color.   C/3-5
    Mirror, imitation ivory color.   C/15-20
    Hairclip.   C/3-5

Meat grinder, attached to plank surface with round legs.   C/20-30

American brass and maple bed warmer, 44 in. long. Bright cut and pierced cover, baluster turned handle with traces of black paint. Ca. 1780.   A/150

Left, **foot-warmer,** wood frame, punched tin, complete door, complete with interior ember box. Wire bale handle, 8 x 9 x 5½ in high.   C/100-150

Right, **dressing table** items Large **mirror,** beveled glass, cast iron frame.
    C/90-125
Comb & brush, set.
    C/20-25

Above, **Fluting iron**, "The Best", by C. W. Whitfield, Syracuse, N.Y. C/15-22.50

Upper right, **Churn**, footed, pine with metal bands. Cast iron handle shaft, wooden dashers inside. C/85-125

Right **Wall match safe**, with container, striking surface and receptacle for used matches; tin, 7 in. high. C/15-25

Bed-warmer, brass, round, intricate punched design. — S-200.00

Bin, pine, dovetailed, two compartments with lift lids and shaped crests; 21¼ x 73½ x 29 in. high. — A-220.00

Bookends, pair, cast iron sheep, 7¼ in. high. — A-40.00

Bookends, pair, cast iron owls, brass layered over iron, expanding periscoping connecting slides, 4 in. high. — D-45.00

Bootjack, bentwood, unusual, 21½ in. long. — A-17.50

Bootjack, handcarved wood, 17 in. long. — D-45.00

Bootjack, wrought iron, 18 in. long. — D-10.00

Calling card tray, aluminum, fancy border, Victorian style. — D-1.50

Carpet stretcher, cast iron, "The Cady", 13 in. long. — A-4.00

Cheese tester, metal, "Moser Signau Rosterei/Switzerland", 6¾ in. long. — D-9.00

Clothes pins, handmade, wood, set of three different. — D-18.00

Clothes pins, wood, two-way unsprung, set of ten. — D-20.00

Clothes-peg, wooden strip with clothes pegs, six hooks, 4 x 37 inches. — A-12.50

Coal hod, slant-front top, tin lining, 22 in. high.　　A-45.00

Comb box, wooden, tole-type decoration with three-color striping, 7 x 9 inches.　　A-17.50

Commode rack, wall-mounted, three-bar, swiveling, brass.　　D-16.50

Cradle, American Sheraton walnut, 41 in. long.　　A-90.00

Cradle, pine, hooded with cutouts, 39½ in. long.　　S-125.00

Crock stand, four-tier, semi-circular, scalloped supports, 21 x 41 x 32 in. high.　　A-115.00

Crumber, tin, for collecting tabletop crumbs after meal, ca. 1890.　　D-4.50

Curling iron, wooden-handled, brass finials, 9 in. long.　　D-6.50

Door-knocker, heavy cast brass, 5 x 5 inches.　　A-37.50

Door-ringer, brass turn-knob and shaft, iron circular bell.　　D-9.00

Door-stop, horse, brass, 11 in. wide, 9½ in. high.　　A-22.50

Door-stop, German Shepard dog, standing, cast iron, 15 in. long, 13 in. high.　　D-32.50

Door-stop, cast iron, Punch, 12½ in. high.　　A-27.50

Door-stop, cast iron cat, black, orig. paint, 8¼ in. high.　　D-36.00

Door-stop, wolfhound, cast iron, 15½ in. long.　　A-75.00

Door-stop, cast iron Spanish galleon, 10½ in. long, 11 in. high.　　D-32.50

Dough box, turned legs and breadboard top, 20½ x 36 x 29 in. high.　　A-115.00

Downspout collection box, tin, with embossed eagle and worn paint and painted date 1849; 21 in. high.　　A-280.00

Dresser bottles, pair, clear pattern glass in flower-form, tulip-shape stoppers, 8 in. high.　　D-22.50

Dresser tray, porcelain, footed, handpainted, 14-k gold leaf, French, 7 x 9½ x 1½ in. high.　　D-89.50

Dryer, boot and shoe, galvanized tin, placed on stove to dry foot-gear overnight; ca. 1930, 5 x 8½ x 26 in. high.　　D-45.00

Drying rack, oak, mortised pegged construction, three bars and shoe feet, 42 x 48 inches.　　A-40.00

Dust pan, stenciled tin, gold berry-leaf, small size.　　D-12.50

Featherbed fluffer, pine, handcarved, 24 in. long.　　A-18.00

Fluting iron, with attached lamp and foot pedal, brass burner, clamps to table, 9 in. long.　　A-30.00

Footstool, pine, primitive chipcarving, refinished, 6 x 12 in. top, 6½ in. high.　　A-25.00

Footstool, poplar, scalloped base, lift lid. Paint worn, 13 x 17 inches, 10½ in. high. **A-70.00**

Footwarmer, soapstone, bail handle, 6 x 8 x 1¼ in. thick. **D-10.00**

Footwarmer, soapstone, bail handle, 8 x 12 x 3-3/8 in. thick. **D-15.00**

Footwarmer, square tin perforated box in wood frame, bail handle, 9½ in. high. **D-125.00**

Glove box, pyrographic, Victorian, beveled edges, 4 x 11½ x 2½ inches. **D-15.00**

Hair floral bouquet, jewelry, ca. 1850, small size. **D-7.50**

Hamper, wicker, corner, pie-wedge shape, wooden bottom, painted pale green, ca. 1880, 14 x 20 x 24½ in. high. **D-45.00**

Hand mirror, wood, chip-carved, 11 in. high. **A-15.00**

Hanging box, pine bottom-board, chipcarved with pinwheels, hearts, leaves, etc., dated 1791. Unfinished, 11 x 11½ x 11¾ in. high. **A-510.00**

Hat rack, folding, walnut, accordain, ten hooks, 23 in. high. **A-45.00**

Hall tree, stained hardwood, wooden clothing pegs, 47 in. high. **D-40.00**

Herb cupboard, Maine, dozens of small compartments, 42 in. high. **D-1,250.00**

Hot water bottle, white metal, oval, 8 x 11½ inches. **A-35.00**

Hot water container, copper, brass cap, 9 in. diameter. **S-40.00**

Hummingbird feeder, blown glass, clear, 7¼ in. high. **A-20.00**

Ice box, two-door, oak, refinished, brass hardware, 40 in. high. **D-300.00**

Ice-cream maker, wood-stave bucket, metal churn, brass parts. **D-45.00**

Ice pick, steel tip, wood handle. **S-5.00**

Ice tongs, scissors type, iron handles, 11 in. long. **D-8.00**

Kerosene carrier, tin over glass, ventilated sides, 10 in. high. **D-19.00**

Kerosene reservoir, glass, red, wire handle. **A-15.00**

Key, wood, for tightening rope beds, 17 in. long. **A-55.00**

Knife box, two-section, straight sides, 8½ x 14 inches. **A-35.00**

Knife box, divided, comb graining, 9 x 12 x 4½ in. high. **A-32.50**

Knife box, two-section, pine, old paint, 8½ x 13½ inches. A-70.00

Lap-board, pine, applied edge moulding, one-board wide, 21¼ x 25¼ inches. A-32.50

Lap-board, walnut, 23 x 27 inches. D-15.00

Letter opener, bone, vertical etched stripes, 10 in. long. D-8.00

Mattress roller, from New Hampshire inn, wood, 5 in. diameter, 28 in. long. D-65.00

Match-holder, tin, wall-hanger, old gold paint. D-40.00

Matchbox holder, tin, lift lid, old red, 1¾ in. deep. D-15.00

Matchbox holder, brass, pedestaled, weighted base, 3¼ in. high. D-25.00

Nutcracker, cast iron, "Little Giant", 1890, 3 in. long. D-15.00

Peg-board, wood, four pegs, 2½ x 26 inches. A-20.00

Plinth, pine, old green paint, 14½ in. square, 46 in. high. A-30.00

Potty, spindleback arm chair, stencil decorated crest. A-35.00

Rug beater, wire with wood handle, Victorian period. D-10.00

Shelves, hanging, pine with scalloped sides, 15 in. wide. A-75.00

Shelves, hanging, whale-end, 20¼ in. wide. A-25.00

Shelves, hanging, triangular with scalloped front moulding and side brackets, 6 x 33 x 27½ in. high. A-305.00

Shelves, hanging, scalloped sides and four graduated shelves, old dark paint; 9½ x 25 x 41¾ in. high. A-225.00

Shelves, hanging, mahogany, "S"-curve ends, 23½ in. high. A-45.00

Shoe stretcher, iron, hinged, ca. 1870. D-12.50

Soap dish, wood, rectangular, 3¾ x 7½ inches. D-33.00

Soap dish, white porcelain, rectangular, 5 in. long. S-14.00

Spinning wheel, well-detailed, turned legs, finials with chip carving; wheel 21 in. diameter, 35 in. overall high. A-260.00

Stovepipe hole cover, metal-rimmed cardboard with handpainted landscape scene, 8 in. diameter. A-25.00

Strong box, dovetailed with bracket feet, 17½ x 33 x 16 in. high. A-65.00

Table bowl, cast iron, 8 in. diameter. D-43.00

Table bowl, cast iron, 12 in. diameter. D-48.00

Table bowl, cast iron, 12½ in. diameter.	**D-60.00**
Table cloth, linen, floral band, 56 x 64 inches.	**D-55.00**
Table cloth, linen, red, white and gold, 70 x 80 inches.	**A-45.00**
Thumb latch, rod and support, no keeper, 6¾ in. high.	**A-8.00**
Towel, linen, four colors, 19 x 32 inches.	**A-22.50**
Towel, linen, three colors, 20 x 34 inches.	**A-22.50**
Towel bar supports, pine, pair; scrolled, 3½ x 13½ inches.	**A-25.00**
Towel rack, turned posts with five bars, 27 x 33½ inches.	**A-25.00**
Trivet, cast brass, lyre and pineapple, 7 in. long.	**A-15.00**
Trivet, cast iron, five-paw, lacy 7 in. diameter.	**D-18.50**
Trivet, wrought iron, wooden handle, 10 in. long.	**A-17.50**
Trivet, wrought iron, handled, 10 in. diameter, 7½ in. high.	**A-30.00**
Wall pocket, two compartments, freehand floral design on top, 6 x 14 x 24 inches.	**A-85.00**
Washboard, all wooden, weathered, 13 x 31 inches.	**A-65.00**
Water distiller, copper, three sections, brass spigots, by Harrison Mfg. Co., 14 in. high.	**D-150.00**
Yarn winder, good turnings and chip-carved detail, 45 in. high.	**A-80.00**

ICE CREAM MOULDS—*Antique Pewter*

(Research information regarding mould manufacturers courtesy Lahaska Antiques, Pennsylvania.)

Eppelsheimer (E & Co.), New York City, in operation after 1880.

Fr. Krauss' Son (K & Co., Krauss), Milford Pennsylvania, in operation after 1860, in which year they took over

Schall & Co. (S & Co.), New York City, founded in 1854. Many Krauss and Schall numbers coincide.

Note: "C C"-marked moulds are of French origin and are of the same time period.

Both Eppelsheimer and Krauss offered the moulds in pure tin (at a higher price), and they were somewhat shinier and less malleable than the standard consistency. Should one encounter these (seldom), they are of comparable value.

Automobile (large early 4-door limosine), K-623	**D-48.00**
Banjo, K-545	**D-52.00**

Basket, (medallion), K-482	**D-32.00**
Basketball, E-1150	**D-34.00**
Bear, Teddy, K-611	**D-34.00**
Beehive, K-250	**D-44.00**
Bicycle, Lady riding, K431	**D-58.00**
Boat, S-229	**D-39.00**
Boat, (Ancient Roman galley?), K-232	**D-35.00**
Bride and Groom (One of the very few double-figure moulds produced, K-627	**D-50.00**
Bull, S-223	**D-54.00**
Cape Cod cottage, K-637	**D-70.00**
Carnation, E-361	**D-24.00**
Cat and Moon, E-1180	**D-65.00**
Christmas stocking, K-590	**D-42.00**
Christmas tree with Star, K-641	**D-43.00**
Clover, four leaf, K-268	**D-28.00**
Clown (full figure), K-624	**D-52.00**
Coat of Arms, British, K-564	**D-43.00**
Colonial lady's skirt, E-1185	**D-28.00**
Cow (standing), S-358	**D-48.00**
Cupid's face in Rose, K-306	**D-29.00**
Cupid on Rabbit, K-561	**D-34.00**
Daisy, E-317	**D-23.00**
Diploma, K-633	**D-26.00**
Dog (pug), K-390	**D-42.00**
Eagle, American, exceptional detail, K-283	**D-58.00**
Egg, K-117	**D-11.00**
Elk's head, (three-part), K-493	**D-46.00**
Fish, Dolphin, K-258	**D-48.00**
Fisherman, E-951	**D-32.00**
Frog on Mushroom, K-180	**D-48.00**
Golf bag with Clubs, K-622	**D-46.00**
Grapes, bunch, K-257	**D-18.00**
Headless Admiral, full figure with binoculars, K-519	**D-39.00**
Heart, to be pierced by Arrow, E-956	**D-16.00**
Lamb, (lying down), K-168	**D-46.00**
Lily of Valley Leaf, E-319A	**D-22.00**
Lion, (rare position, reclining on side), E-674	**D-49.00**
Loving Cup, (three-part), S-569	**D-36.00**
Mandolin, K-547	**D-52.00**
Monkey, E-642	**D-56.00**
Oak leaf with Acorns, S-385	**D-36.00**
Orange. (skin texture nicely detailed), K-120	**D-11.00**
Orchid, dated 1892, K-319	**D-38.00**

Owl, S-175	**D-56.00**
Peach, E-234	**D-15.00**
Pear, E-248	**D-18.00**
Potato, S-154	**D-16.00**
Pumpkin, S-600	**D-14.00**
Rabbit, (crouching), E-675	**D-29.00**
Rabbit in Cabbage, K-584	**D-39.00**
Ring, Wedding, K-608	**D-14.00**
Rose Bud, K-315	**D-29.00**
Sailboat, K-465	**D-54.00**
Sailboat, (dated 1899; sloop "Columbia", third winner of The Americas Cup), K-553	**D-65.00**
Shoe, baby, E-1230	**D-38.00**
Slippers, pair, K-284	**D-42.00**
Strawberry, K-124	**D-27.00**
Swan, (neck down), S-277	**D-36.00**
Thistle Flower, S-430	**D-34.00**
Turtle, K-176	**D-56.00**
Vase, (very fancy), K-294	**D-28.00**
Violin, K-544	**D-52.00**
Martha Washington, K-461	**D-48.00**
Washington's profile on Hatchet, K-336	**D-27.00**
Watermelon, (with slice out), S-566	**D-18.00**
Wheelbarrow, K-480	**D-33.00**
Wishbone, K-322	**D-22.00**

INK CONTAINERS, Etc.

In the days of writing quills, penknives, sanders and other writing accoutrements, the inks were of great importance. These were containers of many sizes and materials, and held the writing fluid. Some were intended for desk-use, others were very large and held the household or business ink supply. Still others were quite small and fitted into a traveler's writing set. The older inks of blown and molded glass are quite collectible, as are earthenware examples and the many patented forms.

Ink, redware, black shiny glaze, chips, 1½ in. high.	**A-13.00**
Ink bottle, pontiled, umbrella-shape, eight-sided, blob top.	**D-25.00**
Ink bottle, blown and sharply pontiled, aqua, ca. 1860.	**D-22.50**
Inkstand, with two crystal wells, walnut, handled, English, late 1800's.	**D-195.00**

194

Inkwell, clear glass in stamped-brass stand. C/12-18

Inkwell, clear blown glass, brass top (paired with matching sander). C/55-80

Ink, traveler's, lignum vitae, Civil War period, 2 in. high. **D-17.00**

Inkwell, umbrella-shaped, ca. 1850, 2 in. diameter, 2¼ in. high. **D-25.00**

Inkwell, hinged brass top, 2-5/8 in. high. **S-60.00**

Inkwell, round, brass, with sander, well and visible ink reservoir; 6 in. diameter. **D-55.00**

Inkwell, blown glass, octagonal, moss green, 2½ in. high. **A-25.00**

Inkwell, blown glass, side spout for pen, 3 in. high. **D-25.00**

Inkwell, brass, two side-by-side containers, glass-bodied, 7 in. wide. **D-60.00**

Inkwell, brass fittings, two clear inkwells, 3 x 3 x 5½ inches. **A-25.00**

Inkwell, pattern glass, nonspillable, paneled base, rounded top, 2 in. high. **D-8.50**

Inkwell, pewter, American, 1 in. square at base, ¾ in. square at top with pen opening, ca. 1750. **D-75.00**

Inkwell, redware, clear glaze has old flakes, 2 in. high. **A-42.50**

Inkwell, soapstone, sculpted top, 2¼ in. square, ca. 1790. **D-45.00**

Inkwell, stoneware, good condition. **A-30.00**

Inkwell, treen, olive green blown insert, pen holes, 1½ in. high. **A-30.00**

Inkwell, treen, glass insert, turned rings, 1¾ in. high. **A-13.00**

Inkwell, turned wood, "Silliman & Co./Chester, Conn.", 4/ in. diameter, 3 in. high.　　　　　　　A-145.00

Master ink bottle, brown pottery, tilted, 6 in. high.　D-12.00

Master ink bottle, yellow pottery, faint signature, 8 in. high.　　　　　　　　　　　　　　　　　　　D-15.00

Master ink bottle, stoneware, mottled brown and beige, 5¼ in. high.　　　　　　　　　　　　　　D-15.00

Master ink bottle, stoneware, brownish glaze, 4½ in. high.　　　　　　　　　　　　　　　　　　　D-12.00

Sander, tin, black japanned finish, round 3 in. high.　D-18.00

Sander, treen, round, old reddish paint, 2¾ in. high.　S-25.00

Standish, silver, English, Birmingham 1838-39, two crystal inkwells and central open pen holder.　A-250.00

INSTRUMENTS—*Precision*

Barometer, English, mahogany "banjo" wall type, made by Cain/Halifax, 19 Century, 36 in. high.　A-310.00

Barometer, English, mahogany "banjo" type, 39 in. high.　　　　　　　　　　　　　　　　　　　　A-300.00

Charting rule, "Adelaide", red brass, 1½ x 24 inches, opens to 6 in. width.　　　　　　　　　　D-95.00

Chronometer, ships; taken apart and not reassembled, all parts present. Rosewood case with brass trim and lifter handles.　　　　　　　　　　　　D-650.00

Compass, brass bowl and marked dry card, in 6 x 6 in. box　　　　　　　　　　　　　　　　　　　D-85.00

Compass, "Riggs and Brother/Philadelphia", 9-inch.　D-195.00

Inclinometer, brass construction on wood backing, to indicate vessel list, 14 in. high.　　　　　　D-75.00

Octant, ebony with brass fittings, ivory scale and name plate. Flat swing arm, orig. keystone case.　D-395.00

Octant, brass and ebony, ivory scales and name plate. Signed, "Imray/London", ca. mid-1800's.　D-375.00

Quadrant, ebony, brass fittings and ivory scale, Flat swing arm, in good overall condition, several small pieces missing.　　　　　　　　　　　　　　D-365.00

Sextant, solid brass construction, orig. black finish, silver scale. Signed, orig. carrying case and extra eyepiece.　　　　　　　　　　　　　　　　　　D-395.00

Telescope, wood barreled long glass, extends to 44 in.; signed, "Dollond/London", complete with two lens caps.　　　　　　　　　　　　　　　　　D-295.00

Telescope, brass with rope covering, optics not good, extends to 36 inches. **D-95.00**

Telescope, mahogany three-draw, brass fittings, extends to 17 inches. **D-97.50**

Telescope, wood barrel, leather-covered, brass fittings. Single-draw, marked "Spencer Browning/London/Improved", 45 in. long. **D-250.00**

Telescope, tripod; solid brass, Queen Anne style legs, 19 in. high, 3 in. diameter, 40 in. long. **D-725.00**

Telescope, tripod; stands 18 in. high, brass, 23 in. long. **D-325.00**

Transit level, brass, "W. & L.F. Gurley/Troy, N.Y.", 13 in. long. **A-90.00**

IRON—Cast (See also **Kitchen, Fireplace,** *et. al)*

Andiron, miniature, stylized figure, 4 in. long. **A-32.50**

Bird, very worn black paint, 4 in. long. **A-12.00**

Birds, pair, 4 in. long. **A-22.50**

Bird, rectangular base, worn and rusted paint, 3 in. high. **A-17.50**

Bookends, lying dogs, pair; 6 in. high. **A-10.00**

Book press, Victorian, wheel-turned, 60-lb. weight. Ca. 1865, 11½ x 17 inches, 15 in. high. **D-75.00**

Cannon, wooden base with old green paint, 5 in. long, 2¼ in. high. **A-40.00**

Cannon, wooden carriage with old blue paint, 9½ in. long. **A-85.00**

Carousel horse, modern polychrome paint, 24 x 26 in. high. **A-105.00**

Doorstop, boxer, orig. paint with wear, 9¾ in. high. **A-30.00**

Doorstop, frog, no paint, 3 in. high. **A-25.00**

Doorstop, horse, 11 in. long, 10½ in. high. **A-47.50**

Duck, worn white paint, 5¾ in. long. **A-12.00**

Ducks, pair; one with head up, one down, height, respectively, 11½ and 6¾ inches. **A-180.00**

Eagle, worn gilt, wingspan 8¼ inches. **A-14.00**

Eagle and arrow, old gilt, 7¼ in. wingspan. **A-17.50**

Fish, solid-cast, 7 in. long. **A-50.00**

Frog, solid-cast, 4 in. long. **A-25.00**

Frog, "I Croak for the Jackson Wagon". Old green and yellow paint, 5 in. long. **A-225.00**

Garden ornament, cast iron grey rabbit, 11½ in. high. **A-85.00**

Eel or fish-spears.
Left, handwrought iron, pointed haft, 10½ in. long.   C/20-30
Center, handwrought iron, hollow-socket haft.   C/20-30
Right, factory cast iron, about half of handle-haft broken.   C/8-15

Beaver or wolf trap, wrought iron, double-spring, with chain and three-prong drag. Trap is 16 in. long, and bait or trip pan is missing.   C/30-45

Kettle, iron, lidded and bailed; height to handle, 13 inches.   C/35-50

Pot, cast iron, one gal. capacity, orig. handled lid.   C/20-30

Fluting set, for ruffles, matched. Cast iron, maker-marked, 6 in. wide.   C/20-30

Hitching post, horse head, to be fastened to top of pole.   A-60.00

Horse tether, round, 6¼ in. diameter.   A-22.50

Kettle, on three legs, iron bail, 16 in. diameter.   A-45.00

Owl, cast iron, miniature, 2½ in. high.   A-12.50

Parrot, on perch, worn polychrome paint, 3¾ in. high.   A-30.00

Paperweight, cast frog, worn green paint. Obviously male, 2¾ in. long.   A-40.00

Paperweight, cast pig, 3 in. long. A-20.00
Popcorn-popper, wire screen top, wooden handle, 8 in. diameter. D-22.50
Porringer, cast, 6¼ in. diameter. A-55.00
Pot, heavy wire handle, 5½ in. diameter. A-15.00
Rabbits, pair; white paint, 10½ in. high. A-95.00
Scotch Bowl, so-marked, two small side handles and tilt ring, 5 in. high. D-12.50
Tassel weights, set of four, 4½ in. high. A-14.00
Trivet, George Washington, 9½ in. long. A-22.50
Trivet, heart with scrolls. A-20.00
Urn, cast, 11¼ in. high. A-25.00
Vases, pair, one with cast name "Clyde", 14 in. high. A-125.00
Windmill weight, cast horse, old white and black paint, welded repair to feet, 17¼ in. high. A-55.00
Windmill weight, cast rooster, painted white. Has remains of wooden base, 9½ in. high. A-135.00

IRON—*Wrought*

Instead of being poured into a mold to form a cast object, wrought iron is shaped by hand, or by hand and machine. Wrought iron is sometimes also called "hand-made" or "hand-forged", or sometimes, merely "forged".

Baker's tongs, for grasping hot pans, 15 in. long. D-20.00
Cleaver, 15 in. long. D-20.00
Ferrier's tong, 15 in. long. A-9.00
Fork, simple tooling on handle, 16 in. long. A-32.50
Fork, delicate proportions, 16 in. long. A-20.00
Fork, tooled handle, 23 in. long. A-45.00
Hoe head, very early, 5 in. wide. D-12.00
Hook, four-prong, wrought, 5½ in. high. A-25.00
Hook, spike driven into wall with hook on underside, ornament above hook of six pieces iron with curled ends, length 5½ inches. A-105.00
Ice tongs, 25 in. long. A-11.00
Kettle set, fork, brass-bowled ladle and strainer, 17 in. long. D-55.00
Latch, curved end is spring, 23½ in. long. A-70.00
Latch and keeper, barn-door size, 15 in. long. A-25.00
Ornament, for top of flag pole, 9¾ in. high. A-25.00
Ring, with four double hooks, 6 in. diameter. A-50.00
Spring latch, 7½ in. long. A-30.00

Thumb latch, double heart finial, thumb piece missing, 11¼ in. long. A-35.00

Thumb latch, tulip on each end, thumb piece alongside, 16 in. long. A-135.00

Thumb latch, with latch rod and staple, good detail, 13½ in. long. A-75.00

Trap, single-spring, orig. pan, chain and hooks, 5 in. jaws. D-30.00

IRON—*Wrought Hinges*

Birds-head ends, pair; plain straps, 18¼ in. long. A-70.00
Double-arm ends, pair; 23¼ in. long. A-50.00
Double swan's head end, single hinge, 17 in. long. A-80.00
Doubles swan's head, pair; 23 in. long. A-55.00
Hinges, pair; 32 in. long. A-45.00
Pitchfork-shaped, pair; 8½ in. long. A-45.00
Ram's horn, pair; 9½ in. long. A-40.00
Ram's horn, pair; 7¾ inches long. A-60.00
Ram's horn, pair; 10½ in. long. A-75.00
Snake's head, single hinge, 15 in. high. A-40.00
Straps, pair; 18½ in. long. A-45.00
Straps, pair; 23½ in. long. A-40.00
T-shape, swordfish ends, single hinge, 12 in. drop, 36 in. long. D-60.00
Turnip-shape, single hinge, 6¾ in. long. A-12.50

IVORY PIECES—*[See also* **Oriental***]*

Box, covered, pouch form with relief of buddha on one side and monkey-like figure on other, deity finial. A-100.00

Candlestick, Chinese, engraved dragon and floral decoration on round wood base. Of 19th Century, 12 in. high. A-100.00

Chess set, Oriental, 32 characters in fitted game board case. A-350.00

Figure, medicine doll; Oriental, 8 in. long. A-160.00

Figure, of Kwan Yien; Chinese, late 19th Century, 26 in. high. A-550.00

Figure, of Kwan Yien; Chinese, with child, each holding prunus blossom, 9¼ in. high. A-275.00

Figure, of lady seated holding book, Oriental, 6 in. high. A-250.00

L. and r. pair of **Oriental carved ivory figures,** of an Emperor and Empress, 23 in. and 21½ in. high.   A/1500

Center, **Oriental carved ivory covered urn,** on pierced and carved wood stand. Height of ivory, 20 in.   A/650

Courtesy Adam A. Weschler & Son, Washington, D.C.; photograph by Breger & Associates.

Figure, of sea goddess, Chinese, goddess standing, holding basket of fish. Overall height, 9½ inches.   A-260.00

Figure of standing Buddha holding lotus blossom, on double-lotus blossom base, dressed in Bodhisattva flowing garments, 16 in. high.   A-950.00

Figure, of standing female deity, Chinese, prob. Ming Dynasty, AD 1368-1644, 9½ in. high.   A-625.00

Figure, of standing goddess, Chinese, with dragon holding basket with flowers, 9 in. high.   A-450.00

Figure, of standing lohan, Chinese, prob. Ming Dynasty, 9 in. high.   A-600.00

Figures of maidens, pair; Chinese, 19th Century, 7½ in. high.   A-350.00

Figures, two, Oriental, of young boy with wisp, other of man carrying buckets, 3¾ in. high.   A-125.00

Carved Ivory: Courtesy Adam A. Weschler & Son
Model of a clam in high relief carving of seated priest above interior with
horse and rider; signed in calligraphy.   A/200
Center left, **Group of mother and child.**   A/175
Center right, **Group with man and monkey on his back.**   A/75
Bot. left, **Study of seated Hotei.**   A/Unknown
Bot. center, **Group of men in fishing boat.** Signed in calligraphy. A/50
Bot right, **Group of old sage with staff and crane.**   A/50

Figure group, Chinese, bearded sage holding septre
and mounted on horse with attendant at his feet.
Height, 9 inches.   **A-300.00**

Figure group, Chinese, three actors, man and two
children, 7 in. high.   **A-200.00**

Figure, Japanese, of two men and boy, 6 in. high.   **A-225.00**

Landscape, Chinese, modeled, trees with buildings,
deity figures, etc. On carved and pierced wood
stand, 6 in. high.   **A-150.00**

Phoenix birds, pair, Oriental, 10 in. high.   **A-400.00**

Phoenix birds, pair, Oriental, 10 in. high.   **A-310.00**

Plaque, Japanese, carved ivory and laquer, circular,
19 in. diameter.   **A-220.00**

Pomegranate, Oriental, interior elaborately carved
with cliff dwellings and figures in wood landscape, 4
in. high.   **A-350.00**

Pomegranate, Oriental, interior carved with figures, 4 in. high.   A-210.00

Tusks, pair, bas relief of crane and serpent, 18 in. long.   A-110.00

Vase, Oriental, covered, dragon finial on domed top neck with foo dog mask and loose ring handles. Height, 9 inches.   A-175.00

Winter melon, Chinese, carved relief trailing vines opens to reveal two erotic scenes in high relief. Length, 3 inches.   A-400.00

JAPANESE COLLECTIBLES

Ball, rock crystal, resting on white brass chrysanthemum form base. Ca. 19th Century, 4½ in. diameter.   A-450.00

Bottles, Imari, pair; late 19th Century. Square tapered form with floral and gilt panels below vignettes, 11 in. high.   A-400.00

Box, lunch; black and gold lacquer, four-part, late 19th Century.   A-150.00

Figure, stone, of Jizo Diety (child god), Jeiji Period. Backed by a relief cloud-form nimbus, on double lotus plinth, 27 in. high.   A-600.00

Figures, stone, guardian, pair; Jeiji Period, each a standing warrior in dress uniform, 26 in. high.   A-1,050.00

Jardiniere, porcelain, octagonal, blue and white, 10 in. high.   A-35.00

Jardiniere, porcelain, footed, Celadon, square. Green, blue and white underglaze decoration, 8½ in. high.   A-120.00

Lantern, garden, stone; triple graduated pagoda form with turned and double lotus pole pediment. Meiji Period, 22 in. square, 81 in. high.   A-1,000.00

Screen, floor; lacquer, two-fold, 66 x 70 in. high.   A-100.00

Screen, table; lacquer, two-fold, polychrome decorated panels, 35 x 31 in. high.   A-120.00

Sword, Samauri, decorated brass tsuba, 17-in. blade. Menuki handle, scabbard, signed Kozuka utility blade 17 in. long.   A-175.00

Sword, of carved ivory, sheath having segmented scenes of ten warriors, bronze tsuba with four warriors on grip, 32½ in. long.   A-300.00

Imperial Japanese lacquer tray, 15½ in. wide and 21 in. long. Oblong, with deep section depicting procession in gold overlay, silver rim. 19th Century.   A/900

Courtesy of Adam A. Weschler & Son

Urns, Imari covered, pair; hexagonal shape panels of buildings, flowers, roosters and peacocks. Removable dome tops with pierced steeple-shaped finials, 17 in. high.   A-1,200.00

Vase, Imari long-neck; two medallions with floral landscape.   A-150.00

JEWELRY

Unlike many other kinds of collectibles, a fine assemblage of jewelry pieces takes up very little space. Good jewelry can be collected for beauty, worn for enjoyment, and is nearly unequaled as a sound investment.

Jewelry—*Antique*

10-K white gold engagement ring, nine tiny diamonds in cluster.   D-35.00

14-K gold ring, three diamonds across top.   D-95.00

14-K gold ring, with diamond approx. 32 pts.   D-110.00

14-K ladies wristwatch, yellow gold, filigree stretch-band.   D-45.00

14-K white gold ring, 35 pt. center diamond and six to sides.   D-140.00

18-K yellow gold plain wedding band.   D-33.00

Above left, **solid gold brooch,** real carnelian cameo, yellow and gold finish. 175-200

Above center, **brooch,** 10k, reconstructed ruby, 2 pearls, 18k white gold front, green gold finish. 80-100

Above right, 10k yellow gold **necklace,** imitation aquamarine, real baroque pearl. 90-110

Left, 10k gold **brooch,** reconstructed ruby, real whole pearls, green gold raised leaves. 80-100

Jewelry—*Art Deco*

Gold earrings, 14-K, each with two rubies and dangling pearl. **D-39.00**

Pink gold lapel watch, 14-K, by Hamilton. **D-165.00**

Ring, 10-K, oval opal with two small opals. **D-35.00**

Ring, yellow 14-K gold, eight tiny turquoises. **D-29.00**

Wristwatch, pink gold, with 14-K gold band, ten diamonds, eight rubies. **D-275.00**

Jewelry—*Art Nouveau*

Earrings, sterling. **D-19.00**

Pendant, sterling chain. **D-13.00**

Pendant, enameled, with three diamonds, on 14-K gold chain. **D-72.00**

Ring, sterling, with garnet at end of curl. **D-10.00**

Ring, 14-K gold with oval top for engraving. **D-52.00**

Ring, 14-K gold wraparound with three diamonds. **D-85.00**

Ring, enameled, 14-K gold, with three diamonds. **D-89.00**

Jewelry—*Bangles, Bracelets*

14-K antique-style tubular bangle, with two rubies.   **D-115.00**
14-K florentined bangle with 21 swirled diamonds.   **D-245.00**
14-K narrow slip-on bangle.   **D-44.00**
14-K slip-on rope-twist bangle in three-color gold.   **D-76.00**
14-K wide bangle, opens, engraved all around.   **D-155.00**
14-K ankle bracelet, with two gold hearts.   **D-16.00**
14-K chain bracelet, thick gold rope, 8 inches.   **D-68.00**
14-K double gold circle linked bracelet.   **D-74.00**
18-K charm bracelet, antique. With twelve pink gold charms in 14-K and 18-K gold; alarm clock, phone, bird, etc.   **D-290.00**

Bracelet and earrings set, gold and onyx.
Set: C/150-200

Necklace/locket, jet and silver, Victorian.
C/45-60
Ring, gold, pearl setting   C/30-40
Brooch, cast metal backing, composition stones.   C/5-10
Brooch, tooled silver back, red stones.
C/25-35

Jewelry—*Chains*

14-K yellow gold cable chain, 12 inches.   **D-14.00**
14-K yellow gold neck chain, 15 inches.   **D-15.00**
14-K yellow gold neck chain, old and heavy, 25 inches.   **D-110.00**
14-K yellow gold man's watch chain, 11½ inches. Antique.   **D-84.00**
14-K fancy link green gold and platinum man's watch chain, 14½ inches long. Antique.   **D-150.00**
18-K yellow gold "S" chain, heavy, 22 in. long.   **D-110.00**
Platinum fancy link watch chain, 13½ in. long. Antique.   **D-80.00**

Belt chain,
10K yellow gold, 10K green gold.   75-90

Gold filled **chain**, 18 in.
35-45

Jewelry—*Charms*

Baby carriage, antique 14-K yellow gold.	**D-29.00**
Comedy and tragedy, old 14-K yellow gold.	**D-12.00**
Convertible car, old 14-K yellow gold, moveable wheels and trunk.	**D-46.00**
Faith, Hope & Charity, 14-K yellow gold.	**D-16.00**
Golf clubs in bag, old 14-K yellow gold, removeable clubs.	**D-31.00**
Moveable carrousel, antique 14-K yellow gold.	**D-40.00**
Moveable baby in playpen, old 14-K yellow gold.	**D-18.00**
Old woman that lived in a shoe, old 14-K yellow gold.	**D-25.00**
Tricycle, antique 14-K yellow gold.	**D-32.00**
Typewriter, moveable, old 14-K yellow gold.	**D-23.00**
Violin, antique 14-K yellow gold.	**D-19.00**

Jewelry—*Custom*

14-K band with five oval turquoises across top.	**D-35.00**
14-K chain, bars and links, 15 inches.	**D-92.00**
14-K chain, interlocking "U"-shaped links, 15 inches.	**D-38.00**
14-K ring with four sapphires and two diamonds.	**D-69.00**
14-K ring with cluster of four rubies.	**D-52.00**
14-K ring, flower-shaped with diamond center and swirl.	**D-115.00**

Jewelry—*Gentlemen's*

10-K ring, with large, square, deep-red stone.	**D-23.00**
14-K man's ring with garnet and diamond each side.	**D-65.00**
14-K oval cufflinks and tie-tac, each set with a black star sapphire.	**D-110.00**
14-K ring with three diamonds (¾ carat).	**D-245.00**
14-K wedding band, size 9¾, of three woven strands.	**D-48.00**

ID bracelet, heavy, 14-K yellow gold.   **D-395.00**
ID bracelet, very heavy, 18-K pink gold.   **D-765.00**

Jewelry—*Precious Stones and Metals*

Blue sapphire and diamond ring. White gold mount
set with oval faceted blue sapphire (approx. 1.60
carats) and six round diamonds.   **A-475.00**

Top, l., **Emerald and diamond brooch.**   A/650
Top, r., **Coral and diamond brooch.**   A/325
Center, **Coral bead, diamond, sapphire, emerald and ruby bracelet.**
                                                            A/750
Bottom, **Cultured pearl, ruby and diamond bracelet.**   A/1000
Courtesy Adam A. Weschler & Son, Washington, D.C.; photograph by
Breger & Associates.

Diamond bar pin, Victorian. Yellow gold mount set
with four mine-cut diamonds weighing appox. 1.25
carats.   **A-425.00**

Diamond brooch, circular. Platinum mount set with
25 round diamonds weighing approx. 12.75 carats.   **A-2,500.00**

Diamond brooch—Lavaliere. Platinum mount set
with 18 emerald-cut diamonds and 126 round
diamonds. Total weight of diamonds approx. 6
carats.   **A-1,900.00**

Diamond flexible bracelet. Platinum mount set with
four round diamonds weighing approx. three carats
and 140 round diamonds weighing 4.90 carats.   **A-2,400.00**

Diamond dinner ring. 14-K white gold mount set with
three round diamonds weighing approx. one carat,
centering 16 round diamonds weighing approx. two
carats.   **A-1,500.00**

Diamond gypsy ring. Set with round canary diamond
weighing approx. one carat.   **A-750.00**

Bot. left
Marquise diamond ring.
A/7900

Bot. right
Man's star sapphire ring.
A/3250

Top left
Blue sapphire and diamond ring. A/1000

Top right
Diamond dinner ring.
A/2300

Courtesy of Adam A. Weschler & Son

Diamond earrings, pair, 14-K four-prong Tiffany-type mountings set with round diamonds weighing approx. 1.30 carats.   A-650.00

Diamond and pearl bangle bracelet. 14-K yellow gold, white gold top, mount set with 38 round diamonds weighing approx. .60 carats, and seven cultured pearls.   A-825.00

Emerald and diamond earrings, pair. Yellow-white gold mounts set with two pear-shaped faceted emeralds, two carved emeralds and six rose diamonds.   A-675.00

Emerald and diamond ring. White gold mount centering round faceted emerald weighing approx. .75 carats, surrounded by 24 round diamonds weighing approx. one carat.   A-700.00

Emerald-cut diamond ring. Platinum mount set with emerald-cut diamond weighing approx. 1.85 carats, centering two tapered baguettes.   A-2,400.00

Emerald pendant and chain. 14-K yellow gold mount set with octagonal faceted emerald weighing approx. 48.50 carats and three round faceted emeralds.   A-475.00

209

Lapis lazuli, coral and diamond butterfly brooch.
14-K yellow gold mount set with 18 cabochon lapis
lazuli, 12 angleskin polished coral and 54 round
diamonds. Total weight of diamonds approx. 2.40
carats.

A-850.00

Mexican opal and diamond ring. Yellow gold mount
set with four polished Mexican opals and five round
diamonds. Total weight of diamonds approx. .35
carats.

A-525.00

Opal and diamond ring, custom design. 14-K yellow
gold mount set with eight marquise cabochon opals
and six round diamonds.

A-400.00

Ruby and diamond bracelet. 18-K flexible floral
mount set with 60 round faceted rubies and 36 round
diamonds. Total weight of diamonds approx. two
carats.

A-1,400.00

Ruby and diamond ring. 18-K yellow gold mount set
with oval faceted ruby weighing approx. 1.35 carats
and 22 round diamonds weighing approx. 1.25
carats.

**Sapphire and diamond flexible straight-row
bracelet.** Platinum mount set with eighteen square
blue sapphires weighing approx. six carats and 18
round diamonds weighing approx. 3.50 carats.

A-3,200.00

Tiger's eye and diamond ring. 14-K yellow gold owl
form mount set with 11 round diamonds weighing approx. .65 carats, and two tiger's eyes.

A-450.00

Topaz and diamond brooch. 14-K yellow gold mount
set with six emerald-cut topaz and 16 round
diamonds. Total weight of diamonds approx. .50
carats.

A-350.00

Right, **antique carved coral flower brooch-lavalier,**
yellow gold mounts, ca. 1870.   A/125
Above left, **antique carved coral zinnia brooch,**
yellow gold mount, late 19th Century.   A/250
Above center, **carved coral "rose" earrings,** pair,
yellow gold screw mounts.   A/175
Courtesy of Adam A. Weschler & Son

KITCHEN COLLECTIBLES—[See also Butter Related]

Apple corer, tin, cylindrical, 7 in. long.	D-8.50
Apple corer, tin, hollow handle, 6 in. long.	S-9.00
Apple peeler, mechanical, "Goodell Co.", direct-pivot model.	D-49.50
Baking tin, set; eight tin pans, various sizes, rolled edges.	D-18.50
Batter beater, mfg. by "A. & J.", metal beater, wood handle.	D-4.50
Batter beater, wireware, marked "Androck", wood handle.	D-6.00
Batter pitcher, stoneware, cobalt blue glazed ring, 8¼ in high.	D-36.50
Beanpot, redware, chocolate glazed, one-half gallon size.	D-15.00
Bread box, tin, orig. japanning, 8¾ x 9 x 12½ inches.	D-18.50
Bread maker, "Universal #4, tin, complete and dated 1904.	D-22.50
Bread peel, handcarved wood, 8½ x 13 inches, 9 in. handle.	D-55.00
Braising pot, cast iron body and handle, 10¾ in. diameter.	D-16.50
Broiler, wrought handle and body, 17½ in. long.	A-65.00
Broiler, revolving, rectangular, wrought iron, 22 in. long.	A-50.00
Cake decorator, tin, brass rod and funnel, 8 in. long.	D-13.00
Cake pan, tin, angel food. Cooling rack, 10 in. diameter.	A-7.00
Cake turner, tinned, with wireware handle, hearts motif.	D-6.00
Candy kettle, copper, double row of brass dovetailing, 25¾ in. diameter.	D-395.00
Candy kettle, handforged iron handles, copper rivets, 7½ in. high.	D-295.00
Candy thermometer, brass-faced, tin-backed, 6½ in. long.	D-19.00
Can opener, "Famous Narragansit".	D-4.50
Can opener, "Edlund Co.", steel blade, wood handles.	D-6.50
Cheese grater, pine, tin surface, 9½ x 14 inches.	A-32.50
Cheese shredder, hopper on board, crank handle, 10 x 11½ inches.	A-52.50

Flour sifter, marked tin, Japanned round handle.
C/8-12
Bread knife, heavy wire handle. C/9-12

Paddle, or flat kitchen ladle, dated 1707. From southern U.S., hardwood, about 14 in. long.
C/60-85

Kitchen grater, "Use Fels-Naptha Soap".
C/6-9

Cornbread mold, cast iron, "Griswold Crispy Corn Stick Pan", 13 in. long.
C/15-20

Cheese strainer, woven woodsplint, 18½ in. diameter. A-135.00

Cherry pitter, twin-pronged plungers, table-top, 8 in. high. S-24.00

Child's knife and fork, steel, inlaid wood handles. A-10.00

Chopping knife, steel blade, wood handle, fine condition. S-13.00

Churn-beater, wire, 11 in. long. D-6.50

Coffee grinder, "Crystal", glass jar, wall mount. D-35.00

Coffee grinder, wall type, "Golden Rule Blend Coffee". D-30.00

Knife tray, handle hole, stained red, 15 in. long.
C/35-45

Can openers, early types.
Right, metal-framed. C/3-5
Left, wood-handled.
C/4-6

Candy mold, consisting of eight 5-bear white-metal units within rectangular metal frame. All units can be removed, total measures 10½ x 19¼ inches.
Private collection.   C/30-45

Center, **spice cannister,** adjustable top opening, tin.   C/2-4
Lower, dipper-like **spoon** with central drainage hole.   C/5-8

Coffee grinder, wood, dovetailed corners, orig. faded lable. Extra-fine condition, 13 in. overall height.   C/75-90

Coffee mill, tabletop, with glass bean bin.	**A-26.00**
Coffee pot, tin, embossed circles, 9 in. high.	**D-60.00**
Coffee pot, tin, made of four pieces, 6½ in. high.	**D-50.00**
Coffee pot, sidehandled, tin, ca. 1840, 8½ in. high.	**D-65.00**
Coffee pot, tin, turned wood handle, 6 in. basal diameter.	**A-12.50**
Coffee pot, side spout, tin, 9½ in. high.	**A-27.50**
Collander, tin, nicely footed, well-punched holes, 10 in. diameter.	**D-10.00**

Collander, tin, metal-legged, wooden roller; 9 in. high. D-14.00

Cook pot, copper, covered; ca. 1830, 4 x 6½ inches, handled. D-125.00

Cookie board, good color, 19¼ x 28½ inches. A-55.00

Cookie board, 13 x 26 inches, pine. A-32.50

Cookie board, pine, 15½ x 40 inches. A-30.00

Cookie board, round, 18 in. diameter. A-52.50

Cookie cutter, stake handle, Vermont, 3 in. diameter. D-10.00

Cookie cutter, tin, bird, 4¼ in. long. A-11.00

Cookie cutter, top-hatted man, German marks, 12¾ in. high. D-54.00

Cookie cutter, tin, bird, 4½ in. long. A-12.00

Cookie cutter, tin, horse with mane and tail, 4½ in. long. A-40.00

Cookie cutter, tin, rooster, 3 in. high. A-21.00

Cookie cutter, tin, fish with crimped fin, 5 in. long. A-15.00

Cookie cutter, very primitive chicken. A-7.00

Cookie roller, solid maple, corrugated head, 10 in. long. D-22.50

Cutting board, heart cut-out handle, 8 x 11¾ inches. A-27.50

Cream whipper, "A. & J.", bowl-type, ca. 1900. D-8.50

Dipper, tin, 9 in. top diameter, 4 in. high. D-24.50

Dipper and spatula, combination tool, iron, 14½ in. long. A-25.00

Dishrack, wire, ca. 1900, 4 x 12½ x 16 inches. D-12.50

Double boiler, two-piece set, copper, 5½ in. diameter. D-75.00

Dough board, pine, 2 in. rear splash edging, 18 x 28 inches. D-25.00

Dough box, poplar, never finished; 9 x 14 x 32 inches. A-25.00

Dough box, pine, dovetailed; 13½ x 14 x 32½ inches. A-65.00

Dough cutters, iron and wood, wheeled, ca. 1910. D-4.50

Dough scraper, wrought iron, 6½ in. long. S-25.00

Dough scraper, wrought iron, handled, 4 in. long. A-17.50

Dough scraper, wrought iron, wood handle, 4 in. long. A-12.50

Drainers, pair, wireware with bowl clips, one tin-toned brass. D-15.00

Eggbeater, cast iron, "Dover", wood handle and tin blades. D-12.50

Kitchen tool, "Castello's Knife / Pat'd 1913". For coring, peeling and slicing apples, 7 in. long. C/10-16

Ladle, wrought iron handle with hanging tip, perforated brass bowl held with copper rivets. C/50-65

Kitchen press, early, oak base, iron frame, screw and wheel. With milled brass container; acquired in Pennsylvania, ca. late 1800's, 15 in. high. C/80-100

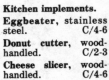

Kitchen implements.
Eggbeater, stainless steel. C/4-6
Donut cutter, wood-handled. C/2-3
Cheese slicer, wood-handled. C/4-6

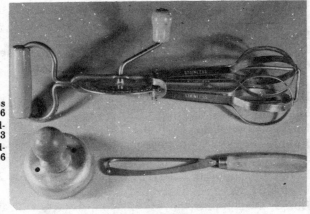

Eggbeater, tin, Pat'd 1923, tin gears, wood-knob handle. **D-10.00**

Ember tongs, brass, oval handle holes, 10 in. long. **A-10.00**

Feeding dish, child's, "Weller", yellow-duckling center. **D-17.50**

Fish-cutting board, old, 13 in. long. **A-22.50**

Fish poacher, copper, copper draining tray, brass lift handles. **D-85.00**

Food chopper, crescent blade, turned hardwood handle, worn. **D-16.00**

Food chopper, tin, double-bladed, 4½ in. high. **S-6.50**

Food chopper, "Rollmans", table clamp, nickeled iron, 6 in. high. **D-12.50**

Food chopper, "Warranted Cast Steel", 6 in. wide. A-12.00

Food cover, tin, dome top with pewter lift finial, 8 in. diameter. D-35.00

Food grinder, "Enterprise", extra-large country store size. D-15.00

Flour sifter, tin, knobbed turner on handle end. S-11.00

Frying pan, sheet iron, wrought handle stamped "Wood". A-50.00

Funnel, handhammered copper, dovetailed, 7½ in. diameter. D-59.50

Funnel, copper, orig. tin liner, 5½ x 6½ inches. D-22.50

Funnel, tin, with pointed juicing spear, and filter. D-5.00

Grater, plated tinware, Germany mark, 12 in. long. D-10.00

Grater, tin, with handle, ca. 1890. D-6.50

Grater, tin, unusual triangular punching, 11½ in. high. A-10.00

Grater, pierced tin, half-round side, 8½ in. long. S-30.00

Grater, tin, "Marvel Kitchen Utility", ca. 1920, 9½ in. diameter. D-10.00

Griddle, soapstone; iron bandings and side loops. Scarce. D-30.00

Herb masher, maple, concentrics on handle, 5 in. long. D-18.50

Hook, wrought iron, four-prong, 8 in. long. A-15.00

Juice reamer, milk glass, "Sunkist", 9 in. handle to lip. D-6.50

Kitchen canisters, pair, "Coffee" and "Tea", old. D-7.50

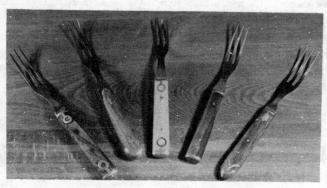

Wood and bone-handled forks, pewter inlaid.   Each: C/4-8

Lar Hothem photo.

Sugar bucket, Shaker, all wood, lapped wood hoops top and bottom. Top diameter 11½ inches, 16½ in. high.   C/125-175

Wooden bowl, large and fine, about 15 in. diameter.   D/35

Vegetable strainer, 12½ in. long.   C/15-20
Grater, grid wires.   C/4-6
Country inn cooker, tin-lined, copper. With lift-lid and steam spout, late 1700's / early 1800's; 18 x 21½ x 17 in. high.   Private collection. C/325-425
Spice cabinet, with orig. drawer pulls, 10 in. wide. Note, back is a later addition, attached for hanging purposes, 17 in. high.   C/60-85

Kitchen cupboard, "Napanee", zinc top, complete with orig. flour bin, swing-out glass sugar, spice set, and label.   **A-275.00**

Kitchenware set, wrought iron, well-tooled, five pieces.   **D-375.00**

Knife box, pine, divider and grip handle, 2½ x 6¼ x 11 inches.   **D-23.00**

Kraut chopper, wood handle, 9¼ in. wide.   **A-25.00**

Kraut chopper, wood handle, 8 in. wide.   **A-20.00**

Kraut cutter, hickory handle, iron blade.   **A-13.00**

Kraut cutter, wood handle, blade 6½ in. long.   **A-7.00**

Ladle, carved wood, well-shaped handle, 6½ in. long.   **A-40.00**

Ladle, hand-wrought handle, iron bowl 6 in. diameter.   **D-37.50**

Lemon squeezer, wood, hinged, 10½ in. long. — A-22.50

Lemon squeezer, two-piece wooden, porcelain receptacle. — D-25.00

Lemon squeezer, wood, replacement handles, 12 in. long. — S-18.00

Maple syrup pot, tin, black, spout filter, 4¾ in. high. Rare. — D-75.00

Masher, wood, 6 in. high. — S-6.00

Masher, wood, round bottom and carved from one piece. — D-6.00

Match safe, cast iron, kitchen-type, 2¼ x 3 x 5 inches. — D-30.00

Match holder, for tabletop, well-turned wood; 4½ in. high. — D-21.50

Measure, copper, wide-band strap handle, ca. 1840, tin lining. — D-99.50

Measure, brass, one-pint capacity, early seaming, rolled edges. — D-110.00

Measure, brass, one-quart capacity, strap handle, rolled edging. — D-110.00

Measure, copper, side-handled, ca. 1800, 8 in. high. — D-100.00

Measure, copper, hooded spout, ca. 1790, 10½ in. high. — D-125.00

Measuring cup, concentric lines, tin, ca. 1890, 3 in. high. — D-5.00

Meat tenderizer, stoneware, wood handle, 9 in. long, chipped. — A-10.00

Meat tenderizer, stoneware, wood handle, 10 in. long. — A-25.00

Mixing bowl, yellowware, brown stripes, 6½ in. diameter. — A-12.50

Mixing bowl, yellowware, blue/white stripes, 9½ in. dia. — A-20.00

Mortar and pestle, maple, 9 in. high, 4½ in. diameter. — D-40.00

Mortar and pestle, turned maple, 4½ x 7½ inches. — D-46.50

Muffin pan, cast iron, six compartments, 5¾ x 9¾ inches. — A-20.00

Muffin pan, cast iron, three legs, handles, 7½ in. diameter. — A-45.00

Nutcracker, plated cast iron, screw-type, ca. 1910. — D-16.50

Nutmeg grater, lift-top for nutmeg storage, 6 in. long. — D-8.50

Nutmeg grater, tin, 6¼ in. high. — A-7.50

Nutmeg grater, 4 in. long, tin. — A-5.00

Kitchen chopper, handforged steel blade, wooden handle, 5 in. wide.
C/9-15

Cutlery sharpener, hardwood base, cast iron water trough and crank shaft. With wood handle, Berea sandstone wheel.
C/35-50

Table set, early, bone handles with pewter inlays.
Set: C/15-25

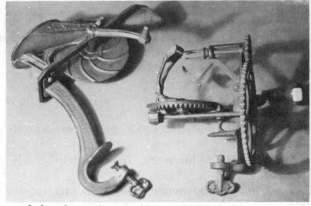

Left, **cherry-pitter,** tabletop clamp model, cast metal. C/18
Right, **apple-peeler,** tabletop clamp model, crank handle, cast metal. C/25

Plunger churn, stave-constructed, iron hoops. Body 21 in. high, basal diameter 11 in.
C/125-175

Kitchen masher, hand-carved hardwood, old, 13 in. high.
C/25-35

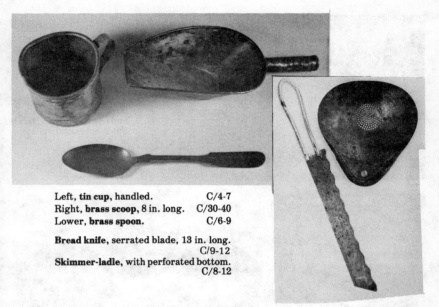

Left, **tin cup,** handled.   C/4-7
Right, **brass scoop,** 8 in. long.   C/30-40
Lower, **brass spoon.**   C/6-9

Bread knife, serrated blade, 13 in. long.
                                                    C/9-12
Skimmer-ladle, with perforated bottom.
                                                    C/8-12

Nutmeg grater, wall-hanging, tin, 5 in. long.	D-7.50
Nutmeg grater, turned walnut case, spring-feed, 2 in. diameter.	A-80.00
Oven peel, wood, 3 ft. long, peel 15 in. diameter.	D-65.00
Pan, tin, oval, rolled edges, 2¾ x 4 x 7 inches.	D-3.00
Pastry board, gallery strip three sides, 17½ x 25¾ inches.	A-17.50
Pastry cutter, brass wheel, wrought iron, 6 in. long.	A-25.00
Pastry cutter, wrought iron, brass wheel, 8¼ in. long.	A-20.00
Pie lifter, wireware, grasps pie top and bottom, 16 in. long.	A-15.00
Pineapple eye snips, for digging and cutting excess; Pat'd 1901.	D-22.50
Plates, two; tin, 10 in. diameter.	A-12.50
Pot holder, crewel work, rose figure, ca. 1870.	D-6.50
Potato masher, wood, one-piece construction.	D-8.50
Potato masher, oak and maple, ca. 1860.	D-7.50
Potato masher, wood and wireware, ca. 1900.	D-4.50
Potato ricer, zinc-plated iron, Pat'd 1881.	D-8.50
Potato peeler and parer, steel, wire and wood, ca. 1900.	D-6.00
Pourer, tin, multi-spout, 8 in. wide.	A-107.50
Pudding molds, set; three nesting, oval, fluted tins.	D-25.00

Noodle board or dough tray, with added side and backboards. Of thick softwood, 26½ in. wide. C/15-25

Egg basket, wireware, collapsible, bottom 6 in. diameter. C/30-40

Cookie cutters, left and center; right, donut cutter, all tin with patina.

L. to r.: C/3-6
C/2-4
C/4-6

Pudding mold, stamped tin, scalloped fluting, 8 in. diameter. **D-6.50**

Pudding pan, tin, three-footed, wire handle, 6 in. diameter. **D-20.00**

Rolling pin, handmade, wood, 16 in. long. **D-24.00**

Rolling pin, wood with some curl, 19½ in. long. **A-12.50**

Rolling pin, cigar-shaped rolling surface, 17 in. long. **S-24.00**

Rolling pin, tin, with wooden handles; 17 in. long. **A-45.00**

Rolling pin, curly, maple, 18½ in. long. **A-42.50**

Rolling pin, all-wood, one-piece, 20 in. long. **D-12.00**

Salt box, poplar, hanging, slant lid, 9 x 9½ x 10½ inches. **A-30.00**

Salt box, pine, hanging, oak lid; 6 x 7 x 14 inches. **A-25.00**

Sauce pot, iron, footed, handled; 5 in. diameter. **D-40.00**

Sausage stuffer, metal, lever-action, Pat'd. 1875. **A-25.00**

Sausage stuffer, tin, round case, wood plunger, 16 in. long. **S-33.00**

Kitchen work table, with enameled-metal top. Left, pastry board, right, cutting board, both removable; table 20 in. high.   C/50-80

Shaker, sterling silver on glass, early 1900's. Star top openings, 2¾ in. high.
                    C/12-18

Cream whipper, tin, by Fries, 9½ in. high. Private collection.   C/45-60

Scouring box, pine, center worn through, 12 x 18½ inches.	A-32.50
Shaker, tin, poss. for salt, 3 inches high.	S-14.50
Sieve, tin, 11¼ in. diameter.	A-18.00
Sieve, dish-shaped with perforated bottom in star pattern.	S-9.00
Sieve, tin, heart-shaped, three triangular feet, 3¾ in. high.	A-67.50
Skillet, cast iron, "S. P. & Co.", 2¼ x 11¾ in. diameter.	D-12.00
Skimmer, wrought iron, 12 in. long.	A-15.00
Skimmer, brass, forged-iron handle, three rows holes; early.	D-95.00
Spatula, wrought iron, 4¾ in. long.	A-42.50
Spatula, wrought iron, 11½ in. long.	A-22.50
Spice box, tin, lift-top, small, ca. 1850.	D-25.00
Spice box, tin, with seven small containers inside.	D-35.00
Spice canister, tin, dome-top, 2¼ in. diameter.	D-6.00
Spice canister, tin, early seaming, 3¾ in. diameter.	D-6.50
Spice container, without individual units, 7 in. diameter.	D-16.50
Spice rack, wood, eight drawers, 10 in. high.	D-48.00
Spice set, six spice cans inside, old hasp, ca. 1870.	D-35.00

Enameled metal kitchen grouping, white with black trim. All left
to right:
    Large funnel, handled.   C/4-6
    Small funnel, handled.   C/3-5
    Cup.   C/2-4
    Spouted pouring container.   C/5-9

Kettle, copper, known as apple-
butter kettle in the Midwest.
Excellent condition, wrought
iron handle, 23¾ in. diameter,
top.
    Private collection.   C/225-295

Pitter, "New Standard Cherry Stoner / Mt. Joy, PA",
11½ in. high.
                                  C/16-22

    Ladle (Germany.   C/4-6
    Fruit press.   C/10-14
    Fork.   C/3-5

Juice squeezer, cast aluminum,
counter-top model. Maker-marked
and 9 in. long.
Private collection.   C/12-16

Fork, iron tines, wooden handle, brass rivets, "Russell /
Green River Works", 18 in. long.   C/15-25

Spoon, kitchen, white metal, sieve bottom, 11 in. long. **S-4.00**

Spoon, curly maple, hand-carved, 7 in. long. **A-22.50**

Steamer, tin, single handle, rolled edges, 5½ in. high. **D-3.00**

Stew pot, copper, brass-dovetailed, ca. 1830; 10½ in. diameter. **D-165.00**

Stirring spoon, wooden, ball-topped handle, 14 in. long. **D-4.00**

Stock pot, copper, brass-dovetailed, 11 in. diameter. **D-145.00**

Stove lifter, old-fashioned, cast iron. **D-1.50**

Strainer, tin, punched design, 6 in. diameter. **A-50.00**

Strainer, wrought iron and brass, small bowl, 9 in. long. **A-80.00**

Strainer, tin, lapping at seams, hand-pierced, 11 in. diameter. **D-30.00**

Strainer, heavy copper, with handles; 15 in. diameter. **A-30.00**

Strainer, brass bowl and brass bottom screen; 6 in. diameter. **S-33.00**

Strainer, brass, white-metal handle, 6½ in. long. **A-20.00**

Sugar bucket, tin, hinged, excellent japanning; ca. 1890. **D-10.00**

Syrup pitcher, tin, covered with wire loop finial, 6¼ in. high. **D-32.50**

Table fork, two-tined, wooden handle, ca. 1850, 6¾ in. long. **D-4.50**

Table knife, bone-handled, "Naylor", 9 in. long. **D-3.50**

Table knife, pewter inlaid handle, 7¾ in. long. **D-4.00**

Taster, wrought iron, handle signed and dated 1843, 10 in. long. **A-150.00**

Taster, wrought iron and brass, 10½ in. long. **A-35.00**

Teakettle, cast iron, gooseneck, four-footed, copper cover. **D-79.50**

Teakettle, cast iron, 8 in. high. **A-35.00**

Teakettle, gooseneck, footed, wrought handle, 10 in. high. **A-115.00**

Teakettle, copper, wirebail handle, 6¼ in. high. **D-37.50**

Teakettle, copper, folding wire handle, 10 in. basal diameter. **D-40.00**

Teakettle, brass dovetailing, American, ca. 1820, 9½ in. high. **D-135.00**

Teapot, tin, punched designs, 5½ in. high. **A-45.00**

Teapot, tin, oval, straight spout, 4¾ in. high. **S-55.00**

Toaster, wrought iron, turned wood handle, 21½ in. long.   **A-180.00**

Toaster, wrought iron, ornamental twisted grill, 20½ in. long.   **A-170.00**

Toaster, wrought iron, bread rack incomplete.   **A-30.00**

Toaster, tapered pencil-post handle, delicate, 31½ in. long.   **A-140.00**

Trivet, wrought iron, rotating top 6 in. diameter, 17 in. long.   **A-70.00**

Utensil rack, wrought iron, 12 in. long.   **A-22.50**

Utensil rack, wrought iron, five hooks, 22 in. long.   **A-95.00**

Vegetable masher, wire head, wood handle, ca. 1920.   **D-4.50**

Vegetable slicer, serrated tin blade, wood handle, 7 in. long.   **D-3.00**

Wafer iron, wrought iron, dated "1860", 32 in. long.   **A-25.00**

Waffle iron, circular, mounted in round iron frame.   **S-17.00**

Waffle iron, wooden handles, overhead bail, unmarked.   **D-16.00**

Warming oven, tin, floor model, dome top, with charcoal oven.   **D-150.00**

Washer, for vegetables, 5½ in. high.   **A-15.00**

Washer, sewer tile, colander with ¾ in. holes; 13½ in high.   **A-55.00**

Lemon squeezers, three varieties.
Top, all-wood, turned handles.   C/30-45
Left, white metal, spring handle opener   C/10-15
Right, japanned cast iron, removabl: ceramic insert.
Private collection.   C/25-35

Food cutters and choppers.
Left, cast iron handle, six steel blades.   C/10-15
Lower right, steel blade and wooden handle.   C/8-12

Canning items.
Fruit jar holders, wireware, each.   C/9-12
Jar filler, clear glass.   C/4-6
Canning jar, ½ gal., Atlas, each.   C/10-13

LAMPS

Aladdin lamp, white milkglass shade, flint glass, oil.　　**D-145.00**

Aladdin, brass base, handpainted milkglass shade with pink roses, old shade with decoration added later; electrified, 21 in. high.　　**D-125.00**

Alcohol lamp, two wicks, twin brass spouts, "H. A.", ½ pint capacity.　　**D-45.00**

Lamps, kerosene, left to right:
Miniature, orig. shade, replaced globe.
C/25-35
Lamp, old but not orig. chimney.
C/35-45
Miniature, frosted base, acorn wick knob.　　C/25-35

Astral lamp, brass fluted column, marble base, prism ring frosted cut to clear shade. No burner, 15 in. high.　　**A-155.00**

Astral lamp, gilt brass petal form, stepped marble and brass base. With burner, two mis-matched prisms, 18¾ in. high.　　**A-145.00**

Bedside oil lamp, brass, pedestaled, tin bottom, blown chimney, 14 in. high.　　**D-65.00**

Betty lamp, attached three-footed saucer, cast iron, 6 in. high.　　**A-85.00**

Bracket lamp, Bristol blue art glass, white enamelled decor, converted to electricity, font 6 in. diameter.　　**D-35.00**

Clear lamp, blown urn-shaped font, minor base chips, 6½ in. high.　　**A-50.00**

Clear lamp, pressed haxagonal base, diamond pattern font, 7½ in. high.　　**A-37.50**

Clear lamp, pressed hexagonal base, tulip pattern font, 6 in. high.　　**A-22.50**

Crusie lamp, double, tin, with pick and hanging hook. Early lapped tin, can be used separately, 8 in. high.　　**D-185.00**

Crusie lamp, iron, rust damage, 7¼ in. high.　　**D-60.00**

Standing lamp,
1870's.
45-50

Standing Lamp,
1870's.
45-50

Hanging Lamp,
1880's.
350+

Footed Hand Lamp,
1890's.
45-50

Footed Hand Lamp,
1870's.
45-50

Footed Hand Lamp,
1890's.
50-55

Figural stem lamp, "Grape Harvest", boy, dog and grapes, font in frosted Dexter pattern, blown chimney. — **D-125.00**

Finger lamp, kerosene, pressed glass, brass cap and burner. — **D-35.00**

Finger lamp, blown-in-mold, shading from clear to sunturned amethyst, pedestal base, applied handle, 3 x 3 x 3½ in. high. — **D-42.00**

Going To Bed Lamps: These held a supply of phosphorus-coated match-like sticks. At bedtime one was removed, struck on the attached abrasive surface and place in hole in lamptop. It remained lighted long enough to get into bed for the night. Examples follow:

> **Ceramic,** in shape of beehive. — **A-35.00**
>
> **Lignum vitae,** threaded cap, ivory receptacle, 3 in. high. — **A-27.50**
>
> **Lignum vitae and satinwood,** two, 2 and 2½ in. high. — **A-47.50**
>
> **Treen,** with transfer scene, ivory receptacle, 3 in. high. — **A-27.50**
>
> **Treen,** with transfer scene, ivory receptacle. — **A-42.50**
>
> **Treen,** with transfer scene, age check in lid. — **A-25.00**
>
> **Treen,** with photographic scene, 2¼ in. high. — **A-35.00**
>
> **Wood,** covered with plaid paper, 2½ in. high. — **A-27.50**

Gone With The Wind lamp. — **A-50.00**

Grease lamp, iron and brass, wick support, 8½ in. high. — **A-215.00**

Grease lamp, adjustable sawtooth trammel a replacement, 3 in. high. — **A-50.00**

Grease lamp, stoneware. — **D-220.00**

Grease lamp, wrought iron with twisted hanger, 6½ in. high. — **A-115.00**

Hurricane lamp, with reflector, brass, 12 in. high. — **D-135.00**

Lamp, kerosene, petticoat base, flint blown chimney, 17 in. high. — **D-45.00**

Lamp, kerosene, brass, brass burner, blown chimney, 8½ in. high. — **D-62.50**

Lamp, kerosene, ruby glass font, marble base, 16¼ in. high. — **D-89.50**

Lamp, opalescent base, clear pressed font, brass collar, 7 in. high. — **A-50.00**

Lamp, oil, brass, weighted base, 10 in. high. — **A-22.50**

Cut Glass, late
1800's.

900+

Standing Lamp,
1890's.

75-85

Lamps, clear flint, pair; Rigler fonts, base chips, 11½ in. high. **A-85.00**

Lamp, clear pressed glass, pewter collar, mismatched whale oil burner, 9 in. high. **A-60.00**

Lamp, tin, double-spout, handle, 8 in. across and high. **A-105.00**

"Meeting house" lamps, pair. Brass wall-bracket lamps, kerosene, from New Hampshire, flint blown chimneys, 15 in. high. **D-175.00**

Miner's lamp, tin, ca. 1860, contoured to forehead, brass spout. **D-57.00**

Miner's lamp, brass, "T. & W. Aberdare", 9 in. high. **A-27.50**

Miner's lamp, tin, 3½ in. high, miniature teakettle type. **A-8.00**

Miner's safety lamp, using wire gauze to prevent flame crossover, built-in wickpick, iron with brass trim, ca. 1890. **D-22.50**

Miniature lamp, handled, clear glass. **A-12.50**

Miniature lamp, kerosene, "Twinkle", 8 in. high. **A-21.00**

Oil lamp, clear pressed font, 9 in. high. **A-30.00**

Peglamp, blown-in-mold, ribbed, panelled, brass hardware, 5 in. high. D-5.00

Peglamp, pattern glass, oil, Diamond and Star, 12¾ in. high. D-45.00

Petticoat lamp, with filler tube, base peg, 4 in. high. D-65.00

Privy lamp, double-spout, tin, whale oil burner, 9 in. long. A-20.00

Skater's lamp, all brass, steel bail, 10 in. high. D-45.00

Sparking lamp, glass, brass parts, 2 in. diameter, 3 in. high. D-60.00

Student lamp, brass, yellow swirled shade, electrified, 20½ in. high. A-200.00

Student lamp, brass, double. Ribbed emeraldite domed shape, converted from oil, ca. 1890, 22 in. high. A-300.00

Student lamp, Victorian, gooseneck, frosted glass shade, 15 in. high. A-70.00

Tavern-wall lamp, tin, tin reflector, brass-hinged burner, handle holed for hanging. D-89.50

Whale oil lamp, tin, saucer base and conical font, traces of dark brown japanning, 6¼ in. high. A-50.00

Whale oil lamp, tin, double-wick burner, orig. graining, 8 in. high. D-125.00

Whale oil lamp, matching pair, guaranteed sandwich glass. In Heart and Thumbprint pattern, pewter collars, pewter burners, twin oil spouts in each lamp, 8½ in. high. D-450.00

Whale oil lamp, pewter, brass collar and double-spout burner, 7½ in. high. A-105.00

Work lamp, cast iron, quart-size torch with 6 in. spout, "Furnace Lamp #1", screw cap, bail handle. D-42.50

LANTERNS (See also Lamps and Lighting Devices)

Barn lantern, tin, blown chimney, brass burner, "L"-shape foot for beam straddling, iron loop holder. D-45.00

Candle lantern, seven glass panels, top with handle; vent hinged for access, 11½ in. high. A-110.00

Candle lantern, glass on three sides, plus tin panel. Ring handle, attached cylindrical match-holder, 10½ in. high. A-40.00

Candle lantern with carrying case, mica in front, tin on sides and back. Whale oil burner fits candle socket; 10 in. high.　　　　　　　　　　　　　　**A-75.00**

Hand lantern, tin, folding; has two mica windows, measures, unfolded, 3-1/8 x 3¾ x 5½ inches.　　　**D-85.00**

Kerosene lantern, bullseye lens, 13 in. high.　　**A-17.50**

Kerosene lantern, clear blown chimney, tin base, 14½ in. high.　　　　　　　　　　　　　　　　**A-24.00**

Lantern, iron and tin, clear glass globe, decorative pattern of holes arranged in circles, 11 in. high.　**A-130.00**

Lantern, early pierced candleholder type, 16½ in. high.　　　　　　　　　　　　　　　　　　　**D-115.00**

Lantern, tin, wall-mounted, removable vent finial, 28½ in. high.　　　　　　　　　　　　　　　**A-90.00**

Lantern, sheet iron with wrought fittings, red glass, brass oil burner and font, 15 in. high.　　　　　**A-55.00**

Lantern, tin, orig. ring and loop, gray-black tin, hand-pierced decoration. Fine condition, ca. 1820, 16 in. high.　　　　　　　　　　　　　　　**D-150.00**

"Lighthouse" lantern, tin, wide armstrap. Lighthouse-shape globe, mold-blown, rows of stars at top vent, whale oil reservoir, ca. 1830, 17 in. high.　**D-195.00**

Policeman's lantern, japanned tin, magnifying bullseye lens about 3 in. diameter. Tin, with blackout slide, whale oil burner.　　　　　　　　　　　　**D-65.00**

LIGHTING DEVICES—And Related Items

Candle arm, tin, from sconce or chandelier, "S"-shaped, 7½ in. long.　　　　　　　　　　　**A-50.00**

Candleholder, tin, peg, square drip-pan.　　　　**D-24.00**

Candleholder, wrought iron, driven into block of pine, 5¼ in. high.　　　　　　　　　　　　　**A-225.00**

Candleholder, "sticking tommy", wrought iron, 9 in. long.　　　　　　　　　　　　　　　　　　**A-42.50**

Candleholder, burlwood, in shape of cap, 2½ in. high.　　　　　　　　　　　　　　　　　　　**A-52.50**

Candleholder, wrought iron, adjustable, three legs, 8½ in. high.　　　　　　　　　　　　　　　**A-35.00**

Candle mold, tin; single long tube for church candles, 20½ in. high.　　　　　　　　　　　　**D-175.00**

Candle mold, three-tube, tin, handled, 9½ in. high.　**A-17.50**

Candle mold, tin, six-tube, handled, 11 in. high.　**A-21.00**

Candle mold, tin, missing handle, twelve-tube, 10¾ in. high.   A-90.00

Candle mold, six rows of four tubes (24), 15½ in. high.   D-210.00

Candle mold, five rows of ten tubes (50), 10½ in. high.   D-305.00

Candle sconce, tin, hanger tab, small shelf, 13¼ in. high.   A-77.50

Candle sconce, tin, crimped semi-circular top, 9½ in. high.   A-55.00

Candle sconce, tin, circular crimped top, 13½ in. high.   A-67.50

Candle sconce, tin, 13½ in. high.   A-75.00

Candle sconce, tin, punched, minor rust, 9½ in. high.   A-20.00

Candle snuffer, wrought iron, scissor handle, ca. 1840.   D-25.00

Candle snuffer, primitive wrought iron, 7½ in. long.   A-27.50

Candle snuffer, scissors, brass tray 3¾ x 8½ inches.   D-45.00

Candle snuffer, tin, pat'd 1852, brass pivot rivet.   D-65.00

Chamberstick, tin, transfer-decorated, 5 in. high.   D-24.00

Chamberstick, brass, rectangular saucer base, polished, 5 x 6 x 3¾ in. high.   A-62.50

Chandelier, candle, six-arm, turned wooden center, electrified.   A-115.00

Chimney cleaner, for lamp, wireware, slide and ferrule, 15 in. long.   D-18.50

Hall light, blown glass, embossed brass fittings, 7 in. diameter, 18 in. high.   A-105.00

Lighting device, wooden, adjustable, iron candle socket, pine base, adjusts to 27 in. high.   A-420.00

Lighting device, brass, conical base, tubular burner, 11½ in. high.   A-65.00

Reservoir, whale oil, tin, syrup-type hinged top, 9½ in. high.   D-75.00

Sconces, tin, pair, old black paint with scratches, 13 in. high.   A-27.50

Torch, tin, three-burner, cone-shaped font, 9 in. high.   A-155.00

Wick trimmer, wrought iron scissors-type, 8 in. long.   A-22.50

Wick trimmer, and tray; both brass, 9¼ in. long.   A-50.00

Wick trimmer, lamp; cast iron frame, "Pat. 1-3-68", 6½ in. long.   D-20.00

Wick trimmer, lamp; cast iron, removable steel blade, 8½ in. long. **D-18.00**

Wick trimmer, wrought iron, 6¼ in. long. **A-17.50**

Workshop light, tin, hanging, with six wicktubes, center brass filler cap, gray tin, 4 x 6 x 12 in. high. **D-140.00**

LOCKS—KEYS

Jail door key, brass, blank key to be cut for particular locks at later time, 3 in. long. **D-4.00**

Leg irons, with tubular key, cast steel, joined by 16½ in. of heavy chain, Marked "Prov. Tool Co.", ca. 1870. **D-85.00**

Lock, iron, 4¼ in. high. **A-7.50**

Shark, brass case, self-locking. 6-8

Empire 6 Lever, brass case, self-locking. 7-9

Y & T, bronze case, self-locking. 6-8

Lock, iron, heart-shaped with heavy solid brass keyhole and plate, 3½ in. long. **D-17.50**

Lock and key, for old wrought iron bear trap, 7 in. high. **A-40.00**

Padlock, hand-made, cylinder and hook type, 9½ in. long. **D-22.00**

Padlock, iron, attached wrought iron eyebolt, 3½ in. high. **A-12.50**

MASONIC

Badge, two-piece, "Claremont Commandery No. 9". **D-7.00**

Badge, 32nd Degree, "New Hampshire Consistory Badge", in orig. folding case. **D-15.00**

Badge, two-piece, silver-colored, "Triennial Conclave/Pittsburgh/1898". **D-7.00**

Masonic.
Commandery sword, etched blade, maker's mark. C/150-200
Commemorative flask, local lodge. C/10-15
Matchbook holder, Masonic symbol. C/3-5

Bookends, bronzed cast iron, each with large masonic emblem in deep relief; pair.	**D-25.00**
Ring, Masonic, man's size set with nine round diamonds.	**A-350.00**
Sash attachments, group of four, sword-shaped, silver plated, ca. 1900.	**D-20.00**
Watch fob, Masonic Temple at St. Johnsburg, Vermont, worn silvering.	**D-10.00**
Whisky flask, with Masonic emblem, aqua, blown, marked "Zanesville", 7 in. high.	**A-400.00**

MEDALS *(All U.S. unless designated otherwise)*

Air Force Commendation Medal, unissued, mint condition.	**D-15.00**
American Legion school award, bronze, 2-7/8 inches.	**D-20.00**
Antarctica Service Medal, mint condition.	**D-12.00**
Boston Evacuation medal, 39mm, copper, 1901.	**D-6.00**
Boy Scouts, 72mm, bronze, Society of Medalists, orig. box.	**D-30.00**
Canadian Nat'l Railways commemorative medal, 33mm, 1973.	**D-8.00**
Championship, U.S. Revolver Ass'n, sterling, 1911.	**D-20.00**
Civil War period die trial, of 52mm medal or campaign token.	**D-50.00**
Diving and Swimming Awards, "Wianno Club", 1917, pair.	**D-12.00**
English Cornation medal, William IV, white metal, 1831.	**D-20.00**
Eureka Octagonal medal, Calif., reverse of $50 gold slug.	**D-15.00**
General Motors medal, 50 millionth car, gilt brass.	**D-4.00**
Harvard University, bronze, 80mm size, orig. box, 1907.	**D-30.00**
Korean Service Medal, mint, in orig. box.	**D-7.00**
Marine Corps Reserve medal, fresh condition.	**D-10.00**

Medal, 30mm, "Removal of the Connecticut Battle Flags", 1897. **D-25.00**

Meritorious Civilian Service Medal, Air Force, mint cond. **D-30.00**

National Defense Medal, mint condition. **D-4.00**

Naval Reserve Medal, mint condition. **D-15.00**

Navy Expeditionary Medal, mint, in orig. envelope. **D-12.00**

New York Stock Exchange, by sculptor H. Augustus Lukeman, 1922. **D-25.00**

Niagara Ass'n Track and Field medals, pair. **D-40.00**

Republic of Viet Nam Service Medal, mint, in orig. box. **D-7.00**

Union Pacific Railroad advertising medal, copy on both sides. **D-5.00**

WW-I, "Myron Therrick/American Ambassador to France". **D-20.00**

WW-I Victory Medal, with edge lettering. **D-20.00**

MEDICAL—PHARMACEUTICAL

Apothecary jar, clear brown glass, matching stopper, 9 in. high. **A-10.00**

Apothecary jar, clear pressed glass, tin lid, 9¼ in. high. **A-20.00**

Apothecary jar, blown, cobalt blue, matching stopper, label incomplete, 9 in. high. **A-17.50**

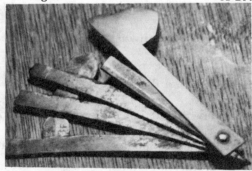

Fleam, an instrument for bleeding; steel blades and razor, brass case, about 4 in. long.

C/45

Apothecary jar, for chemicals, original label, complete with ground glass stopper. From turn-of-century Doctor's office.

C/12-20

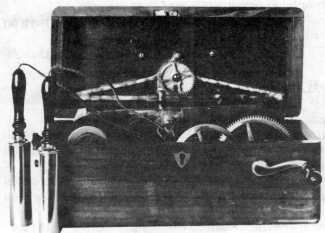

Electromagnetic machine. 1854.
95-120

China Inhaler,
"Acme".
45-50

Cork press,
iron.
35-45

Bag, doctor's; black grained leather, leather handle, full brass lock and hardware. **D-50.00**

Dentist's canister, polished brass with twin cover clamps. Deeply embossed lettering, "De Trey's Dentocoll", ca. 1890. **D-75.00**

Fleam, (bleeder), spring-loaded, brass. Ten steel blades with small orig. horn to catch blood during venesection. **D-50.00**

Fleam, hand-forged blades, pair; in handcarved wood box 5½ in. long with sliding cover. Ca. 1790. **D-59.50**

Medical instruments, complete set for urology, cased. **D-25.00**

Medicinal herb, "Lobelia", full ingredients in package. **D-5.00**

Medicinal herb, "Red Clover Tops", from Penick Crude Drugs Co., full contents. **D-6.50**

Medicinal herb, "Red Oak Bark", full contents. **D-4.50**

Medicinal herb, "Summer Savory", full contents. **D-4.00**

Medicinal herb, "Tansy Leaves & Tops", Penick Drugs, full contents. **D-6.50**

Sterilizer, nickel-plated brass, "U.S.A.M.D./Pioneer, N.Y.", with alcohol heater.   **D-12.00**

Syringe, pewter and wood, 8½ in. long, turned handle.   **D-16.50**

MEN'S TOILETRY

Collar box, embossed leather in cupids and scroll-work, 4 in. diameter; orig. packaged collar inside.   **D-29.50**

Razor, safety, brass, boxed with brass blade holder.   **D-12.50**

Razor, straight-edge, folding, etched blade, European.   **D-25.00**

Razor and case, straight-edge, initialed ivory handle.   **D-65.00**

Razor rack, paperholder of wood and pressed cardboard; handle is a shaving brush 5¼ in. long.   **D-12.50**

Shaving mug, occupational, (attorney), one chip from lip.   **D-120.00**

Shaving mirror, American Chippendale mahogany, ca. 1800. Cheval-type mirror above one long drawer on bracket feet, 20 in. high.   **A-100.00**

Shaving mirror, American Chippendale mahogany, ca. 1810. Cheval-type mirror above two aligned drawers and ending in ogee bracket feet, 7 x 16 x 25 in. wide.   **A-125.00**

MINIATURES

This field has long been a specialty collecting area, with many collectors choosing items in a certain class, as furniture or lamps. Some of the miniatures were made for toys, others as tests of skill, still others served as salesmens' samples to show to prospective customers without taking along unwieldy full-size specimens. It is not always easy to say what purpose a miniature once served, as a small, well-made chest of drawers could have been either a commercial sample or child-size furniture.

Basket, wicker, well-ribbed, handled, 2 in. diameter.   **D-8.50**

Basket, market, for child; plaited splint, 5 in. high.   **D-12.50**

Basket, picnic, nailed rim; 3½ x 5 x 5 inches.   **D-8.50**

Book, children's, color plates; 3½ x 4½ inches.   **D-14.50**

Bootjack, hand-carved wood, one-piece, 7 in. long.   **D-24.00**

Chest, blanket; poplar, 10 x 11¼ x 19 inches.   **A-205.00**

Chest, blanket; pine, six-board, 7½ x 11 x 18 inches.   **A-80.00**

Chest of drawers, flame graining, 7½ x 16 x 18 inches.   A-110.00

Croze, oak, hand-forged blade, 2½ x 5½ inches.   D-165.00

Display case, pine, glass front, 7 x 11¼ x 14 inches.   D-100.00

Document box, tin, loop handle, 2¾ x 2¾ x 5¼ inches.   D-10.00

Doll house cradle, brass, 1¼ in. long, w/celluloid doll.   D-10.00

Duck, handcarved wood, black and white paint, 3½ in. long.   A-30.00

Figurine, bisque, of boy playing drum, 3 in. high.   D-6.00

Goose, handcarved wood, grey and white paint, 3½ in. long.   A-35.00

Horseshoe, salesman's sample, "Snowcleat", spiked bottom.   D-36.00

Irons, pair; cast iron, "Mrs. Potts Irons", 3¾ in. long.   D-36.50

Kettle, salesman's sample, brass, 2¾ in. diameter.   D-55.00

Lamp, pedestaled, glass chimney, 10½ in. high.   D-32.00

Lamp, whale oil, blown-in-mold, 2¾ in. high.   D-42.50

Lantern, tin, whale oil burner, 5¾ in. high.   D-150.00

Mold, copper, for chocolate butterfly, 2 x 2½ inches.   D-25.00

Mug, handled, glazed white porcelain, advertising crest.   D-7.50

Pannekin, copper, ring loop on cover, 4 in. wood handle.   D-75.00

Pitcher, "Schweppes Soda", brown glaze, 1½ in. high.   D-15.00

Sewing machine, orig. box, mint condition, 4½ x 5 inches.   D-32.50

Spool holder, wood, six thread spindles, 4 in. high.   D-15.00

Stein, cobalt blue and gray stoneware, 2½ in. high.   D-15.00

Swan, handcarved wood, neck glued, 3¼ in. long.   A-27.50

Teakettle, brass, tin-lined, 5 in. bottom diameter.   D-48.00

Teapot, tin, early lap seaming, 2¾ in. high.   D-45.00

Teapot, salesman's sample, tin, ca. 1850, 5 in. high.   D-125.00

Teddy bear, glass eyes, jointed appendages, 4½ in. high.   D-22.50

Tool box, oak, tray with five compartments, 6¼ x 9½ x 18.   D-60.00

MIRRORS

Beveled, in birdseye maple frame, 16¼ x 22¼ inches. **A-80.00**

Beveled, pine, one-piece, old black paint, mirror glass cracked, 6½ x 7½ inches. **A-185.00**

Cape Cod, in orig. box, carved frame with openwork crest with fruit, flowers and bird. Old worn gilt, 9 x 20 inches. **A-350.00**

Cape Cod, fine early carved crest with scrolls, flowers and bird reaching for fruit. Worn orig. polychrome and gilt, orig. worn mirror glass, 10 x 22 inches. **A-1,350.00**

Convex, in wooden frame topped by carved wooden and gesso eagle, regilded with gold leaf, 22 x 29 inches high. **A-250.00**

Empire, decorated, turned columns and corner blocks, 12½ x 16½ inches. **A-45.00**

Empire, divided; ornate corner gesso in raised leaf motifs. Upper panel 6¾ x 9 inches, lower 9 x 13½ inches, and is replaced. **D-45.00**

Empire, divided; mahogany veneer with black and gold stenciled pilasters; overall, 18 x 36 inches. **A-95.00**

Empire pier, pilasters with corner blocks in old gilt and black, embossed brass rosettes, 20 x 51 inches. **A-135.00**

Federal, carved, gessoed and gold leafed, ca. 1830-40. Half-turned columns with corner rosettes, 22 x 32 inches. **A-150.00**

Hand, early, pine frame laced together, orig. cardboard case dated 1793. Poor condition. **A-40.00**

Hand, polished brass, Victorian, Art Nouveau decorations, 8¼ in. long, 3 x 4 in. beveled glass mirror. **D-50.00**

Mirror, small, pine frame with old but not orig. painted decoration, 6½ x 9¼ inches. **A-55.00**

Mirror, gold gilt on frame, 2 x 16½ x 20½ inches. **A-27.50**

Mirror, old built-up design incomplete, 4¾ x 7 inches. **A-15.00**

Mirror, in walnut shadow box frame, 15¾ x 18¾ inches. **A-17.50**

Mirror, in old wooden frame 5 x 7 inches. **A-30.00**

Mirror, pine, primitively carved with fleur-de-lis crest, 5¾ x 14½ inches. **A-145.00**

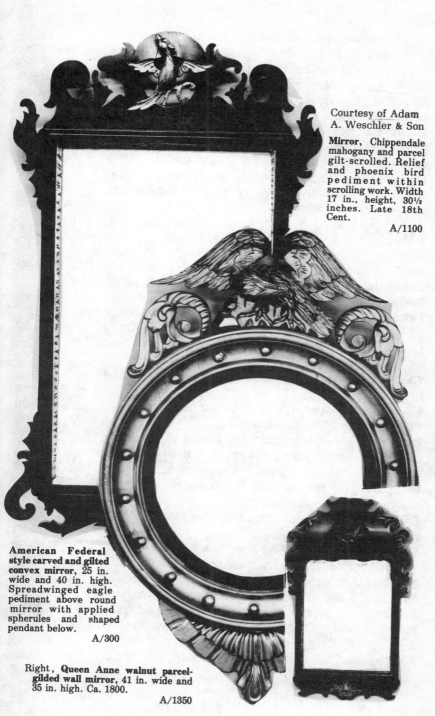

Mirror, Chippendale mahogany and parcel gilt-scrolled. Relief and phoenix bird pediment within scrolling work. Width 17 in., height, 30½ inches. Late 18th Cent.

A/1100

American Federal style carved and gilted convex mirror, 25 in. wide and 40 in. high. Spreadwinged eagle pediment above round mirror with applied spherules and shaped pendant below.

A/300

Right, **Queen Anne walnut parcel-gilded wall mirror,** 41 in. wide and 35 in. high. Ca. 1800.

A/1350

Oval, American carved, gessoed and gold-leafed, ca. 1840, 20 x 23 inches.   **A-100.00**

Scroll ear, Chippendale-style, mahogany, by Biggs & Co., Richmond, Virginia. Concave carved and pierced gilded phoenix bird pediment, 21 x 36 inches.   **A-135.00**

Scroll, American Chippendale walnut, last quarter of 19th Century, 20 x 34 inches.   **A-170.00**

Scroll, Chippendale, mahogany, with applied and incomplete gilded phoenix, 15¼ x 29½ inches.   **A-410.00**

Queen Anne, English, faded mahogany on pine. Small veneer repairs and gilded applied carvings incomplete, 11 x 25 inches.   **A-200.00**

MOLDS

Brick, or poss. molten metal, 6½ x 10½ inches.   **D-25.00**

Cake, aluminum, in shape of lamb, ca. 1920, 12 in. long.   **D-16.00**

Candy, wood, two-part, five different animals, 2½ x 13 inches.   **A-70.00**

Candy, wood, two-part, makes six pumpkins, 1½ x 12 inches.   **A-50.00**

Candy, wood, two-part, makes seven animals, 3 x 14 inches.   **A-120.00**

Cheese, small, footed, and heart-shaped.   **D-135.00**

Chocolate, tin, 5½ in. wide.   **A-29.00**

Chocolate, set of four, animal forms, 3 to 4 in. long.   **D-48.00**

Chocolate, begging figure of rabbit, tin, 6¼ in. high.   **D-22.50**

Chocolate, tin, sitting rabbit, 4¾ in. high.   **D-20.00**

Doll part, cast iron for making 3-in. hands for bisque dolls.   **D-75.00**

Easter egg, tin, three compartments, 7¼ x 15½ inches.   **D-35.00**

Easter egg, rabbits on a swing, 5 x 7 inches.   **D-45.00**

Easter egg, tin, two parts, oval, 2-3/8 in. long.   **D-8.50**

Food, copper, deep-relief cornucopia, 3½ in. high.   **D-55.00**

Food, tin, melon-ribbed, soldered repair, 9 in. long.   **A-21.00**

Food, tin and copper, 6¼ in. diameter, 7 in. high.   **D-95.00**

Food, redware Turks' Head, hairline crack, 2 in. high.   **A-12.50**

Maple sugar, tin, removable separators, 8½ x 15 inches.   **D-35.00**

Maple sugar, tin, 3½ x 5¼ inches.   **D-2.25**

Maple sugar, tin, 5 x 7½ inches.   **D-3.50**

Mould, tin, embossed alligator, edge crimp, 4¼ in. long.

A-7.50

Plum pudding, three-footed, bail handle, excellent condition.

D-15.00

Soap, wood, machine-dovetailed corners, 3½ x 6 inches.

D-22.50

MUSICAL INSTRUMENTS

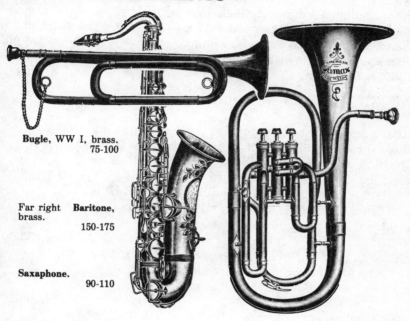

Bugle, WW I, brass.
75-100

Far right **Baritone,** brass.
150-175

Saxaphone.
90-110

Autoharp, 18-string Zimmerman dated 1894, orig. box with label, all strings, tuning key, "Harmonette".

D-45.00

Baby Grand piano, Baldwin mahogany case, bench included, 65 in. long.

A-2,800.00

Baby Grand piano, Chickering, ebony case, first quarter 20th Century, 57 in. by 80 in. long.

A-1,150.00

Baby Grand piano, French Provincial-style, by Sohmer & Co., New York, 58 x 68 in. long.

A-1,600.00

Baby Grand piano, Steinway, ebonized, 70 in. long.

A-6,900.00

Grand piano, and bench, Steinway, mahogany case, ca. 1927, 70 in. long.

A-3,200.00

Guitarr-zither, Columbia, in fitted mahogany case, 19 x 23 in. long.

A-110.00

Harpsichord, Hepplewhite inlaid mahogany, tapered straight legs with embossed-urn roundel brass mounts. Ca. 1830, 60 in. long.   A-500.00

Organ, "Gem Roller" with eight musical cobs, tappet felts need replacing. Mechanically sound, orig. stenciling, excellent bellows.   D-335.00

Organ, late Victorian Gothic Revival, walnut, pump-type. By Story & Clark, Chicago, ca. 1880, 82 in. high.   A-350.00

Piano, spinet, Bressler French Empire mahogany, made in Paris, 1813. Piano 33 x 27 x 67 in. long.   A-2,500.00

Piano, spinet, Louis XV style, walnut, Lester.   A-775.00

Piano, upright, English Regency burl walnut, ca. 1880. By C. Ritter, 50 x 60 in. wide.   A-350.00

MUSIC BOXES—*Cylinder*

Allard-Sandoz, interchangeable cylinders, 19th Century, three cylinders each with eight tunes. Tune sheet on lid underside, fine appearance, needs cleaning. Size, 14 x 35 x 11¼ in. high.   D-3,495.00

Chalet/orchestra, two dancing dolls, six tuned bells and drum, eight tunes. Ornate and an exceptional instrument both musically and visually. Size, 14½ x 33 x 28½ in. high.   D-4,995.00

Heller organ, by Heller of Bern, Switzerland, 19th Century, six tunes. Steel music comb and reed organ section, bellows should be recovered. Walnut box, 10 x 22¼ x 9¼ in. high.   D-2,200.00

Mermod Freres, with two cylinders, six tunes per cylinder. Has mandolin-type tune arrangements in sweet, pleasing tone. Cabinet walnut with inlay of musical instruments, 14 x 32¼ x 12½ in. high.   D-2,495.00

Music box, movement prob. by Debitczek of Prague, six tunes. Excellent movement in newer case, 7¼ x 13 x 5½ in. high.   D-495.00

Swiss, late 19th Century, attractive burled wood, four tunes. Governor missing one blade, box 6¼ x 11½ x 4½ in. high.   D-449.00

Swiss, pre-1870, brass bedplate, four tunes. Governor jewel missing, needs redampering, 6½ x 13¼ x 4¾ in. high.   D-495.00

Swiss, outstanding, ca. 1880, eight tunes. Bright, crisp sound, unusual inlay, plays beautifully, 8 x 16 x 5½ in. high.   D-895.00

Top left, **Cylinder player,** Edison Fireside Model B, with brass horn with end diameter of 7 inches. D/300

Lar Hothem photo, courtesy F. Jacmenovic.

Top right, **Swiss music box,** 16½ in. long. A/600

Upper center, **Swiss music box,** 21 in. long. A/350

Lower, **Swiss music box,** 37 in. long, 14 in. high. Rosewood and ebony satin and vari-wood inlaid medallion top; has three 6 in. interchangeable cylinders. A/600

Courtesy Adam A. Weschler & Son, Washington, D.C.; photograph by Breger & Associates.

Swiss, six-inch cylinder, eight tunes and three saucer bells. Cabinet walnut with floral inlay on lid, needs minor repairs. **D-795.00**

Troll & Baker bell box, on table, ca. 1870-80, three interchangeable cylinders, six tunes per cylinder. Three-part comb, six engraved bells with bee-shaped strikers. Impressive, case with brass inlay on matching table, beveled mirror beneath lid. Plays beautifully, 25 x 48 x 41½ in. high. **D-6,495.00**

MUSIC BOXES—*Disc*

Adler upright, 21¼ in. discs, large, in walnut case. Mild replacement work needed, case needs refinishing, 16 x 30 x 39 in. high. **D-2,295.00**

Celesta, 8 in. discs, case exterior needs refinishing, a scarce example. **D-595.00**

Euterpephon, 12 in. discs, cabinet needs some work, goddess Euterpe on lid underside, blowing two trumpets. Size, 13¼ x 15¼ x 8 in. high. **D-995.00**

Kalliope, 7¾ in. discs, two broken comb teeth, mechanism requires cleaning. Size, 8¾ x 10¼ x 6¾ in. high. **D-535.00**

Kalliope, with six bells, 9¼ in. discs, plays well, one tooth broken, 10¾ x 11½ x 7 in. high. **D-945.00**

Kalliope, 13½ in. discs, brilliant tone. Walnut box, white inlay around border, with zither attachment. Size, 15 x 15¾ x 7½ in. high. **D-1,095.00**

Komet, 10¼ in. discs, pleasant-sounding, needs cleaning and regulation. Cabinet in nice condition, "KOMET" inlaid with ivory, 11½ x 13 x 7½ in. high. **D-795.00**

Perfection, 10½ in. discs, 1897-1901 (New Jersey made), unit in choice unrestored condition. Rare, 13¾ x 15¼ x 8¼ in. high. **D-1,295.00**

Polyphon, 6½ in. discs, nice sound, needs usual cleaning and regulating. Attractive underlid lithograph, 7¼ x 7¾ x 4¾ in. high. **D-439.00**

Polyhymnia, 7¾ in. discs, may have non-original comb, plays nicely. Very rare, 8¾ x 10¼ x 6¾ in. high. **D-595.00**

Polyphon, 9¾ in. discs, superb sound, small piece of veneer missing. Scenic picture under lid, 11 x 12 x 7½ in. high. **D-795.00**

Record player, Standard Machine Company Model A, horn end 15 in. diameter.

D/350

Lar Hothem photo, courtesy F. Jacmenovic.

Polyphon, 15½ in. discs, nice specimen of most popular disc size in medium-size boxes. Walnut cabinet, needs cleaning and regulating, 18 x 21 x 8¾ in. high.   **D-1,195.00**

Regina, 8¼ in. discs, smallest Regina made, more rare than 11 and 15½ in. types. In light oak cabinet, plays well, 9¾ x 12¼ x 8 in. high.   **D-995.00**

Sirion disc-shifting, in contemporary Komet upright case, with mechanism for playing time double that of single disc. Requires start-stop parts, 21 x 34 x 44½ in. high.   **D-3,995.00**

Stella console, 17½ in. discs, ca. 1900, refinished case, rich and resonant tone. A classic specimen, ornate mahogany case, good supply of discs, 22¼ x 29½ x 37¾ in. high.   **D-4,995.00**

Symphonion, 5¾ in. discs, in very poor condition, needing a number of replacements. Size, 6½ x 6½ x 2¼ in. high.   **D-149.00**

Tannhauser, 15 in. discs, disc-shifting to play a different melody. Some of the special mechanism missing, cabinet painted black, 18¼ x 23¼ x 8½ in. high.   **D-1,295.00**

Troubadour, 8¾ in. discs, good-sounding, new end needed for idler arm. Size, 9½ x 10½ x 8¾ in. high.   **D-625.00**

Troubadour, 8¾ in. discs, broken spring, lightly damaged lid. A clean box for the rebuilder, 9½ x 10½ x 6½ in. high.   **D-565.00**

NAUTICAL *(See also* **Scrimshaw** *and* **NAUTICAL (Instruments)**

Nautical (or marine) items have long had a peculiar fascination, both to those who went out on the seas, and to the rest of us land-lovers. Most of the collectibles served specialized functions, whether whaling tool, anchor light or navigational instrument.

Nautical items nearly always command premium prices. There is first the romantic association with powerful natural forces, and the allure of exotic foreign ports. The items are always very well made, for lives often depended on durability and accurate functioning. Finally, the items are often made of, or had major parts of corrosion-resistant materials. These might be brass, bronze or copper, which adds to desirability.

Auger, ships; wood twist handle, 21 in. long.   **D-18.00**
Beckets, pair; with ropework sea chart handles.   **D-65.00**
Bell, ships; brass, with clapper and hanging bracket, 9¾ in. high.   **A-75.00**
Billet head, rough, aged condition, 16 in. long.   **D-425.00**
Billet head, wood carving from ship's bow, 13 in. long.   **D-475.00**
Binnacle, dome-shaped compass housing with kerosene burner for night viewing; compass in good condition, 10 in. high.   **D-135.00**
Binnacle, compass bowl of brass, marked card, mahogany housing. Side light missing, 16 in. high.   **D-195.00**
Blubber knife, hand-forged, wood haft gone, 18½ in. long.   **D-35.00**
Boat lenses, set of three; stern-lights, clear, red and green.   **D-85.00**
Bone box, Prisoner of War-made during Napoleonic War. Box completely covered with cutout intricate panels. 19th Century.   **D-195.00**
Bottle holder, ocean liner(?), brass, 4 in. diameter. **D-25.00**
Cabin light, lens cracked and base dented, brass, 12 in. high.   **D-55.00**
Candle-sticks, ivory, with Justice and Liberty ladies. Matching pair, solid ivory, 9 in. high.   **D-750.00**

Ship's wheel, polished hardwood.   D/95

Nautical container, marked "Distress Outfit". With copper rolled-seam body, brass screw-threads and bronze lid and handle. By the Upson Walton Company, it once held flare pistol and cartridges.   C/35-40

Compass, large size, in reinforced wooden box/case.   D/375

Boat propellor, solid brass, 14 in. across.   D/75

Lar Hothem photos

Chest, sea captain's; dome-top, oval "Wilton Lines" plaque, and interior with 32 pieces officers' dining utensils.   A-225.00

Chest, seaman's; dovetailed pine, rope handles; 15½ x 17 x 45 inches.   A-25.00

Cleat, brass, for securing lines on small vessels; 5 in. long.   D-6.00

Cleat, brass, 8 in. long.   D-9.50

Clock, brass face marked "U.S. Maritime Commission"; solid brass case, works well.   D-275.00

Clock, early Seth Thomas with external bell. Brass construction, wood backplate, most of orig. label, works good.   D-395.00

Clock, brass Seth Thomas, lignum vitae globe.   **D-425.00**

Coat-hanger, ship's, solid brass.   **D-5.00**

Coat-hook, three-way, solid brass.   **D-7.50**

Corn-huskers, two whalebone; 5 and 5¼ in. long.   **A-15.00**

Cribbage board, made from walrus tusk; from collection of a whaling captain, 16 in. long.   **D-325.00**

Display case, for sail-maker tools; under glass. Rosewood lid, selection of tools: Needles, cases, palms, beeswax, etc.   **D-325.00**

Diver's knife, deepsea; double-edge steel blade, knife screws into brass sheath, 13 in. overall.   **D-95.00**

Drawshave, mast-maker's; for trimming mast and spars. Hand-forged blade 14 in. long, piece 22 in. overall.   **D-25.00**

Figurehead, three-quarter form of woman in full dress. Painted, weathered, authentic, 29 in. tall.   **D-4,500.00**

Figurehead, prob. from large admiralty model. Carved boxwood, full-bodied woman, right arm missing, 7 in. high.   **D-1,500.00**

Glass holder, brass, attaches to bulkhead.   **D-7.50**

Half model, ship; nine laminated lifts, 42 in. long.   **D-295.00**

Half model, ship; three laminated lifts, 36 in. long.   **D-175.00**

Hair brush, ivory, with painting of steamship *Brittany.* Brush is old, painting contemporary.   **D-65.00**

Key, solid brass, 4 in. long.   **D-5.00**

Lantern, green-painted metal, red glass front, electric, 13 in. high.   **D-35.00**

Lantern, anchor; copper and brass, 14 in. high.   **D-75.00**

Lantern, masthead; copper construction with brass fittings. Clear lens and orig. oil burner, 22 in. high.   **D-225.00**

Lantern, gimble brass, fancy ring, double-wick burner, globe missing.   **D-125.00**

Lantern, anchor; copper with brass fittings, 19 in. high.   **D-125.00**

Latch, door; polished brass, yacht fitting, 6 in. long.   **D-8.50**

Latch, door; brass sliding latch with lock-end, 5 in. long.   **D-7.50**

Lead pencil, mechanical, bone-handled, 3 in. long.   **D-12.00**

Letter opener, ivory, with whales and banner; contemporary scrim-shaw on old ivory.   **D-45.00**

Log timer, hourglass shape, to determine distance and speed of vessel, Fifteen-minute timer, early 19th Century.   **D-185.00**

Paddlewheel boat model, of wood, wire and brass. Ca. 1900, 20 in. long.
Lar Hothem photos

D/200

Model, boat; New England lobster boat, handcarved;
ca. 1860, 4½ in. wide, 12½ in. long.   **D-69.50**

Model, ship; the brig *Vengence,* 14 in. long.   **D-125.00**

Mortar and pestle, of whale ivory and in good condition. Good age coloring, 19th Century.   **D-95.00**

Navigational ruler, English-made, ivory, 6 in. long.   **D-75.00**

Needle case, sail-maker's, ivory. Either end unscrews, contains three needles; 6 in. long.   **D-95.00**

Needle case, sail-maker's, wood with sliding cover; three sail needles, 8 in. long.   **D-27.50**

Note pad, ivory, with German silver clasp and plaque, daily reminder type.   **D-50.00**

Pistol, Colt model 1860. Matching parts numbers, naval battle scene engraved on cylinder.   **D-495.00**

Port-hole, good glass, hinge pin missing, 9 in. diameter.   **D-25.00**

Port-hole, good glass, bronze, 12 in. diameter.   **D-75.00**

Rope server, sailor's tool for manipulating rigging; rosewood, 9 in. long.   **D-25.00**

Seam-rubber, sail-maker's; brass blade, 4 in. high.   **D-35.00**

Searchlight, German origin, 21 in. high, brass.   **D-450.00**

Sewing basket, ropewoven, covered, painted red; 7½ in. diameter, 4 in. high.   **D-95.00**

Ship in bottle, three-masted vessel, bottle 10 in. long.　D-47.50

Ship painting, signed "T. Willis", of single-masted vessel. Good condition, 18 x 24 inches.　D-395.00

Ship painting, oil on canvas of brig, signed "W. Chambers/89". Some restoration, 20 x 30 inches.　D-975.00

Ship painting, brig sailing in choppy seas, signed "Arthur Anderson/1845", 19 x 31 inches.　D-1,750.00

Ship painting, watercolor of ship flying American flag with pilot boat and building in background. "...Port of Marseilles/December, 1847". Signed by Honore Pellegrim, French, 1800-1870. Painting is in good condition, 19 x 25 inches.　D-4,750.00

Ship portrait, colored lithograph, "Far Horizon/The North America". By Dawson, London, 1941; 18 x 25 inches.　A-325.00

Sign, ship's; carved wood, "Boyd N. Shepard". Weathered blue and yellow paint, 8 ft. 4 in. long.　A-175.00

Speaking trumpet, ship's; solid brass, 15 in. long.　D-185.00

Taffrail log, brass construction and spinner; indicator marked "Walker Patent/Cherub Mark-II Ship Log".　D-145.00

Taffrail log, made by "Fisher Price/Boston Mass.". Three-piece construction, brass, most of orig. paint.　D-115.00

Telegraph, ship's; floor-model, 36 in. high, dial-face only.　D-1,800.00

Telegraph, ship's; table-model, overall height 23 inches.　D-290.00

Whale, carved from whalebone, recent item, half-bodied, 6 in. long.　D-75.00

Whalebone binoculars, brass fittings, one lens cracked, 4 in. long.　D-95.00

Whalebone letter opener, 7 in. long.　D-18.00

Whalebone panel, incised design of flowers in basket.　A-165.00

Whale teeth, pair; antique, with Godey ladies and sentimental inscriptions; 7 in. high.　D-1,250.00

Whale tooth, simply carved with sperm whale outline. Old, good age coloring, 6 in. high.　A-225.00

Wheel, ship's; made of walnut with large brass hub and brass support rings each side. Wheel 36 in. diameter.　D-295.00

Whiskey or rum decanter, flat-bottomed, pale amber glass, brought up from Atlantic shipwreck; 6½ in. diameter.　C-200.00

NETSUKE

Boar, carved ivory, signed, 1¼ in. high. **A-75.00**

Boar, kneeling, signed;, 2 in. long. **D-60.00**

Chick in egg, signed, 1½ in. long. **D-45.00**

Crouching man, with fan. **A-75.00**

Dancer, ivory, with moveable head, old man with hatchet and a samurai, lot of three. **A-90.00**

Horned animal, carved ivory, signed, 1 in. high. **A-125.00**

Horse, kneeling, signed, 1¾ in. long. **D-25.00**

Man, carrying keg; egg enclosing seated man with fan, each signed, lot of two. **A-110.00**

Men, carrying octopus, signed in calligraphy. **A-75.00**

Namazu, in form of large open-mouth carp with tail uplifted, supporting scholar on its back reading scroll, signed. **A-400.00**

Netsuke, carved wood, tiny repair in back, 1-5/8 in. long. **A-45.00**

Puppy with rope, carved ivory, signed, 1½ in. high. **A-170.00**

Two actors, in Kabuki. **A-200.00**

Water buffalo, carved ivory, signed, 1½ in. high. **A-130.00**

OCCUPIED JAPAN (Years 1946-1952)

Angel, ceramic, with drum and gold cymbols, 3¾ inches. **D-6.00**

Ashtray, ceramic, white, heart-shaped, flower sprays, 2¼ inches. **D-3.00**

Ashtray, ceramic, bridge, court musician in diamond costume. **D-4.50**

Ashtray, ceramic, scallop shell, floral and gold, 5½ inches. **D-4.50**

Basket, miniature, applied white flowers, 2½ in. long. **D-3.00**

Bear, porcelain, standing, brown, holding fish, 4½ inches. **D-7.50**

Betty Boop, celluloid doll, moveable arms, 6 inches. **D-10.00**

Bird, porcelain, multi-color, on flower branch, 2¼ inches. **D-4.00**

Bookends, ceramic, girl with watering can, boy with airplane; pair. **D-15.00**

Boy, bisque, sword in belt, 5 in. high. **D-12.00**

Boy, bisque shelf-sitter, bare feet, fishing pole gone, 3 inches. **D-8.00**

Occupied Japan.
Olympus 35mm camera
complete with two-part
leather case. Zuiko 4cm
lens. Both camera and
case marked "Made in
Occupied Japan".
C/30-45

Candy dish, metal, pedestaled, pierced relief, 2½ x 6¾ inches.	**D-15.00**
Castle, goldfish bowl ornament, 3 x 3¼ inches.	**D-5.00**
Cigarette box, ceramic, covered, 1¼ x 4 x 4¼ inches.	**D-7.50**
Cigarette box, with matching ashtray. Gold bamboo jeweled decoration; 4½ x 5 in. and 3¼ x 4 inches. respectively.	**D-14.00**
Cigarette lighter, Aladdin Lamp style, 2¾ x 4 inches.	**D-9.00**
Cigarette urn, silverplated metal, footed, 3¼ in. high.	**D-8.00**
Clock, miniature, grandfather's, floral decoration, 5-1/8 in. high.	**D-6.00**
Coasters, set of three; maroon lacquer on metal, 3 inches.	**D-6.00**
Cocktail shaker, lacquer on metal, red color.	**D-25.00**
Combination, metal pocket compass and magnifying glass, working, chrome-plated, 1½ in. long.	**D-7.00**
Couple, bisque, high-relief sculpted, 5¼ x 6¼ inches.	**D-45.00**
Curio shelf, black lacquered wood, gold decoration, 19 in. high.	**D-30.00**
Deer, porcelain, brown sleeping fawn, ¾ x 2 inches.	**D-5.00**
Dish, oval, metal, silver-plated, 3¾ x 5 inches.	**D-4.50**
Dish, maple leaf, white with gold trim, 3½ inches.	**D-2.50**
Dog, porcelain, white and gray bulldog, 2¾ inches.	**D-4.00**
Dog, porcelain, spotted, with ball, 3¼ in. long.	**D-6.00**
Dogs, porcelain, three puppies in basket, 2-5/8 x 3 inches.	**D-8.00**
Donkey, ceramic, pulling cart, 4 x 5 inches.	**D-8.,00**
Double figures, ceramic, couple walking arm-in-arm, 8 in. high.	**D-19.00**

Double figures, ceramic, man in red coat, lady in ruffled skirt, 6 in. high   **D-17.00**

Double figure, ceramic, lady in flowered skirt, man in waistcoat, 3¼ in. high.   **D-6.50**

Double figures, ceramic, man with oboe, lady with cello, 3-3/8 x 3-3/4 inches.   **D-9.00**

Easter chick, plush, yellow, 1½ in. high.   **D-.50**

Elephant, metal, trunk upraised, 4½ in. long.   **D-8.00**

Elf, ceramic, seated, green and purple, plays mandolin, 3 in. high.   **D-8.00**

Frog, bisque, tan, plays concertina on stump, 3 in. high.   **D-15.00**

Frog prince, bisque, seated, matte green, 2 x 2-7/8 inches.   **D-6.00**

Girl, bisque, holds doll, flowers at feet, 2¾ in. high.   **D-6.00**

Incense burner, Oriental man holds burner-box in lap.   **D-8.00**

Lamp bases, bisque, boy and girl, both leaning against tree trunks, 9¾ in. high; pair.   **D-35.00**

Liquer set, 6 in. decanter (no stopper) with six 2 in. tumblers; gold rims, roses, shield and wreath.   **D-40.00**

Motor launch, ceramic, 4 x 8 inches.   **D-13.00**

Mouse, metal, wind-up, red ears, in orig. box.   **D-14.00**

Musician, bisque, man playing bass viol, 3-3/8 inches.   **D-10.00**

Opera glasses, focusing knob stuck, orig. leather case, 2½ x 3¾ inches.   **D-30.00**

Oriental man, ceramic, gray beard, green cloak, 4¾ in. high.   **D-6.50**

Oriental sage, ceramic, green robe, holds paintbrush, 6¼ in. high.   **D-10.00**

Oriental woman, ceramic, holds flower and basket, 6 in. high.   **D-8.50**

Planter, ceramic, Elsie the Cow, in front of basket, 2½ inches.   **D-5.50**

Salt/pepper, ceramic, yellow pears, 2 in. high.   **D-7.50**

Salt/pepper, shakers, metal, worn silverplate, 1½ in. high.   **D-4.00**

Scottie, celluloid, tan with red collar, 1½ inches.   **D-3.00**

Seal, porcelain, brown, standing, 4-5/8 in. high.   **D-7.50**

Shepherdess, bisque, with lamb and tambourine, 4-3/8 inches.   **D-10.00**

Shoe, ceramic, white, gold trim, colored flowers, 2¼ inches.   **D-3.00**

Souvenir mug, Capital Building, Washington, D.C., 2½ inches. — **D-6.00**

Swan, ceramic, 3¼ x 5 inches. — **D-8.50**

Table set, all melon-ribbed; salt, pepper, mustard with lid, oil, vinegar, and tray. — **D-28.00**

Table set, salt, pepper and stand; orange and blue cabbages with butterflies, on stand. — **D-17.00**

Tea infuser, metal, chrome-plated, teapot-shaped. — **D-4.00**

Toby jug, Indian chief, 2¾ in. high. — **D-14.00**

Toby jug, full-figure, black hat, green coat, 2½ inches. — **D-8.50**

Toothpick holder, white deer and hollow brown stump, 2 inches. — **D3.50**

Tray, metal, oval, 4-1/8 x 8-3/4 inches. — **D-6.00**

Vase, ceramic, gold trim, floral spray, side handle. — **D-5.00**

Wall pocket, cuckoo clock with pinecone. — **D-4.00**

Wall pocket, bisque, figural, lady leaning from window, 2¾ x 3¾ inches. — **D-12.00**

Wheelbarrow, ceramic, white with floral sides 2-7/8 inches. — **D-4.00**

ORIENTAL JADES

Amulet, green, axe-form, animal pediment; 18th Century, 2½ in. high. — **A-60.00**

Animal, fantasy, varicolored, 17th/18th Century, ¾ in. high. — **A-50.00**

Belt Buckle, carved, gray-white, Ch'ien Lung Dynasty, dragonhead decorated. — **A-50.00**

Belt buckle, carved, two-part, green and white jade, Ch'ien Lung Dynasty. — **A-75.00**

Center, **green jade mandarin's hair pin 10¾ in. long.** A/50
Bot. left, **white-green jade treasure lock,** Ch'ien Lung Dynasty. A/70
Bot. right, **green jade carving of Phoenix bird,** 3 in. long. A/125

Courtesy Adam A. Weschler & Son, Washington, D.C.; photograph by Breger & Associates.

Upper left photo, left and right, **pair of Chinese green jade exotic bird figures**, perched on treetrunk plinth; 8 in. high. Late 19th Century.

A/700

Center, **pair of Chinese jade table screens.** Mottled green with relief scenes of flowering branch and bird. Separate carved and pierced wood stand; height overall, 9½ inches.

A/150

Top right photo, **green-brown jade bronze-form amulet** 2 in. diameter.

A/40

Pale green jade Tibetan prayer wheel, 2¼ in. diameter.

A/50

Left, **green-white jade figural group** of two birds perched on limb, 5¼ in. high. A/250

Green-white jade covered hanging urn, 15 in. overall height. A/1800

Two-color green jade covered urn, 9 in. high. A/1000

(All pieces 19th & 20th Centuries)

Courtesy Adam A. Weschler & Son

Bowl, green-black moss jade, early 19th Century. Flared, with ring base, 1¾ in. high. **A-125.00**

Bracelet, brown, Ming Dynasty, etched with geometric design. Gilded silver hinge and locking attachment of later date. **A-100.00**

Bracelet, beige jade, Ming Dynasty, continuous vine decoration. **A-75.00**

Bracelets, lot of two, varicolored jade, Ch'ien Lung Dynasty. **A-125.00**

Bracelets, lot of two, moss green jade, 19th Century. **A-75.00**

Brooch, "spinach" jade, hand-enameled florals on carat-clad sterling, filigreed back, 1¼ x 1½ inches. **D-200.00**

Buckles, lot of two, Ming Dynasty, one white, one green-brown. **A-100**

Buckles, lot of three, carved, Ming and Ch'ien Lung Dynasties. All quality: Mutton fat, onion-brown and bone-colored.   A-125.00

Buckles, lot of four, Ming and Ch'ien Lung Dynasties. One caramel-brown, three gray-green.   A-175.00

Cabinet pieces, lot of twelve, varicolored and carved. Six animal and floral forms, (amulets), five opium pipe ends and one pendant.   A-125.00

Carving, white jade, early 19th Century. Gourd-shaped, 2 in. high.   A-60.00

Carvings, miniature, lot of ten; white-green jade. Buddha, Sennin, Karako boy, bats, pi-ring, etc.   A-150.00

Dish, shallow mutton-fat jade, interior relief carving of flowers and leaves. On wood stand, 5 in. diameter.   A-100.00

Figure, of rearing T'ang warhorse, green-white, 19th/20th Century. With wood stand, 3½ in. high.   A-130.00

Figure, of standing bearded sage, white, Ch'ien Lung Dynasty, 2 in. high.   A-70.00

Figure, of three butterflies flanking good luck character, white jade, Ch'ien Lung Dynasty.   A-60.00

Fish, double, green-brown, late 18th Century.   A-100.00

Foo Lion, varicolored, reclining, Ming Dynasty, 2½ in. long.   A-125.00

Hair pins, mandarin, lot of four; green-white jade, 18th Century, longest 5¾ inches.   A-90.00

Horses, green-black, pair; one galloping, one on its back. With wood stands; 19th/20th Centuries, height of taller, 3 inches.   A-200.00

Pendants, varicolored, carved, lot of four; Ch'ien Lung Dynasty, fruit and floral forms.   A-300.00

Pi-ring, pale green, Ch'ien Lung Dynasty.   A-35.00

Pi-ring, green-brown, rectangular, carved and pierced, surrounded by foliage, Ch'ien Lung Dynasty.   A-50.00

Ring, floral-carved, "spinach" jade, raised floral motifs to sides, 5/8 by 3/4 inch.   D-95.00

Rings, archer's, lot of three; varicolored, Ch'ien Lung Dynasty.   A-100.00

Rings, archer's, lot of three; varicolored jade.   A-175.00

Treasure lock, green-white jade, Ch'ien Lung Dynasty, butterfly form.   A-35.00

PAPER

Cut-out, on black background, deer and birds in a tree, dated 1970. Framed, 9½ x 12½ inches.   **A-25.00**

Cut-out, two hands, tulips and shield with inscription and dated 1882. Faded black background, cherry and pine frame, 10 x 12 inches.   **A-85.00**

Cut-out, folded paper, eagles, hearts, etc.; decorated frame 15½ x 18 inches.   **A-30.00**

Doll, Forbes Victorian girl ice-skating, 1896, 8 in. high.   **D-17.50**

Dolls, uncut sheet, "Betty Bonnet's Little Niece", from 1916 woman's magazine, 14 clothing changes.   **D-6.50**

Scrap book, containing handmade doll clothes, beautifully stitched with applied handmade lace, etc.; 7½ x 11 inches.   **A-25.00**

Soldiers, heavy paper, wooden plinth bases, ca. 1880's, 4 in. high, lot of three.   **D-2.50**

Toy, three children on a sleigh, seven pieces, 1896, 4½ x 8 inches.   **D-8.50**

Toy theatre, Civil War period, stage setting in lithographed color, paper over cardboard, arched, 4½ x 5 inches; overall 2 x 5¼ x 8 inches. Wooden knobs turn endless panels (est. 120 inches of 24 scenic panels, including plantation slaves, Civil War battles, etc.) Ca. 1864, extremely rare.   **D-249.00**

Toys, McCormick Spice radio givaway circus figures, uncut sheet, mint, 1937, pair.   **D-8.50**

George A. Prince & Co. catalog. 1866. Organs.   30-45
Colliers. 1888-1957.   2-4
Marines enlistment poster. 30 x 39.   25-30
Judge. 1881-1939.   10-15
Mickey Mouse Magazine V. 2 No. 8.   20-25
Opposite page. The Silver Bell Mines **certificate** was in a
dealer lot priced at   12 for $6

PAPERWEIGHTS

Bubbles, in rows, on amber base surrounded by
clear crystal. Window cut in top, unmarked, 3½ in.
diameter.   A-30.00
Butterfly on white latticework, blue, marked "Z" for
Zimmerman, 3½ in. diameter.   A-55.00

Amos 'n' Andy paper-
weights, 3½ in. long,
matched pair, cast iron.
Pair: C/20

Lar Hothem photo

Top right.	D/4
Lower right.	D/50
Top left.	D/50
Lower left.	D/50

Candy, jumbled, slight bruises on surface, 3 in. diameter.   **A-52.50**

Clear, numbered on flat bottom, 3 in. high.   **S-30.00**

Floral canes red, white and blue, white latticinio, unmarked, 3 in. diameter.   **A-7.50**

Flower, white, on pistachio ground, St. Louis and marked "1973", 3-3/8 in. diameter.   **A-105.00**

Lily, blue, on white ground with symmetrically arranged air bubbles. "Z", 3 in. diameter.   **A-27.50**

Lily, white, with five clear bubbles, marked "St. Clair", 3¼ in. diameter.   **A-15.00**

Millefiori, patterned, alternate with laticinio, St. Louis, 1972, 3¼ in. diameter.   **A-102.50**

Millefiori, with central fleur-de-lis, St. Louis, 2-7/8 in. diameter.   **A-100.00**

Swirls, pink, alternate with latticinio, 2¾ in. square.   **A-37.50**

Turtle, green, on yellow and white varigated ground. Signed Joe Zimmerman, 3-3/8 in. diameter.   **A-52.50**

PEWTER

Barber's bottle, screw-on top, small split and holes, 6½ in. high. **A-255.00**

Basin, minor dents, London touchmarks, 9¼ in. diameter. **A-135.00**

Basin, repairs, unmarked, 8¼ in. diameter. **A-65.00**

Beaker, 2¼ in. high. **A-40.00**

Beaker, 2¾ in. high. **A-45.00**

Beaker, 3¼ in. high. **A-45.00**

Beaker, unmarked, 4 in. high. **A-47.50**

Candlestick, battered base and top flange, 10¾ in. high. **A-80.00**

Candlesticks, pair; push-ups, unmarked, 9¾ in. high. **A-270.00**

Chalises, pair; unmarked, American, may have had handles, 6¼ in. high. **A-90.00**

Chamber lamp, cast handle has hole, burner gone, 5¼ in. high. **A-70.00**

Charger, worn, unreadable touchmarks, 16½ in. diameter. **A-160.00**

Charger, 16¼ in. diameter **A-160.00**

Charger, Continental touchmarks, small repaired hole, 15 in. diameter. **A-42.50**

Charger, Samuel Danforth touchmarks, 13 in. diameter. **A-350.00**

Chargers, pair; with marriage initials, 15 in. diameter. **A-200.00**

Coffee pot, American, soldered base repair, 11¼ in. high. **A-185.00**

Coffee pot, "Savage/Midd. Ct./No. 3", holed handle base, 10 in. high. **A-185.00**

Coffee pot, pedestal base, American marks. **D-155.00**

Coffee pot, cast finial, 10 in. high. **A-45.00**

Coffee pot, "T.S. Derby", silver plated, hinge pin replaced. **A-190.00**

Creamer, marked "XI", 5¾ in. high. **A-36.00**

Double measure, spirits, ca. 1800. **D-75.00**

Flagon, rim dated 1834, 9 in. high. **A-520.00**

Flagon, not marked, 10 in. high. **A-255.00**

Hot-water bottle, pewter cap screw, 12½ in. long. **A-45.00**

Lamp, burning fluid, rabbit-ear burners damaged, 6¾ in. high. **A-75.00**

Pitcher, marked "Solid Pewter", 11 in. high.

C/35-55

Lamp, brass and pewter, rabbit-ear burners, 5½ in. high.   A-115.00

Pitcher, side-spouted, marked "Quart", touchmark, 6¼ in. high.   A-65.00

Pitcher, covered, acorn finial, cast handle, 12¾ in. high.   A-110.00

Plate, surface corroded, faint touchmark, 7-7/8 in. diameter.   A-45.00

Plate, London touchmark, repaired hole in center, 8-7/8 in. diameter.   A-45.00

Plate, soup, unmarked, 12½ in. diameter.   A-60.00

Porringer, unmarked, 4 in. diameter.   A-65.00

Spoons, two; both with Continental touchmarks, 7 in. long.   A-22.50

Tankard, "James Yates/1/2 pint", 3-5/8 in. high.   A-80.00

Tankard, "Pint/Imperial Measure", English, 4½ in. high.   A-75.00

Tankard, "Pint", worn maker's mark on bottom, 4½ in. high.   A-200.00

Tankard measure, "¼ gil", minor dents, 1¾ in. high.   A-45.00

Teapot, "Sellew & Co./Cincinnati", 8½ in. high.   A-290.00

Teapot, unmarked, repairs, battered, 7½ in. high.   A-50.00

Teapot, unmarked, American, 7¾ in. high.   A-200.00

Tumbler, unmarked, European, 5¼ in. high.   D-55.00

PHOTOGRAPHICA

Ambrotype, Civil War, of soldier standing with musket and bayonet. **A-85.00**

Daquerreotypes, pair; of Quaker man and woman. With 3½ x 4 in. photos is an 1883 handwritten letter from man to his Elders soliciting permission to marry. Ca. 1850's. **D-89.00**

Darkroom lantern, tin, orig. burner, kerosene, prob. Kodak. **D18.50**

Darkroom lantern, plate photographer's, tin, brass trim. In orig. oil state, with blown-glass chimney, red front safety lens, swivel reflector, 6 x 6¼ x 12 in. high. **D-100.00**

Stereoptic viewcards, Spanish-American War.

Each: C/4-10

Above. **Plate-frames,** photo, wood, glass and metal sprung.
    Back, marked "Kodak". C/15-20
    Front, hinged back. C/9-12
Photo courtesy Judy Morehead, Creative Photography, Lancaster, Ohio.

Left, **photographic timer,** Eastman-Kodak, metal, 5 in. high.

C/17.50

Photograph album containing 185 early photographs of the major participants in Civil War. Both Union and Confederate sides portrayed. — A-1,300.00

Photograph on silk, Victorian girl by cast iron fence in garden; with frame, 15 x 18½ inches. — D-27.50

Printing frame, glass face, Eastman Kodak, for 3¼ to 5½ inch film negatives. — D-5.00

Tintype, Civil War, soldier standing with Colt pocket revolver across chest. Locket of hair behind tintype in case. — A-80.00

Tintype in case, soldier standing with musket and bayonet, and with cross-belt and pistol in belt. — A-95.00

Tintype in case of Officer seated, wearing shoulder epaulets. — A-40.00

Tintype in case, Union soldier standing with Springfield musket and bayonet. — A-50.00

Tintype in case, Sargeant holding cap with bugle insignia. — A-50.00

Tintype in case, full-length portrait of Union soldier with Springfield musket and bayonet. — A-75.00

Tintype in case, soldier seated, holding musket. — A-80.00

Tintype in gilt metal frame, seated Corporal in frock coat. — A-45.00

Tintype in gutta percha frame, oval, of Civil War Officer complete with sword; 4¼ x 5½ inches.

PLATES—*ABC*

Glass, "Little Bo Peep," girl with sheep. Complete alphabet and numbers 1 to 9 on rim, 7½ in. diameter. — D-45.00

Glass, clear, and frosted; heron and palm trees in central intaglio. Minor underside flake, 6 in. diameter. — D-30.00

Porcelain, center with "Crusoe Viewing The Island," ABC's around outside rim in brown, 8½ in. diameter. — D-39.50

Porcelain, A through Z on rim in gold, in center, rooster and chickens. Marked Germany, 6¼ in. diameter. — D-39.50

Tin, A through Z in circle, plus ten birds, animals, and a butterfly at center; 8 in. diameter. — D-22.50

Tin, "Hi Diddle, Diddle", embossed alphabet around
rim. Animal characters from rhyme in center. Early
plate.   **D-39.50**
Tin, "Cock Robin", 7-7/8 in. diameter.   **D-65.00**

PLATES—*Baby*

China, white semi-vitreous; Campbell Kids, "Buffalo
Pottery", one bottom-rim chip, 1-3/8 in. high and
7-3/4 in. diameter.   **D-32.00**
Earthernware, light tan; "Baby Plate", four bird
decals, prominent crazing. "W. C. Co." on bottom,
7¾ in. diameter.   **D-32.00**
Earthernware, buff; "Higgedly - Piggedly / My Black
Hen", 1½ x 8 inches.   **D-38.00**
Porcelain, white; Hickory-Dickory-Dock motif, two il-
lustrations. Marked "Noritake / Hand-Painted", 1½
x 7 in. diameter.   **D-35.00**
Pottery, white; goose and gosling decal cartoon
figures, "Won't You Take Me?" Bottom mark, "The
Wellsville China Co. / 227", 1½ x 7¾ in. diameter.   **D-28.00**
Pottery, yellow; "Uncle Wiggly / Grandpa Goosey
Gander", by "Sebring Pottery Co. (for) Fred A. Wish,
Inc.", 1-5/8 x 8-1/2 in. diameter.   **D-28.00**

PLATES—*Collectors' and Limited Edition*

Anna Perenna

Burques "Chun Li"	**D-100.00**
Burques "Chun Li", signed	**D-125.00**
Burques "Firebird"	**D-110.00**
Burques "June Dream"	**D-75.00**
Burques "June Dream"	**D-95.00**
Byzantine Triptych	**D-325.00**
Frame	**D-15.00**
"Empress Gold"	**D-110.00**

Anri Christmas Plates (Italy)

1971 St. Jacob in Groeden, first edition	**D-69.50**
1972 Pipers at Alberobello	**D-77.50**
1973 Alpine Horn	**D-205.00**
1974 Young Man and Girl	**D-59.50**

1975 Christmas In Ireland	D-49.50
1976 Alpine Christmas	D-Out
1977 Heiligen Blut	D-115.00
1978 Klocklersingers	D-77.50
1978 Anri-Ferrandiz Christmas plate, "Leading the Way"	D-69.50
1977 Appleby "She Walks In Beauty"	D-269.00
1978 Avondale Melissa Plate, first edition	D-59.50

Appleby

Unicorn (bronze)	D-125.00
"Bouquet" (bronze)	D-125.00

Avey, Linda

"The Blessing"	D-30.00
"Appreciation"	D-37.50

Avondale

Melissa	D-65.00
"Melissa" figurine	D-25.00

Bareuther Christmas Plates (German)

1967 Stifskirche, first edition	D-87.50
1968 Kappel	D-20.00
1969 Christindelsmarkt	D-8.00
1970 Chapel in Oberndorf	D-12.00
1971 Toys for Sale	D-15.95
1972 Christmas in Munich	D-29.00
1973 Sleigh Ride	D-22.50
1974 Black Forest Church	D-19.95
1975 Snowman	D-22.95
1976 Chapel In Hills	D-23.50
1977 Christmas Story	D-27.95
1978 Bareuther Christmas	D-23.50
1973 Bareuther Christmas Bell, first edition	D-9.00

Belleek Christmas Plates (Ireland)

1970 Castle Caldwell, first edition	D-119.00
1971 Celtic Cross	D-47.50
1972 Flight of the Earls	D-49.50
1973 Tribute to Yeats	D-59.50
1974 Devenish Island	D-165.00
1975 The Celtic Cross	D-49.50
1976 Dove of Peace	D-52.50
1977 Wren	D-54.50
1976 Belleek Bicentennial, rare	D-79.50
1978 Beran Little Blue Horse, first edition	D-105.00

Beran, Lenore

"Softly, the Sun Sets", first edition	D-75.00
Circle of Enchantment (Print)	D-50.00

Berlin Christmas Plates (Germany)

1970 Christmas in Bernkastel, first edition	D-125.00
1971 Christmas in Rothenburg	D-14.50
1972 Christmas in Michelstadt	D-28.50
1973 Christmas in Wendelstein	D-52.50
1974 Christmas in Bremen	D-17.50
1975 Christmas in Dortland	D-29.50
1976 Christmas in Augsburg	D-29.50
1977 Christmas in Hamburg	D-27.50
1978 Christmas in Berlin	D-29.95
1973 Berlin Mother's Plate	D-24.50

Bing & Grondahl Christmas Plates (Denmark)

1895 Frozen Window, first edition	D-2995.00
1896 New Moon	D-1875
1897 Sparrows	D-1195.00
1898 Star and Roses	D-725.00
1899 Crows	D-1275
1900 Church Bells	D-735.00
1901 Three Wise Men	D-375.00
1902 Gothic Church Interior	D-359.00
1903 Expectant Children	D-275.00
1904 Frederiksberg Hill	D-139.00
1905 Christmas Night	D-155.00
1906 One Horse Sleigh	D-102.50

Collection of sixty-three [63] Bing & Grondahl Christmas plates, years 1909-1973.

(Collection) A/1950

Courtesy Adam A. Weschler & Son, Washington, D.C.; photograph by Breger & Associates.

1907	Little Match Girl	D-129.00
1908	St. Petri Church	D-82.50
1909	Yule Tree	D-87.50
1910	The Old Organist	D-95.00
1911	Angels and Shepherds	D-95.00
1912	Going to Church	D-82.50
1913	Bringing Home the Tree	D-87.50
1914	Royal Castle	D-82.50
1915	Dog Outside Window	D-119.00
1916	Sparrows at Christmas	D-74.50
1917	Christmas Boat	D-79.50
1918	Fishing Boat	D-82.50
1919	Outside the Window	D-79.50
1920	Hare in the Snow	D-72.50
1921	Pigeons	D-59.50
1922	Star of Bethlehem	D-59.50
1923	The Ermitage	D-59.50
1924	Lighthouse	D-61.00
1925	Child's Christmas	D-72.50
1926	Churchgoers	D-62.50
1927	Skating Couple	D-92.50

1928 Eskimos	D-64.50
1929 Fox Outside Farm	D-79.50
1930 Town Hall Square	D-82.50
1931 Christmas Train	D-72.50
1932 Lifeboat	D-74.50
1933 Korsor-Nyborg Ferry	D-59.50
1934 Church Bell in Tower	D-59.50
1935 Lillebelt Bridge	D-59.50
1936 Amalienborg Castle	D-77.50
1937 Guests Arrival	D-79.50
1938 Lighting the Candles	D-119.00
1939 Old Lock-Eye, the Sandman	D-159.00
1940 Christmas Letters	D-157.50
1941 Horses	D-315.00
1942 Danish Farm	D-155.00
1943 Ribe Cathedral	D-155.00
1944 Sorgenfri Castle	D-109.00
1945 The Old Water Mill	D-135.00
1946 Commemoration Cross	D-67.60
1947 Dybbol Mill	D-95.00
1948 Watchman	D-69.00
1949 Landsoldaten	D-67.50
1950 Kronborg Castle	D-139.00
1951 Jens Bang	D-8.00
1952 Thorvaldsen Museum	D-67.50
1953 Royal Boat	D-77.50
1954 Snowman	D-88.00
1955 Kalunborg Church	D-94.00
1956 Christmas in Copenhagen	D-139.00
1957 Christmas Candles	D-139.00
1958 Santa Claus	D-102.50
1959 Christmas Eve	D-139.00
1960 Village Church	D-199.00
1961 Winter Harmony	D-109.00
1962 Winter Night	D-69.50
1963 The Christmas Elf	D-135.00
1964 The Fir Tree and Hare	D-39.50
1965 Bringing Home the Tree	D-47.50
1966 Home for Christmas	D-41.50
1967 Sharing the Joy	D-35.95
1968 Christmas in Church	D-37.50
1969 Arrival of Guests	D-18.50
1970 Pheasants in Snow	D-16.00
1971 Christmas at Home	D-15.95

1972 Christmas in Greenland   D-16.95
1973 Family Reunion   D-23.00
1974 Christmas in the Village   D-11.00
1975 Old Water Mill   D-17.00
1976 Christmas Welcome   D-25.95
1977 Copenhagen Christmas   D-26.95
1978 Bing & Grondahl Christmas   D-26.95

Bing & Grondahl Christmas Bells

1974 Roskilde Cathedral, first edition   D-87.50
1978 Notre Dame   D-64.50

Royal Copenhagen Christmas Plates *(Denmark)*

1908 Madonna and Child, first edition   D-1550.00
1909 Danish Landscape   D-145.00
1910 The Magi   D-125.00
1911 Danish Landscape   D-135.00
1912 Christmas Tree   D-139.00
1913 Frederik Church Spire   D-137.50
1914 Holy Spirit Church   D-15.00
1915 Danish Landscape   D-122.50
1916 Shepherd at Christmas   D-85.00
1917 Our Savior Church   D-82.50
1918 Sheep and Shepherds   D-82.50
1919 In the Park   D-79.50
1920 Mary and the Child Jesus   D-74.50
1921 Aabenraa Marketplace   D-69.50
1922 Three Singing Angels   D-68.50
1923 Danish Landscape   D-69.50
1924 Sailing Ship   D-89.50
1925 Christianshavn   D-77.50
1926 Christianshavn Canal   D-75.00
1927 Ship's Boy at Tiller   D-132.50
1928 Vicar Family   D-77.50
1929 Grundtvig Church   D-76.00
1930 Fishing Boats   D-79.50
1931 Mother and Child   D-82.50
1932 Frederiksberg Gardens   D-82.50
1933 Great Belt Ferry   D-107.50
1934 The Hermitage Castle   D-110.00
1935 Kronberg Castle   D-135.00

1936 Roskilde Cathedral	D-135.00
1937 Main Street Copenhagen	D-142.50
1938 Round Church Osterlars	D-259.00
1939 Greenland Pack Ice	D-249.00
1940 The Good Shepherd	D-309.00
1941 Danish Village Church	D-309.00
1942 Bell Tower	D-315.00
1943 Flight to Egypt	D-409.00
1944 Danish Winter Scene	D-152.50
1945 A Peaceful Motif	D-295.00
1946 Zealand Village Church	D-152.50
1947 The Good Shepherd	D-219.00
1948 Noddebo Church	D-149.00
1949 Our Lady's Cathedral	D-165.00
1950 Boeslunde Church	D-185.00
1951 Christmas Angel	D-309.00
1952 Christmas in Forest	D-139.00
1953 Frederiksborg Castle	D-1109.00
1954 Amalienborg Palace	D-135.00
1955 Fano Girl	D-225.00
1956 Rosenborg Castle	D-195.00
1957 The Good Shepherd	D-102.50
1958 Sunshine Over Greenland	D-122.50
1959 Christmas Night	D-157.50
1960 The Stag	D-185.00
1961 Training Ship Danmark	D-185.00
1962 The Little Mermaid	D-215.00
1963 Hojsager Mill	D-79.50
1964 Fetching the Tree	D-64-50
1965 Little Skaters	D-59.00
1966 Blackbird	D-47.50
1967 The Royal Oak	D-44.50
1968 The Last Umiak	D-22.95
1969 The Old Farmyard	D-22.95
1970 Christmas Rose and Cat	D-22.50
1971 Hare in Winter	D-15.95
1972 In The Desert	D-18.95
1973 Train Homeward Bound	D-22.95
1974 Winter Twilight	D-17.50
1975 Queen's Palace (P. C. T., List . . .)	D-30.00
1976 Danish Waterfall	D-29.95
1977 Hunter and Hound	D-23.50
1978 Royal Copenhagen Christmas	D-29.50

Royal Doulton Plates *(England)*

1974 RD Neiman Harlequin Plate, first edition	74.50
1976 RD Neiman Pierrot Plate	D-64.50
1977 RD Columbine Plate	D-67.50
1978 RD Punchinello Plate	D-69.00
1976 RD Fisherman's Wharf (SF) first edition	D-39.00
1977 RD Venice	D-64.50
1975 RD Spring Harmony Plate, first edition	D-46.50
1977 RD Country Bouquet	D-67.50
1976 RD Garden of Tranquility, first edition	D-51.50
1976 RD Valentine, first edition	D-79.50
1977 RD Valentine	D-19.95
1978 RD Valentine	D-29.50

Wedgwood State Seal Plates *(England)*

No. 1, Virginia, set of two plates, first edition	D-9.00
No. 2, Pennsylvania, set of two	D-9.00
No. 4, New York, set of two	D-9.00
No. 6, New Hampshire, set of two	D-10.00
No. 7, Delaware, set of two	D-11.00
No. 9, Georgia, set of two	D-9.00
No. 12, Rhode Island, set of two	D-11.00
No. 13, Connecticut, set of two	D-11.00

Wedgwood Christmas Plates

1969 Windsor Castle, first edition	D-225.00
1970 Trafalgar Square	D-13.50
1971 Piccadilly Circus, London	D-28.50
1972 St. Paul's Cathedral	D-26.50
1973 Tower of London	D-29.50
1974 House of Parliament	D-14.50
1975 Tower Bridge	D-19.50
1976 Hampton Court	D-23.00
1977 Westminster Abbey	D-32.50
1978 Wedgwood Christmas	D-34.95
1979 Wedgwood New Year Bell, first edition	D-34.95
1978 W. Tricolor Decade Christmas	D-299.00

Wedgwood Christmas Mugs

1972 Christmas Mug	D-11.00
1976 Christmas Mug	D-24.50

Wedgwood Bicentennial Plates

1972 Boston Tea Party, first edition	D-17.50
1973 Paul Revere's Ride	D-79.50
1974 Battle of Concond	D-19.50
1975 Across the Delaware	D-52.50
1975 Victory at Yorktown	D-17.50
1976 Signing of Declaration	D-17.50
1976 Wedgwood Colony Set, issue price $175	D-95.00
1976 Bicentennial Six-scene plate, issue price $85	D-42.50
1976 Wedgwood Bicentennial Bell, issue price $65	D-37.50

Wedgwood Calendar Plates

1971 Pastoral Cherubs, first edition	D-7.50
1972 Zodiac	D-7.00
1973 Butterflies	D-119.00
1974 Camelot	D-119.00
1976 Robins	D-20.00
1977 Tonatiuh	D-18.50
1977 Wedgwood Vickers Innocence, first edition	D-105.00
1978 Wedgwood Vickers Cherish Plate	D-59.00
1976 Wedgwood Olympic Montreal	D-39.50

A) **Auction.** These are the top-bid, realized prices from recent auctions.

C) **Collector.** A few listings came from people who have kept up with market conditions for their collecting area(s).

D) **Dealer.** These represent antiques listings from top dealers.

S) **Shows.** A few listings are from important antiques exhibitions and sales.

POLITICAL ITEMS

Badge, FDR-Garner, brass, 25mm, extra-fine. D-7.00
Badge, guest, "Republican National Convention/
1936" D-25.00
Badge, Taft campaign, celluloid picture of Taft, 1¾
inches. D-20.00

Coolidge, 1924.
15-20

Wilson & Marshall,
1912
22-24

Left, **Political.**
Political and entertainment buttons
and badges.
D/Unlisted

Lar Hothem photo

Booklet, Presidential, "Political Information for
1892". D-12.50
Button, Bryan-Sewall, "16 to 1", 7/8 inch. D-12.00
Button, Carter, "Ohio For Carter", 1¾ inches. D-5.00
Button, clothing, tin Teddy Bear, light rust. D-4.00
Button, Coolidge, brown and white, "Keep
Coolidge". D-20.00
Button, Ford, light and dark blue, 1¾ inches. D-5.00
Button, Hoover, black and white, 1¼ inches. D-30.00
Button, Ike, red and white 2¼ inches. D-10.00
Button, Landow-Know, yellow, brown and white, 7/8
inch. D-10.00
Button, Lemke-O'Brien, "Union", ribboned, 7/8 inch.
Scarce. D-35.00
Button, Roosevelt-Garner, brass with blue enamel-
ing. D-12.50
Button, Smith, black and white, 1¼ inches. D-35.00
Button, Stevenson-Sparkman, ribboned, 3 inches. D-8.00

Button, TR, bull moose, "Founder/1912", brass.   **D-6.00**
Button, political, "Hoarding/Helps Communism", 7/8 inch.   **D-5.00**
Button, political, "Vote For Woman Suffrage/Now. 2nd, 1915".   **D-15.00**
Button, Willkie, banner and elephant, "Life Begins in '40".   **D-4.00**
Button, Willkie, "The Hope Of Our Country", 1¼ inches.   **D-7.00**
Clay pipe, Henry Clay bust, "Warranted To Color", fine cond.   **D-85.00**
Elephant head, solid brass in deep relief, pintype.   **D-10.00**
Ferrotype, Grant, brass border, "We Will Fight It Out On This Line", 21mm.   **D-80.00**
Ferrotype, Horace Greeley, book-shaped locket, bold image.   **D-175.00**
Inaugural medal, Taft, 1809, official, bronze, with orig. box.   **D-250.00**
Lapel button, Moses-Winant, blue and gold, ½ x 1¼ inches.   **D-6.50**
Lapel stud, Wm. Jennings Bryan Presidential campaign, 7/8 inch.   **D-27.50**
Medal, Lincoln, bust, "1809—1909" bronze, 61mm.   **D-20.00**
Mourning badge, Garfield, silver-dolar size, ribboned.   **D-25.00**
Mourning ribbon, Harrison, "Our Nation Mourns A Hero Gone", 3 x 8 inches.   **D-150.00**
Name clip, Hoover, blue and gold ¼ x 1 inch.   **D-7.50**
Napkin, campaign, Alf Landon, song words, 13½ in. square.   **D-4.00**
Paperweight, Wm. McKinley, relief of Memorial Building, Canton, Ohio.   **D-22.50**
Paperweight, Nixon-Agnew, triangular lucite, 1973.   **D-15.00**
Paperweight, McKinley, crystal, rectangular, with photo.   **D-15.00**
Paperweight, T.R., slightly used appearance.   **D-15.00**
Pen, glass, T.R., "President Roosevelt/America."   **D-50.00**
Pencil, "Hoover for President/1932", red plastic head at top.   **D-12.00**
Photo, Grant, sepia paper in gilt shell border, tin back.   **D-60.00**
Photo, Harrison, thick two-sided glass pendant case, clear.   **D-40.00**

Pin, Hoover, brass with embossed head, 1 in. diameter. D-12.50

Pin, Lafolette-Wheeler, bronze, extra-fine condition. D-12.50

Pinback button, Warren G. Harding, brown picture 5/8 in. diameter. D-6.50

Pinback button, Landon-Knox, GOP elephant, "1936", ¾ inch. D-4.00

Plaque, Hoover, oval tin, 3¾ x 5¾ inches. D-12.50

Postcard, black and white, "I Like Ike". D-8.00

Postcard, Bryan-Kern, "1903-1913/My Choice", corner tack-holes. D-15.00

Postcard, Taft portrait at Massachusetts summer home. D-4.00

Postcard, T.R., Ex-President addressing crowd, Haverhill, Mass. D-5.00

Postcard, Wilson, "Victory Greetings", minor corner tack-holes. D-5.00

Ribbon, Henry Clay, "The Wagon Boy". A-12.50

Ribbon, Lincoln-Hamlin, "Union And Victory", 2½ x 8¼. D-300.00

Scissors, with portraits of TR and wife on handle sides. D-50.00

Soap baby, McKinley, orig. tag and box, "Campaign Baby . . .". D-75.00

Spinner, Ike, aluminum, half-dollar size. D-5.00

Stickpin, McKinley campaign. D-30.00

Stickpin, McKinley, gold bug, enameled black and cream body. D-50.00

Ticket, inaugural, Truman-Barkley, cancelled, 1949. D-20.00

Ticket, Nat'l Repub. Conv., "1st Day Only", Chicago, 1920. D-10.00

Tie bar, JFK, PT-boat pin, gold color, 1¾ inches. D-10.00

Tintype, Lincoln, "S. J. Lovewell/Photographic Tent", 1½ x 2 inches. D-150.00

Token, Henry Clay, bust and wreath, holed for wearing, 24mm. D-15.00

Token, Millard Fillmore, bust and eagle, brass, holed, 28mm. D-20.00

Token, John C. Fremont, bust and eagle, brass, holed, 23mm. D-17.00

Token, Zachary Taylor, "Mexican War Victories", copper, 25mm. D-25.00

Token, FDR, "Onward America/A New Deal", 7/8 inch. D-7.50

Token, Al Smith, donkey and "1928", gilt brass, 25mm.   **D-7.00**

Torch, tin, campaign torch on wooden pole, 49 in. long.   **A-25.00**

Torch, tin, with brass kerosene filler; without wood handle.   **D-20.00**

Watch fob, "Bryan & Kern/1908", presidential campaign.   **D-24.00**

Watch fob, "T.R.-Fairbanks/1904", dark lettering, broken strap.   **D-15.00**

POPCORN AND PEANUT MACHINES AND VEHICLES

The early peanut/popcorn street wagons and the related theater lobby machines are not only scarce to the point of rarity, but beautiful. Some pieces in as-found condition require years of accurate restoration to retain authenticity and value.

Cretors "Earnmore" model. Unrestored but fairly complete for easy restoration. This model has the peanut roasting equipment in addition to the popping unit. Ca. 1919.   **C-2,000.00**

Cretors "Earnmore" model. Unrestored, mostly complete. Quite rare, and equipped with steam engine and electrical power. Ca. 1934.   **C-4,000.00**

Cretors "Graduate" floor model. Recently restored; Ca. 1915.   **C-1,750.00**

Cretors model #2 wagon. Recently restored; documented history with this original wagon, 1906.   **C-9,500.00**

Cretors model "C" wagon. Restoration just completed, clean, equipped with new Cretors 20 oz. kettle and automatic oil delivery system.   **C-20,000.00**

Cretors model "C" wagon. Magnificent wagon, fine original, with just completed two-year restoration.   **C-28.000.00**

Holcomb & Hoke table model machine. Early automated machine, unrestored but in fine restorable condition.   **C-1,000.00**

Buda/Cretors popcorn and peanut truck. Original, immaculate condition. Extremely rare, only three known to exist. Ca. 1912.   **C-85,000.00**

PORCELAIN—*BOEHM*

Edward Marshall Boehm Porcelain Objects Of Art
  Boehm porcelain figures are considered by many to be the finest ever made. Material is superb and there is great attention to detail. Figures are depicted in typical poses and, with naturalistic bases, are most lifelike.

Baby Cedar Waxwing, printed mark and pattern number, 3¼ in. high. — **A-125.00**

Baby Red Poll, printed mark and pattern number, 4 in. high. — **A-150.00**

Baby Wood Thrush, printed mark and pattern number, issued 1958. (The official bird of the nation's capital.) Width, 3½ in., 4½ in. high. — **A-150.00**

Barn Owl, printed mark, limited edition of 350 issued 1972. Owl is 21 in. high, 12 in. deep and 27 in. wide. — **A-3800.00**

Black Grouse, printed mark, limited edition of 175 issued 1972. Grouse is 15 in. high, 14½ in. deep, and 14 in. wide. — **A-1600.00**

Black Headed Grosbeak, limited edition of 175 issued 1972. Grosbeak is 10 in. high, 9 in. deep, and 13 in. wide. — **A-425.00**

Blue Tits With Apple Blossom, printed mark, limited edition of 350 issued 1973. — **A-1400.00**

Catbird, printed marks and pattern number, limited edition of 500 issued 1965. Catbird 7½ in. wide, 14½ in. high. — **A-1050.00**

Crested Flycatcher, printed mark and pattern number. Limited edition of 500 issued 1967. Flycatcher 18½ in. high. — **A-1800.00**

Fledgling Bird Figures, (two), baby fledgling Chickadee and fledgling Black Burnian Warbler. Each with printed mark and pattern number; 4 in. height. — **A-225.00**

Green Woodpeckers, printed mark. Limited edition of 50 issued 1973, 20½ in. high. — **A-2600.00**

Kestrels, pair, printed mark and pattern number. Limited edition of 500 pairs issued 1968; male, 14 in. high; female, 16½ in. high. — **A-1000.00**

Lapwing, printed mark. Limited edition of 100 issued 1973. Lapwing 17 in. high. — **A-1450.00**

Lazuli Bunting, printed mark and pattern number. Limited edition of 500 issued 1973; 13½ in. high. — **A-1000.00**

Top l., **Boehm Baby Crested Flycatcher**, printed mark and pattern number, 5 in. high. A/150

Bot. l., **Boehm Baby Robin**, printed mark and pattern number, 3½ in. high. A/125

Center, **Boehm Baby Western Bluebird**, printed mark and pattern number, 6 in. high. A/200

Right, **Boehm Baby Blue Jay**, printed mark and pattern number, 4½ in. high. A/150

Lesser Prairie Chickens, (pair), printed mark and pattern number. Limited edition of 300 pairs issued 1962; male, 10 in. high, female, 10 in. high. A-1000.00

Long Tail Tit, printed mark. Limited edition of 350 issued 1973; 12½ in. high. A-1450.00

Nuthatch, printed marks. Limited editions of 350 issued 1971; 8½ in. high. A-450.00

Parula Warblers, printed mark and pattern number. Limited edition of 400 issued 1965; 14½ in. high. A-1850.00

Red Squirrels, printed mark. Limited edition of 100 issued 1972. Squirrels 14 in. high. A-1400.00

Roadrunner, printed mark and pattern number. Limited edition of 500 issued 1968. (State bird of New Mexico.) A-2500.00

Rufus Hummingbird, printed mark and pattern number. Limited edition of 500 issued 1966; with flowers, 14 in. high. A-700.00

Tree Creepers, printed mark. Limited edition of 200 issued 1972. Height, 17 inches. D-1600.00

Trenton Cactus Wren, printed mark and pattern number. Limited edition of 400 issued 1972; height, 13 in. A-1200.00

Winter Robin, printed marks. Limited edition of 225 issued 1971. Robin 9½ in. high. A-650.00

279

Wood Thrushes, printed mark and pattern number. Limited edition of 400 pairs issued 1966; male, 16 in. high, female, 15 inches.

A-5000

Yellow Chrysanthemums With Butterfly, printed mark. Limited edition of 350 issued 1972; height, 8½ inches.

A-500.00

Young American Bald Eagle, limited edition of 850 issued 1969. (President Nixon Inaugural Edition with Presidential Seal.) Height, 9½ inches.

A-1000.00

Boehm Bobcats, printed mark. Limited edition of 200 issued 1971; height, 9 inches.
A/900

Courtesy Adam A. Weschler & Son, Washington, D.C.; photograph by Breger & Associates.

Salts, individual, porcelain, scalloped edge with gold trim. Three of complete set of twelve. Bottoms marked "Royal Austria". The set: C/55-80

POTTERY—American

Abingdon console bowl, pink, 17 inches	**D-9.00**
Bauer carafe, red, lid with under-rim nick.	**D-3.00**
Bauer plate, green, 15 inches.	**D-9.00**
Bennington-type vase, higlaze brown, 5½ x 8 inches.	**D-5.00**
Blue Ridge bowl, blue flowers and buds, 9¼ inches.	**D-3.50**
Blue Ridge platter, 11¾ inches.	**D-4.00**

Blue and white.

Top left, **Pitcher.** Apricots (Embossed). 45-50

Top center, **Salt.** Hanging, Grid (Embossed). 45-50

Top right. **Pitcher.** Daisys (Embossed). 60-70

Left. **Bowl.** 25-30

Burley Winter jardiniere, marked, 10 x 11½ inches.	**D-36.00**
Camark centerpiece, flared shell, 5½ x 12 inches.	**D-10.00**
Camark flower holder, glossy black, 5¾ x 9 inches.	**D-15.00**
Cambridge Art vase, higlaze brown, 10¾ in. high.	**D-120.00**
Cardinal cookie jar, antique wall phone, marked.	**D-15.00**
Cowan vase, square base, green, footed, 5 inches.	**D-15.00**
Floraline vase, footed, dull green, 6½ in. high.	**D-3.00**
Franciscan Ware plate, tan wheat relief, 11 inches.	**D-3.00**
Frankoma bean pot and lid, green/brown, 6½ x 8½ inches.	**D-17.00**
Frankoma jug, brown, 5½ in. high.	**D-5.00**
Frankoma liquer jug, signed, 3½ x 5 x 6½ inches.	**D-16.00**
Frankoma milk pitcher, "Aztec" relief, 4¾ in. high.	**D-2.50**
Frankoma sugar, one-handled, 2¾ inches.	**D-4.00**
Fulper bowl, contrasting blues in and out, 10¼ inches.	**D-45.00**
Fulper centerpiece bowl, turquoise, oval, 17½ inches.	**D-30.00**

Gonder vase, blue lustre, leaves and flowers, 11 in. high. D-20.00

Haeger bud vase, eggshell white, sticker, 7¼ in. high. D-5.00

Haeger candlesticks, blue to green, 4¾ x 5¼ inches. D-12.00

Haeger centerpiece, 6 x 7½ x 23¾ inches. D-20.00

Haeger vase, ivory, running deer, sticker, 9-1/8 in. high. D-12.00

Hampshire vase, mottled blue, cylinder, 4 x 7 inches. D-30.00

Hull Blossomflite basket, square, 5½ x 10¼ inches. D-20.00

Hull Bowknot cornucopia, black to green, 7½ inches. D-24.00

Hull Butterfly planter, cream higlaze, 3 x 4 x 13 inches. D-14.00

Hull Camellia cornucopia, pink and black, 8¾ inches. D-10.00

Hull Continental basket, orange, "Hull/USA/55". D-20.00

Hull Ebbtide vase, pink and gray spatter. D-20.00

Hull Grape Harvest cornucopia, 8¼ in. high. D-16.00

Hull House and Garden creamer/covered sugar, green. D-12.00

Hull Magnolia candlesticks, pink higlaze, pair. D-15.00

Hull Narcissus pitcher vase, ivory and rose, 13-5/8 inches. D-5.00

Hull Open Rose fan vase, handled, footed, 6½ inches. D-15.00

Hull Parchment and Pine vase, "Hull/USA/6-4", 10½ inches. D-25.00

Hull Red Riding Hood cookie jar and lid, light hairline. D-20.00

Hull Regal planter, green and maroon, 7 x 10 inches. D-10.00

Hull Rosella vase, pink and white, 2½ x 5 x 6½ inches. D-18.00

Hull Serenade hat vase. D-14.00

Hull Spatter wall pockets, 7¼ x 7½ in., pair. D-20.00

Hull Stoneware vase, green rim, 8 in. high. D-20.00

Hull Sunflower cookie jar, 8½ in. high. D-9.00

Hull Thistle vase, side-handled, 4 x 6¼ inches. D-25.00

Hull Tokay covered comport, pink, 7 inches. D-20.00

Hull Tulip vase, pink and black, mark illegible, 7 inches. D-18.00

Hull Waterlily vase, pink and turquoise, tiny glaze miss. D-11.00

Hull Wildflower footed vase, 9½ inches. D-18.00

Hull Woodland basket, chartreuse and pink, 9 inches. **D-25.00**

Imperial planter, speckled orange, 3 x 3 x 4½ inches. **D-2.50**

McCoy Blossomtime 700 line vase, ivory, 6¼ inches. **D-4.00**

McCoy Butterfly line footed vase, blue, 9 inches. **D-16.00**

McCoy Harmony line footed dish, green and white. **D-5.00**

McCoy "Pasted Straps" line vase, turquoise, 12 inches. **D-12.00**

McCoy Springwood line jardiniere, pink, 5-3/8 inches. **D-8.00**

McCoy Swirl line orchid planter, footed, 7 in. long. **D-3.00**

Monmouth vase, matte green, 8 inches. **D-7.00**

Monmouth pitcher, tan, 5½; in. high. **D-6.00**

Moorcroft vase, salmon hibiscus, 5¾ x 8¼ inches. **D-105.00**

Mosaic Tile Co. square tile, floral, 4-3/8 inches. **D-4.50**

Muncie vase, green and rose, 5¼ x 9 inches. **D-10.00**

New Jersey Porcelain Company ashtray, "Security National Bank, Trenton, N.J. 1927". **D-15.00**

Niloak ball jug, blue, 3½ in. diameter. **D-6.00**

Niloak ewer vase, gray and pink, 10¼ in. high. **D-22.00**

Niloak pitcher, beige, 5¼ in. high. **D-10.00**

Peters & Reed bowl, Moss Aztec, signed, 2 3/8 in. high. **D-10.00**

Peters & Reed vase, Zane Landsun glaze, 5 in. high. **D-15.00**

Pennsbury creamer, marked, 4¼ in. high. **D-15.00**

Pealtzgraff vase, green, 5¼ in. high. **D-10.00**

Pisgah Forest teapot and lid, "Pisgah Forest/1936". **D-40.00**

Pisgah Forest vase, celadon green, 4¾ x 6¾ inches. **D-13.00**

Redwing bean pot and lid, glazed lid and interior. **D-12.00**

Redwing cookie jar, green banana bunch, 8½ in. high. **D-18.00**

Redwing dish, gray and maroon, free form, 2 in. high. **D-10.00**

Redwing milk pitcher, waffle weave, 4 x 5 inches. **D-4.00**

Redwing pitcher, green and ivory, ice guard, "Red Wing". **D-16.00**

Redwing vase, blue and pink, two leaves, 9 in. high. **D-9.00**

Redwing vase, pansy decoration, handled, 6½ in. high. **D-18.00**

Rockingham urn, mottled brown, 4½ x 6 x 7½ inches. **D-25.00**

Rockwood bowl, rose, leaf and butterfly relief, 3½ in. high. **D-37.00**

Above
Kitchen mixers. Left, "Borden's", graduated-mark side, one quart, wood handle.
C/25-40
Right, "Robert's Lightning Mixer", 9¾ in. high.
C/15-20

Above
Pyrographic boxes, wood-burned decorations.
Top, general-purpose, dated 1910 on bottom.
C/15-20
Bottom, glove gox, late 1800's. C/10-13

Above
Running light, kerosene, all brass, clear front. With red rear and side lens, 'Neverout / Insulated Kerosene Safety Lamp", by Rose. Mfg. Co., and cast iron mount, 9¾ in. high.
C/60-85

Above
Spooner. Mint condition, marked Heisey, 6¼ in. high.
C/24-30

Above
Syrup, RR dining car, "International Silver Company", PRR logo, "Silver Soldered / 8 oz.". C/50-65

Above
Candlestick telephone, brass maker's plate, "Western Electric", pat. dates 1904 & 1913, 11¾ in. high. C/125-150

Above
Coffee grinder, wood, dovetailed corners, orig. faded lable. Extra-fine condition, 13 in. overall height. C/75-90

Above
Ruby flashware, left & right:
  Tumblers, matched pair, sawtooth pattern, 2½ in. high. C/55-70
  Bud-vase, center, inscribed "Mrs. W. G. Freese / 1907 / Jamestown", 8 in. high. C/80-100

Left
Shaker bentwood box, left; 1½ in. high, 4¼ in long.
C/40-60
Tinderbox, right, tin, with orig. steel **striker** (center) for flint. These are also called strike-a-lights.
Pair. C/55-75

Right
Candlebox, walnut, wood-peg construction, dovetailed corners. Heart-shape cutout, box 6½ x 14¼ x 8½ in. high.
C/Unlisted

Pie-safe wall cabinet, oak and ash, one-shelved bottom pie safe with side ventilation holes, screen-covered. Top, two-shelved storage area, ship-lap back, two drawers, wood and brass pulls. Cabinet is 16¾ x 43 x 72 in. high. C/375-475

Below
Tramp art **trinket box,** 6¼ in. wide.
C/30-40

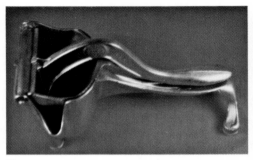

Above
Juice squeezer, cast aluminum, counter-top model.
Maker-marked and 9 in. long.
Private collection.   C/12-16

Right
Glass **whisky jug,** one-half gal. size. "The Bott and
Cannon Co. / Distillers and Wholesale Liquor Dealers",
12 in. high.
Private collection.   C/12-20

Left
Butter utensils, wooden,
longest piece 10 inches.
  Left, **paddle.**   C/8-10
  Top center, **mold.** C/25-35
  Right, hook-handle **scoop**
                  C/15-25
  Bot. center, butter **spade**
                  C/7-11
Private collection.

Right
Country inn cooker, tin-lined, copper. With lift-lid and steam spout; a
rare piece, these were inserted in a
special-built hearth receptacle and
made quantities of stew and por-
ridge. Late 1700's/early 1800's; 18 x
21½ x 17 in. high.
Private collection.   C/325-425

Right
Masonic.
  Commandery sword,
  etched blade, maker's
  mark.   C/150-200
  Commemorative flask,
  local lodge.   C/10-15
  Matchbook holder,
  Masonic symbol. C/3-5

Left
Hunting knives.
  Top, handmade U.S.
  knife for WW-II,
  private issue. C/18-25
  Lower, knife and
  sheath, made in Ger-
  many, pre-1944.
                  C/35-45

Right
Coca-Cola.
  Knife, (World's Fair / 1933).
                  C/8-12
  Concession apron.   C/8-15

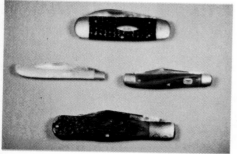

Left
Knives.
  Top, 4¼ in., "Case XX /
  U.S.A.", #6250   C/40-55
  Left, "Case XX / U.S.A.",
  nine-dot, #31049.   C/8-12
  Right, "Anvil / Prov. U.S.A.",
  pat. 3,317,996.   C/9-13
  Bottom, "W.R. Case & Sons,
  Bradford, PA", #61050.
                    C/125-150

Above
Fluting set, for ruffles, matched. Cast iron, maker-marked, 6 in. wide.   C/25-45

Above
Nautical container, marked "Distress Outfit". With copper rolled-seam body, brass screw-threads and bronze lid and handle. By the Upson Walton Company, it once held flare pistol and cartridges.   C/35-40

Right
Tools. Top, **Stanley scraper**, marked orig. blade, reversible head, brass sleeve. Wood handle dated (stamped) 1898, 13½ in. long.   C/30-40
Zax, or "slate axe", hammer used in putting on slate roofs. Device pounded and pulled nails and made nail-holes in slate shingles. Maker-marked, leather-washer handle. Note: Similar items are made today for custom shingleing.
C/25-30

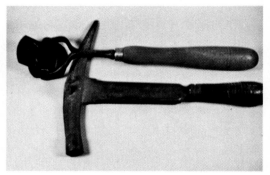

Right
Stone-working tools.
Left, **crandle**, multi-toothed, iron wedge and handle. With stamped name "King", 16 in. long.   C/35-45
Right, **toothed hammer**, wooden handle.   C/15-25

Left
Pencil boxes, top three light wood with lithographed scenes. Respectively, top and left to right: Oriental, "A-B-C", and Jack and Jill.
(Each) C/15-20
Bottom, hardwood (maple) box, with sliding top, turnable, two compartments, decorative decal.
Private collection.   C/20-25

Above
Bells, wood and brass, patina untouched. Scale, first bell is 8¾ in. high.

Top.	C/45-60
Lower right.	C/45-60
Bottom center.	C/30-40
Bottom left.	C/35-45
Left center.	C/100-125

Private collection.

Above
Musical toy in shape of Easter egg, with rabbit. Plays "Peter Cottontail"; by Mattel, Inc., ca. 1952, 6½ in. long.
Private collection   C/15-25

Right
Lidded crocks with wood and wire bail carrying handles; two large specimens each 9¼ in. high. Crock at right marked "Cruikshank Bros. Co. / Preserves, Jellies, Fruit Butters . . .".

Left.	C/20-30
Center.	C/18-25
Right.	C/30-40

Private collection.

Above
Beaded pincushion, heart-shape with bird figures and floral designs. Indian-made tourist item. New England, early 1900's; with beaded loops, 9 5/8 in. high.
Private collection.   C/80-110

Above
Sugar bucket, Shaker, all wood, lapped wood hoops top and bottom. Top diameter 11½ inches, 16½ in. high.
                                    C/125-175

Left
Pre-Columbian artifacts, most late BC centuries, all Meso-american.
Top, effigy **jaguar metate** (ceremonial corn-grinder) of stone, 13 in. long, legs and tail broken. C/100-150
Center left, matched pair of **ear dangles** (?), depicting two unknown animals. Green-white jade, ¾ in. high.   C/60-80
Lower center, jade **bird-man**, 3¾ in. long, of imperial green.
                                    C/350-475
Center, **half bird-man**, longtitudinal stone-cut, quality translucent bluish jade.   C/100-125
Right, **drilled gorget**, dark green jade.   C/60-80
Private collection.

Right
Occupied Japan, all items marked, longest item 5 inches.
Left, **Aladdin lamp lighter** and tray.   C/6-10
Right, metal double-dish with Washington D.C. scenes. C/6-10
Lower center, **Ashtray**, glazed pottery.   C/3-6
Private collection.

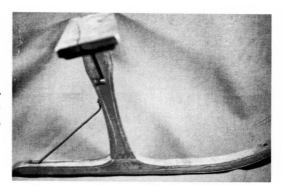

Right
Chair sled or "seat-ski", for
winter sport. Ca. late 1800's,
bottom runner 31 in. long.
Private collection.   C/50-75

Above
Lobby ash receptacle, copper and spun
brass, weighted base. Sand-filled top lifts
off to empty contents; 16¾ in. high, top 11
in. extreme diameter.
Private collection.   C/45-75

Above
Store-size coffee mill, "National / Elgin".
Some decorative paint lines remaining; 27
in. high, wheel diameter 19½ inches.
Private collection.   C/250-325

Left
Baskets. Largest is 11¾ in.
high. All in perfect condition.
Left, **buttocks basket.**
                C/55-75
Lower, **cylindrical,** of
willow.   C/10-15
Right, **Cherokee** or Great
Lakes Indian.   C/75-95
Private collection.

Above
Jewelry:
Necklace/locket, jet and silver, Victorian.
C/45-60
Ring, gold, pearl setting   C/30-40
Brooch, cast metal backing, composition
stones.   C/5-10
Brooch, tooled silver back, red stones.
C/25-35

Above
Egg basket, wireware, collapsible, bottom
6 in. diameter.   C/30-40

Left
Mallets:
Burl head, hand-carved
handle.   C/25-35
Turned head, squared handle.
C/11-17

Right
Wireware:
Vegetable strainer, 12½ in.
long.   C/15-20
Grater, grid wires.   C/4-6

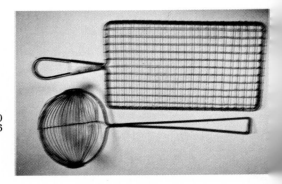

Above
Foot-warmer, wood frame, punched tin, complete door, complete with interior ember box. Wire bale handle, 8 x 9 x 5½ in. high.
C/100-150

Above
Dresser, walnut, burled walnut front, "wishbone" mirror-mount. Marble inset, refinished, glove boxes, acorn pulls. Dresser is 18 x 36 x 66 in high.

C/750-1050

Left
Shooting accoutrements. Clockwise, from top:

Ammunition block, handworked maple, for fifty .22 cartridges. Poss. for competitive target shooting, 3 x 4¾ inches.

C/12-16

Bullet bag, handcarved wooden spout, linen pouch with several lead balls inside. C/7-12

Patch knife, used with muzzle-loading rifles to size patches around ball, antler handle, very old. C/25-35

Primer discs, for Winchester center-fire cartridges, for hand reloading. Original marked tin box. C/11-15

Left
Dropleaf gateleg table, golden oak, unusual twelve-sided top. Fern circle on stretchers, 28½ in. high. C/375-450

Right
Civil War items. Top and bottom, triangular-bladed **bayonet** and brass-appointed leather sheath, all marked. C/60-75

Lower center, **rifleman's knife,** Bowie-type, made in Sheffield, England, marked "Ebro" on bladeback. Bone handle, 9½ in. long. C/55-75

Left and right, four **Minie-type bullets,** cast lead.
Each: C/1-1.50

Left to right, paper cartridge, wax and thread complete. C/9-12

Two cast iron **projectiles,** brass driving bands missing.
Each: C/4-6

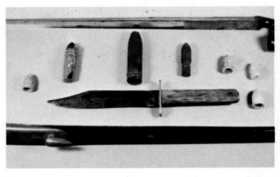

Above
Souvenir spoons, bottom example with gold-washed bowl, all sterling. Each: C/20-30

Above
Smoking stand, golden oak, with match drawer, brass knobbed. Has shelf depression ashtray; stand 7¼ in. square, 24¾ in. high.
C/75-110

Below
Automobilia. Top and bottom, wooden gas tank **depth-measuring sticks.** Half of one side, "For Ford Cars Only", Firestone Tires and local shop ads on other. Each: C/10-15
Center, all-brass **oil-changing pump,** 12½ in. long. C/13-17

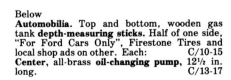

Rookwood bud vase, glossy tan, delicate, 7¼ inches.　**D-32.00**
Rockwood candlesticks, pink, 2¾ in. high, pair.　**D-40.00**
Rookwood chamberstick, dark blue, attached saucer.　**D-25.00**
Rookwood vase, blue, 4½ x 4½ inches.　**D-30.00**
Rookwood vase, rose, seahorse relief, 6½ inches.　**D-30.00**
Rookwood vase, turq., glaze drip one side, 7 5/8 inches.　**D-28.00**
Rookwood vase, higlaze celedon green, 6 x 6¾ inches.　**D-35.00**
Rosemeade creamer/open sugar, set, blue, 3¼ in. high.　**D-7.00**
Rosemeade planter, marked, kangaroo, 6 in. long.　**D-16.00**
Roseville Appleblossom bowl, pink, 3 x 11½ inches.　**D-35.00**
Roseville Baneda vase, footed, base-handled, 7 3/8 inches.　**D-20.00**
Roseville Bittersweet vase, footed, 6½ in. high.　**D-17.00**
Roseville Bleeding Heart vase, repaired flake, footed.　**D-9.00**
Roseville Bushberry vase, footed, 6 3/8 inches.　**D-16.00**
Roseville Carnelian bowl, blue, 3¼ x 8½ inches.　**D-28.00**
Roseville Clematis basket, 7 x 7¼ inches.　**D-30.00**

Rozane Royal, vase, artist signed.
450-600

Lower left
Baneda, Jardiniere, 9½".
125-150

Primrose, vase 8".
50-60

Roseville Columbine bud vase, base-handled, 7¼ in-ches. D-9.00

Roseville Cosmos cornucopia, blue, 7½ inches. D-22.00

Roseville Dahlrose bowl, handled, 4 x 6½ inches. D-16.00

Roseville Dogwood II vase, slant top, 10 inches. D-36.00

Roseville Donatello bowl, stamped, 2½ x 6¼ inches. D-25.00

Roseville Florentine double bud vase, reverse stamp. D-30.00

Roseville Foxglove vase, footed, handled, 6 inches. D-13.00

Roseville Freesia ewer, blue, 6 x 6½ inches. D-12.00

Roseville Fuchsia vase, side-handled, 6 inches. D-22.00

Roseville Gardenia vase, tan, 3¾ inches. D-14.00

Roseville Imperial bowl, handled, 2 x 10½ inches. D-30.00

Roseville Iris bowl, brown, 3 3/8 x 5 inches. D-14.00

Roseville Ivory II fan vase, base-handled. D-13.00

Roseville Ixia bowl, green 4 x 6¾ inches. D-30.00

Roseville Jonquil vase, shoulder handled, 4 in. high. D-30.00

Roseville Larose vase, shoulder handled, 6 in. high. D-10.00

Roseville Laurel bowl, gold, 2½ x 6½ inches. D-35.00

Roseville Lustre bud vase, higlaze, 4 x 8 inches. D-40.00

Roseville Magnolia Blue bud vase, 6 x 7½ inches. D-10.00

Roseville Magnolia Green basket, 9½ x 13 inches. D-75.00

Roseville Ming Tree bookends, turquoise, pair. D-20.00

Roseville Moderne vase, base rim flakes, 13 inches. D-40.00

Roseville Montacello bowl, handle bruise, 5¼ in. high. D-17.00

Roseville Moss bowl, blue, light hairline, 3 in. high. D-8.00

Roseville Mostique bowl, gray, hairline, 2¾ in. high. D-12.00

Roseville Orchid and Turquoise vase, footed, 6 in. high. D-80.00

Roseville Panel bowl, brown, 2 x 6½ inches. D-9.00

Roseville Peony bowl vase, gold, shoulder handled. D-20.00

Roseville Pinecone vase, green, footed, 6½ in. high. D-20.00

Roseville Primrose vase, brown, footed, handled. D-30.00

Roseville Rosecraft Vintage double bud vase, rim nick. D-15.00

Roseville Silouette candlesticks, turquoise, 2¾ in-ches. D-15.00

Roseville Snowberry basket, blue, footed, 8 inches. D-40.00

Roseville Teasel console bowl, tan, 13 inches. D-40.00

Roseville Thornapple bowl, brown, 8¾in. diameter. D-22.00

Roseville Tulip pitcher, early; spout repair. D-20.00

Roseville Tourmaline vase, blue, 6 3/8 inches. D-35.00

Roseville Tuscany lamp, dark blue, pottery 8½ in. high. **D-45.00**

Roseville Velmoss II planter, green, 4½ x 9 inches. **D-30.00**

Roseville Waterlily bowl, pink and green, 7½ in. diameter. **D-20.00**

Roseville Whirlpool window box, apple green, 9 in. long. **D-20.00**

Roseville White Rose bowl, brown and green, 4¼ in. diameter. **D-12.00**

Roseville Wincraft vase, beige, handled, 9 inches. **D-32.00**

Roseville Zephyr Lily ashtray, blue, flake repair. **D-10.00**

RRP Company batter pitcher, yellow, 6¾ inches. **D-9.00**

RRP Company planter, brown, "RRP Co./USA", 3¼ in. high. **D-6.00**

Royal Copely vase, relief flowers, yellow, 7 inches. **D-5.00**

Royal Copely wall pocket, apple, 6 in. high. **D-7.00**

Rumrill salt/pepper, two-tone, silver sticker, pair. **D-5.00**

Ruskin candlestick, iridescent, 6½ in. high. **D-9.00**

Senegal child's cup/saucer, four sets. **D-9.00**

Shawnee teapot, Tom the Piper's Son. **D-20.00**

Stangl (Miscellaneous) carafe and stopper, marked, 7¾ in. high. **D-10.00**

Stangl (Miscellaneous) dish, green, 2 x 7 x 10 inches. **D-5.00**

Stangl Terra Rose cigarette box, with ashtray lid. **D-6.00**

Stangl Terra Rose covered dish, green 5 5/8 inches. **D-10.00**

Stangl Terra Rose vase, heart-shape, 6 in. high. **D-4.50**

Styron bookends, brown and white horse. **D-12.00**

B. Taylor relish dish, three-part, 5½ x 13 inches. **D-10.00**

Trenton vase, higlaze turquoise, ribbed, 7¾ in. high. **D30.00**

USA cookie jar, boy at butter churn, 11 3/8 inches. **D-15.00**

USA covered casserole, light blue, 8 in. diameter. **D-7.00**

USA pitcher vase, maroon, melon-ribbed, 8½ in. high. **D-5.00**

USA planter, green rim, four-footed, 3¼ in. high. **D-5.00**

Van Briggle bowl, turquoise, 4½ x 7¾ inches. **D-35.00**

Van Briggle bowl, rose, berries and leaf band. **D-20.00**

Van Briggle creamer, white, signed "LW", 3 in. high. **D-10.00**

Van Briggle sugar, hexagonal, 2 in. high. **D-5.00**

Van Briggle vase, spiderwort, 6 inches. **D-28.00**

Van Briggle vase, turquoise, lily-shape, 8¼ in. high. **D-15.00**

Weller Alvin double bud vase, eight-hole, 7 in. high. **D-45.00**

Weller Atlantic(?) vase, chess rook, 3½ x 7 inches. **D-30.00**

Weller Baldin vase, inked "F", 6 x 7½ inches. **D-40.00**

Weller Beford Matte vase, thick green glaze, 6 inches.	D-28.00
Weller Blossom vase, side handles, blue, 7 in. high.	D-20.00
Weller Burntwood bowl, mice, 1 7/8 x 3¼ inches.	D-45.00
Weller Cameo vase, blue higlaze, handled, 9½ inches.	D-18.00
Weller Cornish vase, blue, tab handles, 8½ inches.	D-20.00
Weller Darsie vase, ivory, unmarked 5½ in. high.	D-12.00
Weller Drapery vase, cracked, 2 x 4 x 4 inches.	D-5.00
Weller Dupont bowl, four-paneled rose baskets, 2¾ in. high.	D-35.00
Weller Euclid vase, turquoise, hairline, 10 inches.	D-8.00
Weller Evergreen jardiniere, 10½ x 13½ inches.	D-55.00
Weller Flemish vase, corner rebuilt, 5¼ in. high.	D-40.00
Weller Floral console bowl, lavendar and blue flowers.	D-20.00
Weller Florala vase, ivory, cylindrical, 8 in. high.	D-27.00
Weller Florenzo planter, footed. 5¼ in. square.	D-8.00
Weller Forest jardiniere, 4½ x 5½ inches.	D-38.00
Weller frog figure, emerging from lily pad, 4¾ in. high.	D-25.00
Weller Fruitone bowl, green and brown, 2 7/8 in. high.	D-16.00
Weller Hudson vase, Lilies of the Valley, 7½ in. high.	D-40.00
Weller Ivoris jardiniere, ivory, 8 x 9½ inches.	D-45.00
Weller Ivory vase, six oak leaf panels, 12 in. high.	D-28.00
Weller kingfisher figure, reglued beak break, 5½ in. high.	D-10.00
Weller Loru vase, maroon to dark purple, 7¼ in. high.	D-20.00
Weller Louwelsa pillow vase, signed, 5 in. high.	D-30.00
Weller Lustre bud vase, maroon, gray and black, 6½ in. high.	D-10.00
Weller marbleized vase, maroon, gray and black, 6½ in. high.	D-40.00
Weller Mi-Flo Jardiniere, ivory, yellow flowers, 4 in. high.	D-20.00
Weller Olla water jug, green, no top, paint worn.	D-9.00
Weller Panella bowl, blue, no mark, 12 3/8 in. diameter.	D-30.00
Weller Paragon bowl, blue, 4¼ x 5¼ inches.	D-15.00
Weller Pastel vase, blue, three scallops, 5 in. high.	D-20.00

Weller Pierre creamer, sugar and milk pitcher, green. D-22.00

Weller Ragenda console bowl and candlesticks, pair, and set. D-50.00

Weller Roma bowl, triangular, 3½ x 7¼ inches. D-22.00

Weller Roma planter, cream, fruit and floral, 3¾ in. high. D-25.00

Weller Rudlor cornucopia vase, yellow, 8¼ in. high. D-23.00

Weller Seneca vase, green, footed, 9¼ in. high. D-10.00

Weller Silvertone vase, stamped, 3 x 7½ inches. D-20.00

Weller Softone planter, yellow, 3½ x 4½ x 7½ inches. D-9.00

Weller Sydonia cornucopia, green and brown, 8 inches. D-12.00

Weller Tutone triple bud vase, 7 x 7½ inches. D-30.00

Weller Velva vase, side handles, 4 x 6 inches. D-22.00

Weller Wild Rose tankard, green, 12 inches. D-33.00

Weller Wisteria bowl vase, green, 6 x 6 inches. D-18.00

Weller Woodcraft bud vase, five-hole, 8½ in. high. D-25.00

Weller Wood Rose busket, marked "BX", 4 x 4¼ inches. D-25.00

Weller Zona creamer, cream higlaze, 3¼ in. high. D-10.00

West Coast Pottery wall pockets, 9 inches, pair. D-40.00

York pitcher, blue, tilted ribs, "York/488". D-6.00

Zane bowl, blue and brown, impressed "Zaneware". D-18.00

POTTERY—*Historical Blue Staffordshire (Made in England)*

Over 200 factories–pre-American Revolution into the 1850's–made Staffordshire pottery. Most are obscure, but the wares of perhaps a dozen top potteries are especially admired today, such as the Clews brothers of **Cobridge, England.**

Bowl, Washington by the tomb, medium dark blue, 6¼ in. diameter. A-130.00

Bowl, and matching plate, Neptune, dark blue, "Clews" on plate, 6¾ and 4½ in. diameter. A-80.00

Cup and saucer, brilliant deep dark blue, "Clews", hairline and chip. A-60.00

Cup and saucer, "E. Wood and Sons, Burslem", scene of the ship **Chancellor Livingston,** dark blue. A-260.00

Cup plate, arms of the States Series by F. Mayer; South Carolina, 4¼ in. diameter. A-225.00

Cup plate, impressed signature "Stevenson", Boston statehouse mismarked "Scudder's American Museum", 4¼ in. diameter.   A-535.00

Cup plate, Landing of Lafayette, "Clews", dark blue, 3½ in. diameter.   A-235.00

Pitcher, America and Independence, hairline in base, deteriorating edge repairs, dark blue; 9¾ in. high.   A-150.00

Platter, America and Independence, dark blue, "Clews", 13 in. long.   A-500.00

Platter, Landing of Gen. Lafayette..., excellent transfer in dark blue, "Clews", 17 in. long.   A-725.00

Plate, Arms of New York, "Excelsior", dark blue, professional repairs, 10 in. diameter.   A-160.00

Plate, Beauties of America, Library/Philadelphia, I & W Ridgway, dark blue, 8¼ in. diameter.   A-135.00

Plate, "The Escape of the Mouse from Wilkie's Designs", 10 in. diameter.   A-87.50

Plate, "Doctor Syntax drawing after Nature", 10¼ in. diameter.   A-60.00

Plate, "Doctor Syntax mistakes gentleman's house for an Inn", 10 in. diameter.   A-65.00

Plate, "Doctor Syntax painting a portrait", "Clews", 10 in. diameter.   A-90.00

Plate, "Doctor Syntax taking possession of his living", glaze flaking, 10 in, diameter.   A-45.00

Plate, fishing scene, "Clews", hairline and flake, 10 in. diameter.   A-35.00

Plate, "Mambrino's Helmet", Don Quixote, medium dark blue, 10 in. diameter.   A-85.00

Plate, Park Theatre/New York, dark blue, 10 in. diameter.   A-150.00

Plate, Peace and Plenty, "Clews", dark blue, 10 in. diameter.   A-150.00

Plate, Sancho Panza's debate with Teresa, Don Quixote, 9 in. diameter.   A-95.00

Plate, scene of early steamboat, dark blue, 10¼ in. diameter.   A-180.00

Plate, "The Valentine from Wilkie's Designs", 9 in. diameter.   A-100.00

Plate, "Welcome Lafayette, the Nation's Guest and our Country's Glory", embossed border, impressed "Clews", 7¾ in. diameter.   A-320.00

Platter, Winter View of Pittsfield, Mass., brilliant dark blue, "Clews", 16 in. long. — A-675.00

Sauce boat, Landing of Lafayette, base chipped, 5 in. high. — A-200.00

Soup plate, America and Independence, 8¾ in. diameter. — A-110.00

Soup plate, "Playing at Draughts from Wilkie's Designs", 8¾ in. diameter. — A-100.00

Teapot, brilliant dark blue, scene of two dogs, unmarked, 7¾ in. high. — A-145.00

Toddy plate, Peace and Plenty, old edge repair, 5½ in. diameter. — A-175.00

Tray, "The Rabbit on the way from Wilkie's Designs", 9¾ in. long. — A-100.00

Tureen, "Doctor Syntax pursued by a Bull", 9 in. long. — A-60.00

Urn, with open handles, three glaze flakes, dark blue, 5¾ in. high. — A-90.00

POTTERY—*Redware*

Apple butter jar, old base chips, 6½ in. high; base chips. — A-22.50

Apple butter jars, pair; clear glaze, ea. 6½ in. high. — A-130.00

Bottle, black metallic glaze with lipwear, 6½ in. high. — A-40.00

Bottle, greenish shiny glaze, 6½ in. high. — A-60.00

Bowl, brown band with swags of yellow slip and green dots, 2½ in. high. — A-75.00

Bowl, clear glaze with brown speckles, 5 in. diameter. — A-30.00

Bowl, interior with brown sponged rectangles, 3¾ in. high. — A-60.00

Bowl, bullseye design in white slip, clear and orange glaze; 14 in. diameter, 2 in. high. — A-245.00

Bowl, cream slip with three-color glaze, minor wear, 9 in. diameter. — A-30.00

Canning jar, two-tone glaze, clear and cream slip, 8¼ in. high. — A-100.00

Cooler, applied handles, incised horsehead, 14¼ in. high. — A-205.00

Cup, greenish glaze with brown brushmarks, minor glaze flakes. — A-20.00

Pitcher, redware, slight rim and lip chips, 10 in. high.

C/35-55

Dish, handled, green running glaze; Shenandoah, 9 in. diameter. A-210.00

Dog with basket, clear glaze with brown splotches, 4½ in. high. A-165.00

Flower pot, tooled bands and stripes of yellow slip, 6 in. high. A-40.00

Flower pot and saucer, brown splotches, tooled rings, 5¾ in. high. A-45.00

Flower pot with attached saucer, base stamped "LTK", 4½ in. high. A-80.00

Flower pot with attached saucer, cracked, 4¼ in. high. A-22.50

Flower pot with attached saucer, brown splotches, 3½ in. high. A-90.00

Jar, miniature, with flared lip; 1½ in. high. A-11.00

Jar, ovoid, clear glaze, brown splotches, 9¾ in. high. A-135.00

Jar, clear glaze with green, firing imperfection, 12 in. high. A-110.00

Jar with lid, speckled brown glaze, lid and rim chips, 10 in. high. A-155.00

Jug, shiny dark green glaze, large base chip, 8½ in. high. A-32.50

Jug, greenish shiny glaze with orange spots, 7¾ in. high. A-125.00

Jug, dark green glaze with orange spots, 7¾ in. high. A-85.00

Jug, dark green shiny glaze, glaze flakes, 9¼ in. high. A-55.00

Jug, interlocking yellow circles, 6 in, high. A-115.00

Jug, brown splotches and clear glaze, incised shoulder lines. A-65.00

Jug, clear shiny glaze with some green, 11 in. high. A-95.00

Jug, signature "Somerset Potters Works", cobalt design, 11 in. high. A-75.00

Loaf pan, three-line yellow slip decoration, straight and wavy lines with dots. Coggled edge, edge chips, 10½ x 16½ inches. — A-420.00

Mold, Turk's head, clear glaze, 8½ in. diameter. — A-35.00

Muffin pan, ten spaces, clear glaze with some green, 13½ x 16 inches. — A-115.00

Mug, tooled lines around rim and base, 5½ in. high. — A-87.50

Milk pan, flared sides, cream-colored interior, 7½ in. high. — A-45.00

Plate, yellow slip design, coggled edge, 8¼ in. diameter. — A-82.50

Plate, coggled edge with crowfoot design in yellow, edge chips. — A-95.00

Plate, brown and yellow slip, clear glaze, 7½ in. diameter. — A-135.00

Plate, simple tulip design in yellow slip, 8 in. diameter. — A-70.00

Porringer, black shiny glaze, edge flakes, 2 3/8 x 4 inches. — A-40.00

Porringer, shiny black metallic glaze, 3 x 5½ inches. — A-70.00

Pitcher, clear glaze, brown shoulder band, some chips, 7¾ in. high. — A-165.00

Pitcher, yellow slip with brown and green, 8½ in. high. — A-155.00

Shaving mug, old chip on base, 4 in. high. — A-25.00

Vase, two applied ring handles, reddish brown glaze, 6¾ in. high. — A-85.00

Vases, pair; (recent) "L. B./1973", ea. 8½ in. high. — A-40.00

Vase, thick yellow-green glaze, 6¾ in. high. — D-79.00

POTTERY—*Spatterware*

Bowl, kitchen, blue and white, 12 in. diameter, 6 in. high. — A-77.50

Bowl, green and white, 9½ in. diameter, 4¼ in. high. — A-47.50

Creamer, blue and purple, red rose decoration, one repair, 4 in. high. — A-70.00

Creamer, blue and purple, handle with glaze wear and hairlines. — A-75.00

Cup, purple spatterware, hairline. — A-35.00

Cup, peafowl in blue, red and yellow; rim chip. — A-70.00

Cup and saucer, blue, with rooster in four colors. — A-320.00

Cup and saucer, brown, cornflower in red and green. — A-195.00

Cup and saucer, purple, cornflower in red and green. A-230.00

Cup and saucer, blue, peafowl in four colors; rim roughness. A-95.00

Cup and saucer, red, peafowl in blue, yellow, green, black. A-150.00

Cup and saucer, purple, rooster in four colors; cup cracked. A-110.00

Cup and saucer, red, rose in three colors; glaze wear on rim. A-90.00

Cup and saucer, green, plain; hairline in saucer. A-65.00

Jar, blue and yellow, chipped; 6½ in. high. A-35.00

Plate, blue, peafowl in four colors, impressed "Adams", 9½ in. diameter. A-250.00

Pitcher, rainbow, hexagonal, spout repaired, 7½ in. high. A-150.00

Sugar bowl, blue, peafowl in four colors, 4¼ in. high. A-175.00

Teapot, blue, red rose decoration, lid with small edge flakes. A-140.00

Bowl, **spongeware,** brown on cream, 4½ in. diameter.

C/25-35

POTTERY—*Stoneware*

Batter pitcher, bail handle, yellow glazing, Rockingham. D-55.00

Batter pitcher, reddish slip with wear, 9 in. high. A-20.00

Batter pitcher, stylized flower, two-gal. size, "1843", 13¾ in. high. A-280.00

Batter pitcher, floral design in cobalt blue, signed, 10 in. high. A-300.00

Batter pitcher, two-gallon, signed, hairline cracks, 13½ in. high. A-75.00

Batter pitcher, simple cobalt blue decoration, 10½ in. high. A-115.00

Bowl, "Nichols & Co./Williamsport, Pa.", 10 in. diameter. A-80.00

Butter crock, blue feather designs, covered, 8½ in. diameter. A-165.00

Canning jar, blue leaf designs, 8½ in. high. — A-65.00

Canning jar, cobalt blue brushed designs, 9½ in. high. — A-70.00

Canning jar, stenciled cobalt blue shield, 9½ in. high. — A-50.00

Cooler, impressed signature "Somerset Potters Works". Two incised birds highlighted in cobalt blue, applied handles, flared top, with wood, pewter and iron spigot; 19 in. high. — A-1700.00

Creamer, cobalt blue brush marks, rim chip, 3¾ inches. — A-85.00

Crock, two-gal. size, cobalt quillwork flourish, "2". — A-7.50

Crock, cover, five-gal. size, brown and cream glazed. — D-24.50

Crock, cobalt blue feather motif, half-gal. size. — D-49.50

Crock, two-gal., "A.C. Ballard/Burlington, Vermont". — D-24.00

Crock, six-gal., incised cow in blue, 13 in. high. — A-55.00

Crock, three-gal., quillwork decoration, 13½ in. high. — A-75.00

Crock, "New York Stoneware Co.", 8 in. high. — A-105.00

Crock, "4", leaf design, cracked, 11½ in. high. — A-17.50

Crock, ten-gal. size, comic sketch of old woman with curly coiffure in cobalt slip, Albany slip interior, 17¼ in. high. — A-595.00

Crock, four-gal. "Brady and Ryan", 11 in. high. — A-190.00

Crock, three-gal., cobalt hen pecking corn, 10½ in. high. — A-165.00

Flower pot, Albany slip, "Bennington", hairlines, 3 in. high. — A-75.00

Jar, ovoid, small handles, brown-green glaze, 14½ in. high. — A-32.50

Jar, blue horizontal stripes, 6 in. high. — A-42.50

Jar, five-gal., "5" in cobalt blue, 15½ in. high. — A-45.00

Jar, ovoid, basal chips and hairlines, 15½ in high. — A-22.50

Jar, three-gal., signature "T. Reed", rim hairline, 11½ in. high. — A-195.00

Jar, stenciled "3" in cobalt blue, 13 in. high. — A-15.00

Jar, "John P. Eberhart & Co.", minor lip chips, 10 in. high. — A-45.00

Jar, "Jugtown Ware", applied handles, 6½ in. high. — A-85.00

Jar, impressed signature, "Jordan", 13½ in. high. — A-60.00

Jar, brushed blue floral band, applied handles, 13½ in. high. — A-95.00

Jar, "E. A. Montell", cobalt single flower, 10¾ in. high. — A-65.00

Crock, "A. P. Donaghho / Parkersburg, WVA", 12 in. high.
C/28-38

Jar, salt-glazed earthenware, 12 in. high.
C/10-15

Cream crock, light tan color, orig. lid, bail and wooden handle, 10 in. high.   C/18-28

Earthenware kitchen items.
Left, dark green glazed salt container, some bottom edge chips, 6 in. high.   C/40-55
Right, light green glazed mixing bowl.   C/20-28

Photo courtesy Judy Morehead, Creative Photography, Lancaster, Ohio.

Jug, four-gal., thistle-and-swirl design, gray.   **D-175.00**

Jug, cobalt blue floral and swirl design, 11½ in. high.   **D-125.00**

Jug, "Charlestown", one-gal., beige color, 13 in. high.   **D-85.00**

Jug, gray, salt-glazed, cobalt blue feather design, 12 in. high.   **D-85.00**

Jug, Albany slip, 6½ in. high.   **S-45.00**

Jug, three-gal., cobalt blue feather design, 15 in. high.   **S-60.00**

Jug, impressed "H. & C. Nash/Utica", 10½ inches high.   **A-80.00**

Lidded crocks with wood and wire bail carrying handles; two large specimens each 9¼ in. high. Crock at right marked "Cruikshank Bros. Co. / Preserves, Jellies, Fruit Butters ...".

Left.	C/20-30
Center.	C/18-25
Right.	C/30-40

Private collection.

Jug, four-gal., neck and handle chocolate brown, mint. **D-39.50**

Jug, ovoid, one-gal., green slip, hand-thrown. **D-65.00**

Jug, five-gal., "Weading & Belding/Brantford, Ohio". **A-65.00**

Jug, signed "Bennington, Vt.", ovoid, 10 in. high. **A-110.00**

Jug, three-gal., "A. H. Wheeler Co./Boston, Mass.", 30 in. high. **A-175.00**

Jug, "Whites Utica", bird in cobalt slip, 22 in. high. **A-155.00**

Jug, two-gal., stylized floral design, 25 in. high. **A-70.00**

Jug, "M. Hanssling/Newark, N.J.", 14¼ in. high. **A-50.00**

Jug, one-gal. size, three old small rim chips. **S-25.00**

Milk pitcher, cobalt blue glaze, white interior, 7 in. high. **D-50.00**

Pig, white shiny glaze, one foot chipped, 6 in. long. **A-65.00**

Pitcher, miniature, gray and chocolate brown, 1½ in. high. **D-10.00**

Pitcher, Southern green glaze, rim chip, 13¼ in. high. **A-25.00**

Pot, two-gal., "Frank B. Norton/Worcester, Mass.", 9½ in. high. **D-75.00**

Sieve, three-footed, Albany slip, 9 in. high. **A-40.00**

PRE-COLUMBIAN ARTWORKS

The term "Pre-Columbian" has special meaning. It refers mainly to the Central and South American regions and simply means anything made before the arrival of Columbus. Items are pre-1492 by any number of years, and some artifacts date back to three and four thousand BC.

Top-quality pieces made by such admired cultures as Aztec, Maya and Inca have long been collected, and many of the finest artworks have gone to Europe in early years. Among the more sought-after and valuable materials are objects of gold and jade, though effigy pottery and fine hardstone pieces are avidly collected today.

Axe head in human form, stone, 5¼ in. high. A-60.00
Copper celt, cast metal, Guatemala, 3 in. long. C-45.00
Copper effigy pin, eagle(?) form, corroded, Panama. C-15.00
Equadorian burial piece, female torso with head-
dress. A-60.00
Effigy pottery, Panama, double-headed weasel, 5 in.
diameter. A-100.00
Figure of seated man, black glazed pottery, 6 in.
high. A-35.00
Figure of standing man, carved stone, 22 in. high. A-115.00
Gold figurine, frog effigy, from Panama. A-150.00
Gold figurine, Panama, ca. AD 400. A-315.00
Funerary pottery urn, large, Mexico, ca. AD 400. A-225.00
Granite celt-axe, flared blade, polished, 6½ in. long. A-50.00
Jade bead, incised; Guatemala, drilled, 3¼ in. long. C-40.00
Jade "Bird-man", Costa Rica, mottled white/green, 6
in. high. C-200.00
Jade "Bird-man", Costa Rica, translucent sea-green,
3 in. high. C-350.00
Jade carving, Costa Rica, ca. AD 400. A-175.00
Jade carving, Mesoamerican, ca. AD 600. A-550.00
Jar finial in form of priest, 4½ in. high. A-50.00
Kneeling figure, gray carved stone, 9½ in. high. A-60.00
Obsidian bent-blade knife, Southern Mexico, 7 in.
long. C-25.00
Obsidian blade, Southern Mexico, 12½ in. long. C-60.00
Pottery bottle, Chimu culture (Inca Huaco), 7½ in.
high. A-250.00
Pottery bowl, El Salvador, missing tripod legs, 13 in.
diameter. C-50.00
Pottery burial pieces, 14 small pieces, collection. A-120.00
Pottery effigy jug, monkey(?), Peruvian highlands, 5
in. high. C-70.00
Pottery figurine, damaged "Gingerbread man", 7 in.
high. A-30.00
Pottery jug, flared rim with lizard, 6¼ in. high. A-80.00
Pottery polychrome whistle, bird effigy,
Mesoamerica, 2 in. high. C-35.00
Pottery vessel, snake-figure spout, 6½ in. high. A-100.00
Pottery vessel, image of jaguar, El Salvador, 3 x 7½
inches. A-65.00
Pottery vessel, Mexico, ca. AD 100, 3½ x 6½ inches. A-70.00
Pottery warrior figure, Nyarit, Mexico, AD 800, 7 in.
high. A-110.00

Spindle-weight, monochrome terracotta, 3 in. diameter.

C-5.00

Stone-bead necklace, seventeen pieces, drilled and polished.

C-30.00

Stone carving of male figure with hands to ears, 7½ in. high.

A-60.00

Stone sculpture of standing man, Huaco, 12 in. high.

A-100.00

Stone "seal", wheeled disc with rim impressions, 1 in. diameter.

C-12.50

PRIMITIVES

Apple-butter stirrer, long-handled, wooden, 89 in. long.

A-27.50

Apple-peeler, all wood, homemade, on 8 x 14½ in. pine plank, mortised construction, 8½ in. high.

D-65.00

Bed-warmer, sheet iron pan with wrought handle, brass-hinged lid with punched holes and stamped designs, 37½ in. long.

A-105.00

Bench, primitive, oak, 11 x 12 x 43½ in. long.

A-50.00

Bench, bucket; pine, several coats of worn paint, last two blue and grey, 11½ x 42 x 56 in. high.

A-215.00

Canteen, stave-constructed, worn red paint, 9 in. diameter.

A-30.00

Carved man, horse-hair coiffure, 20th Century, 13 in. high.

A-62.50

Carving, of bearded man wearing turban, 5 in. high.

A-25.00

Cheese dryer, woven splint, bentwood frame, 22½ in. diameter.

A-55.00

Cheese press, wood, shoe feet, pegged construction, 21 in. high, 21¾ in. wide.

D-78.00

Cleaver, butcher's, 15½ in. long.

A-35.00

Conestoga wagon and two horses, wood, 22 in. long.

A-65.00

Cranberry scoop, early, tin and wooden prongs, 23 in. long.

D-42.00

Cranberry picker, hickory handle, iron teeth, 43½ in. long.

A-30.00

Crutch, wooden, 51 in. high; handcarved.

A-17.50

Dipper, wooden, primitively carved, 10¼ in. long.

A-17.50

Dish-draining rack, pine board ¾ in. thick, New England, 2¾ x 9½ x 16 inches.

D-29.50

Dry sink, dovetailed box, tapered board legs, old red paint, 20 x 27½ x 37½ in. long.

A-200.00

Doughbox, poplar wood, with top suitable as kitchen work surface. Size 14 in. deep, 28 in. long.　　C/125-150

Grain measures.
Upper, **one-peck size,** 13 in. high, old alligatored paint.　　C/45
Bottom, ¼-**peck size,** original unfinished surface.　　C/30

Lar Hothem photo.

Firkin, (sugar bucket), large, old skim milk white paint, bentwood handle pegged in, 11½ in. high.　　**D-35.00**

Fishspear, four tines, wrought iron, 13 in. long.　　**S-15.00**

Flax-winder, eight-armed, wooden pegged, 4 ft. high.　　**D-125.00**

Flint and steel, early, hand-forged.　　**D-15.00**

Grain stake, handcarved, to hold top bundle in stack.　　**D-35.00**

Hand-adz, metal strap-on blade, nicely carved handle, 12 in. long.　　**D-75.00**

Hay rake, wood, 68 in. wide, 70 in. long.　　**A-65.00**

Herb drying basket, splint, with cover, wrapped rims, sliding cover, 12¼ x 22 x 28¾ in. long, rare.　　**D-225.00**

Herb drying rack, wooden frame with a net shelf, 29 in. square, 30 in. high.　　**A-295.00**

Herb grinder, rolls between hands, round bottom disk with wear, 11 inches.　　**D-41.00**

High chair, made from forked tree branch, doll-size, 19¾ in. high.　　**A-40.00**

Hobby horse, pine, old worn brown paint, old repair to one rocker and other has broken end, 47 inches.　　**A-235.00**

Kneeling figure, carved wood, good primitive detail in hands and face, white body, modern wooden base, 29½ in. high.　　**A-475.00**

Grease horns, with metal-bound wooden ends with central holes, linked together by chain. Used with very early wagons for wheel lubrication. Matched pair. C/30-40

Shock-rope winder, Midwest, 17 in. long. Used by lone worker to secure standing bundles of corn. Item had rope knotted to hole, was tossed around bundle, and rope was caught in groove and twisted in "V"-shaped slot. The bundle was tied with twine, and the winder and rope removed. C/5-8

Marionette, fully jointed wooden horse, white and black paint, 9 in. high. **A-40.00**

Marionette, fully jointed wooden horse, primitively carved, leather saddle, tape halter, cloth and carpet mane and tail, 20 in. long, 24 in. high. **A-500.00**

Mouse trap of wood and tin, early, intricate entrance with moving floor and door that closes behind mouse. **S-45.00**

Niddy-noddy, wood, 18 in. long. **A-22.00**

Niddy-noddy, (yarn-winder), hand-pegged maple, each wrapping head at different angle, connected by single shaft. **D-33.00**

Open salt, well-turned wood, 2½ x 2½ inches. **D-38.00**

Potato carrier, pine, trough with end handles, 10½ x 21 x 78 inches. **A-25.00**

Rabbit, carved wood, weathered, age cracks, 15 in. long. **A-125.00**

Rake, all wooden, pioneer, 69 in. long. **A-60.00**

Sap bucket, four-finger lap, twist hoops. **D-18.50**

Sausage stuffer, wood, base slab, wooden lever arm 30½ in. long, 13 in. high, with tin plunger and wooden mallet. **D-82.00**

Scrub board, wood, sawtooth surface, 3½ x 27¼ inches. **A-29.00**

Snowshoe thong cutter, Maine, handmade and pegged, forged table clamps, 26 cutting blades, two 15-in. handles, 28 in. long. **D-70.00**

Spinning wheel, for wool, wheel 49½ in. diameter. **A-135.00**

Spinning wheel finger, lignum vitae, unusual. **D-12.50**

Spoon, wide carved handle, refinished, 14½ in. long. **A-15.00**

Step-stool, pine, scalloped base, old worn brown and yellow comb graining on blue, 10 x 15 x 18¾ in. high. **A-130.00**

Stool, pencil-post legs, old grey paint, 18 in. high. **A-45.00**

Stool, three-legged, 29 in. high. **A-80.00**

Stool, square top and spindle legs, 19½ in. high. **A-27.50**

Stool, three-leg burl top, 15 in. diameter, 26 in. high. **A-40.00**

Sump mortar, hollowed from one log, maple, 21 in. high. **D-175.00**

Vise table, harness-maker's, wooden pressure handle, 28½ in. high, ca. 1860. **D-30.00**

Wagon jack, for a Conestoga wagon, old red paint. **D-100.00**

Walking stick, with snake around shaft, 35½ in. long. **A-25.00**

Walking stick, eagle with serpent in beak, surmounted by Liberty cap, 36 in. long. **A-55.00**

Yarn winder, floor type, turned legs, chip-carved, 40 in. high. **A-75.00**

Yarn winder, four tall legs, four arms, pegged, 37 in. high. **D-125.00**

Prints—*American Sporting*

COLORED PRINTS OF "SPORTING INCIDENTS". Designed by W. S. Vanderbilt Allen. Printed in New York, 1893. Limited Edition, published by Henry J. Thomas. Each print is 16 by 19 inches.

The Essex County Hounds. Morristown. September, 1893. **A-225.00**

The Gymkhana Races, Rockaway Hunting Club. The Umbrella Race. Cedarhurst. July 5, 1890. **A-110.00**

The High Jump. National Horse Show Association. New York, November, 1892. **A-200.00**

The Meadow Brook Hunt. Westbury, Long Island. November, 1892. **A-175.00**

The Meeting Of The Coach Club. York. May 27, 1893. **A-100.00**

Mr. P. Suffern Tayler's Coach At The Country Club. October, 1892. **A-225.00**

AMERICAN SPORTING PRINT: **Judging Hackney Stallions, National Horse Show Association Championship Prize. November, 1892.**

A/150

Courtesy Adam A. Weschler & Son, Washington, D.C.; photograph by Breger & Associates.

Polo Match For The Westchester Cups Between Meadow Brook And Rockaway Teams. Newport, Rhode Island, 1892.

A-130.00

Pony Race For Polo Ponies At Hempstead Farms. October 19, 1893.

A-125.00

The Queens County Hunt. Mineola, Long Island.

A-300.00

Races Of The American Hunt And Pony Racing Association For The Championship Stakes. Linden, New Jersey. November 5, 1892.

A-75.00

The Road Coach. Acquidneck, Newport, Rhode Island. August, 1892.

A-100.00

Steeplechase At Hempstead Farms. October 21, 1893.

A-225.00

Tandem Shooting Cart. Newport, Rhode Island. August, 1892.

A-250.00

The Tuxedo Road Coach, Republic. Nyack, New York. 1892.

A-200.00

The Westchester Hunt. White Plains, New York. November, 1892.

A-100.00

VIVIPAROUS QUADRUPEDS OF NORTH AMERICA, by John James Audubon and John Woodhouse Audubon. Published by J. J. Audubon, New York, 1848; Copyright, 1845. Printed and colored prior to Publication by T. Bowen, Philadelphia.

Columbia Folio; each approx. 21¾ x 28 in.

American Marsh Shrew. Males, natural size. No. 25, Plate CXXV, 1847.   **A-125.00**

Annulated Marmot Squirrel. Natural size, No. 16, Plate LXXIX, 1845.   **A-125.00**

Bridled Weasel. Males, natural size. No. 12, Plate LX, 1845.   **A-150.00**

AUDUBON PRINT: **Pine Marten** (Mustela Martes, Linn.) Male and female, in winter pelage. Natural size. No 28, Plate CXXXVIII, 1848.
A/250

Courtesy Adam A. Weschler & Son, Washington, D.C.; photograph by Breger & Associates.

Brown, or Norway, Rat. Natural size, male, female and young. No. 11, Plate LIV, 1845.   **A-150.00**

Californian Hare. Natural size. No. 23, Plate CXIL, ca. 1847.   **A-325.00**

Canada Otter. Gray male. No. 25, Plate CXXII, 1847.   **A-175.00**

Canadian Lynx. Three-quarter natural size. Male. No. 4, Plate XVI.   **A-325.00**

Colliaes Squirrel. Natural size. No. 21, Plate CIV, 1847.   **A-225.00**

Fremont's Squirrel. Natural size, Fig. 1. **Sooty Squirrel,** Fig. 2, natural size. No. 30, Plate CXLIX, 1848.   **A-250.00**

Little Chief Hare. Natural size. No. 17, Plate LXXX-III, 1846. — A-125.00

Missouri Mouse. Natural size No. 20, Plate C, 1846. — A-150.00

Mole-shaped Pouched Rat. Natural size. No. 22, Plate CX, 1847. — A-125.00

Pouched Jerboa Mouse. Males, natural size. No. 26, Plate CXXX, 1847. — A-150.00

Richardson's Spermophile. Natural size. No. 10, Plate CXLIX, 1848. — A-125.00

Tawny Lemming. Natural size. **Black's Lemming.** Natural size, Figs. 2 and 3. No. 24, Plate CXX, 1847. — A-150.00

Texan Skunk. Natural size. No. 11, Plate LIII, 1845. — A-150

Townsend's Arvicola. Male, natural size, Fig. 1. — A-150.00

Sharp-nosed Arvicola, natural size, Fig. 2. **Bank Rat,** natural size. No. 29, Plate CXLIV, 1848. — A-100.00

Yellow-cheeked Meadow Mouse. Natural size. No. 23, Plate CXV, 1847. — A-125.00

Yellow-bellied Marmot. Male, natural size. No. 27, Plate CXXXIV, 1848. — A-125.00

QUILTS & BEDCOVERINGS

Bedspread, geometric popcorn pattern, hand-crocheted, cotton, 90 x 95 inches. — A-110.00

Comforter, pieced and knotted; nine-part squares on yellow fabric, 64 x 70 inches. — A-70.00

Coverlet, double-weave two-piece, with bird, tree and church borders. Center has stars and four rose medallions, signed and dated 1861, 73 x 83 inches. — A-120.00

Coverlet, double-weave, two-piece. Pine tree pattern in brick red and white; fringe missing, worn, 76 x 78 inches. — A-90.00

Coverlet, jacquared, single-weave, two-piece. Blue and white, signed and dated 1845, worn, fringe missing, 76 x 92 inches. — A-65.00

Coverlet, single-weave, two-piece, blue and white. Overshot pattern, unusual borders separately woven, 98 x 102 inches. — A-145.00

Coverlet, American hand-loomed wool and flax. Blue, purple and white, 78 x 92 inches. — A-175.00

Coverlet, two-piece, intricate pattern in dark red and blue, 70 x 86 inches. — A-105.00

Coverlet, seamed center in geometric pattern, two shades of blue; attractive, unusual combination, fringed, 72 x 90 inches.   A-165.00

Coverlet, jacquared, two-piece, blue, gold, red and white single-weave pattern. Dated 1853, worn, 70 x 86 inches.   A-105.00

Coverlet, jacquared, single-weave, blue on white. Signed and dated 1853, 78 x 88 inches.   A-125.00

Coverlet, jacquared, roses and stars in four colors, with bird border, 78 x 89 inches.   A-105.00

Coverlet, jacquared, two-piece, single-weave. Blue and white, signed and dated 1843, worn, 76 x 86 inches.   A-75.00

Coverlet, overshot, two-piece, in four colors including bright moss green. Beautiful condition, 80 x 96 inches.   A-230.00

Coverlet, overshot, two-piece. Blue, brown, red and white, 76 x 88 inches.   A-155.00

Coverlet, overshot, two-piece. Applied knotted fringe, red and white, 71 x 88 inches.   A-115.00

QUILTS—*Applique*

Baskets of Tulips, vining border in five colors, feather quilting. Beautiful condition, 84 x 96 inches.   A-305.00

Central Medallions, meandering floral border in three colors. Medallions are red and green, some wear, 88 in. square.   A-155.00

Flower Baskets, in red and yellow-green on white ground, 72 x 88 inches.   A-75.00

Oakleaf Variant, red and dark brown calico. Embroidered signature, 81 x 96 inches.   A-265.00

Pinwheels, serrated leaves in green and red, feather quilting, meandering border, green faded, 80 x 82 inches.   A-245.00

Princess Feather, design in red and green, meandering border. From New York state, 86 in. square.   A-155.00

Quilt, red squares with three leaves on corners, red border, some machine restitching, 80 in. square.   A-65.00

Stylized floral design, green, tan and orange. Well-made, 84 in. square.   A-225.00

Stylized floral design in gold and red, feather quilting in the white, 73 x 88 inches.   A-170.00

Stylized floral, in four colors, 82 in. square.   **A-230.00**

Stylized pots of flowers, in green and yellow print with gold. Three additional colors, good quilting, 82 x 98 inches.   **A-235.00**

Stylized roses, blue-green, ruffled stitches on red, meandering border. Minor stains, 72 x 86 inches.   **A-245.00**

Stylized whig rose, three colors, some wear, repair necessary, 81 x 86 inches.   **A-185.00**

QUILTS—*Chintz*

Print, in red, brown, white and blue, 67 x 75 inches.   **A-65.00**

Floral pattern, birds of paradise in three colors against yellow ground. Corners cut out for bed posts, 100 x 104 inches.   **A-130.00**

Floral pattern, six large stars pieced from calico and chintz, all on brownish ground. Back fabric with Greek temple in four colors, 98 in. square.   **A-260.00**

Star in a Diamond, alternating squares of brown floral chintz, homespun, 72 x 83 inches.   **A-75.00**

QUILTS—*Patchwork*

Quilt, tic-tac-toe squares, white and colors, multicolor knotting, edge machine stitched. Good hand-quilting, 70 x 83 inches.   **D-55.00**

Quilt, green background with white figure, vari-colored patterns. Machine-stitched edges, 76 x 90 inches.   **D-145.00**

Quilt, with gaily-colored butterflies, early flour-sack backing. Has 42 irregular-size patches, 67 x 80½ inches.   **D-125.00**

Quilt top, all hand-sewn, white cotton border, 30 x 80 in. patchwork center, overall 76 x 96 inches.   **D-75.00**

Quilt top, multi-shaped panels done in pure silk. Large, 73 x 96 inches.   **D-400.00**

QUILTS—*Patterned*

Bride's friendship type, dated 1876, medium-size.   **D-450.00**

Double Irish Chain, deep pink chain squares, 62 x 68 inches.   **D-65.00**

Eight-Point Star, Amish, single border.   D-250.00
Irish Chain, Mennonite, blue and white.   D-175.00
Log Cabin, Pennsylvania, ca. 1890.   D-325.00
North Carolina Lily, handmade, old, unused, 74 x 90
inches.   D-195.00
Ohio Star, hand-quilting, Amish, ca. 1880, 68 x 76 in-
ches.   D-150.00
Texas Star, Mennonite, double border.   D-500.00
Trapezoidal, diamond-quilted, many tiny prints, ca.
1920, 67 x 82 inches.   D-45.00
White Wedding Ring, 1930's, hand-quilted, 90 x 98
inches.   D-150.00

QUILTS—*Pieced*

Black and Navy grid on maroon, black border.
Amish, child-size, 37 x 53 inches.   A-195.00
Amish, navy blue with black stripe and border.
Brown homespun backing, 60 x 72 inches.   A-165.00
Amish crib quilt, four colors, edge machine-bound,
remainder hand-done. Never used, 33 x 45 inches.   A-185.00
Amish, tan and black pattern of squares, faded
salmon band, magenta binding, 66 x 76 inches.   A-220.00
Amish, dark plain colors, never used, 72 x 86 inches.   A-175.00
Amish, tan, light blue and brown on one side,
medium blue and tan on the other, green border, 64
x 76 inches.   A-225.00
Basket of Flowers, three shades of blue, and
maroon. Quilted flowers, homespun back, 66 x 72 in-
ches.   A-135.00
Bow-tie, in vivid dark colors, white thread quilting in
four distinct colors. Stitched initials and date, 1932,
76 in. square.   A-355.00
Blocks and Bars, Pennsylvania, red, white and blue,
youth's size, 62 x 76 inches.   A-85.00
Chimney Sweep, Amish indigo prints, old blocks but
put together in 1950-60's, hand-quilted, unused.   D-115.00
Central Star, background of small squares, striped
border. Color-floral prints, corner dated 1925, 84 in.
square.   A-405.00
Compasspoint, Pennsylvania, gold and white, 75 x 90
inches.   A-170.00
Crib quilt, pieced, pink calico border around colorful
squares, 37 in. square.   A-65.00

Crib quilt, solid colors on white with blue border. Modern metal frame, 28 x 37½ inches.   **A-100.00**

Crosses in Squares, pink and brown on grey field, homespun backing, some wear, 70 x 76 inches.   **A-95.00**

Diamonds in Diamonds, colorful floral prints, edge wear.   **A-65.00**

Eight-Point Starburst variant, in dark colors of wool and cotton, prob. Ohio, 74 x 88 inches.   **A-425.00**

Geometric design, red, white and black print used with white, 72 in. square.   **A-165.00**

Geometric pattern, four colors, Amish, quilted hearts, circles, 64 x 78 inches.   **A-135.00**

Geometric pattern, in six colors, black back, 67 x 82 inches.   **A-210.00**

Log Cabin, in blue and brown prints with red accents, white homespun back, 81 x 84 inches.   **A-165.00**

Log Cabin, in blue, red, white, yellow and green calico; back with stripes of red and yellow, 80 in. square.   **A-145.00**

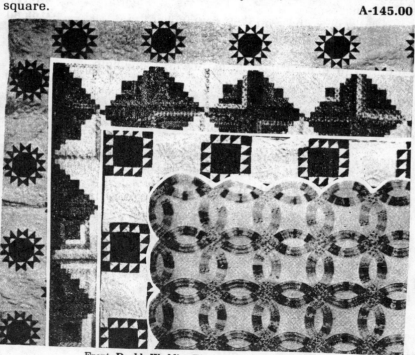

Front, **Double Wedding Ring.**   150-170
Second, **Double Saw Tooth.**   100-115
Third, **Log Cabin.**   125-140
Fourth, **Rising Star.**   100-115

Lone Star, multi-colored calico, 79 x 80 inches.   A-85.00

Ocean Waves, in grey and white with goldenrod, goldenrod borders. Scalloped edge, backing homespun, 78 in. square.   A-205.00

Optical Stars, New Hampshire, red and white, 65 x 77 inches.   A-125.00

Quilt, applique swags and tasseled border, green and white calico with red tassels, 82 x 84 inches.   A-175.00

Quilt, one-strip fabric border with stars, printed pattern, remainder all hand-pieced, colorful, 83 in. square.   A-225.00

Quilt, blue and red print squares on white ground, blue border; machine-stitched binding, 85 in. square.   A-140.00

Sawtooth, gold and brown, stains, 84 x 86 inches.   A-45.00

Single Star, in pastel shades with deep pink border, on white. Quilt 84 x 92 inches.   A-225.00

Single Star, pastel shades with red center on white, 80 x 82 inches.   A-90.00

Snowflake, pink and white, 69 x 80 inches.   A-85.00

Squares, in blue, green and red calico, 79 in. square.   A-185.00

Squares, Amish, green and pink on blue ground. Border with quilted baskets of flowers, sawtooth edge, 73 in. square.   A-255.00

Square within a Square, purple and green, Amish, prob. Ohio. 70 x 85 inches.   A-255.00

Star, in blue, coral, purple, etc. on white, 78 x 102 inches.   A-125.00

Triangles and Squares, all wool, minor moth damage, Amish, dark colors, 83 x 96 inches.   A-225.00

Triple Irish Chain, harlequin border in colorful prints on white ground, 57 x 88 inches.   A-85.00

Tulip, gold, green, white and pumpkin colors, 81 in. square.   A-325.00

Turkey Tracks, in red and black with green and white print, minor edge wear, 83 x 94 inches.   A-215.00

Zig-Zag, green vines with purple and deep rose flowers, 68 x 84 inches.   A-45.00

RAILROADIANA

Air horn, brass, Leslie Tyfon, 21 inches, No. 125.   D-125.00

Ash tray, brass, "Pullman", 2½ x 4½ inches.   D-35.00

Ash tray, SP, cobalt blue, 3½ x 6 inches.   D-65.00

Bell, locomotive, brass, 15 in. high.	**A-600.00**
Builder's plans, complete set, Louisiana depot.	**D-45.00**
Builder's plate, brass, "Fairbanks-Morse", 1953, 8 x 17 inches.	**D-125.00**
Builder's plate, steel, "American Locomotive", 1947.	**D-50.00**
Butter chip, Pennsylvania RR, "Purple Laurel".	**D-5.00**
Can, kerosene; one gal., galvanized, B & O.	**D-28.00**
Can, kerosene; one gal., galvanized, Lehigh Valley RR.	**D-25.00**
Can, water, RE Lines, one gal. top.	**D-20.00**
Candle lamp, brass, 1907, 5 in. globe.	**D-55.00**
Celery dish, CMST & P, Syracuse, 5 x 10 inches.	**D-22.00**
Cereal bowl, CMSTP, 1937, "Traveler", 7 in. diameter.	**D-20.00**
Clock, Seth Thomas, locomotive, windup, brass, 8 in. diameter.	**D-150.00**
Coffee pot, silver, SP Co., 4 x 6 inches.	**D-40.00**
Compote, SF, Mimbreno.	**D-25.00**
Creamer, Pullman, Syracuse, 2 x 2¾ inches.	**D-35.00**
Cup and saucer, B & O, 1st Vintage, 1927, "Philip E. Thomas".	**D-75.00**
Dinner plate, MKT, "Old Abbey", 10 in. diameter.	**D-135.00**
Dinner plate, NYC, "Mohawk", Salmon color, black strips, 10 in. diameter.	**D-65.00**
Dish, Pullman, Syracuse, 7½ in. diameter.	**D-40.00**
Dome cover, CMST & P, Syracuse, 7 inches.	**D-18.00**

Syrup, RR dining car, "International Silver Company", PRR logo, "Silver Soldered / 8 oz.". C/50-65

Brakeman's lantern, "H.V.Ry", on globe and stamped on lantern top; wick adjusts from bottom center of base; rare. C/150-200

Document seal, lever-type, brass impression plate. For local lodge, "Brotherhood of Locomotive Firemen and Engineers". C/45-65

Railway Paper Collectibles

Top, **lock and chain** with copper dated (26) nail; rare. Brass lock, "C & M V RR", no key.   C/55-65
Bot right, **lock**, brass hasp, H.V.R.R. Co.", for section shanty, no key.   C/30-40
Badge, "Pennsylvania / 1921", Keystone mark.   C/15-20

Cap badge, "Brakeman", passenger car brakeman's.   C/10-13
Key, (left, solid brass, caboose, "Adlake".   C/14-19
Key, (right), C&N, by "Fraim", for switch lock.   C/8-12
Lantern, D. & H. RR, Adlake-Kero   C/50-65

Fire bucket, IC, 15 in. high.	**D-30.00**
Fire extinguisher, brass, Erie RR, 14 in. high.	**D-40.00**
Fire extinguisher, brass, IC RR, two gal.	**D-100.00**
Fork, silver, UP.	**D-8.50**
Funnel, AT & SF, large size.	**D-18.00**
Hand lantern, (Adams & Westlake/1922), globe etched "ACL".	**D-35.00**
Hand lantern, CM & St. P. RR, (Handlan), fair condition.	**D-45.00**
Hand lantern, CM & STP RR, amber and green lights.	**D-120.00**
Hand lantern, (Dietz/Standard), bell bottom, 5 3/8 in. globe.	**D-42.00**
Hand lantern, etched "FRISCO" on globe, no maker marked.	**D-65.00**
Hand lantern, Keystone P.R.R. (Union Carbide Oxweld/Model A).	**D-60.00**
Hand lantern, Keystone P.R.R. (Trackwalker/1909), rear white and red lens.	**D-75.00**
Hand lantern, N.Y.C.S., (Dressel), red globe 3¾ inches.	**D-35.00**

Hand lantern, Santa Fe embossed in square bell bottom, 10 in. diameter globe. — D-125.00

Hand lantern, Southern Ry., (Adlake-Kero), red rib globe. — D-35.00

Hand lantern, St. L.S.F. Ry., (250 Kero/1923), amber globe. — D-70.00

Ice cream dish, silver, CMST & P, 5 inches. — D-30.00

Inspector's lantern, T & P, 7½ x 14 inches. — D-75.00

Key, brass, Nashville, Chatanooga & St. L. — D-22.00

Key, brass, Parkersburg Branch RR Co. — D-25.00

Key, brass, Yazoo & Mississippi Valley. — D-40.00

Knife, silver, MKT. — D-9.00

Ladle, silver, Pullman. — D-22.00

Lock, signal; NKP, brass. — D-35.00

Lock, signal; Southern Ry., brass. — D-45.00

Lock, switch; C of P RR (Calif.), brass, very old. — D-75.00

Lock, switch; N & W Ry. Co., brass, embossed name. — D-55.00

Lock, switch; RPP, brass, unmarked brass key. — D-75.00

Marker lantern, ACL, (Armspear), three amber lights, 5 in. globe. — D-115.00

Marker lantern, St. L. I.M.RR, (Adlake), two white lenses. — D-115.00

Marker lantern, St. L. S. F., (Adlake), one blue lens, brass plate. — D-90.00

Marker lantern, U P RR, (Handlan), amber globe. — D-75.00

Marker lanterns, SP Lines, matched pair; by Handlan, one amber, one green. Each: — D-85.00

Menu holder, silver, Great Northern, marked, 5 x 5 inches. — D-35.00

Menu holder, silver, Milwaukee Rd., marked, 5 x 5½ inches. — D-60.00

Oval dish, ACL, 5½ inches. — D-22.00

Paperweight, Burlington Rte., 1945, 2½ x 7¼ inches. — D-55.00

Paperweight, Philip E. Thomas, 1927, 4½ x 7½ inches. — D-65.00

Pitcher, glass and silver, ACL, 7¼ x 10½ inches. — D-125.00

Pitcher, NYC, "DeWitte Clinton", 5 x 5 inches. — D-45.00

Salad plate, N & W, Lamberton Scammell, 6½ in. diameter. — D-25.00

Saucer, Pennsylvania R.R., "Broadway". — D-25.00

Soap dish, brass, 3½ x 5½ inches. — D-35.00

Soup bowl, Western Pacific, Shenango, 6½ in. diameter. — D-30.00

Spittoon, Frisco, porcelain. — D-40.00

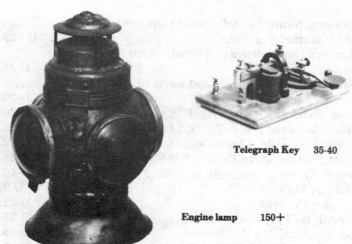

Telegraph Key   35-40

Engine lamp   150+

Spittoon, MK & T, nickel plated.	**D-50.00**
Steam whistle, brass, three-chime, "Lunkenheimer", 5 x 20 inches.	**D-300.00**
Step stool, NYC System.	**D-125.00**
Step stool, Pullman.	**D-90.00**
Sugar bowl, silver, NYC, 4 x 4 inches.	**D-45.00**
Sugar tongs, silver, Southern RR, 4 in. long.	**D-16.00**
Switch-stand lantern, (Adlake), two amber and two blue lights, target style.	**D-100.00**
Tablespoon, silver, RI.	**D-9.00**
Torch, N & W, heavy iron, 5 x 6 inches.	**D-23.00**
Torch, St. L. S. F., 6 x 8 inches.	**D-18.00**
Towel rack, brass, UP RR, 6½ x 25 inches.	**D-65.00**
Track level, wood with brass, 60 inches.	**D-75.00**

RUGS—*Eastern and Oriental*

Eastern and Oriental rugs have been used and collected in Europe for centuries, and in the 19th and first half of the 20th Centuries by affluent Americans. Recently there has been a surge of interest along the entire collecting spectrum, as people have become aware that some well-made rugs can be had for less than a thousand dollars.

There is the added factor of inflation, or antiques and collectibles purchased for security and investment reasons. Whatever the major purpose, there is now a brisk market in the rugs. Note that "Antique" rugs are considered to be over one hundred years old, while "Semi-Antique" rugs may be over 60 years old. Regional varieties, as listed here, may be of less age.

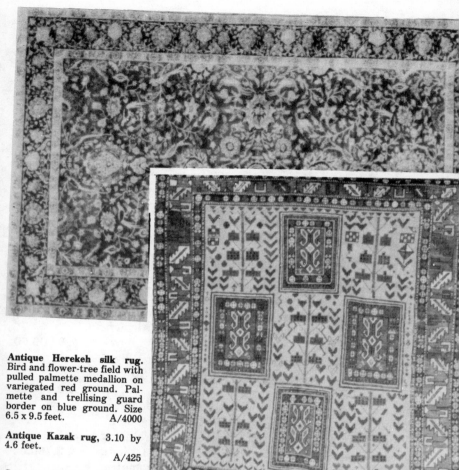

Antique Herekeh silk rug.
Bird and flower-tree field with
pulled palmette medallion on
variegated red ground. Palmette and trellising guard
border on blue ground. Size
6.5 x 9.5 feet.   A/4000

Antique Kazak rug, 3.10 by
4.6 feet.

A/425

Courtesy Adam A. Weschler
& Son, Washington, D.C.;
photographs by Breger &
Associates.

Eastern and Oriental Rugs—*Antique*

Antique Cabistan Rug. Diagonal paisley design on
red ground, three guard borders and intermittent
floral and stylized animal design. Size 4.4 x 6.1 feet.   A-1,600.00
Ant. Daghestan Rug. Palmette field on variegated
blue ground, geometric floral guard border on sand
beige ground. Size 3.10 x 5.2 feet.   A-400.00

Ant. Kazak Rug. Blue ground with animal and latch-hook medallions centering three double latch-hook medallions. Serrated and floral guard border on ivory ground. Size 4.4 x 6.10 feet.　　　　A-2,300.00

Ant. Kerman Rug. Star pulled medallion on beige ground, all within floral and animal design on burgundy ground. Complementary border on burgundy ground. Size 10.6 x 15 feet.　　　　A-1,300.00

Ant. Kerman Rug. Blue ground with pulled medallion and paisley spandrels, complementary guard border on old rose ground. Size 5.11 x 8.9 feet.　　　　A-1,600.00

Ant. Keshan Rug. "Tree of Life" pattern on gold ground, floral guard border on dark blue ground. Size 8.7 x 11.6 feet.　　　　A-2,900.00

Ant. Keshan Rug. Marquise shape medallion with all-over floral design on brick red ground, floral design guard border on dark blue ground. Size 7.3 x 10.3 feet.　　　　A-1,800.00

Ant. Kuba Rug. Trellising palmette field on variegated blue ground, three guard borders in intermittent trellising floral and serrated "S" design. Size 6 x 15.8 feet.　　　　A-5,000.00

Ant. Laver Kerman Rug. Paisley design on light green ground, complementary guard border. Size 4.6 x 7.4 feet.　　　　A-3,900.00

Ant. Laver Kerman Rug. Millefleur field on ivory ground with pulled lobed medallion on red ground. Pictorial spandrels, serpent and floral trellising guard border on ivory ground. Size 11.6 x 13.7 feet.　　　　A-3,700.00

Ant. Oushak Rug. Ivory ground with geometric medallions on pastel pink ground, complementary guard border. Size 6 x 9.1 feet.　　　　A-1,250.00

Ant. Oushak Rug. Trellising floral and leafage field on turquoise ground, complementary guard border on red ground. Size 8.4 x 12.9 feet.　　　　A-1,700.00

Ant. Sarouk Rug. Star medallion with floral devices on cream ground within a large marquise pulled medallion on dark blue ground, all on brick red ground with floral pattern, ivory spandrels, wide variegated blue guard border with intermittent floral and vase of flower devices. Size 11 x 13.10 feet.　　　　A-4,800.00

Ant. Senna Rug. Serrated pulled medallion with stylized human and fish design on light blue ground, within marquise shape pulled medallion with all-over floral trellising design. All on ivory ground with complementary designs, complementary guard border on light salmon ground. Size 12.1 x 17.3 feet.　　**A-4,900.00**

Ant. Serapi Rug. Red ground, with geometric pulled medallion on green ground, ivory spandrels, floral trellising guard border on variegated red ground. Size 8.7 x 12.1 feet.　　**A-2,700.00**

Ant. Tabriz Rug. Floral medallion flanked by half-medallions on light green ground, all within sand beige ground. Wide guard border with geometric and floral designs on brick red ground. Size 3.11 x 5.4 feet.　　**A-2,500.00**

Ant. Tabriz Rug. Central pulled floral medallion within a marquise shape pulled medallion on brick red ground. All on variegated blue ground with floral bouquests, ivory spandrels, floral trellising guard border on brick red ground. Size 4.3 x 6 feet.　　**A-1,050.00**

Ant. Tabriz Rug. Floral field with double pulled medallion on ivory-to-red grounds, all on sand beige ground. Complementary spandrels on blue ground, floral trellising guard border on sand beige ground. Size 8.7 x 13.2 feet.　　**A-1,300.00**

Ant. Yomud Saddle Mat. Irregular; ivory field filled with latticed geometric floral medallions on variegated ground, latched hook guard border with animal trappings and tasseled fringe. Size 2.5 x 4.3 feet.　　**A-1,900.00**

Eastern And Oriental Rugs—*Semi-Antique*

Semi-Antique Afshar Rug. Red ground with geometric floral medallion centered by vased flowers and geometric spandrels. Floral guard border on variegated red ground. Size 5.2 x 6.8 feet.　　**A-500.00**

Semi-Ant. Agra Rug. Gold ground with pulled central medallion, lavender spandrels, complementary guard border on ivory ground. Size 12 x 16.6 feet.　　**A-250.00**

Semi-Ant. Bijar Rug. Brick red rectangular panel with latticed and floral field within a pulled geometric medallion on blue ground. Ivory trellising guard border. Size 3.8 x 4.11 feet.　　**A-1,200.00**

Semi-Antique Anatolian prayer rug, with Mosque on red ground framed by guard border in celadon green ground with gold and salmon devices. Rug 4.4 x 5.7 feet.   A/1225

Courtesy of Adam A. Weschler & Son

Semi-Ant. Caucasian Prayer Rug. Stylized animal and floral field on blue ground within rectangular prayer mosque with pulled medallion on old rose ground. Floral trellising guard border on variegated blue ground. Size 4 x 5.8 feet.   **A-525.00**

Semi-Ant. Daghestan Rug. Two rows of floral bouquets on variegated rose field. Complementary trellising guard border on blue ground. Size 3.9 x 9.8 feet.   **A-775.00**

Upper left, **Semi-antique Heriz rug**. Herati field on old rose, blue and pink ground, complementary spandrels. Floral trellising guard border on variegated blue ground; 12.6 by 9.5 feet. A/2700

Above left, **Semi-antique Kazak rug**, 4.5 x 7.5 feet. A/510

Above right, **Semi-antique Kuba rug**. Rectangular panel with windowpane field of geometric latched hook medallions on variegated ground. Three guard borders with floral serrated and wine cup design on red-to-ivory-to-green ground. Rug 4.3 x 9.3 feet. A/1300

Courtesy Adam A. Weschler & Son, Washington, D.C.; photographs by Breger & Associates.

Above right, **Kerman rug.** Sunburst medallion with paisley and pulled design on ivory ground, complementary guard border; 9 x 12 feet.   A/1900
Above left, **Heriz rug.** Herati field on ivory, blue and red ground. Floral and palmette guard border on navy blue ground. Size 11.1 x 19.10 feet.   A/2000

Courtesy of Adam A. Weschler & Son

Semi-Ant. Ferreghan Rug. Blue field with palmette trellising field, complementary guard border, 9.3 x 13.3 feet.   **A-475.00**

Semi-Ant. Goum Rug. Ivory ground with diagonal paisley field, floral trellising guard border on blue ground, 4.9 x 6.7 feet.   **A-625.00**

Semi-Ant. Hamadan Rug. Three floral medallions surrounded by floral bouquets on brick red ground. Floral guard border on navy blue ground, 2.8 x 9.9 feet.   **A-375.00**

Semi-Ant. Heriz Rug. Red ground with Herati pattern, floral and palmette guard border on blue ground. Size 12.8 x 16.3 feet.   **A-4,700.00**

Semi-Ant. Isphahan Rug. Floral trellising field on ivory ground, central pulled star medallion on blue ground. Floral trellising guard border on variegated rose ground. Size 4.5 x 7.5 feet.

A-900.00

Semi-Ant. Isphahan Tree-Of-Life Rug. Brick red arabesque centered by tall flowering tree and two smaller trees each of which have intertwined winged serpents within a bird and floral field. Palmette guard border. Size 4.7 x 7.3 feet.

A-3,000.00

Semi-Ant. Kazak Rug. Red ground with floral field centering three geometric medallions on blue ground with complementary field, double "E" guard border on ivory ground. Size 3.6 x 6 feet.

A-1,800.00

Semi-Ant. Kazak Prayer Rug. Within mosque, trellising star field on ivory ground, trellising wine cup guard border on red ground. Size 3 x 6.1 feet.

A-1,000.00

Semi-Ant. Kazak Rug. Red ground with three geometric medallions on alternating sand beige-to-blue ground, serrated and wine cup guard border. Size 5 x 8.8 feet.

A-900.00

Semi-Ant. Kazak Rug. Diagonal medallion field on variegated blue ground, stylized bird guard border on ivory ground. Size 3.9 x 8.2 feet.

A-550.00

Semi-Ant. Kerman Rug. Brick red ground with flowering and vine field, palmette guard border on blue ground. Size 9 x 11.4 feet.

A-3,000.00

Semi-Ant. Keshan Picture Rug. Deer in extensive multi-colored floral landscape, wide guard border with continuing scenes of deer in landscape, with dwellings on light blue ground. Size 4.5 x 7 feet.

A-1,800.00

Semi-Ant. Keshan Garden Carpet. Windowpane field with flowering trees, animals, birds, etc. on vari-colored grounds. Palmette guard border on complementary grounds.

A-1,800.00

Semi-Ant. Keshan Rug, silk. Lavender ground with floral trellising field, palmette trellising primary border on blue ground and five borders with paisley and arabesque design. Size 4.2 x 6.8 feet.

A-10,700.00

Semi-Ant. Keshan Rug. Red ground with pulled lobed medallion within floral leaf field, light blue spandrels, complementary guard border on blue ground. Size 4.7 x 6.9 feet.

A-950.00

Semi-Ant. Kuba Rug. Blue ground with stylized animal and floral field, two guard borders with floral and bat design on red-to-sand beige ground. Size 6.2 x 10.9 feet.　　　　　　　　　　A-1,300.00

Semi-Ant. Laver Kerman Rug. Millefleur field on ivory ground, floral bouquet guard border on navy blue ground. Size 10.1 x 18.4 feet.　　　　A-2,900.00

Semi-Ant. Laver Kerman Rug. Floral trellising field with pulled lobed medallion and paisley design on blue ground. Complementary spandrels on rose ground, paisley and floral guard border on blue ground. Size 11.6 x 15.10 feet.　　　　　A-2,600.00

Semi-Ant. Lillihan Rug. Two floral medallions surrounded by floral trellising designs on red ground. Complementary guard border on blue ground. Size 2.7 x 13.6 feet.　　　　　　　　　　A-400.00

Semi-Ant. Mahal Rug. Rose ground with stylized animal and floral field, palmette guard border on beige ground. Size 9.2 x 11 feet.　　　　A-800.00

Semi-Ant. Perpedil Rug. Blue field containing perpedil figures and snowflakes, all within buff border with star and diagonal design in blue-to-rose-to-ivory grounds. Size 3.11 x 5.5 feet.　　　A-900.00

Semi-Ant. Sarouk Rug. Red ground with all-over floral and vine field, palmette and floral guard border on blue ground. Size 8.9 x 11.3 feet.　　A-3,400.00

Semi-Ant. Sarouk Rug. Two rows of connecting medallions with floral trellising designs on dark variegated blue ground. Floral and scrolling leaf borders on brick red ground. Size 8.9 x 12.5 feet.　　A-1,900.00

Semi-Ant. Senna Rug. Ivory ground with milli-fiori field centering pulled geometric medallion on blue ground. Complementary spandrels, floral palmette guard border on red ground. Size 4.5 x 6 feet.　　A-1,100.00

Semi-Ant. Senna Rug. Rectangular ivory panel with floral field centering two pulled medallions on ivory-to-salmon ground. Blue spandrels, trellising guard border on salmon ground. Size 4.3 x 6.3 feet.　　A-1,800.00

Semi-Ant. Serapi Rug. Herati field on old rose, blue and ivory ground. Size 9.8 x 10.11 feet.　　A-2,700.00

Semi-Ant. Shiraz Rug. Blue ground with latched hook elongated medallion on red ground with all-over floral design. Complementary guard border on variegated ground. Size 3.6 x 5.3 feet.　　A-1,200.00

Semi-Ant. Shirvan Rug. Sand beige ground with all-over palmette field, stylized floral guard border on brick red ground. Size 4.6 x 7.2 feet. A-1,100.00

Semi-Ant. Tabriz Animal Carpet. Sand beige ground with all-over animal and floral landscape. Trellising palmette guard border on salmon ground. Size 10.1 x 12.7 feet. A-400.00

Semi-Ant. Tekke Bokhara Rug. Diagonal gull field on wine ground, latched and serrated guard border on ivory ground. Size 7.3 x 10.8 feet. A-2,900.00

Eastern And Oriental Rugs—*Regional*

Afghan Bokhara Rug. Traditional Bokhara pattern on wine ground, 7.9 x 11.5 feet. A-425.00

Afghan Rug. Trellising field on brown ground with pulled geometric medallion on red ground, complementary guard border. Size 3.7 x 6.10 feet. A-180.00

Bokhara Rug. Traditional Bokhara pattern on red field, 7.1 x 10.10 feet. A-825.00

Goum Rug. Blue ground with all-over flowering and leaf field, complementary guard border on gold ground. Size 3.4 x 5.5 feet. A-425.00

Heriz Rug. Herati field on blue, red and cream grounds, trellising floral guard border on navy blue ground, 6.5 x 8.10 feet. A-650.00

Indo-Tabriz Rug. Flowering tree field on navy blue ground, floral trellising guard border on red-rust ground, 9 x 12 feet. A-1,900.00

Isphahan Rugs, pair. Floral and leaf field on ivory ground with pulled eight-point star medallion, blue spandrels, floral and vignette guard border on red ground. Size 4.10 x 7.9 feet. A-8,600.00

Kashmar Rug. Diagonal floral medallions segmented by floral bouquets on navy blue ground. Wide old rose guard border with intermitent floral and geometric devices, 10.1 x 13.1 feet. A-2,000.00

Kazak Rug. Turquoise ground with ram's horn design and geometric medallion within, on red ground, trellising and ram's horn guard border on ivory ground. Size 3.5 x 5 feet. A-475.00

Kerman Rug. Pulled central medallion with floral trellising devices on ivory ground, complementary wide guard border. Size 11.1 x 16.6 feet. A-1,550.00

Kerman Rug. Ivory ground with floral medallion, complementary pastel guard border. Size 7.10 x 10.2 feet. A-1,300.00

Kerman Rug. Rose ground with floral medallions, complementary guard border in pastel colors, 3 x 3.1 feet. A-175.00

Kerman Rug, signed. Ivory ground with pulled marquise medallion in pastel colors, complementary guard border. Size 11.11 x 19.5 feet. A-4,200.00

Keshan Animal Carpet. Five rows of lobed medallions with birds and animals on blue ground segmented by marquise medallions with animal designs on ivory ground, complementary guard border. Size 10 x 15.9 feet. A-2,600.00

Keshan Prayer Rug. Within mosque, vased floral field on wine red ground, flowering tree and bird guard border on blue ground. Size 4.1 x 7.1 feet. A-850.00

Keshan Prayer Rug, silk. Within mosque, flowering tree field on ivory ground, blue spandrels, floral trellising guard border on lavender ground. Size 4.4 x 6.9 feet. A-1,400.00

Keshan Rug. Millefleur field on red ground, pulled lobed medallion on blue ground, blue spandrels, floral trellising guard border on blue ground. Size 4.2 x 7 feet. A-1,350.00

Kurdish Rug. Five octagonal serrated medallions with intermittent gold-to-red-to-blue grounds. Floral bouquet guard border on red ground, 3.7 x 10.2 feet. A-300.00

Princess Bokhara Rug. Traditional Bokhara pattern on burgundy ground. Size 4.2 x 5.9 feet. A-350.00

Princess Bokhara Rug. Traditional Bokhara pattern on red ground, 4.2 x 6 feet. A-375.00

Sarouk Rug. Burgundy ground with vased flower and palmette field, trellising guard border on blue ground. Size 2.9 x 12.6 feet. A-1,100.00

Tabriz Rug. Palmette field on ivory ground with pulled eight-point star medallion, complementary spandrels. Floral trellising palmette guard border on ivory ground. Size 9.4 x 12.10 feet. A-2,100.00

Turkish Rug. Royal blue ground with palmette field centering pulled lobed medallion, complementary guard border on burgundy ground. Size 8 x 10 feet. A-1,100.00

Turkish Silk Hunting Carpet. Pulled lobed central medallion with birds on black ground and centered by animals, trees and birds on ruby ground. Three guard borders, red-to-black-to-red grounds with animals and trees. Size 4.4 x 7 feet.　　　　　　A-525.00

SABERS And SWORDS

American sword with iron scabbard, hilt has cast eagles; engraved blade 32 in. long.　　　　　A-125.00
Cavalry saber, 1860, 35¼ in. blade.　　　　　A-70.00
Cavalry saber, Confederate, broken blade.　　　A-120.00

Officers Sword　　150+

Cavalry saber, iron scabbard, 35½ in. blade.　　　A-65.00
Cavalry saber, by Ames, iron scabbard, dated 1863.　A-125.00
Cavalry saber, Civil War, black iron scabbard, 38¾ in. blade.　　　　　　A-95.00
Cavalry Officer's saber, 1860, by Ames, also signed iron scabbard.　　　　　A-265.00
Cavalry Officer's sword, iron scabbard, by "I.A.R. & C.", engraved blade 32¾ in. long.　　　A-175.00
Cavalry sword, ca. 1860, metal scabbard.　　　A-75.00
Cavalry sword, U.S., "Emerson & Silver/Trenton/1864", with scabbard.　　　A-105.00
Cavalry sword, U.S., "Ames/1864", with scabbard.　A-115.00
Cavalry sword, U.S., model 1913, "LF & C."　　A-40.00
Cavalry sword, metal scabbard, half-basket hilt, French inscription on blade, 37½ in. long.　　A-185.00
Foot artillery sword, fishscale grip, 18¾ in. blade.　A-60.00
Foot Officer's sword, Model 1850, leather scabbard with brass mounts, 30 in. blade.　　　A-225.00
Foot Officer's sword, by Ames, 1850 Model. A presentation piece, 30½ in. blade.　　　A-295.00
Foot Officer's sword, Model 1850, 30 in. blade.　A-145.00
Foot Officer's sword, "Soligen", scabbard engraved to owner, a Civil War U.S. captain, 32½ in. blade.　A-295.00
Fraternal sword with scabbard.　　　A-22.50

NCO sword, for non-commissioned Officer, by Ames, dated 1863.   **A-90.00**

NCO U.S. sword, metal scabbard.   **A-35.00**

Officer's sword, iron hilt with eagle, "U.S.", 30 in. blade.   **A-115.00**

Officer's sword, by Emerson & Silver/Trenton, N.J., iron scabbard with fancy mounts. Presentation grade, engraved blade 31½ in. long.   **A-755.00**

Officer's sword, in mismatched metal scabbard, "U.S." on blade 33 in. long.   **A-125.00**

Officer's sword, U.S. Navy regulation, gilt metal mounts with eagle head pommel and ivory grip. Inscribed blade 32½ in. long.   **A-300.00**

Saber, U.S., Dragoon model 1840, "Ames/1851", with scabbard.   **D-85.00**

Staff Officer's sword, 1850, C.W. presentation inscription. Blade has small nicks, 31½ in. long.   **A-165.00**

Staff Officer's sword, by Horstmann, 1850 model.   **A-165.00**

Staff Officer's sword, by Ames, "U.S.", iron scabbard, engraved blade 31¾ in. long.   **A-205.00**

Staff Officer's sword, by Ames, with both iron scabbard and sword signed. Blade is 30 in. long.   **A-370.00**

Staff Officer's sword, by Horstmann Bros., engraved blade 29¼ in. long.   **A-125.00**

Sword, Russian Cossack, blade dated 1940, with scabbard.   **A-135.00**

Sword, Wilkinson, with scabbard.   **A-85.00**

Sword cane, bamboo holder, 25 in. blade.   **A-70.00**

Turkish short sword, wooden scabbard, brass hilt, 22 in. blade.   **A-65.00**

SAMPLERS

Sometimes also called "Samples", these early needleworks were made by girls as projects signifying they knew both sewing and their ABC's. Many date in the first part of the 19th Century, and a large number bear both name of maker and the date; religious motifs are common, along with sentimental poems. Most samplers are marketed in frames, and many of these in turn are both old and attractive. They are classified here by a major attribute.

Adam and Eve, with tree and serpent, dated 1797, 19 x 24 inches.   **A-300.00**

Adam and Eve, with birds and animals, "1822", 13¾ x 14¼.   A-150.00

Alphabet, "Washington/April 22nd 1815", 12 x 18 inches.   A-120.00

Alphabet and baskets of flowers, on homespun, 15 x 16½ inches.   A-220.00

Alphabet and birds, flowers and trees, "1865", 19 x 22 inches.   A-125.00

Alphabets and borders, partial genealogy, 1780's, 16¾ in. square.   A-250.00

Alphabets and butterflies, dated 1891, 16 x 17 inches.   A-10.00

Alphabets and flowers, dated 1821, 11 x 13 inches.   A-105.00

Alphabets and house, pine frame, no date, 23 x 23½ inches.   A-190.00

Alphabet and motto, bandings of animals and birds, 8½ in. square.   A-135.00

Alphabets and pine trees, modern grained frame, 15 x 17 inches.   A-130.00

Alphabets and poem, floral border, no date, 17¾ x 18¼ inches.   A-85.00

Alphabets and poems, colorful, "1862", 16¾ x 20½ inches.   A-185.00

Alphabets and prose passages, faded colors, "1831", 7 x 15½ inches.   A-80.00

Alphabets and sets of initials, "1872", 14 x 14½ inches.   A-25.00

Alphabets and two women, "1826", 11¼ x 16½ inches.   A-185.00

Alphabets and verse, pine frame, "1831", 12¾ x 16¼ inches.   A-460.00

Alphabet and verse, vining border, "1839", 19½ x 20½ inches.   A-215.00

Alphabets and verse, floral designs, 14½ x 17¾ inches.   A-160.00

Alphabets and willow trees, no date, 17½ x 18¾ inches.   A-95.00

Dog and tree, 1830's, name flanked by eagles, 9 x 18½ inches.   A-55.00

Exercise showing various stitches, old frame, 8 x 10¼ inches.   A-115.00

Floral border, religious phrases, "1825", 16¼ x 19 inches.   A-470.00

Flowers and birds, crowned angels, "1808", 14 x 18½ inches. **A-400.00**

Flowers and lions, parrots and maze, "1741", 8 x 12½ inches. **A-330.00**

House and tree, faded color, "1837", 15 x 18 inches. **A-65.00**

Panel and quotation, maple frame, no date, 12 x 16½ inches. **A-160.00**

Poem, framed, "1832", 15½ x 17 inches. **A-90.00**

Poem with animals, walnut frame, no date, 10¾ x 11½. **A-180.00**

Rare mourning sample, fine beadwork, 11 colors; young boy kneeling at a tomb. Dated 1855, initials, framed, 5½ x 8 inches. **D-450.00**

Religious poem, on homespun, "1835", framed, 14½ x 20 inches. **A-230.00**

SCALES

Balance scale, tin platforms, chain suspensions. **D-20.00**

Beam scale, heavy duty, taking weights up to 320 pounds; without weights. **D-18.50**

Brass-faced scale, polished, weights up to 28 pounds, "Frary Improved"; 1 in. long. **D-22.50**

Brass-faced scale, "Frary's Imported Spring Balance - Warranted", up to 25 pounds. **D-22.50**

Brass-faced scale, John Chatillon & Son, "Not Legal For Use In Trade"., 10 in. long. **D-18.50**

Brass-faced scale, with large iron spring between scale and hook, 13 in. long. **D-29.00**

Brass-faced scale, 120 pound capacity, with hook, 16 in. long. **A-19.00**

Cast iron, with brass scale bar, weights to 300 pounds. "The Plantation Scales/ARC Scale Co.", 28 in. high. **S-175.00**

Coffee counter scale, cast iron; 9 in. long, tin scale pan is 6½ x 11½ inches. **D-65.00**

Hanging scale, steel-faced, marked in metric kilos and pounds. By C. Forschner, New York. **D-25.00**

Jeweler's scale, marble top, porcelain balance pans, 16 in. long, 7 in. high. **S-75.00**

Postage scale, brass bar and pan, U. S. Post Office, 1955. **S-25.00**

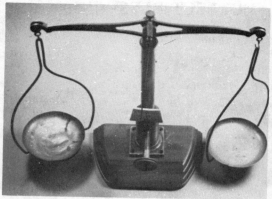

Scale, balance, arm and pan design. This came from an
old drug company, Midwest. All brass, marker face is
ivory; walnut base is not original, 8¼ in. high.
C/75-95

Brass-faced scales, three sizes, with top example 15 in.
long, overall.
Left, Texas Cotton Scale by Hanson, with 160-lb.
capacity. C/35-45
Top right, Landers Improved Balance No. 2. C/10-15
Lower right, cylinder scale, unmarked, brass face.
C/10-12

Round scale, metal case with brass face, 12 in. long. **D-20.00**

Spring hanging scale, "Chatillon's Improved",
weights up to 50 pounds, 13 in. long. **D-15.00**

Stillyard scale, "Whitmore/52", hooks and weight
complete. **D-18.50**

Stillyard scale, hooks and weight, 25 in. long. **S-22.00**

Scale weight, "C. I. Ball", held by thumbscrew, 4 in.
diameter. **D-5.00**

Weights, nickle-plated brass, 100 to 4000 mg., fitted
wooden box with advertising by Whiting Machine
Works, Mass. **D-25.00**

Weight scale, brass arm graduated to ounces, illegible label, tin platform. **S-25.00**

Additional: Scale catalog, by E. & T. Fairbanks & Co.,
Johnsbury, Vermont. Printed 1854, and 54 pages
describing and picturing the Fairbanks scale line.
Woodblock illustrations. **D-35.00**

SCHOOLHOUSE COLLECTIBLES—[See also Bells]

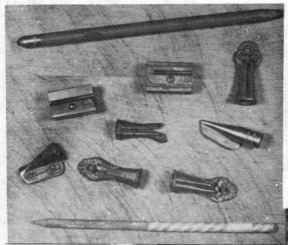

School collectibles.
Top, **pencil**, soft-graphite type. C/1-3
Bottom, **slate pencil**, original paper wrap. C/3-5

Sharpeners.
Four **cast-lead** examples, each: C/7-10
Two **conical**, steel, each: C/3-5
Two **rectangular**, top left, Brass, C/7-10
Top center, aluminum. C/4-7

Molded inkwells, each; fine. C/4-7
Non-spill ink, blown in mold. C/9-12
Dip pens, each: C/2-4

School slates.

Top, **double slate**, hinged, fair condition on edges, good slate. C/28-35
Left, **walnut-framed slate**, fine. C/20-25
Right, **lined slate**, fine condition. C/20-25

Book carrier, brass, wood and iron, braided twill straps.

D-16.00

Book carrier, metal with wooden handles, japanned, leather straps.

S-14.00

Chalk box, orig. label, wood, machine-dovetailed, 4 in. long.

D-9.00

Crayons, for "Blackboard Use". Chalk, six colors for 1¢.

D-1.50

Chalk and crayon boxes. Left, Japanned tin, "Excel-All / Dustless Crayons". C/9-12
Right, dovetailed wooden box, "Occupational Material for the Kindergarten", by Milton Bradley Co. C/15-20
Lower, dovetailed wooden box, "Old Faithful Colored Chalk", by American Crayon Company. C/15-20

Teaching aids, walnut wood, 3-dimensional.
Top, sectional, leather-strapped cylinder: C/30-40
Sectional, conical: C/25-35
Smaller, solid forms, each: C/4-8

Pencil boxes, light wood with paper-covered tops, in fair to good condition. Left to right:
Oriental C/12-15
Jack & Jill C/16-22
ABC (made in Germany) C/15-20
Geometric and floral C/12-15

Lunch bucket, oblong, old paint, wire handles, 9 in. long.	**D-25.00**
Lunch bucket, tin, folding; can slip into pocket, opens to 2¼ x 4¼ x 7¾ inches; dated 1908.	**D-22.00**
Schoolhouse key, nearly 6 in. long, folds to 3 inches.	**D-10.00**
Schoolmaster's desk, pine, turned legs, one dovetailed drawer, lift lid and gallery. Stencil decoration and dated 1853, 22 x 26½ x 38 in. high.	**A-350.00**
Schoolmaster's desk, pine, slant front, one drawer. Ca. 1820, 20 x 32 x 41 inches high.	**A-275.00**
Schoolmaster's desk, one long drawer, ca. 1860, 23 x 31 x 34 in. high.	**A-150.00**
Schoolmaster's desk, pine, lift-up lid, 24 x 27 x 38½ in. high.	**A-180.00**
School seat, folding, (no desk), dated 1916, 30½ in. high.	**A-20.00**
Schoolteacher's desk, on turned legs, walnut, 31¾ in. high.	**A-245.00**
Pencil box, painted wood with stenciled childhood scene, 9 in. long.	**D-14.00**
Pencil box, walnut, tray and lower compartment, 9¼ in. long.	**D-23.00**
Pencil case, tin, worn red paint with yellow stenciling, "A Present", 7½ in. long.	**A-17.50**
Pencil sharpener, conical with wide flat end, cast lead.	**D-4.50**
Pencil sharpener, cast brass, rectangular, 1 in. long.	**S-5.00**
Slate pencil, never used, ca. 1870, perfect condition.	**D-1.50**

SCOUTING MEMORABILIA

A variety of Scouting items are collectible today, especially earlier items. These range from badges to books, posters to patches. Considering the great number of persons who have been Scouts, and the positive publicity of the organization in this country, this may well be an under-collected field.

"Adventuring for Senior Scouts", 4/39, very good condition.	**D-7.00**
Air Scout manual, 6th prt., 10/43, fine.	**D-9.00**
Armband, Emergency Service Explorer.	**D-2.25**
Ash tray, Philmont Kit Carson House, good.	**D-4.50**
Baden-Powell portrait patch, National Office BSA.	**D-2.50**

The Boy Scout's Hike Book, N.Y.: Doubleday, 1913. D/20

The Boy's Camp Book, N.Y.: Doubleday, 1914. D/20

"Best From Boys' Life" comics, #4. **D-1.50**

Book of the Camp Fire Girls, "War Call to the Girls of America", 1917. **D-25.00**

Bookbinding Merit Badge pamphlet, 7/41, good. **D-2.50**

BSA membership card, 1928, three-fold. **D-3.00**

Boy Scout bugle, Rexcraft, chrome-plated, in dust bag; very good condition. **D-18.00**

Boy Scout ring, Tenderfoot emblem, sterling. **D-4.00**

Campaign hat, Scout leader's, in hat press. **D-6.50**

Community strip, red on khaki. **D-1.00**

Cub Scout Parent Orientation Chart. **D-1.50**

Dan Beard, "American Boys Book of Wild Animals", poor. **D-2.50**

Deep Sea Scout Handbook, England, 1933, good. **D-5.00**

Eagle Scout patch, square cut green khaki, very good. **D-12.00**

Explorer field cap, wings-anchor-compass emblem. **D-2.00**

First-Aid tin, Bauer & Black/BSA. Gray, original contents, 1932, good. **D-11.00**

Fishing permit/button, celuloid, 1973 National Jamboree. **D-5.00**

Forty-year Service pin.	**D-3.00**
The Game of Boy Scouts, Parker Bros. Complete, with instructions, 1912, very good.	**D-60.00**
Girl Scout Handbook, 3rd Edition, 9/30, very good.	**D-3.00**
Glass ash tray, with World Scouting emblem.	**D-3.50**
Handbook for Boys, 4th Edition, 38th prt., 9/45, fine.	**D-8.00**
Handbook for Scoutmasters, 1913-14, 1st (Jameson) Edition, fine.	**D-35.00**
Handbook for Skippers, 2nd Ed., 1st prt., 5/39, fine.	**D-8.00**
Lead figure, Scout signaller, 4 in. high, very good.	**D-10.00**
Lifeguard patch, very good.	**D-1.50**
Metal belt buckle, "Gilwell".	**D-12.50**
National Jamboree backpatch, 1960, mint.	**D-12.00**
National Jamboree lapel button, 1957.	**D-4.50**
National Jamboree map, 1964 (Sunoco).	**D-6.25**
National Jamboree neckerchief, 1957, used.	**D-11.00**
Nature Collections, Service Library, 1929, very good.	**D-3.50**
Norman Rockwell cover, "Scouting" magazine, 5/30, good.	**D-7.00**
Patrol medallions, complete unused set on red twill.	**D-30.00**
Philmont arrowhead patch (and) Philmont Story booklet.	**D-4.00**
Philmont award plaque, "We All Made It".	**D-10.00**
Philmont Bicentennial patch, 1976, very good.	**D-5.00**
Philmont neckerchief, red with gold border.	**D-2.00**
Pinback button, Italian National Scout Camp, 1978.	**D-4.50**
Region Seven metal slide, official.	**D-7.50**
Region Seven Tie-bar.	**D-7.50**
San Francisco Council heavy metal slide.	**D-2.50**
Schiff Scout Reservation, plastic slide.	**D-4.50**
Scout bank, Tin coin building-shaped bank, 3½ in. high. Good.	**D-40.00**
Scout Executive patch, wreath style, round-cut edge.	**D-7.50**
Scoutmaster's tie, narrow green.	**D-1.50**
Scout Musician patch, 1950's, used.	**D-1.75**
Scout Week paper poster, 1940, 18 x 26 inches, good.	**D-10.00**
Scout whistle, nickel-plated, current shape.	**D-4.00**
Scouting action photos, twelve, 18 x 24 inches. On heavy cardboard with easel backs. (Lot)	**D-20.00**
Sea Scout manual, 6th Ed., 4th prt., 10/43, good.	**D-4.00**
Southeast region patch, "Southeast", used.	**D-4.00**
Staff Management manual, 1941, fine.	**D-1.25**

Scout ring, sterling silver, ca. 1950.
C/9-15

Tenderfoot emblem, ½-inch pinback button. D-1.00
Troop charter, 1936. D-2.50
The Wolf Cubbook, 3/45, good. D-3.00
Wonderful World of Scouting coin, 1964 NY
World's Fair.
World Jamboree patch, Typhoon Refugee, 1971, D-8.00
mint.
Zippo lighter, with World Scouting emblem. D-5.00
D-5.00

SCRIMSHAW

Scrimshaw is the art of carving scenes or figures on whale teeth, and the making of small useful objects from whale "ivory" or whalebone. Sailors, the scrimshanders, passed the long, lonely hours at sea by making or decorating the objects as gifts for those at home, or for themselves.

Most scrimshaw objects date from the 1800's, the great days of the whaling vessels, when raw materials were easy to obtain.

Alphabet Set, each letter of the alphabet on whalebone blocks; complete with fine box inlaid with a
variety of wood.

D-195

Rare scrimshaw powder horn, 19 in. long. Has continuing scenes of eagle,
Boston harbor, whaling, fish, and four ships. Dated, 1836.   A/2300
Courtesy of Adam A. Weschler & Son

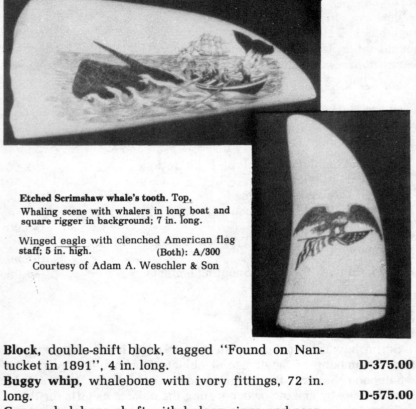

Etched Scrimshaw whale's tooth. Top,
Whaling scene with whalers in long boat and
square rigger in background; 7 in. long.

Winged eagle with clenched American flag
staff; 5 in. high.   (Both): A/300
Courtesy of Adam A. Weschler & Son

Block, double-shift block, tagged "Found on Nantucket in 1891", 4 in. long. — **D-375.00**

Buggy whip, whalebone with ivory fittings, 72 in. long. — **D-575.00**

Cane, whalebone shaft with baleen rings and rosewood section; mid-1800's, 33 in. long. — **D-245.00**

Jewelry box, inlaid with various woods, whale ivory heart in front center. Complete with tray, 12 in. long, 8 in. high. — **D-235,00**

Knife holder, etched scenes of deer in landscape, 20 in. long. — **A-110.00**

Pie crimper, popular scrimshaw item, also called "jogging wheel"; ivory, handle with "D" swordguard, 6 in. long — **D-425.00**

Pie crimper, ivory, very ornate, with heart cutouts, 5 in. long. — **D-795.00**

Plaque, miniature whaling tools in whalebone, 22 in. long. — **D-125.00**

Razor, whalebone handle with ship on one side and man's name on the other. — **D-50.00**

Razor case, leather and ropework, complete with scrimshaw whalebone straight razor.   **D-115.00**

Rope-block, walrus ivory, 2½ in. long   **D-150.00**

Seam-rubber, for creasing sails, 5 in. long. Old.   **D-150.00**

Seam-rubber, scrimshaw, of rosewood.   **D-85.00**

Swift, whalebone and ivory, red and black scribe line, 15 in. long. For yarn-winding.   **D-495.00**

Swift, whalebone with ivory fittings, 19 in. long.   **D-675.00**

Swift, pictured in "Scrimshaw and Scrimshanders", very well made and executed in detail.   **D-2,200.00**

Whale, miniature scrimshaw object, *not* antique, 6 in. long.   **D-75.00**

Whale tooth, with likeness of a lady, mid-1800's, 6½ in. high.   **D-325.00**

Whale tooth, Godey lady done with color tinting, reverse with scene of Fair Haven, good-size bull tooth.   **D-650.00**

Whale miniature, fine age coloring, 3 in. long.   **D-95.00**

SEWING

Button-hole cutter, iron, punch-type used with mallet.   **D-35.00**

Darning eggs, lot of two; one black, other white and red, wood.   **A-20.00**

Needle case, covered with crewel embroidery in four colors.   **A-98.00**

Needle case, German, maple wood, pincushion top, rotating needle dispenser below.   **D-18.50**

Needle holder, wood, urn-shape, pedestaled, 3 in. high.   **D-16.50**

Needle threader, and scissors sharpener; orig. cost, 1¢.   **D-1.00**

Pin case, turned wood, red, advertisement on bottom.   **D-4.50**

Pincushion, crochet pink heart with ribbon trim.   **D-2.00**

Pincushion, miniature basket, woven sweetgrass, 1½ in. high.   **D-8.50**

Pincushion, half-doll, miniature, Germany, yellow dress, 1 3/8 in. high.   **D-30.00**

Pincushion, beaded, loop-fringed, "Niagara Falls" in beads, ca. early 1900's, 3½ in. high.   **D-25.00**

Pincushion, turned wood case, pink tape around green cushion.   **D-10.00**

Pincushion, velvet top, black trim, double spool compartment. **D-27.50**

Pincushion, wood, clamps to table, cushion 2¼ x 5 inches. **D-20.00**

Pincushion, embroidered face of girl with large hat, ca. 1900. **D-3.50**

Pincushion doll, blonde hair, porcelain, sateen cushion, 5 in. high. **C-25.00**

Scissors basket, sweetgrass, Indian-made for tourists, 2¼ in. long. **D-12.50**

Scissors, button-hole, "Ideal", 1885 patent. **D-9.50**

Scissors, stork, with head of person for maker's mark, unusual, 3½ in. long. **D-15.00**

Scissors, stork, "Germany", lightly gilted feathers, 4½ in. long. **D-12.00**

Sewing bird, polished brass, feathers deeply embossed, pincushion pad at top, patented 1853. **D-85.00**

Sewing book, by Clarks O.N.T. Spool Cotton Co., illustrated, 1935. **D-5.00**

Sewing box, pine, two-tiered; lower with single drawer, top with lift-opening for eight spindles, 7 in. long. **D-32.50**

Sewing box, wood, two tiers of thread-holders, whale bone tops to spindles. Painted black with colored flowers, 12½ in. high. **A-130.00**

Sewing box, wood, lift-out compartment, black lacquer, 8¼ in. long. **A-15.00**

Sewing box, golden oak, machine dovetailed corners, lift top exposes 20 spool holders. Box is 3 x 12 x 12 inches. **A-60.00**

Sewing box, Victorian, folk art decoration, two drawers, hand-painted, with lower tier 7 x 10 inches. **D-75.00**

Sewing box, with six-spool thread caddy on top, 8 in. high. **D-42.50**

Sewing box, with Victorian "gingerbread", black walnut with inlays of light wood, eight spool holders, 8½ in. square. **D-60.00**

Sewing box, single-drawer, rounded, with combination spool holder and velvet cushion, 5½ in. square. **D-65.00**

Sewing box, wood, one-drawer, will hold six spools, old green wash over white, 4¼ x 4½ x 7½ inches. **A-90.00**

Sewing cabinet, three-tiered, double lift top, footed, ca. 1880, bottom 6 in. square, middle 4½ in. square. **D-65.00**

Sewing clamp, whalebone, 2¾ in. long. A-50.00

Sewing giveaway, "The Home Needle Case", lithographed, ca. 1920. D-3.50

Sewing lamp, glass, zipper pattern, pale blue with cobalt blue frilled top chimney, blown cobalt chimney, lamp 17½ in. high. D-175.00

Sewing novelty, oak, with four attached spools, two on a side. D-8.50

Sewing stand, two-tiered, top lifts off to reveal eight spindles. D-54.00

Sewing stand, eight-shelf, American, late 19th Century. A-50.00

Sewing table, Empire, mahogany, rectangular top above three long drawers raised on square tapered legs on platform base. Ormolu mounts, 13 x 19 x 28 inches. A-350.00

Sewing tape, reverse advertising "Our Native Herbs", 36 in. long. D-8.50

Sewing tree, for thimble holder, maple, three-tiered, revolving, takes 19 thread spools. Top post with holder, 8½ in. high. D-49.50

Sock darner, wood, double-ended, shaped like dumbbell. D-4.50

Spool holder, blond maple, circular, pincushion top, 6½ in. diameter. D-30.00

Spool stand, one long drawer and 27 spindles, pegged into top. Dark pine, dated 1911, 3¾ x 5 x 10 inches. D-49.50

Stocking darner and needle holder, handle unscrews for needles. D-8.50

Thread caddy, pincushion top, two levels, midsection with guidewires, underside revolving tin disc. D-30.00

Thread and thimble holder, mahogany, holders are handwrought nails, 5½ in. high. D-32.00

Thimble, gold plated, script initials, size 7. D-27.50

Thimble, sterling, paneled border and concentrics, size 9. D-15.00

Thimble, sterling, wide band of six panels with concentrics. D-12.50

Thimble, sterling, embossed concentrics, size 11. D-16.50

Thimble, sterling, quilting; open-topped, unusual. D-15.00

Thimble, sterling, plain band on tip of concentric band. D-16.50

SHAKER PIECES

Shaker pieces have long been admired and collected, and for several valid reasons. They specialized in hand-gathering the best available materials and the finished object was shaped with loving care and great attention to details. Design is both simple and pure; each piece is invariably esthetically complete. This is so whether the object was made for the Shakers' own use, or was an item intended for sale to the surrounding community.

Ash-carrier, sheet iron with wrought handle, 22 in. long. **D-35.00**

Basket, splint, square bottom, round mouth, 7½ in. high. **D-130.00**

Basket, picnic, black ash splint, 6 in. high. **D-85.00**

Basket, egg, carved handle, 2½ x 4 in. bottom, 5 in. high. **D-69.50**

Basket-strainer, woven cane, 14½ in. high. **A-235.00**

Bonnet, woven, black cloth binding and shawl, 10 in. high. **A-10.00**

Bottle, ink, green; Canterbury, 9½ in. high. **A-20.00**

Box, candy, "Flagroot", cardboard, East Canterbury, N.H. **D-10.00**

Box mold, for making fingerlap bentwood boxes. Hardwood, oval, 8 inches. **D-45.00**

Box, nut, "Sugared nuts... Prepared by the Shakers", cardboard. **D-10.00**

Box, pantry, satin-lined, copper nails, lapped, 7 5/8 inches. **D-55.00**

Box, dovetailed construction, 6 x 7½ x 12 inches. **D-55.00**

Box, storage, lid is repaired, oval, 9 in. long. **A-60.00**

Box, storage, stitched joints, old green paint, 6 in. long. **A-47.50**

Bucket, multi-banded, handled, open, 8¾ x 11 inches. **D-102.00**

Bucket, interwoven laps, high ears, handled, 7 x 8¾ inches. **D-105.00**

Butter scales, wood platforms and bar, repaired split, 24½ in. high. **D-100.00**

Carpet beater, North family, Mt. Lebanon, authenticated. **D-50.00**

Chair, side, ladderback, high seat, front posts 18½ in. high. **A-235.00**

Chair, side, ladderback, three slats and turned finials.   **A-230.00**

Chair, ladderback youth's, simple turned finials; Hancock.   **A-160.00**

Chair, ladderback, for sliding under table; rush seat.   **A-280.00**

Chair, ladderback youth's, ¾ in. of one finial replaced.   **A-55.00**

Churn, Maine colony, square, wooden, 23 in. high.   **D-195.00**

Clothes hanger, one-piece handcarved honey maple, Canterbury.   **D-22.50**

Coffee pot, tin, attributed to Enfield, 6½ in. high.   **A-25.00**

Cupboard, pine and tin, rebuilt drawers, 17½ in. wide.   **A-525.00**

Cupboard, pine and basswood, three drawers. Turned ball feet, simple moldings and beaded door frames. Orig. wooden knobs; from Maine or Groveland, 16 x 41½ x 79 inches.   **A-1,500.00**

Drying rack, mortised and pegged, three bars, shoe feet, 48 in. high.   **A-50.00**

Footstool, needs new tape or splint seat, 9 x 10 x 12½ in.   **D-24.00**

Funnel, tin, braced handle, hanging ring, 12¾ in. high.   **D-30.00**

Hamper, loom room, ash splint, oval, ca. 1850, 22¾ in. long.   **D-125.00**

Keg, interwoven laps, age-darkened, 9 in. diameter, 7½ in. long.   **D-132.00**

Lamp filler, tin, side-handled, 5½ diameter, 6 in. high.   **D-65.00**

Mailing label, pre-1917, for Canterbury products and catalogs.   **D-7.50**

Mirror, retiring room, cherry on pine frame, 8½ x 10½ inches.   **A-85.00**

Peg board, pine, nine turned hanging pegs, 9.35 feet long.   **A-105.00**

Reed splitter, wood, iron and brass, for making bonnets.   **D-25.00**

Rocker, armchair, childsize, woven-tape seat, size "O".   **A-380.00**

Rocker, ladderback, four slats and turned finials, rush seat.   **A-230.00**

Rolling pin, one-piece birch, groove rolling surface ends, 19 in. long.   **D-39.00**

Sewing basket, oval, reversible swing top, 4 x 6¼ x 8¾ inches. **D-125.00**

Sewing basket, black ash splint, scissor loop, 7¼ x 11½ inches. **D-135.00**

Sewing basket, oval, bentwood, "Sabbath Day Lake/-Maine" stamp; lid missing, 6¼ x 9¼ inches. **D-95.00**

Stove tools, wrought iron, Canterbury, set of three. Authentic. **D-150.00**

Towel bar, tapering cherry rod mortised into pine block, 41 in. long. **A-195.00**

Transom opener, maple, brass window hook 35½ in. long. **D-21.50**

Yarn swift, standing, Tyringham, 39¼ in. high. **A-95.00**

SHEET MUSIC

Printed single-title music sheets, generally for piano and voice, may be a "sleeper" collecting field. Value determinants include the popularity of the song and the performer(s), and, to some extent, the age of the piece.

Condition is extremely important, and tears, stains and missing sections adversely affect value. Cover illustrations pertaining to the performer and/or subject matter of the music contribute to value.

Written by Al Jolson and Saul Chaplin, this tune from the 1946 motion picture of The Jolson Story is valued at about $3 by collectors and dealers.

Written by Mana-Zucca. 1919. 2-2.50

341

Written by Irving Berlin. 2-2.50

Written by Benny Davis and Harry Akst, 1926. 2-2.50

All I Have To Do Is Dream, Everly Brothers (picture) D-2.50
Andante Con Moto, plain cover. D-1.00
A Blossom Fell, (Boy and girl holding hands) D-1.50
Bonnie Rose, Hetty Urma (picture) D-3.00
Careless Love, Lena Horne (picture) D-2.50
Comin' In On a Wing And a Prayer, Eddie Cantor (picture) D-4.00
Dear Old Daddy Long Legs, Mary Pickford (picture) D-5.00
Desertland, Delyle Alda (picture) D-3.00
Every Little Movement, Lina-Abar Banell (picture) D-3.00
I'm Making Believe, Goodman-Darnell-Oakie-Bart D-3.00
Little Girl Blue, Day-Boyd-Durante-Kaye (picture) D-2.50
Little Lady Make Believe, Dorothy Lamour (picture) D-2.50
Marching Along Together, Kate Smith (picture) D-1.50
Melody in 'F', Anton Rubinstein (plain cover) D-1.50
Memories Song, (tall lamp) D-1.50
Rebecca of Sunny Brook Farm, Lysa Graham (picture) D-3.00
Remember, Irving Berlin (picture) D-3.00
Shades of Night, (Lovers overlooking bay) D-1.50
Smilin' Through, Souvenir Edition; Norma Talmadge (picture) D-3.00
Some Sunday Morning, Brice and Kine (picture) D-3.00
Sweetheart of All My Dreams, Thirty Seconds Over Tokyo, Johnson-Tracy-Thaxter D-2.50

That Old Girl of Mine, Margaret Flavin (picture) D-3.00
The Third Man Theme, The Third Man; Cotten-Valli-Welles D-2.50
To Love Again, The Eddy Duchin Story; Power-Novak (picture) D-2.50
The Twelfth of Never, Johnny Mathis, (picture) D-1.50
Underneath the Stars, (Fountain in park) D-1.50
When I Dream of You, Dora Pelletier (picture) D-3.00
Wild Flower, musical play; Hammerstein D-1.50
A Wonderful Thing, framed song, cover only; Clara Kummer D-2.00
Yearning Just For You, Glenn C. Smith's Paramount Orchestra; (picture) D-2.50

SHOOTING ACCOUTREMENTS

Technically, these are the equipments other than arms and dress issued to soldiers, so the term is military in origin. However, it has also come to mean items pertaining to civilian shooting and firearms.

Ammunition box, wood, label reads "Winchester Black Powder Shells"; machine dovetailed, ca. 1873. D-20.00
Bullet mold, cast steel, for cal. 100 (one-inch) projectile. D-35.00
Bullet mold, for round ball .50 caliber, steel, Civil War era. D-27.50
Bullet mold, solid brass, .45 caliber, pincer action, 4½ inches. D-31.50
Bullet mold, conical ball, iron, pliers type, 5 in. long. D-8.00
Bullet mold, conical ball, iron, pliers, 6 in. long. D-10.00
Bullet mold, "Ideal", detachable casting block, cal. .467. D-12.00
Bullet mold, for Remington pocket pistol, iron. D-35.00
Cannon ramrod, old, wood, brass and iron, 37 in. long. D-45.00

Reloading tool, cast iron with brass fittings, wooden handle knob. Unmarked, 11 in. extreme length. Used to crimp shotgun shells. C/16-22

Shooting bag, powderhorn, priming horn for a flintlock rifle. C/75-100

Left, **shooting accoutrements**. Clockwise from top: **Ammunition block**, handworked maple, for fifty .22 cartridges. Poss. for competitive target shooting, 3 x 4¾ inches. C/12-16
Bullet bag, handcarved wooden spout, linen pouch with several lead balls inside. C/7-12
Patch knife, used with muzzle-loading rifles to size patches around ball, antler handle, very old. C/25-35
Primer discs, for Winchester center-fire cartridges, for hand reloading. Original marked tin box. C/11-15

Cartridge pouch, Civil War, missing tin, leather, pistol size.   D-25.00

Cartridge pouch, Civil War, for musket, "U.S.", with tins.   D-45.00

Case, walnut, for matching pistols; 5¼ x 10½ x 11¾ inches.   A-25.00

Gun parts, unlabeled wooden box of one hundred, plus.   D-12.00

Hunting pouch, with powder horn, leather, tin cap boxes, bullet mold, etc.   D-85.00

Powder flask, "Am. F. & C. Co.", large, leather-covered.   A-30.00

Powder flask, brass, embossed hanging game scene, "Dixon".   D-85.00

Powder flask, copper, "G. & J.W. Hawksley", 8 in. high.   A-55.00

Powder flask, copper, embossed with ivy leaf decoration.   A-65.00

Powder flask, "Dixon/Sheffield", leather-covered.   A-30.00

Powder flask, shell pattern, with charger.   A-15.00

Powder flask, pistol, shell pattern.   A-40.00

Powder flask, small, plain brass, "Hawksley".   A-20.00

Powder flask, "Dixon", lacquered, with cord.   A-32.50

Powder measure, hollowed section of deer antler, 3 in. long.   D-15.00

Percussion caps, tin box of 100, copper, ca. 1873.   D-14.00

Powder horn, with simple carved details at nozzle, 12 in. long.   A-20.00

Powder horn, curved, notched cap, charger, 10 in. long. **A-35.00**

Powder horn, wood base and plug, 11 in. long. **D-20.00**

Powder horn, scrimshaw folk art carving, various western scenes including birds, animals and Indian tepees; ca. French and Indian War era. **D-400.00**

Powder horn, very rare piece with folk art map of New England. Well curved, etched scrimshaw details, ca. 1635-1700, 15 in. long. **D-600.00**

Powder horn, pewter, Continental, simple tooled designs, 13 in. long. **A-40.00**

Reloading tool, "Winchester cal. .32 W.C.F./Pat. Oct. 20, 1874". **D-20.00**

Reloading tool, "Winchester cal. .40-60 W.C.F./Pat. Sept. 14, 1880". **D-20.00**

Scope, Winchester rifle model A5, Pat. 1909, complete with mounts. **A-25.00**

Shot cabinet, for dispensing lead shot, eight compartments, 16 in. high. **D-155.00**

Shot flask, brass and copper, "J. Matthewman", 10 in. long. **A-35.00**

SILVER—Coin

Bowl, sugar; hollow handles, embossed floral bands and basket of fruit finial. Monogrammed and dated 1821; by Peter Chitry, New York, 1815-1836. Bowl 9¼ in. high. **A-235.00**

Bowl, urn-shaped; covered, monogrammed, 10¼ in. high. **A-600.00**

Creamer, embossed bands of thistles, acorns and foliaged. Marked "B. C. Frobisher", monogrammed, 7¼ in. high. **A-275.00**

Creamer, marked "Moore and Ferguson", monogrammed, 7 in. high. **A-350.00**

Knife, butter; marked "Fessenden/Pure Coin", monogrammed, 6¾ in. long. **A-12.50**

Ladle, soup; American in old English pattern, ca. 1800. **A-325.00**

Ladle, soup; American in Fiddle pattern. By Nathaniel Munroe, Baltimore, ca. 1830. **A-100.00**

Spoon, master salt; English, fiddle handle, hallmarked, just over 3 in. long. **D-15.00**

Spoon, serving; name-marked, 8¾ in. long. **A-20.00**

Spoon, serving; name-marked, monogrammed, 9 in. long.　　　　　　　　　　　　　　　　　　　　　**S-35.00**

Spoons, soup; pair. American Fiddle pattern, by R. & W. Wilson, Philadelphia, ca. 1820.　　　　　　　**A-60.00**

Tablespoon, tipped Fiddle, initialed, by Kimball & Gould.　　　　　　　　　　　　　　　　　　　　**D-15.00**

Tablespoons, two, "E. Kinsey" and monogrammed, 7¼ in. long.　　　　　　　　　　　　　　　　　　**A-35.00**

Tablespoons, two, "Palmer Bachelders & Co.", 7¼ in. long.　　　　　　　　　　　　　　　　　　　　**A-22.50**

SILVER—*Plated*

Candelabras, English three-light, pair; height, 16 inches.　　　　　　　　　　　　　　　　　　　**A-200.00**

Candleabras, five-light, pair; removable tops to form single candlesticks. By Gorham & Co., 22 in. high.　**A-250.00**

Dish, serving; Sheffield hors d'oeuvre. Dome top with removable lid on hot water base, ca. 1810.　　**A-125.00**

Dish, warming; English, double. Gadroon border, two covered entree dishes on rectangular stand with spirit burner, 16 in. long.　　　　　　　　　　**A-175.00**

Fish set, Victorian; with 12 knives and 12 forks, each with reeded ivory handles and engraved blades. Encased, 24 pieces.　　　　　　　　　　　　　　**A-320.00**

Wick trimmers, silver-plated scissors type, 6¾ in. long.　　　　　　　　　　　　　　　　　　　　**A-55.00**

Salt-and-pepper shakers, individual, silver-plated, 1 in. high, set of four.　　　　　　　　　　　　Set: C/15-20

Match-box holder, silver plate over brass, Lion crest, "H.M. Grace Affie", three unknown touchmarks; 2¾ x 5 inches.　　　　　　　　　　　　　　　　　　　C/20-35

Bud vase, silver-plated, 5 in. high. C/9-15

SILVER—*Sterling*

Basket, sugar; George III, by A. Calame, London, 1777. Vase form, shaped beaded rim, stylized pierced body with oval medallions interlocked with festoons. Height 5 inches, weight 5½ oz.　　A-350.00

Beaker, touchmarked "W. H. -90", engraved presentation message, 5 in. high.　　A-285.00

Bowls, covered, pair; American, inverted pear shape with slightly flared incised grooved rims, raised on step dome base. Separate top with gadroon lip and urn-melon finial. Ca. 1790, weight 20 oz., 7¼ in. high.　　A-700.00

Bowl, footed; Italian, oval, tapered swirl body raised on trifid double scroll feet. Ca. 1771, 5½ in. long.　　A-120.00

Candlesticks, pair; George II style, French, retailed by San Francisco firm. Octagonal baluster form stem on step base, 10¼ in. high.　　A-450.00

Chocolate pot, repousse; by Dominic & Haff, ca. 1903, 9 in. high.　　A-225.00

Coffee set, after-dinner; by Gorham & Co. Coffee pot, covered sugar, and creamer, 24 oz. weight, three pieces.　　A-170.00

Cruet stand, eight-bottle; George III. Eight assorted cut crystal bottles, London, 1810.　　A-270.00

Desk accessories, Baltimore repousse, late 19th Century. Five piece lot.　　A-105.00

Courtesy of Adam A. Weschler & Son

Left to right:
George III silver teapot, 6 in. high, by Henry Chawner, London, 1792.
　　A/425
George III silver covered urn, 14½ in. high, by Thomas Graham, London, 1792.
　　A/450
George III silver teapot, 7 in. high, maker's mark "WH/DW". London, 1766.
　　A/600

Left bottom, **Sterling oval meat platter.** Pierced repousse border, 18½ in. long, by Gorham. Weight 53 oz.   A/425

Right top, **sterling rococo style footed monteith.** Height, 13 inches, weight 68 oz. Wallace Silversmiths. ca. 1900.   A/625

Right, **Sterling flat table service,** Old Newbury Crafters, handwrought Moulton pattern. Service totals 99 pieces.   A/650

Courtesy of Adam A. Weschler & Son

Sterling three-piece after dinner coffee set and round tray. Consists of coffee pot, creamer, sugar and tray. Total weight 48 oz.   A/500

American silver two-handle covered sugar and creamer, 34 oz. weight. By Peter Chitry, New York, ca. 1814.   A/300

Courtesy of Adam A. Weschler & Son

Left and center, **French silver covered sugar bowl and undertray.** Bowl
5 in. high, and with Paris First Standard Mark. A/450
Right, **French silver side handle coffee pot,** 5½ in. high. Paris First
Standard Mark. A/550

American sterling five-piece silver tea service, with hot water kettle on
spirit burner base, teapot, covered two-handle sugar, creamer and
waste bowl. By Frank Whiting, "Strasbourg" pattern. A/700

Courtesy Adam A. Weschler & Son, Washington, D.C.; photographs by
Breger & Associates.

Dish, bonbon; 5 in. diameter, 4 in. high.   **A-60.00**

Dishes, butter; set of six.   **A-70.00**

Dish, meat; George III, by Wakelin & Taylor, London, 1776. Oval-shaped and gadroon borders with engraved armorial crest, 20 in. long.   **A-950.00**

Dish, sweetmeat; Dutch, round, footed. With five etched crystal compartments, early 19th Century.   **A-100.00**

Dishes, vegetable; pair. Shaped rims with tapered reeded corners, 8¾ in. long.   **A-150.00**

Fish slice, American, fiddle handle. By John B. Jones & Co., Baltimore, ca. 1840.   **A-100.00**

Flagon, American Victorian, ca. 1860. Eastlake style with applied portrait medallions, one inscribed, surrounded by scrolling and leafage design. Hinged dome lid, 10½ in. high.   **A-800.00**

Fork, pickle, Joan of Arc, 4½ in. long.   **D-10.00**

Funnel, wine; George IV, prob. by John Angell, London, 1826. Removable strainer with gadroon and applied shell border, body with armorial crest, multilobe decoration. Length 5½ inches.   **A-475.00**

Goblet, George III, by John Emes, London, 1804. Beaded stringing and bright-cup lip on plain urn-shaped body, 5¾ in. high.   **A-250.00**

Goblet, American, by Hayden, Louisville, Kentucky, ca. 1840. The plain urn-shaped body with beaded lip and step dome base, 5½ in. high.   **A-225.00**

Grater, nutmeg; George III, Irish. By David Peter, Dublin, 1763. Repousse inverted pear shape on round base, 1½ in. high.   **A-280.00**

Knife, butter; presentation piece. Blade embossed the full length with attractive motifs, elaborate handle, initials.   **D-17.50**

Ladle, soup; by George Baker, Providence, R.I., ca. 1825. In fiddle pattern.   **A-100.00**

Ladle, soup, very plain example with curved handle, 11 in. long.   **D-60.00**

Ladle, toddy; English, twisted whalebone handle, ca. 1820.   **A-125.00**

Master salts, pair; George II, London, 1773-1774, with cobalt crystal liners.   **A-90.00**

Mug, George III, by Hester Bateman, London, 1780. Baluster-shape body with leaf-capped double scroll handle, slightly flared lip, molded pedestal base. Weight 10 oz., 5½ in. high.   **A-1,600.00**

Pitcher, water; repousse, four-pint size, 20 oz. weight.   A-175.00

Rattle, baby's; sterling, hollow, 5 in. long.   A-32.50

Server, pie or cake, excellent condition.   D-15.00

Service, coffee-tea; four-piece, by B. Gardiner, New York. Coffee pot, teapot, covered two-handle sugar and creamer. Each with multilobe floral repousse body raised on stepped dome base with gadroon waist, ca. 1840.   A-2,600.00

Skewers, corn, pair; ornate, heavy.   D-12.50

Spoon, baby's; has the curled finger loop handle.   D-10.00

Table plateau, American, repousse, by Jacobi & Jenkins, with mirror inset. Silver weight 23 oz., 12½ in. diameter.   A-225.00

Service, table; flat, Wallace "ROSE Point" pattern, ca. 1934. The usual pieces, plus bouillon spoons, master butter knife, sugar spoon and salt spoons. Total, 83 pieces.   A-825.00

Teapot, George III, London hallmark, 1813. Gadroon rim above fluted and reeded neck on melon-shape body with scroll and chased work handle on ball, feet, 6 in. high.   A-375.00

Teaspoon set, three teaspoons marked "A. Stowell & Co."   D-29.00

Teaspoons, six; George III, by Peter & William Bateman, London, 1808. Bright-cut engraved decorations.   A-170.00

Toast racks, pair; Edward VII, by William Hutton & Sons, London, 1903. Total weight 12 oz.   A-260.00

Tongs, George III, by Hester Bateman, London, ca. 1780, bright-cut decorated.   A-150.00

Tongs, asparagus; George III, by Randall Chatterton, London, ca. 1825, in plain pattern.   A-180.00

Tray, oval, Gorham, 60 oz. silver, 20 in. long.   A-360.00

Tray, service, two-handle; Baltimore, by A. E. Warner, Baltimore, Maryland, ca. 1820. Raised and gadroon border with engraved decoration, interior with armorial crest with leaf and grape framing on bright-cut rosette ground. Weight 192 oz., 34 in. long.   A-2,750.00

Tureen, Gorham, Adam style, 38 oz.   A-375.00

Water kettle, tilting, repousse, by Dominic and Haff. Ca. 1903, weight 73 oz.   A-400.00

SNUFF CONTAINERS

Agate bottle, carnelian stopper, 19th Century, 2¾ in. high.
A-75.00

Amethyst crystal, jadeite stopper, 19th Century, bottle.
A-80.00

Box, enameled; cobalt blue with white bird on lid, 1¾ in. long.
A-130.00

Carved glass, Peking, red-to-white, four sennin with disciples boarding boats on waves.
A-250.00

Cloisonne, double-bottle, 19th Century, millefleur decoration.
A-150.00

Cloisonne, flask-shape, noir with dragon and bat decorations.
A-100.00

Enamel, double-bottle, famille jaune ground with four medallions with female figures.
A-130.00

Hardstone, carved black-to-coral fish in waves.
A-70.00

Hornbill, carved; salamander side panels, engraved landscape with boat front panel, agate stopper, signed.
A-200.00

Ivory, carved, ivory stopper, floral motif, 1 7/8 in. high.
S-125.00

Jade, Oriental, double gourd-shaped with bat and leaf decoration.
A-125.00

Jade, pebble-shaped bottle, jade stopper, 19th Century.
A-50.00

Jade, carved, Chinese, silver band base and top set with coral and turquoise shell, 3¼ in. high.
A-140.00

Lacquered, flask form, for Persian market, overlay of gold, silver and mother-of-pearl.
A-50.00

Malachite, gilt etching of two ladies and Emperor, gold aventurine stopper, 19th Century.
A-160.00

Lapis lazuli, in form of T'ang warhorse, 19th Century.
A-170.00

Peking glass, interior painting of landscape with pagoda, signed on shoulder with red seal, tiger-eye stopper.
A-250.00

Porcelain, Chinese, blue and white, landscape with fishermen, malachite stopper, 18th Century.
A-110.00

Silver, Chinese, relief decorations of fish in waves, turquoise inset decorations with coral stopper, 19th Century.
A-130.00

SODA FOUNTAIN COLLECTIBLES

There has always been an interest in certain fountain collectibles, like the tables and chairs used to decorate the home. Now collector interest has focused on nearly anything once used in soda parlors, from advertisements to ceiling fans.

Ice cream dishes, metal, set of five. D-10.00
Malted milk dispenser, "CARNATION", milk glass with tin lid. D-60.00
Mug, "DAD'S ROOT BEER", heavy clear embossed glass. D-6.00
Soda glasses, bell top, old pressed glass. Per each: D-2.50
Straw-holder, sterling, excellent condition. D-45.00
Syrup dispenser, "BUCKEYE ROOT BEER", china, white letters on black. D-325.00
Syrup dispenser, "HIRES ROOT BEER", china, hourglass shape. D-350.00
Syrup dispenser, "MISSION LIME", green glass top, no lid. D-75.00
Syrup dispenser, "NESBITS", pink frosted glass, date 5/22/26. D-50.00
Table, "wire" legs, fair condition. D-75.00
Table and two chairs, "wire" legs and backs, matched set. C-225.00
Unusual set: Ice cream parlor advertising, Fro-Joy Ice Cream. Nickel-silver sundae dishes, wooden ice cream spoons, hot chocolate pot. Total of 27 pieces, all marked. D-145.00

Ice cream collectibles.
Wooden spoons, festival, group: C/2-3
Metal spoons, mold-pressed, group, 30 spoons. C/12-16
Ice-cream self-release scoop, thumb-operated, brass band, wood handle. C/25-35

Above, **Soda fountain items.** Left and right, early aluminum counter holders for paper cups.
Each: C/2-3
Glass fountain cold-drink container, old nickel size.
C/3-6

Ice cream dippers;
cast metal.   C/6
wood and metal.   C/16

SOUVENIR SPOONS

Baltimore, in fancy script in bowl, silver-plated.   **D-8.50**

Battleship Maine, silver-plated, "Homer/Boston", 4½ in. long.   **D-10.00**

Battleship Maine, silver-plated, "Destroyed Feb 15, 1898".   **D-8.50**

Bremen, brass, crown over crest with key handle, 4¼ in. long.   **D-6.50**

Bridgehampton, sterling, "1856-1956", bridge on bowl, 5 in. long.   **D-12.00**

Columbian Exposition, quadruple plate, teaspoon, ornate.   **D-11.50**

Cruiser Olympia, silver-plated, "May 1, 1898/Manila".   **D-10.00**

Detroit, sterling, shell motif handle and entwined vine.   **D-12.50**

Souvenir spoons, bottom example with gold-washed bowl, all sterling. Each: C/20-30

Lachine Rapids, Montreal; sterling master salt spoon.   D-14.50

London, sterling, openwork crest with lion, hallmarked.   D-13.50

Machias, Maine; sterling, ornate handle with state shield.   D-15.00

Munchen, (Munich), sterling, figural maid, 5½ in. long.   D-13.50

New Haven, sterling master salt spoon, floral handle, 4 in. long.   D-14.50

Norfolk, VA; sterling, fleur-de-lis on handle tip, 4 in. long.   D-14.50

Paris, sterling, shield in crown of Paris, 4½ in. long.   D-12.00

Portland, ME; sterling, scroll in bowl, 4 in. long.   D-15.00

State Normal School, (Keene, N.H.), sterling with gold-washed bowl. Ornate figural handle with many motifs.   D-24.50

University of Wisconsin, sterling, gold wash, 5¾ in. long.   D-15.00

Washington's Mansion, (Mt. Vernon), sterling, English hallmark, 5½ in. long.   D-10.00

White Sulphur Springs, sterling, hammered handle, 5½ in. long.   D-12.50

SPORTING GOODS

Bear trap, cast and wrought iron, "No. 15" on trippan, 35 in. long.   A-145.00

Bicycle lamp, carbide, Germany, aluminum reflecter, 6 in. high.   D-33.00

Bicycle trumpet horn, rubber squeeze bulb, 6¾ in. long.   D-5.00

Boat pump, wood with brass faucet tap, 36 in. long.   D-27.50

Camping stove, tin, wire handles, brass-plated burner, 4 in. diameter.   D-15.00

Child's sled, wooden including runners, paint traces, 30 in. long. **A-45.00**

Cricket box, tin, green paint, perforated lid and extension for fastening to fisherman's belt; 3½ in. long. **D-13.00**

Cricket cage, copper, square, sheet top and bottom, screen sides, round opening with lid at top. **D-47.50**

Eel light, tin, strap bail handle, wick tube with wick, 6 in. long. **D-47.50**

Eel spear, hand-forged iron, seven tines, all barbed, 7 in. long. **C-25.00**

Falconer's chain glove, leather one side, thumb in chain mail. **D-24.00**

Folding cup, bicyclist's, brass, 1897, folding handles, 3 in. high. **D-14.50**

Folding tumbler, bicyclist's, black souvenir transfer image. **D-5.00**

Fish decoy, carved wood, bluegill with tack eyes and metal fins, 9 in. long. **A-150.00**

Fish decoy, carved wood, perch, by Miles Smith; 9 in. long. **A-220.00**

Fish decoy, wood body, metal fins and tail, old paint, 7¾ in. long. **A-52.50**

Fish decoy, green, 10 in. long. **S-20.00**

Fishing reel, circular, fly-casting type, black metal, 4 in. diameter. **D-9.00**

Fishing reel, bait-casting type, solid brass, no gears. **D-28.00**

Fish reel winder, all wood, drum with handle, 6 x 12 inches. **D-25.00**

Fishing rod basket, wicker, Victorian, oval, hinged, 40 in. long. **D-55.00**

Fishing rod holder, cast iron, pat. date 1888, with clamp. **D-11.50**

Fish-spearing light, tin, long wooden handle, three wicks, from Maine; 13 in. wide. **D-85.00**

Ice skates, pair, wood with steel runners, brass heel and toe plates. **D-18.00**

Ice skates, pair, early wood and iron with upturned blade tips. **A-42.50**

Lobster bait hook, old wooden handle, New England. **D-16.50**

Pigeon carrier, tin, old green paint, 14 in. long. **A-35.00**

Shooter's seat, monolegged, folding, prob. British. **D-55.00**

Snowshoes, set, orig. webbing in place, ca. 1880. **D-45.00**

Tennis racket, old, four different woods in construction.　　　　　　　　　　　　　　　　　　**D-14.50**

Walking stick, carved ivory horsehead handle, silver fittings, ebony shaft.　　　　　　　　　　　　**D-325.00**

Wheelman's medal, bronzed, dated 1895, 1¼ x 1½ inches.　　　　　　　　　　　　　　　　　　**D-19.00**

STOVES

Boat stove, "Shipmate's", oven and cooktop, restored.　　　　　　　　　　　　　　　　　　　**S-895.00**

Box stove, four-footed, cast iron, ash platform, overall: 13 x 18 x 25½ inches.　　　　　　　　　**D-150.00**

Footwarmer stove, wood and perforated tin, charcoal pan, bail handle, early.　　　　　　　　　　**D-99.00**

Parlor heater, "New Delta", restored.　　　　**S-695.00**

Parlor heater, "Radiant", cast iron, restored.　**S-1,495.00**

Parlor stove, "Peninsular", base-burner, restored.　**S-3,995.00**

Pot-bellied stove, out-kitchen, mild rust, 4½ ft. high.　**D-600.00**

Schoolhouse stove, rectangular cast iron, coalshelf by door.　　　　　　　　　　　　　　　　　**D-325.00**

Stove, "Gem Starlight", restored.　　　　　　**D-995.00**

Stove, "Midget", cast iron, laundry stove variant, removable top for clothes boiler, "Atlanta Stove Works".　　　　　　　　　　　　　　　　　　**D-145.00**

Stove, "Monarch Mallable", with ovens and sideshelves, restored.　　　　　　　　　　　　**D-1,495.00**

Stove, "Radiant Home Baseburner", with windows and tiles, restored.　　　　　　　　　　　　**D-3,995.00**

Tackroom stove, used to heat barn utility and storage room.　　　　　　　　　　　　　　　　**D-125.00**

Tinsmith's stove, copper and tin, 15 in. high.　**D-85.00**

Tinsmith's stove, bottom-burner, brass kettle in top, 14 in. high.　　　　　　　　　　　　　　　**D-75.00**

TIFFANY ART PIECES

Bowl, glass, lily-form, favrille, green iridescent. Signed "L.C.T./Favrille", and numbered, 6 in. diameter.　　　　　　　　　　　　　　　　　**A-240.00**

Bowl, glass, wide-rim, iridescent purple-gold, favrille, 9½ in. diameter.　　　　　　　　　　**A-225.00**

Bowl, sterling, round, footed, plain contemporary style. Size, 2½ pint, 8½ in. diameter, 33 oz. weight.　**A-200.00**

Left, **Handell desk lamp**, 14 in. high. Frosted and autumn landscape decorated swivel shade. A/425

Center, **Tiffany art glass and bronze lamp**, 23 in. high. Base impressed "Tiffany Studios / New York", and numbered. Shade unsigned. Domical shade with two bands of molded green-white tiles flanking central wide band of yellow-green-amber flowers and foliage; on a baluster reeded and gadrooned circular domed base, raised on five ball feet. A/1800

Right, **Tiffany brass lamp**, 15 in. high. Base impressed "Tiffany Studios, New York", and numbered. Peppermint green feather iridescent shade signed "L.C.T.". A/425

Bracelet, diamond and enamel, flexible, Art Deco style. Platinum mount set with 20 square diamonds approx. .20 carats each, 135 round diamonds approx. .04 carats each, and 90 single-cut diamonds. Total weight approx. 10 carats. Tiffany & Co.   A-3,900.00

Bracelet, diamond, wide, Art Deco style. Platinum mount set with 15 French faceted square diamonds approx. .30 carats each, 80 round diamonds approx. .12 carats each, and 152 round diamonds approx. .03 carats each. Total weight approx. 19 carats. Tiffany & Co.   A-8,100.00

Candlestick, bronze and glass favrille, molded stylized roots on spreading domed base. Enclosed green glass candle holder is supported by elongated rod. Impressed "Tiffany Studios/New York", 18 in. high.   A-425.00

Candlesticks, silver-soldered, set of four; 10 in. high.   **A-350.00**

Centerpiece, sterling, round deep bowl resting on four scroll arms cresting in candlesticks. Tiffany & Co., 20th Century, 16 in. diameter, 4 in. high.   **A-375.00**

Clock, desk, double-faced, square, on oblong green onyx base.   **A-110.00**

Clock, mantel, brass and crystal, white enamelled numeral dial with floral festoon within four bevelled glazed panel housing. Tiffany & Co., early 20th Century, 12½ in. high.   **A-225.00**

Compote, glass, opalescent, favrille; opaline face with red-to-white iridescent cup. Signed and numbered on base, 4½ in. high.   **A-325.00**

Desk set, patinated bronze, four-piece; Moorish design, pair of blotter ends, easel-back calendar frame and pin tray. "Tiffany Studios/New York".   **A-150.00**

French brass repeating carriage clock with alarm, 7½ in. high. Signed "Tiffany & Co., New York". French, ca. 1900.

A/1900

Courtesy Adam A. Weschler & Son, Washington, D.C.; photograph by Breger & Associates

Desk set, gilted bronze, Art Deco style, four-piece; inkwell, blotter, pen tray and easel-back calendar, "Tiffany Studies/New York". A-200.00

Desk set, gilted bronze, Moorish design. Two blotter holders, stationery rack, calendar holder, photo frame, hinge-top double inkwell, letter opener and pen tray. All numbered and marked. A-600.00

Dresser set, sterling; hand mirror, hair brush, clothes brush, shoe horn, soap box, powder box, toothbrush box, necessary box, and seven additional items. A-225.00

Humidor, gilt bronze, hinge-top, relief and repousse tree design. Numbered and marked on base. Ca. 1915, 6¼ in. square. A-125.00

Liqueur, favrille glass, signed "L.C.T.", 2 in. high. A-75.00

Pepper-pots, pair, vermeil silver, Georgian-style, 20th Century. Octagonal shape with urn finial, 4 in. high. A-230.00

Purse, evening, emerald, diamond and mesh gold. Early 20th Century, 14K gold set with 30 French-cut emeralds, 30 round diamonds, tassel with 10 seed pearls, looped mesh gold chain attached. A-1,200.00

Spoons, sterling, set of 12; "Tiffany & Co.", ca. 1884. A-160.00

Spoons, tea, set of six; sterling, raised motif on handles, mint condition. D-110.00

Tray, sterling, round, "Tiffany & Co.", 22½ in. diameter, 110 oz. weight. A-700.00

Vase, glass floral-shape, green, feathered. Signed and numbered on base, 12 in. high. A-550.00

Vase, bronze and favrille glass, trumpet-form; Tiffany Studios, 12 in. high. A-400.00

TIN COLLECTIBLES—[See *also* **Kitchen and Tole**]

Beaker, early seaming, lapped edges, two-quart, 6¾ in. deep. D-9.50

Birdcage, perch, ring, felt-covered bird, cage 11 in. high. A-45.00

Box, worn japanning, clasp incomplete, 2¾ x 2¾ x 4 inches. A-7.50

Bucket, wire bail handle, covered, 13¼ in. high. D-15.00

Coffee pot, punched decoration with urn of flowers and tulips on each side. Brass finial, tip of spout damaged, 11¾ in. high. A-975.00

Left, **Tin pitcher,** hand-soldered, one-quart capacity.
C/12
Kitchen measures, graduated set, nested, to one-cup
size; maker-marked. C/9
Right, **Mould,** bread or pudding, hollow central
cylinder in bottom. From Maine, 10 in. high, tin.
C/25-35

Document box, japanned tin, original
key, 14 in. wide. C/16-24

Tin, personality, Rudy Vallee, 5 in.
diameter. D/9.50

Tin horn, lapped and soldered seams, black japanned body, red
and natural patina on mouthpiece. Working condition, 12¾ in.
long. C/20-30

Cream separator, on legs, cover with brass mesh
screen, 39 in. high.   D-65.00
Cup, marked "U.S." on bottom, large size.   D-10.00
Cup, small, worn green japanning, 1¼ in. high.   A-4.00
Cup, with flat tin strap handle, 4 in. diameter.   D-5.50
Dinner plate, rolled edge, mint cond., ca. 1880, 8¼
in. diameter.   D-3.75
Dipper, bowl with wire-turned rim, hanging loop,
12½ in. long.   A-15.00
Dustpan, old, cylindrical handle soldered to pan
backing.   D-20.00
Funnel, handled, 15 in. high.   D-10.00
Grater, pat'd. 1870, one-piece, 7½ x 11¾ inches.   A-20.00
Horn, with brass mouthpiece, 64½ in. long.   A-105.00
Kerosene can, wire handle with wooden grip, 15 in.
high.   A-20.00
Pail, shaped like tea caddy, cover, lapped seams.   D-22.50
Pail, old blue paint with smoked decoration, 8½ in.
diameter.   A-42.50
Popcorn holder, wire handle, holed cover.   D-11.00
Pudding molds, set of 10; each 1½ to 3 in. diameter,
1¾ in. high.   D-7.50
Scoop, food or grain, round wooden handle, 13 in.
long.   D-14.00
Shaker, condiment, worn brown japanning, 4 in.
high.   A-10.00
Spice box, six round cannisters and central nutmeg
grater, box 7 in. diameter.   A-30.00
Squirrel cage, folk art decorated, attached wire
drum exerciser, shaped like old schoolhouse. Brass
hardware, 8 x 14 x 21 inches.   D-145.00
Tray, cut-out handles, old tin but new paint, 18 x 24
inches.   D-17.50

TOBACCO COLLECTIBLES

Ash tray, cast iron, 75% orig. paint, figural, 2¼ in.
high.   D-15.00
Ash tray, brass, made from base of WW-I artillery
cartridge.   S-20.00
Advertising sign, lithographed tin, "Just Say J. A.
Cigars", cobalt with red lettering, ca. 1920, 3 x 20
inches.   D-15.00

Cigar band dish, 50 different mounted under glass 6½ in. diameter. D-19.00

Cigar box, top and four sides inlaid with five kinds of wood, brass hinges, "Golden Rule Cigars". D-50.00

Cigar box, tin, 9 in. wide, "Humo". D-7.50

Cigar case, tin, brass clip, ca. 1870, holds three cigars. D-14.00

Cigar cutter, pocket squeeze-type, circular disc blade. D-10.00

Cigar cutter, pocket scissors-type, "Black & White 5¢ Cigars". D-7.50

Cigar cutter, folding pocket-type, brass, cigar-shaped. D-15.00

Cigar cutter, folding pocket-knife-type. D-12.00

Cigar-maker's outfit, five pieces: Cutting board, guide, cutter knife, mold, and cigar press. D-125.00

Cigar mold, tin mounted on wooden two-part mold, makes 20 cigars, handforged nails, Pat'd 1871. D-39.50

Cigarettes, "Egyptian Deities", mint orig. contents, 1920's. D-5.00

Cigarettes, package, orig. contents, "La Calpense/Gibralter". D-3.00

Cigarette tin, "British Consols", flat. D-3.50

Cigarette tin, "Chesterfield", clean, flat. D-5.00

Cigarette urn, opaline glass, table-top, nicely decorated. D-9.00

Match box holder, pedestaled, polished brass, 2¾ in. high. D-25.00

Match box holder, pedestaled, brass, weighted base, 3¼ in. high. D-22.50

Lunch box, "The Main Brace/Cut Plug", tin, paper labels, 4¼ x 5¼ x 7¾ inches. D-30.00

Pipe, briar; with hand-carved bowl in shape of Turk's head. D-12.00

Pipe, pressed white clay, Colonial, bowl intact, stem broken. C-10.00

Pipe, Meerschaum, amber color, plain, 5¾ in. long. D-18.00

Pipe lighter, copper and metal, 1920's, 3½ in. high. S-22.00

Pipe rack, old, space for six pipes, brass trim corners. D-15.00

Pipe stand, walnut, humidor holder and top drawer, Victorian, 29 in. high. S-125.00

Pipe stand, hardwood, top pull-drawer and pipe holder on side. D-45.00

Stencils, brass, sets of three; for labeling wooden cigar boxes. Stencils designate brand name or quantity, 4—7½ in. long. **D-25.00**

Tobacco bag, "Just Suits/Cut Plug", 4½ x 5 inches. **D-3.00**

Tobacco box tin, 6 in. wide, "Sweet Burley". **D-3.50**

Tobacco cutter, wooden base, turned handle, 12 in. long. **A-35.00**

Tobacco cutter, wrought iron, wooden handle and attached chopping blade, 5½ x 12 inches. **A-55.00**

Tobacco cutter, cast iron, "P. Lorillard & Co.", counter-top. **D-26.00**

Tobacco cutter, metal cutting blade, "Black Beauty". **D-40.00**

Tobacco flags, felt, lot of 12 assorted sizes, ca. 1906. **D-7.50**

Tobacco humidor, lithographed tin, "Cinco Handy", 5 in. square. **D-21.00**

Tobacco humidor, copper, hand-hammered, two brass bands and brass Marine Corp insignia, ca. 1918, 7¾ in. high. **D-42.50**

Tobacco jar, glass, pewter cover and handle in shape of dog. **D-17.50**

Tobacco jar, figural in shape of monk's head, hairline crack. **D-7.50**

Spittoon, miniature, tin, 3¾ in. diameter, rare. **D-35.00**

Spittoon, silver over brass, Reed & Barton touchmark, four pounds, marked "Plaza" (Plaza Hotel, NYC), ca. 1890. **D-125.00**

Tobacco tin, "American Navy", 3 x 4½ x 6½ inches. **D-45.00**

Tobacco tin, "Beeswing Flaked Gold Leaf Cavendish, pocket-size. **D-12.50**

Tobacco tin, "Brandon Mixture/Richmond, Va.", pocket-size. **D-15.00**

Tobacco tin, "Briggs Pipe Mixture", pocket, 1926 tax stamp. **D-6.00**

Tobacco tin, "Dutch Masters Special Quality Cigars", 5½ in. diameter. **D-16.00**

Tobacco tin, "Edgeworth Extra High Grade/Ready Rubbed", pocket. **D-5.00**

Tobacco tin, "The Elm" cigars, litho. elm and village, scarce. **D-90.00**

Tobacco tin, "Hi-Plane Smooth-Cut", monoplane, 5 x 6¼ inches. **D-40.00**

Tobacco tin, "Honest Labor Cut Plug", very fine condition. **D-17.50**

Tobacco tin, "Idle Hour Cut Plug", 1 x 2¾ x 4¾ inches. **D-21.00**

Tobacco tin, "J. C. Dills Best/Cube Cut Plug", 1910 tax stamp. **D-5.50**

Tobacco tin, "Landmark Cut Plug", bail handle, orig. label. **D-16.00**

Tobacco tin, "North Pole Smoking Cut Plug Tobacco", 6 in. high. **D-45.00**

Tobacco tin, "Pippins 5– Cigars", box for 25 cigars, 3 in. square. **D-35.00**

Tobacco tin, "Schinasi Bros. Natural Egyptian Cigarettes". **D-22.50**

Tobacco tin, "Tuxedo", pocket-size, full orig. label. **D-8.00**

TOLE—*Paint-Decorated Tin*

Box, worn blue japanning, brass bail handle, 6 x 6 x 8½ inches. **A-15.00**

Canister, orange-red with yellow stripes, some wear, 5¼ in. high. **A-22.50**

Canister, black ground, colorful decoration of fruit and foliage is heavily painted, 8½ in. high. **A-120.00**

Canister, black ground with red and yellow decoration. Lid has old soldered repair, 8 in. high. **A-47.50**

Canister, black paint with yellow green and red decoration, paint flaking; 3 in. diameter, 6½ in. high. **A-52.50**

Coffee pot, black ground with very worn floral painting on sides, 9¾ in. high. **A-85.00**

Coffee pot, orig. decoration, worn black ground. Freehand floral decoration in red, yellow, green and black, in good condition, 8½ in. high. **A-525.00**

Deed box, orig. dark brown japanning with yellow and orange-red decoration. Some wear, 9 x 4¼ in., 5½ in. high. **A-80.00**

Deed box, brown japanning with polychrome floral decoration. Some wear, 4½ x 6 x 10 inches. **A-200.00**

Deed box, brown japanning, 4 x 5½ x 9 inches. **A-15.00**

Document box, dark brown japanning with nicely painted floral front in red, yellow, green and white. Lid and ends have additional decoration, minor wear, 5¾ x 7½ x 9¾ inches. **A-500.00**

Hanging box, flowers on green paint, 3 x 7½ x 8 inches. **A-50.00**

Lamp, old paint, clear ribbed glass, electrified, tin decorated, 19½ in. high.

A-60.00

Spice caddy, six small cylindrical tins in tin case with handle. Red-brown ground with floral decoration in three colors, 5½ in. diameter, 3½ in. high.

A-75.00

Tray, miniature, orig. blue japanning with yellow rimmed scalloped border, freehand decoration. Some wear, 3½ x 4½ inches.

A-55.00

Tray, miniature, octagonal, blue with freehand floral decoration. Faded signature on back, 3 x 4 3/8 inches.

A-37.50

Tray, stenciled leaves and flowers on a black ground, 19 x 26 inches.

A-50.00

Tray, octagonal, 9 x 12½ inches.

A-35.00

Tray, scalloped edge, Victorian floral decoration, 19½ x 25½ inches.

A-30.00

TOOL BOOKS And CATALOGS

Aladdin Homes catalog, well illustrated, 120 pp, 1921.

D-4.50

American Training School Equipment, early machinery, ca. 1900.

D-8.50

The Art And Science Of Carpentry Made Easy, 118 pp, 1891.

D-12.50

Broderick & Bascombe Rope Co. catalog, 1944.

D-3.50

Brown & Sharpe Small Tools, well illus.,448 pp, 1926.

D-10.00

Disston Handbook On Saws, many illus. of old tools, 1917.

D-10.00

The Disston Saw, Tool & File Book, 48 pp, 1927.

D-8.50

Elementary Mechanical Drawing, 250 pp, 1915.

D-2.50

Elementary Turning, tool illus., 197 pp, 1907.

D-5.00

Elementary Woodwork, hardcover, 206 pp, 1906.

D-6.50

Elementary Woodworking, early tool illus., 133 pp, 1904.

D-8.50

Elements Of Plane Surveying, (inc. leveling), 255 pp, 1913.

D-8.50

Handbook Of Statistics, Park Steel Company, 1909.

D-1.50

How To Sharpen, Norton Abrasives, mint cond., 1935.

D-3.00

Jim Brown's Catalog, The Brown Wire & Fence Co., 128 pp, 1935.

D-5.00

Jigs And Fixtures, Colvin & Haas, many old tools, 168 pp, 1913.

D-8.50

King's Woodwork & Carpentry Handbook, 134 pp, hardcover. — D-3.00

King's Woodwork & Carpentry, old tools illus., 150 pp, 1911. — D-5.00

Mechanical Drawing, freehand drawings, 148 pp, 1895. — D-3.00

Mechanical Drawing Problems, hardcover, 153 pp, 1917. — D-3.50

Modern Milling Machines, (design, etc.), 304 pp, 1906. — D-8.50

Pexto Mechanics Hand Tool Catalog, mint cond., 96 pp. — D-10.00

Problems In Woodworking, 50 pp. blueprints, etc; 1905. — D-8.50

Shop Projects, hardcover, 382 pp, 1915. — D-6.50

Small Tools #30, Brown & Sharpe Tool Catalog, comprehensive. — D-9.00

Stanley Wrought Hardware Catalog, 353 pp, 1926. — D-9.50

Starret Tool Catalog #24, many old tools, 368 pp, 1927. — D-8.50

Starret Precision Tools, (dial indicators, etc.), 288 pp, 1946. — D-5.00

Starrett Tools 50th Anniversary Catalog, 383 pp, #25. — D-9.50

Story Of David Maydole, The Maydole Hammer Co., 71 pp, 1923. — D-10.00

Wood Utilizations, U.S. Dept. of Commerce, 52 pp, 1929. — D-2.50

Woodworking Machine brochure, well-illustrated, ca. 1900. — D-2.00

Woodworking Machinery catalog, "The Lightning Line", 1915-16. — D-8.50

Young Bros. Ladder catalog, ca. 1900. — D-3.50

TOOLS—*[See also* **Farm***]*

Tools are a major collecting field. Some persons have a general assemblage of many different kinds, while others specialize as in certain types (broadaxes) or tools of a trade like carpentry. Wood and metal tools are especially favored, and the presence of copper and brass is always a plus factor.

Pulley, wooden frame and hardwood wheel, cast iron suspension parts. C/9-12
T-bevel, carpenter's wood, steel and brass; 9 in. long. C/11
Lower, three **try and mitre squares,** Each: C/9-15

Adz, orig. handle, good condition 8 in. blade height. **D-20.00**

Adz, cooper's, "D. R. Barton/1892", 9 in. blade height. **D-26.00**

Adz, cooper's, with very short (9-in.) handle. **D-30.00**

Adz, ship carpenter's, full length handle. **A-22.00**

Adz, large, 5 in. blade, handle 37 in. long. **D-35.00**

Adz, small, once used in the making of dugout canoes. **D-35.00**

Adz, straight-edge blade 2 in. across. **D-25.00**

Anvil, miniature, iron, 3¾ in. long. **D-14.00**

Anvil, full-size, blacksmith's. **D-55.00**

Auger, hollow; "Stearns & Co.", 6¾ in. high. **D-18.00**

Auger, hollow; "The A. A. Wood & Sons Co.", 6½ in. high. **D-22.00**

Auger, wood handle with central brass casting, 27 in. long. **D-40.00**

Axe, duo-blade; head only, "Sager", 12½ in. long. **D-15.00**

Axe, mortise; for rail fence postholes, etc., 35 in. long. **D-75.00**

Axe, felling, handwrought head, ca. early 1800's, 6 in. head. **S-40.00**

Beading tool, brass stop, good blade, 7½ in. wide. **D-18.00**

Beetle, iron-bound wooden maulhead, orig. handle, 37 in. long. **D-7.00**

Bit, bullnose; "Pat. 1887", 8½ in. high. **D-18.00**

Bolt headers, hand-forged, used by blacksmith for heading bolts. **D-20.00**

368

Top left, **cobbler's hammer**, 7½ in. long. C/4-6
Bottom, unusual **hand-vise**, turn-screw closure, japanned wood handle. C/10-15
Right, **Axehead**, old handle, factory-made cast iron, head about 7 in. high.
Private collection C/15-25

Tobacco cutting blade, 11 in. long.
C/8-12

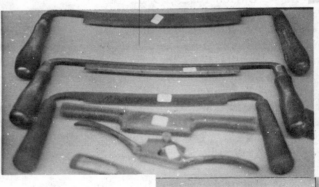

Drawknives, shavers and scrapers. D/25-40

Hand plane, two-piece hardwood, steel blade. "Thistle Brand / New York Tool Co. / Auburn, N.Y.", 7 in. long.
C/20-30

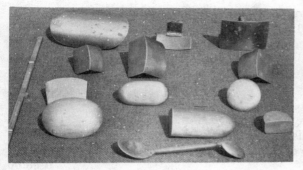

Mold-maker's tools, part of 41-piece set. All items shown are either stainless steel or cast brass. Group:
C/70-90

Hook, multi-purpose, used for hay and straw bales in the Midwest. Hand-forged.
C/2-5

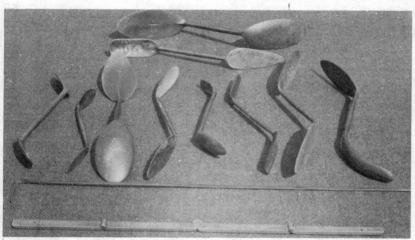

Mold-maker's tools, part of 41-piece set. All items of quality steel and one of cast brass, most with maker's marks and script signature of original owner. Scale: Folding rule is one foot long.
C/80-90

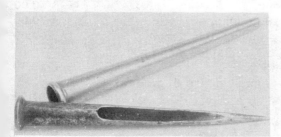

Grain thief, used to take grain samples from closed bags. "Chas. Stager & Co. / Toledo", chrome cover, iron shank, brass rim, 4½ in. long.
C/9-12

Boring tool, "Grand Rapids Sash Pulley", from sash and door factory, 8½ in. long. — D-20.00

Brace, angle attachment, "Millers Falls", 17 in. high. — D-18.00

Brace, brass ferrule on pad, 15 in. high. — D-15.00

Brace and bit, fine wood, brass chuck and button, 18 in. high. — D-70.00

Brace, chuck marked "Harrold, U.S.A.", 11 in. high. — D-22.00

Brace, screwdriving; "Drummonds Pat. 1870", brass cap on wood handle, 12 in. long. — D-30.00

Branding tools, set of ten, by cabinet-maker; 20 to 25 in. long. — D-65.00

Broadaxe, "D. R. Barton/Rochester #2", old handle. — D-70.00

Broadaxe, head only, blade edge 12½ in. long. — D-48.00

Broadaxe, dated 1832, old and slanted handle. — A-27.50

Broadaxe, old handle, unusual wrought head with decorations. — D-70.00

Broadaxe, New York, old handle; head 13 in. at blade edge. — A-27.50

Broadaxe, with handle, head marked "Special/IXL". — D-65.00

Broadaxe, head marked "J. Godfrey/Warms", 30 in. long. — D-75.00

Broad-hatchet, handle 16 in. long. — D-12.00

Bung auger, orig. wood handle, metal and wood 6 in. long. — D-15.00

Bung borer, orig. wood handle, 11 in. long. — D-18.00

Bung borer, unusual, with auger and four cutting blades, 16 in. long. — D-45.00

Caliper, "Stanley/#36½", brass and boxwood, brass hinge. — D-19.50

Caliper, "Union Tool Co./Orange, Mass.", 6¼ in. long. — D-6.00

Calipers, "Starrett/Pat. 4-16-1901", 4½ in. long. — D-6.00

Calipers, "P. Lowentraut Mfg. Co./Newark", 4 in. long. — D-5.00

Calipers, wrought iron, initialed, one side with measuremarks, 20 in. long. — A-50.00

Calipers, double; iron, 18 in. long. — A-70.00

Calipers, leg; "Starrett—Jenny", 6 in. long. — D-7.00

Caning vise, chairmakers, maple, hand-pegged, wrought clamps, 24 in. long. — D-22.50

Caulking mallet, with six caulking irons, graduated sizes. — D-97.50

Chamfer knife, cooper's, "White/Buffalo", 19 in. long. — D-45.00

Broadaxes, with old (if not original) short and canted handles. No maker's marks, both with steel cutting edges, iron body.
Each: S/40-60

Chamfer knife, cooper's, orig. handle, 16 in. long. D-40.00

Chime maul, cooper's, heavy 19-in. bar for knocking on the metal barrel bands. D-36.50

Chisel, 3/16 in. blade, "Fulton Special", 12½ in. long. D-14.00

Chisel, swan-neck; brass ferrule, 3/8 in. blade width. D-22.00

Chisel, corner; "O. V. B.", 15½ in. long. D-24.00

Chisel, ¼ in. wide blade, "Lakeside", 9 in. long. D-16.00

Chisel, 1 in. blade, "Greenlee", 14 in. long. D-18.00

Chisel, 1¼ in. blade, "Barton", 15 in. long. D-22.00

Chisel, 7/8 in. blade, "Douglas Bottom & Co.", 9½ in. long. D-18.00

Chisel, 1¼ in. blade, "P. S. & W. Co.", heavy duty. D-24.00

Chisel-gouge, 5/32 in. channel, 17 in. long. D-12.00

Clamp, harness-maker's, 6 in. wide. D-12.00

Clamp, metal; "Jint Co.", 10 in. lever-style. D-14.00

Clamp, metal; "E. C. Stearns & Co./#4/Syracuse, N.Y." D-22.00

Clamp, wood; jaw length 22 inches. D-13.00

Clamp, wood; 24 in. with opposing handle turns. D-8.00

Coachmakers router, maple or beech with 9½ in. brass sole plate and brass fittings on screw control and router top. D-115.00

Cobbler's tools, set of sixteen pieces. D-35.00

Cutter, circle; hand-forged, 16 in. long. D-30.00

Cutting tool, for leather; crescent, "Newark/1826", 7 in. wide. A-50.00

Depth stop, "Stanley/Pat. oct. 11, 04", 6 in. high. D-8.00

Dividers, "Lufkin Rule Co", 9½ in. high. D-14.00

Dividers, "Peck, Stow & Wilcox Co.", brass joint, 12 in. high. D-18.00

Dividers, "Pexto 8", 8 in. high. D-12.00

Drawknife, adjustable handles, 15½ in. wide. A-11.00

Drawknife, cooper's; blade width 3½ inches, 18 in. long. — **D-26.00**

Drawknife, "Hart Mfg.", 18½ in. wide. — **D-14.00**

Drawknife, wood bladeguard, "Eskilstuna", 14½ in. long. — **D-30.00**

Drill, chain; "Grabler & Co./Cleveland/Pat. 2-18-09". — **D-32.00**

Drill, hand chain; "Millers Falls", 12 in. high. — **D-30.00**

Drill, mechanism; automatically feeds bit into metal. — **D-35.00**

Froe, iron, for splitting shingles, 15 in. blade. — **D-13.00**

Froe, blacksmith-made, orig. handle, blade 11 in. long. — **D-22.00**

Fleshing tool, tanner's, double-handled, 20 in. long. — **D-12.00**

Guage, butt; "Stanley #94", 3½ in. long. — **D-8.00**

Gauge, marking and mortise; brass scale, fence and screw. Rosewood shaft, 10½ in. long. — **D-28.00**

Gauge, plate, tap and drill; 1/4 to 5/8 inches. — **D-15.00**

Gauge, panel; wooden screw, 20 in. long. — **D-12.00**

Gauge, panel; two-color wood, brass plate and lined fence, 21 in. long. — **D-30.00**

Gauge, slitting; roller below handle, wedged blade, 18½ in. long. — **D-32.00**

Gauge, slitting; one roller missing, 20 in. long. — **D-35.00**

Gauge, stripping; saddle-maker's, "C.S. Osborne & Co.", 6 in. long. — **D-24.00**

Gauge, stripping; cast iron handle, "Osborne/1876", 6 in. long. — **D-22.00**

Grafting knife, wooden handle, 10¼ in. long. — **A-5.00**

Gouge, bent; "W. Butcher", cast steel, 11 in. long. — **D-12.00**

Gouge, "Buck Bros.", cast steel, 15 in. long. — **D-10.00**

Hammer, crating; "E. Bonner/1901", 10 in. long. — **D-8.00**

Hammer, farrier's, "Heller". — **D-7.00**

Hammer, file-maker's; rare, with good haft, 9 in. long. — **D-85.00**

Hammer, hoof; horseman's, nickel-plated, with pick, — **D-28.00**

Hammer, snowball; for cleaning horses' hooves, 10 in. long. — **D-20.00**

Hoof-leveling gauge, farrier's; "Hood & Reynolds/Boston", scale marked on brass. — **D-38.00**

Hammer, log-marking; good handle, impressed metal head. — **D-45.00**

Jointer, cooper's; bolted to bench. Double iron, "Stanley", 35¾ in. long. — **D-85.00**

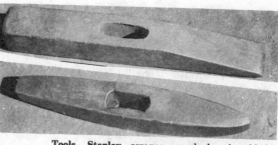

Tools. Stanley scraper, marked orig. blade, reversible head, brass sleeve. Wood handle dated (stamped) 1898, 13½ in. long.   C/30-40
Zax, or "slate axe", hammer used in putting on slate roofs. Device pounded and pulled nails and made nail-holes in slate shingles. Maker-marked, leather-washer handle. Note: Similar items are made today for custom shingleing.   C/25-30
Hammerheads, hand-forged iron, with largest 4½ in. long.   Per each: C/2-3

Mallets:
Burl head, hand-carved handle.   C/25-35
Turned head, squared handle.   C/11-17

Level, "Henry Disston & Sons", brass ends, good glass, 28½ in. long.   **D-32.00**

Level, "O.V.B #100/Pat. 5-8-06"; brass ends, rosewood, vertical bubble missing, 3 x 27½ inches.   **D-40.00**

Level, "Stanley Rule & Level Co.", glass good and brass ends. "Pat. 11-11-1862", 27 in. long.   **D-38.00**

Level, "Stanley #36/Pat. 6-23-96", perfect, 9 in. long.   **D-32.00**

Level, "Stanley #37", perfect, 2 x 6 inches.   **D-35.00**

Level, "Stratton", brassbound, two glass bubbles with wire center-markers, 8½ in. long.   **D-55.00**

Level, "Stratton Bros./Pat. 7-16-1872", brassbound, 6¾ in. long.   **D-70.00**

Level, "Winchester W-104", very fine, 18 in. long.   **D-40.00**

Lumberstick, graduated rod for measuring length and diameter of cut timber. Brass tips, "F.A. Hazelton, Maker".   **D-25.00**

Mallet, carpenter's; burlwood, 10 in. high.   **A-17.50**

Mallet, head enclosed with brass tube, wood handle, 14 in. long.   **D-22.00**

Mallet, carpenter's, burlwood, 14 in. long.   **A-15.00**

Mallet, lignum vitae wood with patina, 14 in. long.   **D-35.00**

Mallet, carver's; heavy head 5 in. diameter.   **D-10.00**

Maul, wood, heavy burl base, 9 in. diameter.   **D-25.00**

Measuring device, brass, from fabric factory; linen tape, body 8 in. long.   **D-45.00**

Measuring tool, cooper's, iron with wood handle, 20½ in. long. **A-40.00**

Micrometer, 1 to 2 inches, "J. T. Slocumb/Prov. R.I.", 5½ in. long. **D-12.00**

Mill pick, used for dressing and "freshening" grooves in millstones, iron head, 9 in. handle. **D-24.00**

Mitre box, adjustable, on legs. **D-45.00**

Mold-maker's tools, bronze foundry, initialed, set of fifteen. **A-85.00**

Nail claw, metal, 14 in. long. **D-8.00**

Nail holder, cobbler's; cast iron, "USMC", top 10 in. diameter. **D-30.00**

Odd jobs tool, "Stanley #1/Pat. 1-25-87", 4½ in. high. **D-38.00**

Plane, wood, 15 in. long. **A-15.00**

Plane, with reversible rockers, metal, 10 in. long. **A-35.00**

Plane, wood, handle at rear, 10 in. long. **A-18.00**

Plane, adjustable molding, beautifully made from exotic wood. Positioning screws have ivory knobs, 12 in. long. **A-127.50**

Plane, "Auburn Tool Co.", with thistle mark, 16 in. long. **D-10.00**

Plane, dado; "Ohio Tool Co.", brass knob, 9 in. long. **D-30.00**

Plane, "D. Kennedy", modified with side extension, 16 in. long. **D-25.00**

Plane, "D. R. Barton/Star Trade Mark", 9 in. long. **D-12.00**

Plane, "Ohio Tool Co.", 16 in. long. **D-9.00**

Plane, scrub; "Stanley #10", 1½ in. blade, 10 in. long. **D-15.00**

Plane, scrub; "Stanley #40/1896", 10 in. long. **D-30.00**

Planes, tongue and groove; pair. "Sandusky Tool Co.", ea. 13 in. long. **D-65.00**

Pipe reamer, log pipes, orig. handle, screw lead, 12 in. long. **D-20.00**

Pipe rod, metal tool, "J. Casper/5-6-13", 12 in. long. **D-18.00**

Pliers, combination; "Diamond Edge", 9 in. long. **D-8.00**

Pliers, saw-set; metal, for angling teeth, 13 in. long. **D-8.00**

Pliers, stamping; metal, "H. J. Schmidt...Wisconsin", 10 in. long. **D-12.00**

Plowplane, beech and boxwood, brass trim, "Porter A. Gladwin/Boston, Mass.", ca. 1860; brass screw stoplever. **D-135.00**

Plumb-bob, brass with steel point, mercury-filled, 6 in. long. **D-40.00**

Plumb-bob, steel tip, top unscrews for lead lines, 3 in. high. **D-16.50**

Punch, adjustable; handheld metal, "Apex", 7 in. long. — D-7.00

Punch, harness-maker's; "Everson/N. Y.", 7 in. long. — D-5.00

Punch, iron, ½ in. diameter, 4 in. long. — A-2.00

Punch, "Samson #4", pliers grip, 7½ in. long. — D-12.00

Quarry spoon, to remove powdered drill-hole debris, 4 in. spoon, 40½ in. long. — D-18.50

Raft auger, handforged, for holing logs before pinning together, 5 feet long. — D-15.00

Rasp, cobbler's; wood handle, 20½ in. long. — D-12.00

Reamer, smith-made, wood handle, 4½ in. long. — D-12.00

Router, old, cuts 7/16 in. wide. — D-60.00

Router, "Stanley #71/1884", 7 in. wide. — D-20.00

Router, "Stanley #71" with depth gauge and fence, 6½ in. wide. — D-25.00

Router, "Stanley #71½/1901", 7 in. wide. — D-18.00

Rule, shrinkage; "Kuffel & Esser Co./N. Y.", brass ends, 24 in. long. — D-18.00

Saw, back; old, wood handle, 17 in. long. — D-6.00

Saw, dehorning; all metal, 16 in. long. — D-8.00

Saw, keyhole; handle repair, old, 9½ in. long. — D-8.00

Saw, mitre; early, 7 x 35 inches. — D-30.00

Saw, pruning; cast iron frame, 16½ in. long. — D-24.00

Scorp, cooper's; blade on forked wood, old, 17 in. long. — D-38.00

Scraper, adjustible; "Bennett Specialty Mfg. Co./1-5-09", 11½ in. long. — D-18.00

Scraper, butcher-block; 6 in. wide, handforged. — D-8.00

Scraper, handled, triangular blade, "Vaughan & Bushnell Mfg. Co.", 17½ in. long. — D-17.00

Scraper, "Stanley #80", good blade, 12 in. long. — D-20.00

Scraper, "Stanley #81", mahogany sole, 10½ in. long. — D-32.00

Scraper, "Stanley #151", marked blade, 10 in. long. — D-17.00

Screw-driver, brass ferrule, "Peck & Hickman, Ltd./London", 9 in. long. — D-12.00

Scribe, wooden marking; adjustable gauge and handle, 20 in. long. — A-21.00

Shingle tool, for removing bad shingles, "Keystone Saw Works/Philadelphia", 25 in. long. — D-20.00

Shipwright's razee, smoothing plane, "Heald & Spiller", open jack handle, 8½ inches long. — D-25.00

Shoe sole cutter, cast iron, two pounds, 10½ in. long. — D-15.00

Slater's breaking bar, straightedge, for sizing slate, 18 in. long. — C-25.00

Slater's hammer and tool, for holing slate, pounding in
and removing nails, leather handle, 12½ in. long.   **C-30.00**

Slick, steel, 3½ in. wide blade, "T. H. Witherby", 31
in. long.   **D-65.00**

Soldering iron for one-armed man, "England/1920".
Gas-fired, original box, 15 in. long.   **D-100.00**

Spoke pointer, iron, wheelwright's, sharpens
wheelspoke ends.   **D-10.00**

Spokeshave, handmade, old, 11 in. wide.   **D-18.00**

Spokeshave, bell metal, polished   **A-15.00**

Spokeshave, double; "Seymour Smith & Son", 9½ in.
wide.   **D-17.00**

Square, angle; marked "B. Stone", folded, 14 inches.   **D-6.00**

Square, angle; "Star Tool Co./Pat. 1867", folded, 8 in-
ches.   **D-8.00**

Stake, tinner's; blow-horn, metal, 24 in. long.   **D-55.00**

Stitching head, saddle-maker's, 15 in. long.   **D-12.00**

Stonemason's dessing tool, solid teeth, cast iron, 10 in.
long.   **D-12.50**

Stonemason's tool, iron handle, adjustable teeth, 18
in. long.   **C-35.00**

Stonewall tool, wrought iron, 28 in. long, for building
stone walls in New Hampshire ca. 1877.   **D-20.00**

Swedges, eye; set of six. Handmade, iron, used to drive
broken handles from tools, average 4 in. long.   **D-100.00**

Tap, for cutting wood threads 2¼ in. across; 12 in.
long.   **D-65.00**

Tinker's tool box, orig. green paint, rings for shoulder
straps.   **D-47.50**

Tobacco leaf cutter, blade, shaft and wood handle, 10
in. long.   **D-12.50**

Tongs, for holding clamshells in button-cutting lathe,
10 in. long.   **D-25.00**

Tool; for artificial flower maker, brass ferrule, 9 in.
long.   **D-9.00**

Traveler, wheelwright's; has pointer, wheel 8 in.
diameter.   **D-28.00**

Traveler, brass wheel and pointer, wood handle, 7 1/8
in. diameter.   **S-35.00**

Traveler, hand-forged, wheel 5½ in. diameter.   **D-22.00**

Try square, copper, rare, 12 in. long.   **D-18.50**

Try square, brass bound, iron measure 6 in. long.   **S-12.00**

Turnscrew, "Shefield and Broad Arrow Combination
Plier & Cutter".   **D-22.00**

Turning chisel, gauged, delicate curved blade, 19 in. long.   **D-65.00**

Vise, bench-type, 9 in. high.   **D-7.00**

Vise, metal, handheld, 4½ in. long.   **D-8.00**

Vise, saw; clamp type, 8 in. high.   **D-7.00**

Water pipe auger, for boring log holes, ¾ in. diameter, iron, 84 in. long.   **D-45.00**

Wedge, powder and cap, for splitting logs.   **D-46.00**

Wedge, splitting, marked "WPA", 14 in. long.   **D-18.00**

Wheelwright's reamer, to enlarge hub holes, hand-forged, 16 in. long.   **D-29.00**

Wood-graining tool set, "Lowe Bros. Co.", orig. box.   **D-28.00**

Woodworking scorp, "Norway/1865", 6 in. long.   **D-28.00**

Wrench, adjustable; "Coes Wrench Co.", 7 in. long.   **D-9.00**

Wrench, adjustable; "Girard Wrench Co.", 11 in. long.   **D-10.00**

Wrench, adjustable; "Keen Kutter/Pat. 1896", 22 in. long.   **D-18.00**

Wrench, double-head; "Case Eagle", 20 in. long.   **D-20.00**

Wrench chain; "Stansbery/Pat. 1901", 29 in. long.   **D-28.00**

TOYS

Airplane, cast iron, 3 inches.   **A-40.00**

Airplane, Hubley, cast iron, no propeller, 3 inches.   **A-15.00**

Airplane, cast iron, blue with silver motor and wheels, prop spins, 5 inches.   **A-47.50**

Airplane, Marx "Roll-over", tin wind-up, 5½ inches.   **A-25.00**

Andy Gump in Car, Tootsietoy, metal, mechanical, orig. paint, 3 inches.   **A-100.00**

Animated toy, paper dancing girl and musicians move as sand filters through reservoir. Glass front, 2¼ x 7¼ x 9¼ inches.   **A-100.00**

Asparagus Bug tin toy, 2 inches.   **A-2.50**

Auto, cast iron, no wheel, no paint, 5 inches.   **A-20.00**

Auto, Chrysler Air Flow, cast iron, pink orig. paint, 4½ inches.   **A-20.00**

Auto Racer, "Oh-Boy", tin, Kiddies Metal Co. Red with black trim, 19 inches.   **A-55.00**

Auto, streamlined; metal, wood wheels, orig. paint, 7 inches.   **A-4.00**

Auto, toy; four-door sedan, 75% orig. paint, by A.C. Williams Co. Cast iron, 2¼ x 3¼ x 6½ inches.   **D-145.00**

Bank, tin, 4 in. high. Lithographed, "Little Folks Cash Register / Old King Cole". C/12-15

Dollhouse, ca. 1920's, 18 in. high. D/125

Cannon, cast-iron toy; WW-I, brass barrel, spring-driven mechanism, by George Carlin Fine Toys / Pittsburgh, PA, 15 in. long. D/100

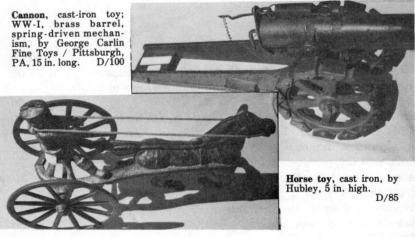

Horse toy, cast iron, by Hubley, 5 in. high. D/85

Balancing clown, metal, 9 inches.	A-17.50
Battleship, Tootsietoy, cast metal, marked, 6 in. long.	D-10.00
Bellringer, horse-drawn, cast iron, broken wheel, no paint, 4 inches.	A-2.00
Blow-pipe, metal, bird calls in water base, 2½ inches.	A-8.00
Boat, penny-toy, German, tin, 2¾ inches.	A-3.00
Boiler, fire engine, cast iron, 5¼ inches.	A-7.50

Barclay, L TO R: Officer with sword, short stride (Marine or American Legion) 708; Officer with sword, tin helmet 708; Marine, short stride 722; Marine, long stride 722; American Legionaire in overseas cap 953; cadet officer with sword, short stride 713; cadet with rifle, short stride 714; cadet with rifle 714. Photo Courtesy Don Pielin C/6-12

Manoil, L TO R: Firing heavy machine gun up 80; Firing AA gun up 46; Firing AA gun through viewer 82; Firing rocket 83; Standing with searchlight 47. Photo Courtesy Don Pielin
C/ 5-7

Bulldozer, cast iron, green with silver wheels.	A-5.00
Bulldozer, Hubley, cast iron, red orig. paint.	A-27.50
Bulldozer, Hubley, cast iron, green orig. paint.	A-32.50
Bus, Arca de Fageot, cast iron, "Compliments of the Fageot Co.", blue orig. paint, 8 inches.	A-110.00
Bus, cast iron, blue orig. paint, silver wheels, 6½ inches.	A-90.00
Bus, cast iron, red orig. paint, 6 inches.	A-25.00
Bus, cast iron, blue with silver wheels, orig. paint, 4¾ inches.	A-20.00
Bus, cast iron, no wheels, red orig. paint, 5¾ inches.	A-5.00
Bus, cast iron, red with silver wheels, orig. paint, 4 inches.	A-37.50

Built Rite Doll House Set No. 10. 25
Photo by Jonathan A. Newman
Courtesy Barbara and Jonathan Newman

"Li'l Abner and his dogpatch band.
Photo Courtesy Garth's Auctions Inc.
150

Musical toy in shape of Easter egg, with rabbit. Plays "Peter Cottontail"; by Mattel, Inc., ca. 1952, 6½ in. long.
Private collection   C/15-25

Bus, cast iron, rusty, no paint, 5 inches.	**A-15.00**
Bus, metal, blue, 6¼ inches.	**D-12.00**
Cadet, West Point, cast iron, no paint, 3½ inches.	**A-1.00**
Cannon, Lionel, cast iron, with red wheels, black orig. paint, 7 inches.	**A-12.50**
Cannon, cast iron, drilled barrel, no paint; barrel 5½ inches, length, 8 inches.	**A-10.00**
Cannon, cast iron, drilled barrel, no paint, 4 in. long.	**A-5.00**
Cannon, cast iron, 3 in. wheels, shoots firecrackers, 7 in. long.	**A-15.00**
Cap bomb, Chinese two-face head, cast iron, 1¾ inches.	**A-75.00**
Cap cane, National Repeater, cast iron and wood, 30 inches.	**A-10.00**
Car, with decal, cast iron, "Airflow Chrysler/A Century of Progress/Chicago—1934". White rubber wheels, red paint, 4 inches.	**A-42.50**
Car, metal, 4¼ inches.	**A-1.00**
Car and cannon, metal, 6 inches.	**A-3.00**

Hubley Ice Wagon, cast iron, two-horse, black horses pulling green wagon, with driver. Circa, 1906. 15½ in. long. 220

"**Dry Goods**", cloth and wood two-horse drawn wagon pull-toy circa 1860, 26 in. long. 180

Photo Courtesy PB84

Carriage, open, cast iron, two-horse, repainted, 11¼ inches. A-10.00

Chariot, horse-drawn, blue, cast iron, orig. paint, 5¼ inches. A-20.00

Convertible, metal, with five people, 3 inches. A-10.00

Coupe with rumble seat, cast iron, black rubber wheels, orig. paint, 6 inches. A-45.00

Coupe, cast iron, red orig. paint, 5 inches. A-25.00

Coupe, Arcade, cast iron, rumble seat and decal, blue orig. paint. A-47.50

American National Company **"Juvenile Auto"** Dump Truck Pedal Car, red and yellow, 57 in. long.   180

Coupe, Ford, Tootsietoy, blue and green orig. paint, 3 inches.   A-32.50

Coupe, Ford, Tootsietoy, black and blue orig. paint, 3 inches.   A-22.50

Coupe, metal, orange orig. paint, 3 inches.   A-15.00

Coupe, Model-T, cast iron, 4 inches.   A-8.00

Coupe, "Structo-like", metal, yellow stripes and gray orig. paint, 17 inches.   A-47.50

Destroyer, Tootsietoy, cast metal, 4½ in. long.   D-8.50

Dick Tracy Squad Car No. 1, Marx, tin, 11 inches long.   A-6.00

Dirigible, Navy, cast iron, orig. paint, (some rust), 4½ inches.   A-32.50

Dirigible, Navy, cast iron, silver wheels, blue orig. paint, 4½ inches.   A-37.50

Dirigible, Cast iron, silver orig. paint, 6 inches.   A-45.00

Elephant, Schoenhut, wood.   A-25.00

Finger-activated toy, wood, covered with printed paper, "The Chicken Dispute", 4 x 8½ inches.   A-65.00

Firecart, ladder, pulled by horses, cast iron, red orig. paint, 5½ inches.   A-17.50

Fire engine, metal, with boiler whistle, orig. paint, 4 inches.   A-10.00

Fire truck, red cast iron, damaged, 6½ inches.   A-15.00

Fire truck, metal, 2¾ inches.

Fire truck, metal, red orig. paint, one ladder, 7 inches.

A-3.00

Fire truck, red and blue orig. paint, damaged, 3½ inches.

A-6.00

Frame, horses and tongue, cast iron for large iron toy.
Orig. paint, 9½ inches.

A-4.00

A-20.00

Ferris Wheel carrying eight gondolas, the gondolas containing a total of 16 small
bisque dolls. Height 33½ in.

1350

Photo Courtesy PB84

384

G-Man, Marx, wind-up, automatic sparkling pistol. — A-10.00

Goose, tin, painted yellow, 5 in. high. — D-15.00

Goose that lays the golden egg, Marx wind-up, tin, orig. paint and box, 9 inches. — A-20.00

Gun, artillery, metal, shoots peas; olive drab orig. paint. 6 inches. — A-5.00

Handcar, railroad, tin wind-up, "Girard Toys". Lithographed tin 95% orig. paint, two pumping figures, 1920's, 5½ x 6 inches. — D-89.00

Horn, tin, red, white and blue, 16 in. long. — D-15.00

Horn, tin, conical, painted red, 22 in. long. — A-22.50

Horse, cast iron, orig. black paint, 7 inches. — D-19.00

Horse and buggy, cast iron, yellow orig. paint, 5 inches. — A-17.50

Horse and sulky, cast iron, no paint, 9¼ inches. — A-17.25

Hook and ladder, cast iron, horse missing, 4 inches. — A-100.00

Ice wagon, cast iron, horse missing, 4 inches. — A-9.00

Ice wagon, cast iron, horse-drawn, green with yellow wheels, orig. paint, 8½ inches. — A-52.50

Jack-in-the-box, wood, two white-haired men with painted composition heads; 2 x 4 inches. — A-95.00

Jack-in-the-box, cardboard barrel, man's head with spring-loaded top hat, barrel 4¼ in. high. — A-140.00

Kazoo, tin, 4¾ inches. — A-1.00

Keystone Cops, Tootsietoy, metal, orig. paint, 3 inches. — A-105.00

Kiddy Cyclist, Unique Art Company, tin, wind-up, 9 inches. — A-50.00

Locomotive, cast iron, black, cowcatcher broken, 6 inches. — A-10.00

Locomotive, cast iron, missing wheels, 8½ inches. — A-12.50

Locomotive and two passenger cars, cast iron, 15 inches. — A-25.00

Locomotive 444, cast iron, orig. black paint, parts missing, 9¼ inches. — A-12.50

Locomotive and tender, cast iron, 5 in. long. — A-7.50

Locomotive and tender, cast iron, pat'd June 8, '80, 10 inches. — A-30.00

Marble weight toy, tin, soldier climbs shot tower for cannonball, returns to ground. — A-75.00

Manure spreader, McCormick Deering, Arcade mfgr., cast iron, with decal, tongue missing, 8½ inches. — A-52.50

Men, set of five, cast iron, small. — A-17.50

Monoplane, red, cast iron, "UX 33", orig. paint, propeller missing, 3½ inches. A-17.50

Motorcycle, cast iron, green, parcel post sidecar, handlebars and door flap missing; motorcycle 9½ inches. A-50.00

Motorcycle cop, Champion, cast iron, orig. paint, 5 inches. A-17.50

Motorcycle, Champion, cast iron, driver missing head, 5 inches. D-10.00

Motorcycle, Harley-Davidson, cast iron, man's head moves, green orig. paint, 5 x 7½ inches. A-50.00

Motorcycle, with sidecar and passenger, cast iron, 4 inches. A-25.00

Motorcycle, three-wheel, cast iron, "Crash Car", blue orig. paint, 4¾ inches. A-20.00

Mule, Schoenhut, wood. A-15.00

Noah's Ark, wooden, ten animals and two people, red roof, 8¾ in. long. A-80.00

Novelty lighter, Planters Peanuts, metal, 2½ inches. A-7.50

Passenger car, RR, two axles and wheels missing, 11¾ inches. A-15.00

Passenger car, Pennsylvania RR Co., cast iron, no wheels, 12 inches. A-12.50

Pip-squeak, chicken, felt-covered in wooden cage, 5 in. high. A-42.50

Pip-squeak, pair of children, squeak when composition heads are pushed down; 4 in. high. A-50.00

Pip-squeak, parrot, colorful, clothcovered base damaged, 6¼ in. high. A-50.00

Pip-squeak, rabbit, composition head and real white rabbit fur. Works, 5½ x 6½ inches. A-105.00

Pneumatic pistol, white metal, paper ammunition roll. D-20.00

Plow, cast iron, twin blades, orig. red paint with silver wheels. Has tractor-pull; 2¼ x 3¼ x 6 inches. D-24.50

Pull toy, bear, wooden wheels and grey plush covering 17 in. long. A-75.00

Pull toy, cow, composition, nodding head, 5½ x 7 inches. A-20.00

Pull toy, horse, papier mache with wooden base and iron wheels, horse mane incomplete, 17 in. high. A-55.00

Pull toy, horse, orig. white paint, wood. One turned wheel replaced, 20 in. long, 20 in. high. A-155.00

Pull toy, horse, wood, with worn green paint. Orig. leather harness incomplete, brass disc wheels, 9½ in. long and high. **A-70.00**

Pull toy, six bells, metal, one bell missing, 8 in. diameter. **D-16.00**

Push toy, tin, animated horse, orig. paint with one brown and one black horse. Yellow and red striping for harness and red wheels. Paint has some wear; 15 in. high and long wire handle. **A-360.00**

Race car, cast iron, orig. blue paint, rubber tires, 6 inches. **A-15.00**

Race car, cast iron, gray, some rust, 5½ inches. **A-20.00**

Race car, Hubley, cast iron, mechanical moving flames from exhaust, red and yellow orig. paint, 8¾ inches. **A-75.00**

Race car, Hubley, cast iron, orange orig. paint, silver man and wheels, 5¼ inches. **A-30.00**

Race car, Hubley, cast iron, no wheels, blue orig. paint, 5½ inches. **A-10.00**

Roadster, black, cast iron, repainted, 5½ inches. **A-20.00**

Roadster, cast iron, white rubber wheels, blue orig. paint, 5 inches. **A-25.00**

Roadster, Tootsietoy, metal, 5¾ inches. **A-4.00**

Sedan, cast iron, red with silver wheels, orig. paint, 4½ inches. **A-32.50**

Sedan, cast iron arcade toy, Chevrolet 4-door. **A-1,400.00**

Sedan, four-door, cast iron, white rubber wheels, red, 6½ inches. **A-35.00**

Sedan, Ford, Tootsietoy, metal, black orig. paint, 3 inches. **A-10.00**

Sedan, metal, green orig. paint, 3½ inches. **A-15.00**

Sedan, metal, rear axle support broken, green orig. paint, 2 inches. **A-5.00**

Sedan, metal, white rubber tires, green orig. paint, 3 inches. **A-7.00**

Sedan, Tootsietoy Buick, metal, red and black orig. paint, 3 inches. **A-5.00**

Signal, Arcade stop & go street indicator, cast iron, with decals. **A-27.50**

Soldier, cast iron, no paint, small. **A-1.00**

Soldier on horse, cast iron, 3¼ inches. **A-4.00**

Steam engine and tender, cast iron, front wheels missing, 6 inches. **A-5.00**

Steamroller, cast iron, red wooden front roller and silver rear wheels, orig. paint, 3 inches. **A-20.00**

Steam shovel, Marion, tin, black orig. paint, red roof, 19 inches. **A-10.00**

Tractor with driver, Arcade, cast iron, no paint, 4½ inches. **A-22.50**

Tractor with driver, Arcade, cast iron, one tire missing, 5½ inches. **A-15.00**

Tractor, cast iron, silver wheels, red orig. paint, 4½ inches. **A-20.00**

Tractor, Arcade, cast iron, red wheels with decal, orig. paint, 6 inches. **A-35.00**

Tractor, Ford, cast iron, red wheels, green orig. paint, 6 inches. **A-22.50**

Tractor and trailer, "Playboy Trucking Co.", metal. Yellow orig. paint, black and green wheels, electric lights. **A-50.00**

Tractor and trailer, cast iron, red orig. paint with silver wheels, 7 inches long. **A-45.00**

Threshing machine, metal, blue orig. paint, 3 inches. **A-3.00**

Toy balancing man, wooden, iron counterweight, man 7 in. high, overall length 17 inches. **A-120.00**

Toy top, "Improved Mechanical Spring", tin, 3¾ inches. **A-3.00**

Toy, tin, miniature gavel style, whistle in handle plus rattle. **D-22.00**

Toy, tin wind-up, bird with plush covering, 4¼ in. long. **A-210.00**

Trolley car, tin, wind-up, "Rapid Transit Co.", lithographed, 8½ in. long. **D-81.00**

Truck, Hercules Mack Motor Express, metal, yellow orig. paint, some rust, 20 inches. **A-22.50**

Truck, bakery, metal, blue, 3 inches. **A-4.00**

Truck, delivery, with driver; tin, flywheel powered, six wheels, red orig. paint, 10¼ inches. **A-22.50**

Truck, delivery, small, metal. **D-19.00**

Truck, dump, Arcade, International, cast iron, dual rubber wheels, front left bumper missing, green orig. paint, 10½ inches. **A-135.00**

Truck, dump, Wyandott, metal, white rubber tires, green orig. paint, 6 inches. **A-8.00**

Truck, fire, ladder; cast iron, red with yellow wheels, 5½ inches. **A-5.00**

Truck, flatbed, cast iron, 60% orig. red paint, marked "Arcade", ca. 1930, 5 in. long. **D-79.50**

Truck, gasoline; Mack, cast iron, open cab, green with silver wheels, front axle damage, orig. paint. **A-45.00**

Truck, gasoline, Mack, cast iron, blue and orange orig. paint, 5 in. long. **A-27.50**

Truck, Mack Bulldog; metal, orig. paint. Large, child's riding size, steerable, hand-operated dump bed. **A-245.00**

Truck, Mack Bulldog, cast iron, rubber wheels, orig. paint, 4½ inches. **A-27.50**

Truck, pickup; Arcade, cast iron, front axle support repaired. Red orig. paint, 8½ inches. **A-37.50**

Truck, stake; metal, white rubber tires, 3½ inches. **A-6.00**

Truck, stake; cast iron, red orig. paint, 6¾ inches long. **A-37.50**

Truck, stake; Fred Green, metal, red paint, 4½ in. long. **A-16.00**

Truck, stake; Mack, cast iron, open cab, no paint, 3½ inches. **A-15.00**

Truck, stake; Mack, cast iron, open cab, no paint, 3½ inches. **A-15.00**

Truck, tank; cast iron, rubber wheels missing, 5¾ inches. **A-12.50**

Truck, open, tow; cast iron, "No. 1965", orig. paint, 4 inches. **A-15.00**

Truck, tractor; Arcade, cast iron, 3¾ inches. **A-7.50**

Van, moving storage, cast iron, green orig. paint, 4¾ inches. **A-35.00**

Wagon, farm; Tootsietoy, metal, orange with red wheels, orig. paint. **A-17.50**

Wagon, patrol; cast iron, 10¼ inches. **A-30.00**

Wagon, Girard, red, metal, orig. paint. **A-10.00**

Wagon, stake; cast iron, black and white horses, red orig. paint, 10¼ inches. **A-35.00**

Wheelbarrow, cast iron, red orig. paint, 4½ inches. **A-5.00**

Wheelbarrow, Kilgore, cast iron, 3¾ inches. **A-3.00**

Wheelbarrow, Lansing, cast iron, 9 in. long. **A-10.00**

Wind-up toy, "Donald Duck Duet", by Marx. **D-155.00**

Wrecker, Austin, cast iron, front wheels missing, green orig. paint, 3½ inches. **A-17.50**

Wrecker, Hubley, cast iron, white rubber tires, green orig. paint. **A-25.00**

A most unusual toy set was auctioned at Garth's (Delaware, Ohio), certainly one of few in the country. It consisted of a complete Schoenhut circus including the large oval tent.

There were over 18 different animals, five clowns, plus lion tamer, lady bareback rider and ringmaster. Included were the circus wagon, and ladders, chairs, pedestals and balls. The tent measured 18 x 44 inches and the typical figure was 9 inches high. Further, the original booklet was present, "Schoenhut's Marvelous Toy Circus. Copyright 1904".

A-3,250.00

TOYS—*Foreign* (Cast Lead)

British medical officer, early high-ranking, mint cond.
D-19.50

Capetown Highlander with rifle, mint.
D-11.00

Colonial, kneeling position, firing.
D-4.50

Gordon Highlander, at firing stance, very fine.
D-7.50

Hussar with separate horse, one arm missing.
D-6.00

Infantry charging with fixed bayonet, gas mask, WWI.
D-7.00

1st Madras Infantry, very rare, good cond.
D-10.00

Middlesex Regiment Officer, WWI, extremely mint.
D-11.00

New Zealand Infantry, WWI, very fine and scarce.
D-11.50

Princess Patricia's Canadian Light Infantry, mint.
D-11.00

Royal Air Force, WWI, extremely mint.
D-13.00

Royal Armor Gunner, Artillery, kneeling with shell, WWII.
D-10.00

Royal Navy Midshipman, very scarce, very good cond.
D-16.00

Royal Tank Corp, WWI, very good.
D-11.00

Royal Welch Fusiliere, mint.
D-14.00

Russian Infantry, rare, WWI.
D-13.00

Seaforth Highlander, ca. 1901, fine to very fine.
D-5.00

Swiss Guard with long halberd, mint.
D-8.00

West India Regiment, rare, very good.
D-10.00

Yoeman of the Guard, with halberd.
D-11.50

Boxed Set: Eight British Infantry, pre-1916 in mint cond. All original paint, each 1¾ inches tall. Gold helmets, red and blue tunics.
(Set) D-10.00

Middlesex Regiment eight-piece Marching Band. Extremely rare to find in this magnificent condition. Consists of leader with baton, bass drummer, two on smaller drums and four buglers. Ca. 1895—1909.

(Set)   **D-175.00**

TRADE SIGNS

Barber pole, painted, turned wood with iron mounting bracket. Old worn blue, and white paint, 36 in. high.   **A-240.00**

Boot-maker's sign, wood, old black paint, heel replaced. Wrought iron brace, 28 in. high.   **A-75.00**

Boot-shaped, vertical lettering "Boots", white on black paint. Wrought iron hanger, 30 in. high.   **A-85.00**

Butcher shop sign, lamb, papier mache, part replaced. Lamb 18 in. high, 33 in. long.   **A-250.00**

Country store, porcelain on tin, advertising stock feeds. Black on yellow lettering, 10 x 20 inches.   **D-32.00**

Drug store, "Steven's Pharmacy", with directional arrow. Tin, black on white lettering. 11½ x 24 inches.   **D-17.50**

Drugstore, suspended cutout of mortar and pestle, ¾ in. wood, black and white lettering, 23 in. high.   **D-150.00**

Fish, wood, painted silver with faded scale-marks. Prob. bait or fish store, New England, 9½ x 21 inches.   **A-90.00**

Sign, sheet metal, horse forequarters, rusty, 34 x 35½ inches.   **A-55.00**

Sign, "Kincaide & Co./Auctioneers/Quincy", 16 x 30½ inches.   **A-25.00**

Tavern sign, oval wood with wrought iron framework, black paint with crescent moons, star, and "D. W. Taylor" in yellow, white horse with red reins and harness, yellow saddle; sign 38 in. high, 57 in. wide.   **A-325.00**

Wooden sign, "Ohio No. 11" in red and yellow paint, brown background.   **A-21.00**

TRAINS

American Flyer O-gauge five-piece set, electric engine No. 1218 with passenger cars.   **A-42.50**

American Flyer Standard-gauge steam engine No. 350.   **A-32.50**

American Flyer Standard-gauge work train set, Electric locomotive, gondola car, caboose, crossing bell signal, signal light and crossing marker.   **A-125.00**

HO-gauge steam engine.   **A-17.50**

HO-gauge, lot of two, passenger cars.   **A-10.00**

Ives O-gauge three-piece set limited, Vestibule Express.   **A-92.50**

Lionel O-gauge Accessories 151, semaphore.   **A-8.00**

Lionel O-gauge caboose.   **A-5.00**

Lionel O-gauge car.   **A-42.50**

Lionel O-gauge crane.   **A-6.00**

Lionel O-gauge diesel, Erie.   **A-55.00**

Lionel O-gauge diesel, New York Central ABA units.   **A-150.00**

Lionel O-gauge diesel, Rock Island, 2-A units.   **A-52.50**

Lionel O-gauge flatcar, with submarine.   **A-11.00**

Lionel O-gauge four-piece set, electric engine with three passenger cars.   **A-55.00**

Lionel O-gauge, lot of six miscellaneous cars.   **A-22.50**

Lionel O-gauge passenger set, three pieces.   **A-40.00**

Lionel O-gauge steam engine, 675.   **A-32.50**

Lionel O-gauge steam engine, 2025.   **A-35.00**

Lionel O-gauge switch engine.   **A-40.00**

Lionel O-gauge tank car.   **A-9.00**

Lionel O-gauge tender.   **A-14.00**

Lionel Standard-gauge baggage car.   **A-27.50**

Lionel Standard-gauge caboose.   **A-17.50**

Lionel Standard-gauge car.   **A-15.00**

Lionel Standard-gauge engine.   **A-47.50**

Lionel Standard-gauge passenger train, consisting of steam locomotive, tender, two Pullman cars, observation car, signal, and lumber car; seven pieces.   **A-475.00**

Lionel Standard-gauge series tank car.   **A-17.50**

Lionel Standard-gauge seven-piece set, steam engine with tender and five cars.   **A-370.00**

Railroad engine and tender, tin, flywheel powered. "L. V.", Pat'd. AP27, 09; red orig. paint, 17 in. long.   **A-20.00**

Toy train catalog, Lionel Electric, color illustrations, ca. 1920's, 46 pages.   **D-15.00**

TRAMP ART

Box, made of quarter-inch pine stock, 7 in. high.   **A-20.00**
Box, ca. 1910, 10½ x 12 x 15½ inches.   **D-75.00**
Box, jewelry, lift-out interior tray and one drawer. Elaborate work with three embossed brass lion-head pulls and inset green velvet panels, 9½ x 11½ x 12½ inches.   **A-90.00**
Box, sewing, octagonal, four drawers, open top, 6 x 13 x 13 inches.   **A-40.00**
Comb case, 3½ x 8¼ x 11¾ inches.   **A-17.50**
Frame, one corner damaged, old varnish finish, 17 x 22½ inches.   **A-22.50**
Frame, cross-corner, old red and gold paint, mirror glass, 15 x 17½ inches.   **A-27.50**
Frame, painted gold, stitchery picture of American eagle and flag, 27 x 32 inches.   **A-45.00**
Humidor, octagonal 6½ in. high.   **A-50.00**

TREENWARE

"Treen" or treenware are objects carved from solid wood, and they are often quite old. The names come from the original source of the material, the tree.

Bowl, interior red, exterior green, 7¼ in. diameter.   **A-45.00**
Bowl, exterior blue and bottom branded with initials, 7¾ in. diameter.   **A-50.00**
Bowl, interior with traces of paint, 12¾ in. diameter, 3¼ in. high.   **A-70.00**
Butter paddle, with age-crack in bowl, 9 in. long.   **A-30.00**
Butter paddle, 7½ in. long.   **D-18.00**
Canister, turned rings with brown stain, inset bottom, matching turned lid, 9½ in. diameter.   **A-37.50**
Chalice, turned, two-color laminated wood, 5 in. high.   **A-10.00**
Dipper, handle hook for edge of pot, 10¾ in. long.   **A-40.00**
Egg cup, white lignum vitae, hand-turned.   **D-11.50**
Goblet, footed, old red paint, carved, 3½ in. high.   **A-25.00**

Jar, covered, footed, old red varnish, 7¼ in. high. A-15.00

Sander, old blue paint, bottom with initials, 2¾ in. diameter, 3 in. high. A-152.50

Toothpick holder, blonde to chocolate brown, 3½ in. high. D-19.50

WAR

Some brief notes about the main collecting areas in this field might be of interest. Bayonets were usually carried on belt or knapsack, and always had provision for attachment to the muzzle end of the military "shoulder arm". "Short arms" were kept at the side, and hence are often called "side arms", the pistols and revolvers.

Carbines were generally of the same, or similar caliber (bullet diameter, measured in hundredths of an inch) as the rifles. Carbines were shortened and lightened versions of rifles, originally used by mounted troops, later by various frontline soldiers.

Muskets were large-bore (high caliber) shoulder arms, usually firing black powder (later, smokeless) and with separate loading of powder and shot. Early varieties ignited the charge by flintlock or caplock, while later types used a firing pin with a metallic cartridge. Like shotguns, muskets had a smooth inner barrel surface and fired round or conical bullets.

Pistols range from early single-shot and multiple barrels to modern types with cartridges held in the handle. Revolvers, as the name implies, have a revolving cylinder that turns to feed a fresh round in front of the barrel breech.

Rifles received the name because the barrel interior, the bore, has twists or spiral grooves (rifling) that cause the conical bullet to spin in flight, increasing accuracy. A special license is required for a U.S. citizen to possess a fully automatic weapon, one which fires continuously when the trigger is depressed. Examples would be submachine guns and the various assault rifles.

WAR—*Weapons*

Bayonet, British triangular Martini, with scabbard. A-20.00

Bayonet, dress, Mauser Eickhorn with tarnished sheath. D-28.00

Bayonet, Mauser 1886 short sawtooth, with scabbard. A-20.00

Bayonet, sawtooth, German engineer's, leather scabbard. D-40.00

Bayonet, shore-dress Mauser with sheath, nickel-plated. **A-25.00**

Carbine, Sharps and Hankins, Civil War, .52 caliber. **A-175.00**

Carbine, Spencer, Civil War, .56 caliber. Saddle ring, elevating sights, barrel 20¼ in. long. **A-325.00**

Carbine, Spencer, Civil War, Boston model 1865, barrel 20 in. long. **A-190.00**

Carbine, Triplet and Scot "Kentucky" cavalry, barrel twists to load. Caliber .56, barrel 30 in. long. **A-205.00**

Carbine, Warner brass frame, .56-50, barrel cavalry length. **A-320.00**

Dagger, Nazi Luftwaffe 1st model, leather sheath, silvered chain. **A-130.00**

Dagger, Nazi Storm Trooper model 1934, "Alles Fur Deutchland". **A-85.00**

Musket, Austrian, single-shot Werndl, llmm. **A-105.00**

Musket, Colt's pat., U.S. model 1864, barrel 40 in. long. **A-380.00**

Musket, European flintlock, cutback stock, barrel 31½ in. long. **A-85.00**

Musket, Mason, model 1861, with bayonet, barrel 40 in. long. **A-230.00**

Musket, Norwich, U.S. 1861, dated 1863, ramrod gone, barrel 40 in. long. **A-165.00**

Musket, Pomeroy, model 1835, with bayonet, flint conversion. **A-180.00**

Musket, Sharps-Borchardt .45-70, barrel 31 in. long. **A-345.00**

Musket, Springfield 1855 dated 1858, Maynard type, .58 caliber, 40 in. barrel. **A-460.00**

Musket, Springfield 1861 dated 1862, .58 caliber, barrel 40 in. long. **A-275.00**

Musket, Springfield model 1861, missing ramrod. **A-185.00**

Musket, Springfield, model 1864, silver shield inlaid in stock. **A-320.00**

Musket, Starr, U.S. model 1816, converted, dated on lock 1836. **A-100.00**

Musket, Trenton, U.S. model 1861, .58 caliber, with bayonet. **A-175.00**

Pistol, Astra, Spanish, 9mm, model 1921, holster and extra clip. **A-145.00**

Pistol, automatic, Colt model 1911, Army .45 caliber. **A-250.00**

Pistol, boxlock, U.S.; lock and barrel marked "Ames/Springfield 1845". **A-300.00**

Pistol, Colt, New Service .455 Eley with holster, British proofed. A-105.00

Pistol, .45 caliber, model 1911-A1, with holster. A-185.00

Pistol, flintlock, U.S. model 1816, 15½ in. long. A-210.00

Pistol, flintlock, U.S. model 1816, lock marked "S. North, Middleton, Conn". Missing ramrod, visible inspector's marks. A-240.00

Pistol, French martial, model 1822; St. Etienne, .72 caliber. A-290.00

Pistol, Japanese, Nambu model 1914, 8mm with holster, clip with matching serial number. A-145.00

Pistol, conversion to percussion, U.S. model 1836, lock marked "Johnson/1839". A-170.00

Pistol, Luger, German, dated 1940. Matched 1936-type holster and two matched clips, all with same serial number. A-375.00

Pistol, Mauser, .32 automatic, Nazi proofmark. A-175.00

Pistol, percussion, U.S. model 1841, visible inspector marks. A-225.00

Pistol, Radom, Polish, Nazi-marked 9mm with holster and extra clip. A-155.00

Pistol, Walther, Nazi-marked P-38 with marked holster and extra magazines (clips). A-340.00

Revolver, Colt Army .44 caliber, 1860, full-fluted cylinder)one chamber blown, barrel 7½ in. long. A-300.00

Revolver, Iver-Johnson .22 caliber, fine condition; training. A-55.00

Revolver, Webley, Mark 5, 1914 D.A., .455 caliber. A-55.00

Revolver, Webley & Son, Mark 3 double action, .38 caliber. A-75.00

Rifle, bolt-action. .30-05, elevating peep sight. A-100.00

Rifle, Burnside, Civil War, S.R.C. 4th model. A-200.00

Rifle, Burnside, Civil War, S.R.C. 4th model, as above. A-360.00

Rifle, Enfield Mark I, .303 caliber, British, dated 1915. A-67.50

Rifle, Japanese WW-II 7mm bolt action. A-65.00

Rifle, Mississippi, Harpers Ferry 1841 model dated 1853, with brass patchbox. Lock replaced, U.S.N. stamp in barrel. A-250.00

Rifle, Pottsdam percussion, full stock with brass trigger guard. A-135.00

Rifle, Rock Island Arsenal, 1906, .30-06 caliber, bolt action. A-115.00

Rifle, sniper, German, model G-43, semi-automatic, scope and sling.   **A-400.00**

Rifle, Spencer, .52 caliber, model 1860, S.R.C., barrel 22 in. long.   **A-240.00**

Rifle, Spencer, 1865, .52 caliber, S.R.C. with Stabler cut-off.   **A-310.00**

Rifle, Springfield trapdoor, model 1873, .45-70 caliber, dented stock.   **A-205.00**

Rifle, Springfield .45-70 rifle, model 1889, ramrod bayonet.   **A-170.00**

Rifle, Springfield, model 1903-A3, marked "Natl Ord".   **A-125.00**

Rifle, Springfield, model 1878, .45-70 caliber.   **A-160.00**

Shell casing, brass, steel projectile, 37mm.   **D-12.50**

Shell casing, inert solid head, German 88mm, WW-II.   **D-45.00**

Sword bayonet, brass hilt, black leather scabbard tipped with brass, blade marked "Collings & Co./Hartford, Conn."   **A-185.00**

Sword, short, Luftwaffe Eickhorn, with sheath and belt.   **A-130.00**

WAR—Related Items

Army knapsack, WW-I U.S.A., canvas with leather straps.   **D-13.00**

Belt buckle, Civil War, Union Army affiliation.   **A-17.50**

Belt and buckle, Civil War Officer's.   **A-90.00**

Canteen, bullseye, Civil War.   **A-37.50**

Canteen plate, and cookpot cup, copper, 8½ in. diameter; set.   **D-225.00**

Cap, Civil War Officer's, embroidered with U.S. wreath.   **A-105.00**

Cartridges, strip of twenty-six, for 7.7mm Japanese machine gun.   **A-20.00**

Cartridge box, for Indian Wars, ca. 1870.   **A-17.50**

Cartridge boxes, matching pair; WW-I, tin, 2 x 3½ x 7 inches.   **D-10.00**

Catalog, Civil War, of military goods; by Ridabock & Co., N. Y., 48 pages illustrating uniform parts, spurs, etc.   **D-35.00**

Dispatch pouch, Civil War, "U.S. Dispatch/1862", 12 in. long.   **D-45.00**

Epaulettes, Civil War, Officer's, missing rank insignia, pair.   **D-45.00**

Nazi Germany **military caps** each with swastika at front.
Each: C/15-25

Nazi-items, **armbands**; Left, swastika, black against red and white.
C/15-25
Right, **"German Army"** with added stamp.
C/10-20

Civil War folding mess set, cased, stag handles, made in Sheffield, England. D/175

Flare pistol, German Navy WW-I, single shot, 27mm, brass. A-45.00

Flare pistol, German (Nazi), WW-II, 27mm, "Erma Erfurt". A-35.00

Gas pistol, Perplex, 12mm, 2 in. barrel. A-15.00

Gauntlets, pair, Civil War Officer's. A-45.00

Gauntlets, pair, Civil War, fine condition. A-70.00

Helmet, iron, WW-I, Lincoln Brigade. A-22.50

Periscope, removed from German WW-II tank. A-20.00

Powder flask, brass and copper, Civil War, Chain-secured stopper, 4 in. long. D-35.00

Presentation cannon, Civil War, brass barrel marked to recipient and dated 1862, wood carriage, 16 in. long. D-650.00

Powder flask, pistol, brass   110-120

Sighter, artillery, old, mahogany with brass fittings, 49½ in. long.   **A-40.00**

Signal cannon, muzzle-loading, small, mounted on wooden block, 7 in. long.   **A-40.00**

Siren, Japanese WW-II, hand-held, round metal body with handle and crank, 13 in. high.   **D-55.00**

Training aid, model 1919 Browning .30 caliber machine gun.   **A-115.00**

Training aid, M-I carbine, sectional views.   **A-115.00**

Training aid, Browning automatic rifle (BAR .30).   **A-105.00**

Training rifle, Mauser 4mm single-shot, bolt action.   **A-100.00**

Writing supplies, Civil War, collapsible holder with small inkwell and sander.   **D-40.00**

WATCHES

American Waltham, 15-jewel, 14k gold case early excellent quality movement; excellent dial with red track.   **D-335.00**

Ball, 19-jewel, white gold-filled case by Keystone, openfaced, white finish dial.   **D-155.00**

Ball Official Standard, 19-jewel, Keystone base metal case, adjusted five positions.   **D-150.00**

Ball Official Standard, 19-jewel, Keystone base metal case, adjusted five positions.   **D-150.00**

Ball (Hamilton), 21-jewel, adjusted five positions, ball case, excellent RR watch.   **D-200.00**

Ball (Hamilton), 21-jewel, Ball dial, adjusts to six positions, 10k yellow gold-filled case, damaskeened movement.   **D-215.00**

Ball (Hamilton Grade 999), Ball Official Standard, 21-jewel, good dial, case by Defiance, five positions.   **D-180.00**

Ball (Waltham), 17-jewel, Gold Seal, five positions, Official Standard dial.   **D-150.00**

Ball (Waltham Gold Seal), Official Standard, orig. Keystone base metal case with stirrup bow.   **D-180.00**

Gold watch and chain, by Rockford, hunter case. Made in Rockford, Illinois, case by C.W.C. Company.   C/115-140

Elgin, BW Raymond, 19-jewel, Grade 372, early, silveroid case, made for RR service.   **D-125.00**

Elgin Father Time, Grade 454, 21-jewel, base metal case.   **D-150.00**

Elgin, Grade 372, 19-jewel, early movement with jeweled barrel, yellow gold-filled case, RR grade.   **D-125.00**

Elgin Model 270, 21-jewel, three-finger bridge movement; adjusted, damaskeened movement, gold gear train.   **D-230.00**

Elgin National, Roman numeral dial, snap bezel, coin silver case. Mainspring broken.   **D-80.00**

Elgin National #349, 21-jewel, engraved movement, yellow gold-filled.   **D-140.00**

Elgin National Watch, gold, open-face. Lever movement, Roman numerals and second hand, engraved back.   **A-225.00**

Elgin Veritas, 23-jewel, adjusted, extra-fine quality movement. Porcelain dial, silveroid glass-backed display case.   **D-280.00**

Hamilton 924, 17-jewel, Keystone case, microregulator.   **D-85.00**

Hamilton 940, yellow gold-filled, RR, engraved case; adjusted five positions to conform to RR standards, chip under bezel at 6.   **D-130.00**

Hamilton 952, bridge movement, 19-jewel, five positions, yellow, gold-filled case. In this grade, 5800 made.   **D-190.00**

Hamilton Grade 990, 21-jewel, engine-turned case, damaskeened movement, adjusted five positions.   **D-175.00**

Hamilton 992, 21-jewel, red seconds track, snap bezel and back, Fahy's 25-year case.   **D-135.00**

Hamilton 992B, Railroad Special, 21-jewels, RR dial.   **D-180.00**

Hamilton 993, hunter case, 21-jewel, engine-turned hunting case, double-sunk dial with faint hairline.   **D-290.00**

Hamilton Grade 996, 21-jewel, jeweled motor barrel, damaskeened movement, bold RR dial.   **D-200.00**

Waltham Chrono-
graph   Rare

Ladies watch - Due-
ber, solid gold.
400-500

Gold Inlaid Silver
Case, Fahys. 150-200

Left, Gold Inlaid
Silver Case, Fahys
"Jockey". 150-200

Right, 20 Year Gold
Filled, Boss, "Loco-
motive".
Hunting case 200-250
Open case   150-200

Hamilton 4992B, Military, white dial with seconds, hack feature, adjustable temperature and six positions.   **D-125.00**

Hampden, 21-jewel, silveroid case, adjustable five positions.   **D-115.00**

Hampden John Hancock, RR, heavy case with thick beveled glass crystal badly scratched, Fahy's case pat. 1884.   **D-130.00**

Hampden Special Railway, 23-jewel, yellow gold-filled, case by Philadelphia, RR dial with red track. **D-240.00**

Howard, 17-jewel, Howard case, excellent dial and condition. · D-185.00

Howard Hunter Case, 17-jewel, engine-turned yellow gold-filled case with Howard logo, Roman numeral dial. · · · · · · · · · · · · · · · · · · D-285.00

Howard Railroad Chronometer, Series Eleven, yellow gold-filled swing-out case, "E. Howard Watch Co./Boston". · · · · · · · · · · · · · · · · · D-330.00

Howard Series Ten, yellow gold-filled, double-sunk dial, RR watch. · · · · · · · · · · · · · · · · · · D-310.00

Howard Series Eleven, RR chronometer, 21-jewel, engraved bezel, yellow gold-filled.

Illinois Bunn, 19-jewel, yellow gold-filled, adjusted five positions. · · · · · · · · · · · · · · · · · · D-175.00

Illinois Bunn Special, 21 ruby jewels, silvered dial, lightly designed case. · · · · · · · · · · · · · · D-130.00

Illinois Sangamo, 21-jewel, yellow gold-filled case, RR grade. · D-180.00

Illinois Victor, Montgomery railroad dial, silveroid case by star, 21-jewel. · · · · · · · · · · · · · · D-130.00

Rockford, hunter case, 15-jewel, gilt movement, micrometer regulator, yellow gold-filled engraved case. · D-165.00

Rockford, 21-jewel, adjusted to temperature, grade 918, orig. porcelain dial. Keystone silveroid case, RR dial. · D-235.00

Seth Thomas, 21-jewel, highly engraved case, double-sunk dial, adjusted to six positions, scarce; small chip at center post. · · · · · · · · · · · · D-345.00

Seth Thomas Century, silveroid case, porcelain dial with chip under bezel at 6, hairlines. · · · · · · D-80.00

Southbend 227, 21-jewel, rayed movement, safety pinions, adjusted to temperature and five positions, RR dial and movement. · · · · · · · · · · · · · · · D-150.00

Southbend Model 347, 17-jewel, micro-regulator, Royal 20-year case with wear, red seconds track. Dial patch repairs. · · · · · · · · · · · · · · · · D-75.00

Universal, (Geneva), open pocket watch, white metal case with 14k chain. · · · · · · · · · · · · · · · A-110.00

Waltham, 23-jewel, up/down indicator, orig. metal dial, yellow gold-filled, adjusted five positions, very impressive. · D-390.00

Waltham Crescent Street, up/down indicator, 21-jewel, yellow gold-filled, engraved bezel and back edge. Two small repaired chips. · · · · · · · · · D-450.00

Waltham Grade 645, RR styled dial, 21-jewel, yellow gold-filled.   **D-120.00**

Waltham Riverside, 10k rolled gold-plated, Keystone case, RR watch.   **D-110.00**

Waltham Santa Fe Route, 17-jewel, dial marked "Santa Fe Route/Waltham", hunter movement in hunter case. Movement winds at 3, Keystone Boss case with dust cover, engraved movement.   **D-390.00**

Waltham Vanguard, 23-jewel, up/down indicator, adjusted five positions. Orig. Crescent yellow gold-filled case, 1908 model.   **D-395.00**

WATCHES—*Character Head*

Apollo Space Pacer. Man at controls of space ship, orig. box.   **D-15.00**

Apollo Space Pacer. Space ship in flight near moon, orig. box.   **D-15.00**

Ballerina. Bradley, blue dress dancing on toes.   **D-15.00**

Barbie. Head left, yellow outer dial, full head, 63 Mattel.   **D-12.00**

Barbie. Small Head, gold case, yellow hair, 64 Mattel.   **D-12.00**

Batman. Gilbert, 1966, orig. box and orig. card.   **D-35.00**

Cinderella. Name only, round.   **D-10.00**

Cinderella. Hair on top of head, evening dress, metal band.   **D-15.00**

Cinderella. Bradley, Walt Disney Production, pink band.   **D-15.00**

Dale Evans. Inside horseshoe with horse, orig. box, round face, Bradley.   **D-45.00**

Dale Evans. Inside horseshoe with horse, oblong face.   **D-35.00**

Davy Crockett. Bradley, buckskin and rifle, silver case.   **D-35.00**

Davy Crockett. Green plastic case, no band.   **D-25.00**

G. I. Joe Combat Watch. Gilbert, 1965, orig. box.   **D-25.00**

Hopalong Cassidy. Orig. band, no stem.   **D-25.00**

Hopalong Cassidy. Not orig. band, no stem.   **D-20.00**

James Bond 007 Spy Watch. Gilbert, orig. box, 1965.   **D-35.00**

Mary Marvel. Fawcett Pub. 24C, 1948, orig. band with price sticker.   **D-85.00**

Mary Marvel. Fawcett Pub. 24C, 1948, black band, different case.   **D-75.00**

Mickey Mouse. Ingersoll, oblong, one homemade hand. **D-35.00**
Minnie Mouse. Bradley, late, round. **D-15.00**
Peter Pan. Round. **D-15.00**
Roy Rogers and Trigger. Plain band. **D-50.00**
Roy Rogers and Trigger. Snake band. **D-50.00**
Snow White. Grey band, no stem, metal case. **D-20.00**
Snow White. Black band, metal case. **D-25.00**
Snow White. Yellow plastic case, orig. box. **D-35.00**
Superman. Oblong, orig. band, metal case. **D-100.00**
Zorro. Name only, not orig. band. **D-15.00**
Zorro. Name only, one-half orig. band. **D-20.00**
Zorro. Name only, orig. box. **D-35.00**

WORLD'S FAIR

Album, by Imperial Portrait Co., Chicago World's Fair, 1894. **D-25.00**
Ash-tray, "Firestone Champion", tire-shape, New York W.F., 1939. **D-10.00**
Banner, gray and orange, 12 in. long, New York W.F., 1939. **D-8.00**
Book, "Official Guide to the World's Fair", 200 pp, St. Louis, 1904. **D-15.00**
Book, "The World's Fair at St. Louis", Reid publisher, 1904. **D-15.00**
Book, "World's Fair Photographed", 528 pp, Shepp, Chicago, 1893. **D-35.00**
Broach, mother of pearl, New York World's Fair, 1939. **D-10.00**
Compact, woman's; Hall of Science, Chicago W.F., 1934. **D-3.00**
Compact, woman's; Fair scenes, New York W.F., 1939. **D-8.00**
Dust pan, souvenir, 3½ in. long, Chicago W.F., 1933. **D-5.00**
Elongated cent, Crystal House, Chicago W.F., 1934. **D-4.00**
Encased cent, "Stork Club", New York W.F., 1939. **D-5.00**
Jigsaw puzzle, New York W.F. 1964-65, "Tent of Tomorrow". **D-3.00**
Knife, glass; "Vetex-Glas", 8½ in. long, New York W.F., 1939. **D-10.00**
Medal, brass color, 50c-size, New York W.F., 1939. **D-4.00**
Medal, bronze, 2¾ in. diameter, St. Louis W.F., 1904. **D-50.00**
Medal, gilt brass, New York W.F., 1939. **D-7.00**

Medal, "Official Souvenir Medal", brass, St. Louis
W.F., 1904.   **D-20.00**
Medal, RCA Exhibit, 64mm, New York W.F.,
1964-65.   **D-7.00**
Patch, 2½ x 3¼ inches, New York W.F., 1964-65.   **D-4.00**
Patch, black and orange, New York W.F., 1939.   **D-6.00**
Spoons, set of five; head of Columbus, plated, dates
1492-1893, with "World's Fair City", Columbian
W.F.   **D-50.00**
Stick pin, celluloid flag, St. Louis W.F., 1904.   **D-10.00**
Tray, "New York World's Fair/1964-1965", picture
of Unisphere.   **D-8.00**
Tray, picture of Federal Building, World's Fair,
Chicago, 1934.   **D-10.00**
Tray, picture of Union Station, St. Louis; square,
metal, 1904.   **D-15.00**

PUBLICATIONS—*Antiques and Collectibles*

ACQUIRE
170 - 5th Avenue
New York City, 10010

AMERICAN ANTIQUES
RD #1
New Hope, Pennsylvania 18938

AMERICAN ART
  & ANTIQUES
One Worth Avenue
Marion, Ohio 43302

AMERICAN COLLECTOR
PO Box A
Reno, Nevada 89506

AMERICAN COLLECTOR'S
  JOURNAL
PO Box 1431
Porterville, California 93257

ANTIQUE COLLECTING
PO Box 327
Ephrata, Pennsylvania 17522

ANTIQUE GAZETTE
929 Davidson Drive
Nashville, Tennessee 37205

ANTIQUE TOY WORLD
4419 Irving Park Road
Chicago, Illinois 60641

THE ANTIQUE TRADER
PO Box 1050
Dubuque, Iowa 52001

ANTIQUES & COLLECTIBLES
525 N. Barry Avenue
Mamaroneck, New York 10543

THE ANTIQUES JOURNAL
PO Box 1046
Dubuque, Iowa 52001

ANTIQUES WORLD
PO Box 990
Farmingdale, New York 11737

COLLECTORS NEWS
PO Box 156
Grundy Center, Iowa 50638

COLLECTOR'S WEEKLY
209 N. Oak Street
Kermit, Texas 79745

THE ENCYCLOPEDIA OF COLLECTIBLES
Time-Life Books
TIME & LIFE Building
Chicago, Illinois 60611

HOBBIES
1006 S. Michigan Avenue
Chicago, Illinois 60605

JOEL SATER'S ANTIQUES
   & AUCTION NEWS
Box B
Marietta, Pennsylvania 17547

MAINE ANTIQUE DIGEST
PO Box 358
Waldoboro, Maine 04572

MILITARY COLLECTORS NEWS
PO Box 7582
Tulsa, Oklahoma 74105

OHIO ANTIQUE REVIEW
PO Box 538
Worthington, Ohio 43085

ORNAMENT
PO Box 35029
Los Angeles, California 90035

THE SPINNING WHEEL
Everybody's Press, Inc.
Hanover, Pennsylvania 17331

TRI-STATE TRADER
PO Box 90
Knightstown, Indiana 46148

WEST COAST PEDDLER
PO Box 4489
Downey, California 90241

DIRECTORY

Contributor and Mailing Address	Information area(s) for book
William P. Weschler Vice President ADAM A. WESCHLER & Son 905-9 E Street N.W. Washington, D.C. 20004	Auctions

Aileen Wissner
AILEEN'S JEWELRY
PO Box 342
Pelham, New York

Antique and
   estate jewelry

Barbara and John Rudisill
ALT PRINT HAUS
3 Lakewood Drive
Medfield, Massachusetts 02052

Early American
   prints, Currier
   & Ives

Bonnie Tekstra
President
AMERICAN INTERNATIONAL
   GALLERIES, Inc.
17792 Fitch Street
Irvine, California 92714

Automatic musical
   instruments

Palmer V. Welch
ANTIQUES FOR DEALERS
213 Alexander Avenue
Scotia, New York 12302

Antiques and
   collectibles

Sallie and Bob Connelly
AUCTIONS/APPRAISALS
666 Chenango Street
Binghamton, New York 13902

Toys

Conway Barker
AUTOGRAPH DEALER
PO Box 30625
Royal Lane Station
Dallas, Texas 75230

Autographs

Hugh W. Parker
BRITISH HOLLOW ANTIQUES
Rte. 1, Box 90
Potosi, Wisconsin

Antique tools

Carol Secrist
Deerfield, Missouri 64741

Carnival glass

E. London
EDWARD LONDON
9408 N. W. 70th Street
Tamarac, Florida 33321

Limited edition
   plates

Osna and Jim Fenner
FENNER'S ANTIQUES, Inc.
2611 Avenue S
Brooklyn, New York 11229

Glass, pottery,
and other

Tom King, Tom Porter
GARTH'S AUCTIONS, Inc.
2690 Stratford Road
PO Box 315
Delaware, Ohio 43015

Auctions

Keith Schneider
GASOLINE ALLEY ANTIQUES
6501 - 20th NE
Seattle, Washington 98115

Comic characters
and collectibles

Linda and George LaBarre
GEORGE H. LABARRE
   GALLERIES
111 Ferry Street
Hudson, New Hampshire 03051

Professional numismatist
& antiquarian

Barbara and Ron Hoyt
HOYT'S ANTIQUES
14 Jerome Drive
Glen Cover, New York 11542

Antique clocks
& watches

Jack Cory
12700-C Knott Avenue
Garden Grove, California 92641

Popcorn machines
& wagons

Richard Merlis
President
JERAL, Inc.
28 Forsyth Street
New York, New York 10002

Antique & estate
jewelry

John Sadler
PO Box 508
Tucker, Georgia 30084

Antiques &
collectibles

KERN COUNTY MUSEUM
3801 Chester Avenue
Bakersfield, California 93301

Historical village

Dagmar and Spencer House LAHASKA ANTIQUES Route 202 Lahaska, Pennsylvania 18931	Ice cream moulds
Larry Eisenstein 87-13 — 30th Avenue Jackson Heights, New York 11369	Collectible gift items
Walter Marchant, Jr. LIL-BUD ANTIQUES 142 Main Street Yarmouthport, Maine 02675	Early American pattern glass
Linda Roberts PO Box 962 Westbury, New York 11590	Unusual jewelry
Charles DeLuca MARITIME ANTIQUES Route 1 York, Maine 03909	Nautical items & scrimshaw
M. Nasser MAURICE NASSER New London Shopping Center New London, Connecticut 06320	Collectors' plates
MYSTIC SEAPORT, Inc. Mystic, Connecticut 06355	Maritime museums
Peggy and Stan Hecker OLD ADVERTISING 5010 Cadet Street San Diego, California 92117	Advertising collectibles
Clara Jean and Stan Davis THE OLD PARSONAGE RFD #1, Hopkinton Concord, New Hampshire 03301	Primitives

Dee and Ron Milam
SCOTTSDALE GALLERIES
6518 Van Nuys Blvd.
Van Nuys, California 91401

American Indian items

Bea and James Stevenson
THE STEVENSONS
90 W. Thacker
Hoffman Estates, Illinois 60194

Scouting memorabilia

Corinne and Sheldon Tucker
T & L RR/GALLERIE T
4512 Montrose
Houston, Texas 77006

Antiques and
railroad items

F. W. Watson
WATSON'S
135 E. Michigan Avenue
New Carlisle, Indiana 46552

Collectors' plates

Nancy and Al Schlegel
WILLOW HOLLOW ANTIQUES
185 S. Main Street
Penacook, New Hampshire 03301

Antiques, collectibles,
& primitives (large
listings)